Psychology and Everyday Life

Karon Oliver

Hodder & Stoughton
A MEMBER OF THE HODDER HEADLINE GROUP

To Chris

Orders: please contact Bookpoint Ltd, 78 Milton Park, Abingdon, Oxon OX14 4TD. Telephone: (44) 01235 827720, Fax: (44) 01235 400454. Lines are open from 9.00–6.00, Monday to Saturday, with a 24 hour message answering service. Email address: orders@bookpoint.co.uk

British Library Cataloguing in Publication Data
A catalogue record for this title is available from The British Library

ISBN 0 340 779977

First published 2000

Impression number	10	9	8	7	6	5	4	3	2	1
Year	2005		2004		2003		2002		2001	2000

Cover photo from Jacey, Debut Art.
Typeset by Multiplex Techniques, St Pauls Cray, Kent
Printed in Great Britain for Hodder & Stoughton Educational, a division of Hodder Headline Plc, 338 Euston Road, London NW1 3BH by J.W. Arrowsmiths Ltd.

Contents

Introduction	iv
1 **Investigating people**	1
2 **Cognitive psychology**	21
3 **Social psychology**	103
4 **Children's development**	171
5 **Physiological psychology**	257
6 **The psychology of individual differences**	333
Answers	413
Bibliography	420
Index	431

Introduction

I wrote this book primarily because I think psychology is such a brilliant subject and I want to share my love of the discipline with everyone. I have enjoyed reading psychology for myself, and I have loved sharing it with others. The best buzz for me is to see light dawning on the faces of my students when they begin to understand that psychology is a real subject which does relate to us all, rather than a set of theories which should be left in academic text books.

The fact that some areas of psychology are still open to discussion can be very disconcerting when you start to study the subject because it would be much nicer to know what you are learning is all undisputed truth. Although there are some theories which are undisputed, other areas, however, are still open to further speculation and this in itself can be a source of excitement. It means that everyone has the potential to contribute to further understanding of of the way we work.

Encouraged by past students, I decided to write this book because they said that when they started to study psychology at A Level they found many of the set texts were quite difficult to relate to real life. I have aimed, therefore, to share some everyday applications of psychology to new students of the subject. There are sufficient theoretical elements to give the new student an understanding of many of the areas of psychology in some depth, alongside much of the most important research in that area. The key studies we look at also include key questions (with answers at the back of the book) to stimulate classroom debate and to focus revision thoughts.

My intention was to encourage thought and critical evaluation but, at the same time, to make reading enjoyable, and for that reason I have included a number of anecdotes and little stories to illustrate the concepts under discussion – after all, if you enjoy or chuckle at something, you are far more likely to remember it. Many of the stories are true, as you will see, and so really do illustrate the interaction between psychology and everyday life.

Although the book is aimed primarily at the content of the first year of the OCR A Level psychology syllabus, I hope that others will read and derive some kind of benefit from the information. If I succeed in encouraging and inspiring anyone to continue with the subject, this past year of constant writing will have all been worthwhile!

Acknowledgements

The author and publisher would like to thank the following for permission to use images: BFI Films: Stills, Posters and Designs, page 39; BFI Films: Stills, Posters and Designs, page 76; Peter Jordan - PA Photos, page 111; Associated Press, page 145; Popperfoto/Reuters, p147; PA Photos, p160; PA Photos, p194; The Advertising Archives, page 214; Science Photo Library, page 217; Corbis-Bettman, page 232; Ronald Grant, page 243; Science Photo Library, page 292; Science Photo Library (x4), page 294; Corbis (x2), page 365; Associated Press, page 368; Andrew Ward - Life File, page 383; The Far Side © Creators Syndicate International, page 394; BFI Films: Stills, Posters & Designs (x2), page 402. All vignette cartoons by Michael Ryan at www.CartoonStock.com.

The publishers would like to thank the following for permission to base key study material on the following studies: Academic Press Inc. for 'Reconstruction of automobile destruction: an example of the interaction between language and memory' by E.F Loftus and J.J. Palmer from the *Journal of Verbal Learning and Verbal Behaviour* Vol 13, 1974; The American Psychological Association for 'Good samaritanism: An underground phenomenon' by I.M. Piliavin, J.A. Rodin and J. Piliavin from *Journal of Personality and Social Psychology* 13, 1969, for 'Transmission of aggression through imitation of aggressive models' by A. Bandura, D. Ross and S.A. Ross from the *Journal of Abnormal and Social Psychology*, 63, 1961, for 'Cognitive, social and physiological determinants of emotional state' by Stanley Schachter and Jerome Singer from *Psychological Review* 69, 1962, for 'Black is beautiful: a reexamination of racial preference and identification' by Joseph Hraba and Geoffrey Grant from the *Journal of Personality and Social Psychology* 16, 1970, for ' A case of multiple personality' by Corbett Thigpen and Harvey Cleckley fom the *Journal of Abnormal and Social Psychology* 49, 1954; Elsevier Science for 'Does the autistic child have a "theory of mind"?' by Simon Baron-Cohen, Alan M. Leslie and Uta Frith from *Cognition* 21, 1985; Mrs A. Milgram for 'Behavioural study of obedience' by Stanley Milgram from the *Journal of Abnormal and Social Psychology* 67, 1963; W.W. Norton & Co. for 'A nation of morons' from *The Mismeasure of Man* by

S.J. Gould, 1981; Pergamon Press for 'Asking only one question in the conservation experiment' by Judith Samuel and Peter Bryant from the *Journal of Child Psychology and Psychiatry* Vol. 23, No. 2, 1984 and 'Social and family relationships of ex-institutional adolescents' by Jill Hodges and Barbara Tizard from *Journal of Child Psychology and Psychiatry*, 30, 1989; Science for 'Teaching sign language to a chimpanzee' by R.A. Gardner and B.T. Gardner from *Science* Vol.165, No. 38994, 1969, for 'On being sane in insane places' by D.L. Rosenhan from *Science* Vol. 179, 1973; Scientific American Inc. for 'Pictorial perception and culture' by Jan B. Deregowski from *Scientific American* 227, 1972 and for 'Experiments in intergroup discrimination' by H.Tajfel from *Scientific American* 223, 1970; Sigmund Freud Copyrights Ltd, the Institute of Psycho-analysis and the Hogarth Press for 'Analysis of a phobia in a five-year-old-boy' from *The Standard Edition of the Complete Works of Sigmund Freud* translated and edited by James Strachey; US Naval Institute for 'A study of prisoners and guards in a simulated prison' by C. Haney, C. Banks and P. Zimbardo from *Naval Research Reviews* 30, 1973. While every effort has been made to trace copyright holders, this has not been possible in all cases; any omissions brought to our attention will be remedied in future printings.

Index compiled by Frank Merrett, Cheltenham, Gloucester.

Investigating people

1

You have decided you want to know more about the subject of psychology. You want to understand how people function, both physically and mentally and what makes them behave the way that they do. I could simply write down all the information I know about psychological theories and research for you to read. The trouble is, even though many of these theories are *accepted* as being true, we can never actually get inside people's heads to find out. This causes an obvious dilemma. If the theories aren't true, how can we possibly find out what is true – how can we discover how people really 'work'.

I could tell you that most people do *this*, or only a few people do *that*, and I could give you examples of research which has shown *this* to be the case, but seriously, how can I *really* know that the people who were under investigation were actually being honest in the way that they behaved or answered questions. Even if we question our own motives as a way of understanding human behaviour, this may make us no closer to understanding because we frequently fool ourselves or make excuses as to why we do things. This kind of introspection has a place in psychology, but I am sure you will realise, the results are going to be quite subjective.

So when you study a subject like psychology, you must learn to question and to evaluate the research that has been done and make your own decisions as to whether you accept the findings of past researchers. You also have to be fair about it because it is very easy to say it is all rubbish! However, unless you can come up with an alternative explanation, you really have to take what others have found seriously.

You have to remember that you are probably going to be biased in some way too. If a researcher is 60 years old, you will probably think he's a bit out of date. When I was a teenager I would have agreed with you, but now I'm actually over half way there, 60 doesn't seem *that* old anymore and I would try and look at the research done by him more positively by stating that he has much more experience than I have.

There is also something known as 'gender bias'. I am female, therefore all females are far superior to males, more intelligent, more able to do lots of tasks at the same time, more sympathetic and so on. However, if I was a male, I would argue that women are much weaker than men, burst out crying too often, become totally irrational around the same time every month and all the other stereotypical characteristics attributed to women.

We can take all these factors into the research situation with us if we are not careful. Therefore in order to try and study people who will *also* have these biases and prejudices, we have to make sure that we are as objective and scientific as we can possibly be. Even then, we can't remove the hidden biases – things we aren't actually aware of doing – like fluttering our eyelashes (if we are female) at attractive male subjects (or the 'vice versa' equivalent), or being extremely negative to the older subject who smells of mothballs and has bad breath.

In order to counteract these situations (most of which have names) or at least keep them to a minimum, we have lots of different designs for research. We also have statistical tests to remove the 'extra bits' of bias mathematically and to tell us if our results really are relevant, or just due to chance. Now read on, bearing in mind what I have just told you.

Alison is going to take her GCSEs next summer and she is already wondering where to go to college to study 'A' Levels. She has decided that she has had enough of school. Yeah, OK the schools not that bad, but she really doesn't fancy having to wear 'sensible' clothes for another two years, and all the boys at the college down the road are so cute!

It's open day at the college and she decides to go and see what it is really like, plus the fact that she hasn't really made up her mind what subject she wants to study. Well, some of these weird subjects that she hasn't done before look quite interesting, especially psychology. That's the one that is all about people and why they do what they do, and body language and aggression and mental illness and stuff – isn't it?

When she gets to the college, along with lots of other students from all different schools, she feels quite nervous. Then she sees Sally, her best mate and this makes it much better. The college has arranged a day where you can go and do sample lessons and find out a bit more about the subject. Along she goes to the psychology department with Sally and quite a few others to hear what the teachers have to say. She is about quarter of an hour early, but she isn't worried because she has a lot of catching up to do with Sally who went to a party with her new boyfriend last weekend. Just as they are about to go into the classroom, two boys come up to them. At first Alison thinks their luck has changed when one of them says, 'Hello, we are psychology students here and we wondered if you would mind taking part in an experiment as part of our coursework?'

Alison looks at Sally, and Sally looks at Alison and they both giggle.

Sally says, 'How long will it take?'

'About ten minutes,' says the dark haired one, who has such gorgeous eyes.

'Will it hurt?' says Alison, fluttering her eyelashes and showing off her cleavage.

The student grins, 'Not this time'.

How do you think the girls feel about the situation? Do you think they have expectations about what they are going to be asked to do? Do you think they could be nervous? What about the male students?

This is a classic example of how people who agree to become subjects in psychological research may actually enter the experiment with expectations or concerns which will in turn affect the way they behave (or perform).

Imagine the same situation with the students asking two boys to take part. They would behave in a completely different way. They may be defiant or act as if they have no fear.

Again, imagine the situation if the researcher was a middle aged man in a white coat and the location was a prestigious university.

By now I hope you will be able to see that psychologists must *carefully* consider ways of investigating people if they want their results to have any value at all. Unfortunately, they don't always get it right, but I hope you will begin to realise that it is not as easy as it seems to put right the mistakes they have made. Whenever you criticise research, you should try to work out how it *should* have been done or whether there was actually an alternative method which wouldn't have resulted in even more problems.

So where do we start?

First of all, we want to try and find out why people behave as they do or why certain things occur. In order to investigate this, we must use a process which is objective and reliable and will produce results which are relevant to everyone – or at least that is what we aim to do.

The way that psychologists investigate the things that interest them is by using 'the scientific method'. This method is really no different to the techniques taught in science at school where you can investigate anything from 'do plants grow without light?' to 'do pH levels affect the rate of enzyme controlled reactions within cells?'

The scientific method actually has four parts to it, and these are things that you will probably have done but not necessarily been aware of.

The scientific method

1 You must make objective observations of the phenomena that you are interested in, for example the differences in gender behaviour or the effects of caffeine on memory.
2 From these observations you will have a good idea of what you want to study. In order to do this you should work out a testable hypothesis on the basis of these observations. A hypothesis is really an educated guess about why people are behaving or reacting in a certain way.
3 You then have to devise a method to test this hypothesis and carry out the research.
4 You should then make both the methods you used and your results available to the public so that others can assess them, replicate them or even extend your findings.

One of the reasons for this is because people can make wild claims which may have a huge effect on our society. A striking example of this was the work of Sir Cyril Burt. He was responsible for the supposed research that resulted in the setting up of the eleven plus exam (an examination used to decide whether schoolchildren should be sent to grammar school or should go to secondary modern school). Grammar schools were very academic and secondary moderns were intended to teach practical skills for the students who were less academically able. After the eleven plus had been in place for a number of years, another researcher started to ask questions about Burt's research. He was interested in why Burt believed it was valid to test eleven year old school children and decide their future.

Sir Cyril Burt was supposed to have carried out a great deal of research about the eleven plus and the fact that your IQ level was supposed to remain the same from age 11 to the end of your life, and that this level was inherited so would never vary. His argument was that if it was always going to be the same, testing people at 11 would be the best way to fit them into an educational system which would be best for them, rather than trying to push them to achieve more that they were capable. But what had happened was that Cyril Burt believed so strongly that this was true that he made up the evidence to prove it. At this point the 11+ was phased out. If it had been possible to give his evidence to the world, he would not have been discredited and millions of children would not have been disadvantaged.

Research methods

There are a number of methods of investigation which come under the umbrella of the scientific method and these are:

1 Experiments
2 Observations
3 Case studies
4 Surveys/questionnaires/interviews
5 Neurophysiological measurements
6 Correlations (worth mentioning although they are really more of a statistical technique than a method)

All of these techniques will be covered in this book. Each one has advantages and disadvantages and each one is suited to specific types of investigations.

The problem lies in the fact that sometimes researchers get it wrong. Perhaps they have poorly designed their study and the participants are not representative of the population as a whole. Perhaps the sample is biased in terms of culture – can you generalise from white, middle class American undergraduate students to the population as a whole? Perhaps the sample just guessed what the study was about and acted accordingly. You also need to consider if the studies have any real value in today's society.

In order to have some idea of the good and bad parts to each methodology it will be useful to go through them, so that when you read the method of each key study you will already have an awareness of the aims of the person undertaking the investigation and what could have gone wrong with their design. We will start with experiments because they are the method everyone always associates with science, and will go through the other techniques in this chapter. The last one, neurophysiological measurements, are actually detailed in the section on biopsychology.

I do hope you will forgive me if some of this seems a little simplistic but I thought, in order to make the subject easier to understand, I would use a very simple type of experiment as an example. It actually has nothing to do with psychology, although our past experiences and beliefs may influence the results but I figured that it would be better to start with something simple in order to look at the possible problems that can arise.

A new company has been formed to develop a new shampoo. Up till now, society has only had one kind of shampoo known as 'Wash' which is a kind of browny-grey colour and smells of disinfectant. This new shampoo, called 'Lustrelocks', obviously needs to be carefully tested in order to find out if it really is better than the others. It smells better and is pink in colour and everyone is waiting with anticipation to find out how good it really is. The company claim that 'Lustrelocks' will make hair shiny and manageable and full of bounce, whereas 'Wash' simply makes it clean.

The executives have appointed a number of scientists to carry out research to decide what method to use to test the shampoo. The leader of the scientific team is called Dr. Kurler. Their hypothesis is that 'NEW LUSTRELOCKS WILL MAKE A SIGNIFICANT DIFFERENCE TO THE SHINE AND MANAGEABILITY OF HAIR' and they will now have to work out some way of testing this hypothesis.

Shall we carry out an experiment, Dr. Kurler?

With an experiment it is important to be able to compare two things in order to see if one has a greater influence than the other. Experiments also need participants, so the question of participants is brought up in my description of this kind of research although it is actually relevant in many respects, in the other different types of methodology. I also ought to mention here that some people use the term participants and others use the term subjects to describe the people who take part. I tend to use the word subject more often, because when I studied psychology that's what they were called. I do understand that some people feel the word subject implies that those taking part are 'subjected' to something and can be considered objects to be manipulated at the researcher's will!

In this particular study, what the researchers are comparing is the two different types of shampoo and how they work on people's hair. They will therefore have two types of condition:

People who use 'Wash' and people who use 'Lustrelocks', and they will be looking to see if their hair is any different afterwards. Therefore:

- One variable (thing that changes) is the different types of shampoo.
- The other variable (thing that changes) may be the way the hair looks before and after shampooing.

(These are known as the **independent variable** – the variable that is being changed or manipulated by the researchers, i.e. the shampoo – and the **dependent variable** – the result.)

It may be that the hair will not be any different but in order to decide whether this shampoo is any good or not they will need to try it out.

First of all, they must ensure that the appearance of the shampoo doesn't influence the subjects. If you were offered nice-smelling, pink shampoo compared with the browny-grey, disinfectant-smelling stuff, it's quite likely that you would automatically be biased. You will probably have a preference for the pink stuff and, as a result, you may have the expectation that it will be better. This **expectancy bias** can have quite an influence on any results. In order to get over this the researchers would have to ensure that the subjects could not smell or see the shampoo.

It is quite likely that the subjects will also have an idea what the experiment is about – and even if they are wrong they may well try and guess. They may be right and realise that by being told to wash their hair twice, the study will have something to do with the shampoo. On the other hand, they may think that it is something to do with their hair texture, or even the techniques they use for washing – do they massage the shampoo into the scalp and so on. Whatever conclusion they come up with, it will probably influence the results because they will no longer be behaving normally. They may either try to help the experimenter or actually try and go against what they think the study is about depending on their interpretation of the worthiness of the study. These extra influences on the results are called **demand characteristics** and can actually ruin the results of a study.

I think the classic example of demand characteristics was demonstrated by studies carried out by Orne, who was interested in the fact that people behave very differently in a psychological study to the way they behave in everyday life. In one study he asked a number of people whether they would carry out five push-ups as a personal favour and, not surprisingly, they all refused. However, when he played the role of research psychologist, they all became very obliging and willing to help. Although the behaviour was the same, and the reasons for asking were the same (to see how people would behave), the responses were totally different.

The most amusing of Orne's studies was carried out in 1962 when he was trying find out whether subjects who were hypnotised were more obedient. He never did find out whether they were because he became more fascinated by the fact that people act in a totally different way if they think they are taking part in a psychological experiment.

Before Orne started the study, he took away their watches. He then asked his subjects to add up rows of numbers on sheets filled with numbers that had been randomly generated. Each subject was given 2000 sheets and each sheet meant they would have to make 224 calculations. He told them to continue to work and that he was leaving the room but would be back later. After five and a half hours they were still working which he found extraordinary. They must have believed that the study was worthwhile, otherwise they wouldn't have continued but he wondered if there was another reason for their continuing to work. He wondered if they were simply being obedient.

In order to get round this, he decided to make the task so ridiculous that he felt they couldn't possibly agree to go on. He told them that once they had finished a sheet, they had to pick a card up from a pile which would tell them what to do next. The card they had to pick up said: 'You are to tear up the sheet of paper which you have just completed into a minimum of 32 pieces and go on to the next sheet of paper and continue working as you did before. When you have completed this piece of paper, pick up the next card which will instruct you further. Work as accurately and rapidly as you can.' How long would it take you to realise that the whole episode was simply a waste of time? Probably not very long – but that is because you are not taking part. If you had been there, you would have been trying to work out the purpose of such a study. Well, presumably Orne's subjects did the same because they all carried on, adding up numbers and tearing up the sheets just as they had been instructed!

There is one further problem that could influence the results which it is worth mentioning here and this is that the experimenter can actually influence the results. If our researchers went up to people with the two bottles of shampoo they themselves would expect the new 'Lustrelocks' to work better, wouldn't they? After all, they have probably spent months working out this secret formula and have great expectations about how good it is going to be.

'Come in subjects. Do sit down. I am going to tell you what I want you to do. There are two bottles on the table in front of you and I want you to wash your hair with both of them. Before you wash your hair you must put on the blindfold and nose clip. Use the first one tomorrow, the one with Number One on the label, and see how your hair feels and whether it feels as if it has more body and bounce.' The experimenter smiles at the subjects and gives them an approving nod. Then, almost as an afterthought, he says, 'Use the other one the next day.'

Do you think subjects would have some idea which one is supposed to be best? This influence, although it is unconscious, can also totally influence the results. This influence is called an **experimenter effect**.

If the researchers have managed to control these problems, the next question crops up: whose hair is going to be washed?

Look at these subjects – do you think they are all going to have the same type of hair? Is this going to be relevant?

Think about your own hair. Is it the same length as your friends or family? Is it the same colour or texture? Are you all the same ages? What have you done to your hair before – have you coloured or bleached it? Do you wear hair gel or mousse? Are you male or female (because that might make a difference)? Do you go swimming a lot and get chlorine in your hair? Have you had your hair permed?

Now think about this in terms of subjects for any kind of experiment rather than simply the shampoo study. No two people are the same, are they? Not only are people not the same in terms of what they look like, but they will not have had the same experiences as each other, they will not necessarily be as intelligent as each other, they may not be the same ages or gender, or they may have come from different parts of the country. Some may be tall and some may be extremely short. Some may have had normal family lives and some may have been in institutions. Some may have broken bones, or suffered with illness. Some may get migraines while others may never have had an ache or pain in their lives. Some may come from one cultural group while others may have totally different codes of behaviour.

What an experimental nightmare!

No, the researchers won't give up at this point and go home – they will try to do the best they can. There are three possible options.

Matched pairs

They can either try and match the subjects so that the ones in each group are as similar as possible. Obviously, the ideal way is to use clones, but as clones are not readily available to researchers at the moment, identical twins are the next best option. The only problem is that there aren't that many available identical twins around. So what they will do is to match the pairs as far as possible for the factors they are interested in. For this experiment it will probably be first of all for hair type, then age and possibly gender. They will have, say, 10 men and 10 women in each group and there will be, say, one long haired in each group, one short haired in each group, one red head in each group and so on. In real psychological experiments, they would match the two groups as far as possible for the factors they are interested in, which again could be gender and age, but may also be IQ or background. The study by Hodges and Tizard gives a good example of matched pairs.

Repeated measures

Perhaps they could make the subjects try both shampoos and do a 'before and after' comparison. The trouble is the hair wouldn't be dirty the second time so we might have to wait for a while before we do the next shampoo. In the meantime the person may have done all sorts of other things with their hair which could affect the results. I guess a way round this would be to shampoo half with 'Wash' and half with 'Lustrelocks' as their first shampoo, and then alternate with the second shampoo. This would at least give us a slightly better idea.

Effects like these can happen when any person has to do different things as part of a study. They may use the experience of the first trial as a kind of practice for the second trial – known as **practice effects**. The things they do between the trials may also influence the results. They may simply be tired the second time around, which again may affect how well they do – known as **fatigue effects**. So if you read about studies where subjects have to do more than one thing, bear this in mind.

Independent subjects

Here they could simply have a huge number of people, randomly divided into two groups who we hope would balance each other out. After all, if there are enough of them it would seem likely that there would be people of all types in both groups, wouldn't it? I don't need to tell you that logistically, if we are to make this work, we would need a lot of people and this is one disadvantage of this method.

Each of the designs has problems – but it is the researcher's choice as to what method he uses. You should always look out for the type of design used for research and consider the subjects, the way they were chosen and whether or not they represent the population as a whole. After all, if our researchers chose, say, six year olds, they would all have hair – sure enough – but probably their hair will be much healthier and less affected by all the preparations we use on our hair as we get older. In this case they may be good subjects but are unlikely to represent the population as a whole.

Sampling

Choosing people for any kind of research should not really be that difficult, except that lots of people don't like the idea of taking part in research, whereas others think it's great fun. This should make you aware that even this small difference can mean we have two different groups of people – the 'don't like's and the 'it's fun's. I have to admit that I am one of these sad people who are willing to be a subject if it involves filling in questionnaires, especially if I think I am going to get something out of it, like a free holiday or shopping vouchers. On the other hand, if I am in a hurry in a shopping centre and someone approaches me with a clipboard, I tend to run for it! However, lots of my friends think I am mad to waste my time on any type of questionnaires and say that no matter what the survey was about, they wouldn't bother to get involved.

Here we have an example of what is known as a **self-selecting sample** – people who want to take part. Maybe there's something about me that makes me want to do it, and that something is enough to affect the results of what ever it is that I do.

The Milgram study is one of those which uses a self-selecting sample. Other studies have also enticed their participants with promises of either money or credits on psychology courses – look out for the one that involves financial rewards.

Ideally, the best kind of sample is a **random sample**, taken from the **population** of people you are interested in investigating. A random sample means that every person has an equal chance of being selected. The ideal way is to put everyone's name in a hat and draw out the relevant number of names. I will never forget one student saying in a test paper, 'A random sample is where you put everyone in a hat and take out the ones you want.' It must have been one immense hat!

In the shampoo experiment, the population the researchers are interested in would be anyone and everyone, because the shampoo is not targeted at any particular group of people. However, if the company decided it should be for teenagers, the **sampling frame** would be teenagers and the sample would be taken from all the teenagers there were. In most research, there would be a more limited sampling frame, like all the teenagers in a certain area, but here it is obvious that that area might not be the same as another area, so we would have to bear that in mind.

Stratified samples are where you take the same proportion of people in your sample as there are in the population. Let's return to our hair experiment here. If 30% of the population have black hair, 30% have blonde hair, 20% have red hair and 20% have mousey hair, the sample would have to contain the same proportions. If the researchers wanted a sample size of 100, 30 would have black hair, 30 would be blonde, 20 would be red heads and 20 would be mice.

Quota samples are a bit like stratified samples. You identify the different types of people, but simply have the same number of each, e.g. 25 of each hair colour to make up a sample of 100.

The last type of sample is the one used by most psychology students when carrying out their research and these are **opportunity samples**. This means that you grab anyone available to take part, but the weaknesses of this kind of sample are fairly obvious – do you think the people you come into contact with every day are representative of the population as a whole?

Whatever design is chosen and whatever sample is decided upon, it must be remembered that where the experiment is carried out will also influence the subjects, and they will have expectations of what is going to happen from their past experiences. Sometimes you can help to get over this by doing a **field experiment** – no this is not an experiment in a field, but one in a naturalistic setting (although one candidate in an exam described it as a study undertaken in a field!). Perhaps a field study would help to get over the effects of pollution on the hair of our subjects.

But how are the researchers going to measure the differences in their hair (as I'm not a trichologist I have absolutely no idea)? The problem with some studies is that the chosen measurement of the effects are sometime a little worrying, so make sure when you are designing and evaluating studies that you take into account whether the results are actually measuring the effects of the manipulation of the independent variable (or in English, is the way the researchers want to get their results – for example, hair shine and static electricity – actually measuring the effects on the hair of the two different types of shampoo).

Perhaps an observational study would be preferable

Here the researchers may have decided that perhaps they could simply watch the behaviour of the subject's hair after they have washed it. They would have to work out what sort of categories of behaviour hair is likely to fit into before they conducted their study. Will it be very static, or just hang lankly? What will happen when the wind blows and will the knots come out easily after washing? Obviously when the study is designed, the type of study will influence whether to watch the behaviours or calculate the results in some other way. If it is a study looking at the effects of something on behaviour, then observing that behaviour is essential. For other studies, observations would be totally inappropriate such as a study on memory – watching people remembering lists of words would not be very helpful.

Observations are used for studies of things like aggressive behaviour or behaviour between groups of people. They can be done by observing the behaviour of your subjects either overtly or covertly, or occasionally research has been done using a method called participant observation. The observation can take place in a laboratory or 'in the field'.

Overt observation

Subjects know they are being observed but this can be a problem as it may change behaviour. Usually subjects get used to being watched after a while and it is said that they have **habituated** to the researcher. Think of 'fly on the wall' documentaries as an example of how people habituate to situations. You may say that you could never behave as people do in these documentaries if they were being filmed, but after a while the people cease noticing that the camera is there.

Covert observation

This is where people hide in trees or behind walls or one way mirrors, so they can't be seen. They could also secretly video the people they are watching. If this is done, you must make sure you don't get arrested for being a peeping tom.

Participant observation

This is where the person observing actually becomes part of the group of people they want to watch. In fact, the film 'I.D.' is a good example of this as it is the story of a couple of policemen infiltrating a gang of football hooligans in order to find out how they operate.

One real life study was undertaken by Whyte (1943) who joined an Italian street gang in Chicago. It was obvious that he was not a normal gang member but he used the cover that he was writing a book. The study is most famous because of his statement 'I began as a non-participating observer. As I became accepted into the community, I found myself becoming almost a non-observing participant.'

If an observational study is undertaken there are some things that must be taken into consideration. You must make sure that the behaviours you are expecting to see actually exist, and that there aren't so many of them that you spend more time trying to work out where to tick on the chart and miss World War Three going on in front of you. You must also make sure that the observations are objective so, for example, you the researchers would design it so that the shampoo manufacturers wouldn't be able to see what they wanted to see and needed to use objective criteria. Finally, you must make sure that observers don't get so bored that they fall asleep. The objectivity can be sorted by having more than one objective observer and then checking that they agree with each other's scores – known as inter-observer or inter-rater reliability. The boredom factor can be solved by something known as time sampling, where you watch for five minutes, say, and then rest for five and so on. The other thing you must remember is that you should never observe someone in a place where they would not normally be on public display unless you have their permission – so stuffing a one way mirror in people's bathrooms is a no go!

Perhaps we should carry out a case study, Dr. Kurler?

Here our intrepid experimenters decide that they will look at someone's hair over a period of time and document when it is washed and what shampoo was used, making copious notes in graphic detail about every possible piece of information. They would then be able to look at any strange or unusual phenomena which may occur as a result of the different types of shampoo.

Case studies do actually have a specific purpose in psychology. They are generally carried out over a long period of time and involve looking in detail at either one or possibly a couple of subjects. They are usually used to look at interesting and unusual phenomena for example Freud's study of Little Hans. The main problem is that they can be quite subjective. If you get to know someone really well over a period of time, they are going to behave in a slightly different way towards you compared with other people, and you will perhaps be less objective about their behaviour as you would have been at the onset of the study.

Perhaps we could simply go for a survey, questionnaire or interview

These methods are frequently used in psychology often to accompany other research. In our shampoo study, we could certainly ask the subjects how they feel about their hair after using the new shampoo and this would give us quite a lot of valuable information to work on. The trouble is that in any kind of questioning people aren't always honest and they may tell us that the shampoo is excellent when they really chucked it down the drain.

There are two different types of questions used in these methods: **open** and **closed questions**. The first is really difficult to analyse but can give lots of very interesting information. After all, some people go on and on about all sorts of things when asked certain questions, and yet you have to actually discard it because it doesn't fit into a scoring system. Others produce great insights into causes and effects. However, these methods are often used as they may give the opportunity of finding out information from a large number of people (questionnaires or surveys) or allow interviewers to focus on one particular area in much greater detail (interviews with open questions).

Whatever happens, the questions must be understandable. Have you ever been given a questionnaire which is really difficult to answer and seems to be totally meaningless or you just don't understand the questions. Another problem is using what is known as 'an answer set' where you *always* tick a's or b's. The other really annoying fact is that some questionnaires are so obvious that you can work out what the right answer is and can mark it accordingly to try and make yourself seem 'very popular', or 'a good lover' and so on.

Perhaps the only way to do it is to measure their brains, Dr. Kurler?

This is where we actually measure people's responses or behaviours using instruments but the problem here is that they aren't going to be very useful for our shampoo research. What I have done is to talk about these types of measurements in the sections relating to sleep and to murderers' brains.

All methods of neurophysiological measurement use specialised equipment. The idea is that the equipment cannot lie, so that if there is something different about a person's responses it can be objectively measured.

Examples are EEGs which measure the changes in electrical activity in different areas of the brain. CT scans are useful to see structural abnormalities. MRI scans are similar to CAT scans but are more accurate because they can pick up smaller details. PET scans allow researchers to examine the relationship between brain activity and mental processes. You will find more information about these types of measurement and how they are carried out in the section on physiology.

Maybe the only thing left to do is a correlation

Correlations are not really a design but more of a statistical procedure. They look for a **relationship** between two variables such as TV watching and aggression. For example, does TV watching affect the amount of aggressive behaviour children display?

The trouble is, **correlations can't actually prove anything** because there could always have been another variable which was not taken into account. Our child may well watch lots of violent TV programmes and may demonstrate huge amounts of aggressive behaviour but the poor child was beaten regularly by its father throughout its life but we haven't taken that into account because it is not one of the variables we are concerned with. Therefore the relationship exists but the TV is probably not the cause. You can see from this how dangerous it is to accept a correlation as being a factual cause.

There are lots of other examples I could cite to make the point here such as the relationship of hot weather to aggressive behaviour. The problem is that when it is hot, we often drink more, and that drink may well be ice cold lager which can lead to people getting aggressive because they are under the influence of alcohol.

Correlations aren't all bad and actually raise a number of potential research questions in psychology. If you find a relationship between two variables, you can then go on to investigate that relationship further. They are also used to check the reliability of psychometic tests (see below) or to compare scores on different types of tests such as how life-stress test scores relate to illness.

Positive and negative correlations

There are two different types of correlation, positive and negative. A positive correlation shows that as one thing goes up, so does another. Supposing we wanted to investigate whether eating lots of steak makes you run faster, we would have to look at the speed of running of athletes and see if there was a relationship between their speed and the number of large rump steaks they ate every week. This could be done by drawing a scattergram.

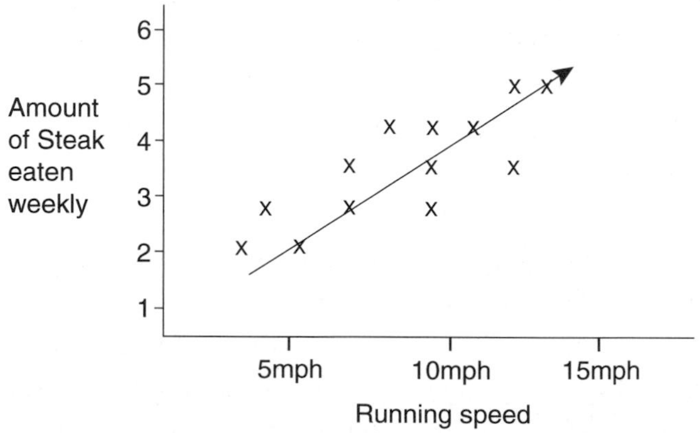

Can you see from the generalised direction that the more steak people eat the faster they seem to run? This would indicate that there is a positive relationship between the amount of steak you eat and your speed of running.

On the other hand supposing we looked at the number of plates of chips you eat and the speed you can run. We would expect the opposite relationship here with speed slowing in relation to the number of bowls of chips you eat.

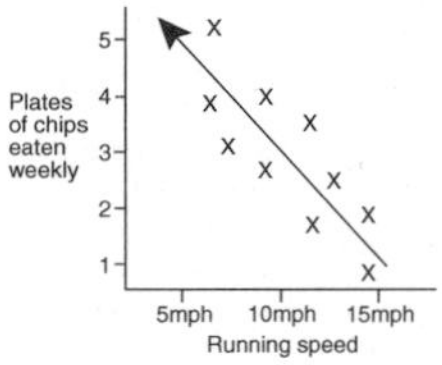

If the amount of food you ate had no bearing at all on your speed of running, the scattergram would show no pattern at all.

Can you see from these examples that we are assuming that the food influences running speed, but we haven't taken into account the athlete's build, or the amount of training they do, and these could be far more relevant to the overall performance of the athlete; the food could have very little relevance.

What about reliability and validity?

One of the things you will hear a lot about in psychology is reliability and validity. **Reliability** means: is the test going to give consistent results? If you measure people one day and then again a week later, will you get the same set of results?

Reliability is checked by doing a test and then retesting sometime later (making sure that your subjects can't remember the results of the first test!).

For a test to be valid or have **validity** means that it is measuring what we want it to measure. For example, if I gave you a passage to read and said I was measuring your intelligence, would you think that a bit odd? What the passage would actually be measuring is your reading ability.

Validity can be assured by first of all looking to see if it looks like it is measuring what we want it to measure (face validity). We could get experts to check it (content validity) or check it against a test that is supposed to be measuring the same thing (criterion validity). We could also check for predictive validity – is the test a valid predictor of future outcomes? An example here would be whether GCSEs are a valid predictor of A Level results.

Let me give you a practical example of reliability and validity. Supposing I told you that I was going to measure the circumference of your head with my tape measure because I had been told that intelligence and head circumference were related to each other – the bigger the circumference, the more the brain. Obviously this is untrue, after all, Einstein didn't have a particularly large brain, but he was very intelligent. Therefore the test would be a reliable test because your head circumference would not vary from year to year (test/retest) but it bears no relationship to intelligence, therefore it is not a valid test of intelligence.

Ethical considerations

I am sure you will realise that it is not really ethical to make your subject do all sorts of things that they would find unpleasant or embarrassing. You can't shave their hair off in order to analyse them without their prior consent. You can't stick electrodes in their heads while pinning them down, even if it is for the advancement of science. You can't push your best friend out into the oncoming traffic to look at whether men or women drivers have quicker reaction times. You mustn't wrench small babies from mothers to investigate children's development, and you can't frighten people by throwing buckets of spiders over them, just to see what the effects of over-arousal are. I know this is probably a bit disappointing but that's the way it is. However, people have not always conducted research that followed the accepted ethical guidelines, as you will see from the key studies. In order to be able to evaluate these studies, you must have an idea of what the ethical guidelines are, and if you are in a position to carry out psychological research you must follow them.

The British Psychological Society issued revised principles in June 1990 and these are the ones that we use to evaluate our studies and to guide further research.

Although there are actually ten principles, they can be reduced to the following most important points:

Consent

- Have the subjects given their informed consent to take part? This means: have they agreed, knowing what the study is about?
- Have the parents of child subjects given informed consent to the research procedures?
- Have payments been used to induce risk-taking behaviour?

Deception

- Have the subjects been deceived about the nature of the study?
- Was there any way to carry out the study other than by using deception?
- Have the procedures been approved by other psychologists?

Welfare

- Has the physical and psychological welfare of the subjects been maintained throughout the whole study?
- Have they left the research in the same condition as they entered?

Debriefing

- Have the subjects been effectively debriefed?

(Adapted from OCR Psychology syllabus, 1999)

Back to the shampoo!

So now we have decided what design we are going to use for our hair study, we have looked at whether there were any ethical considerations that needed to be taken into account, and we can now get our subjects to do what is required. We really need to try to make sure that all our subjects' hair is as dirty as each other, and that they haven't secretly washed it the night before – so they don't look so grotty on the day of the study. The trouble is, there will be some things we can't account for, like the fact that some of them have had flu recently, which may make the hair out of its normal condition. We also can't account for the fact that some of them may have come across a city to get to where we are going to do this study, battling their way through the grime and pollution of city life, while others have come from the countryside where the air is much more pure. These things that we can't account for are called **extraneous variables** or rather extra variables that we don't know about which can affect our results. Extraneous variables are very similar to **confounding variables** and sometimes the terms are used interchangeably. Confounding variables are so called because they might confound or confuse our results and make us think that, say, the shampoo is causing the changes in hair condition, whereas it might be something like the hardness of the water.

Statistical tests are used to mathematically remove the effects of some of these unwanted variables. How they work, I don't really know, but eminent mathematicians have spent hours working out complicated formulas which serve this purpose and that's good enough for me! The main thing you need to remember about statistical tests is that they are able to show whether, for example, any differences in the results between two sets of scores are **significant** differences. It's like saying that one group scored 36 at a test and another group scored 37 but that one score difference may have simply been a fluke – it was not a difference that had any real significance, it may well have been due to chance.

In order for a statistical test to show a significant difference or relationship, we have to be 95% sure that the results are due to what we have done. We can cope with 5% being due to chance, but any more than that makes the odds too high. In our experiment we would be looking for new 'Lustrelocks' to have made a significant difference to the hair of our subjects – whether that change is for better or worse!

I hope this romp through the methodology used in psychological research has given you some insight into the kinds of problems that can be experienced. It should also help you to understand the studies in the book. Many of the key studies that you will read about were well designed while some leave a lot to be desired. Samples were not always representative, or were relatively small, and this certainly influenced many of the results. Look at when the studies were done as many of them were done some years ago now, and perhaps the result would be different nowadays. Ethics, too, were not always of prime consideration.

At least you have a basis on which to evaluate these studies and an understanding of how they could, perhaps, have been improved.

Cognitive psychology

2

Almost everything we do causes us to think. We think about what we are going to do and then think about what we have done. We plan, we discuss, we imagine, we remember, we try to make sense of the world around us and even when we can't, we try and work out why. Sometimes working out why produces the wrong answer, but the processes involved are all interlinked. All these processes involve cognition.

I remember entering my second year at university, still not really understanding what was meant by cognition. What an awful thing to admit! The concept of cognitive psychology continued to seem so obscure and indefinable until one day one of the new first year students asked me what cognitive psychology actually was. I suddenly thought that it is really like the cogs of your brain, whirring away in your head, interconnecting and driving other cogs, a bit like a clock. Of course this is too simplistic for such an amazing set of complex abilities, but at least it's a start.

Cognitive psychology covers a number of areas: memory, perception, language, thinking and attention. All these processes are interconnected because you will find it very difficult to do one without involving another. You cannot identify a seen object without thinking what it is called. In fact you won't even try to identify it unless you happen to be looking in the right place at the right time (paying attention to it), and if you do identify it as something frightening you will have to work out how to escape. There is also a huge debate about the fact that you cannot think without language although I will not go into it here as it is briefly mentioned later in the section on language at the end of this chapter.

One of the questions psychologists frequently ask is whether we are actually born with cognitive skills or whether we acquire them as we mature? Most psychologists believe that we are born with very basic skills, but the majority develop through a process of maturation and experience. This nature-nurture debate constantly appears in all areas of psychology but it is particularly evident in the area of cognition.

The following sections of this chapter focus on four key areas of cognition. The topic of memory is addressed by looking at its structure and function and how accurate it really is. Perception is considered by investigating, among other things, whether our abilities are innate or learned and whether there are cross cultural differences in how we interpret the same stimulus. Thinking is addressed by considering how children begin to work out that other people do not see the world in the same way as they do. The last section is focused on whether language is an innate ability in humans or is simply learned.

Memory

We will begin by looking at one of the most fundamental and complex of human cognitive abilities, the human memory. In fact it is hard to start anywhere else with psychology because what we have stored in our memory is the basis of what makes us who we are, and dictates how we behave. It is for this reason that the section on memory is the longest in this book.

It is difficult to find a precise defintion of 'memory' but it is often referred to as 'the ability to retain information and demonstrate retention through behaviour'. If we could not retain and use information that we have already discovered, it would mean that we would have to process huge amounts of information all the time.

> On his way home last week, Kit encountered a large grizzly bear walking down his road. He knew as a result of the information he had already stored that large grizzly bears have a nasty habit of eating people, and therefore he realised that he should, at all costs, escape. He also remembered that bears like honey, and he just happened to have a jar of honey in his bag. He threw the jar of honey on the pavement as he ran in the opposite direction, and managed to escape whilst the bear was sidetracked by the honey splattered all over the pavement.

Lucky for Kit that his memory was intact. If he had not already stored that information, he would have taken a while to work out what this huge wooly creature actually was, and whether or not it was dangerous, by which time he may have become dinner.

Now imagine what life would be like if you lost the ability to store information.

Henry woke up at 7 o'clock on a Tuesday morning with the sound of the alarm clock blasting in his ears. The problem was he seemed to have lost all of his memory. What was that dreadful noise he said to himself as he looked at the square object on the thing by the side of the thing he was lying on. What is it? How do I stop it? He wasn't sure whether to be frightened of it or annoyed by it. He picked it up, not too sure of what to do next, and threw it across the room. It stopped.

Where am I? Who am I? Suddenly a flat rectangular shape to his side opened and a creature shouted something to him. He realised that this creature was telling him to 'Get up', but he wasn't quite sure where he should get up, or even how to get up... He put the two flat things which seemed to be located at the end of the long things attached to his body onto the soft coloured cover below him and pulled himself into a vertical position.

He suddenly felt the urge to do something, but he wasn't sure what he should do or even where he should do it. 'Do you want the bathroom first before your darling sister gets in there?' said the loud, slightly high-pitched voice. He noticed the creature standing in the door had lots of hair and bumps in strange places. What's a bathroom, he thought? He looked down and suddenly noticed that there was a wet patch on the floor in front of him.

Just imagine what it must be like to have no recollection of anything. Think of all the things you do automatically everyday which rely on stored knowledge such as getting dressed, finding your way around, talking, writing and reading. Is there anything you can do without referring to your memory?

In fact I have painted a very bleak picture for Henry because even very serious amnesic patients (patients who have lost their memory) do not suffer such a large memory loss. Henry had not lost his linguistic skills, although he was having problems remembering names, but he could still talk. Amnesics also remember how to talk and understand language. They will often remember how to dress themselves and how to eat and drink and do things that are well practised. We will return to them later.

From the little we have considered so far, it is obvious that memory helps us to know who we are, it helps us to make sense of the current situation we are in and it enables us to make plans for the future.

I remember being asked to write an essay, 'Is memory like a tape recorder?' and my initial reaction as I started to study psychology was that I thought it was. I used to believe that everything that happened to us was stored in our memories, even though we could not always get access to it. This would help to explain why hypnosis managed to help people recall information that they thought they had lost. I hope you realise by the end of this section how wrong

I actually was, and how memory is a dynamic process which is constantly being updated or changed by the experiences we have.

Psychologists who are interested in memory not only consider what happens when memory becomes disrupted but are also interested in how memory is structured and how it actually works. The structures are the various component parts, like short term memory and long term memory, and the processes are how information is taken in and how it is stored and then recalled.

They have also discovered that there are a number of factors which influence whether information is stored or simply forgotten. I am sure that you have already experienced this because you don't remember all the information you are told, or you may only remember it for a limited amount of time. However, it has been found that we tend to store information if it is very different to other information, if it is rich in detail, if it is connected to other things we know or if it is personally important to us.

The three processes of memory

The next section is going to look at how we take in information and store it and how we can then get at it when we need it. These processes are known as the three processes of memory.

In order to understand what these processes are I would like you to imagine looking up a telephone number in your local directory. Then, being a tidy sort of person, you put the directory away and finally write the number down.

1 ENCODING

First of all you encoded the information, that is you took the relevant numbers into your memory system. Therefore encoding is 'the acquisition of knowledge and creation of an internal representation to be stored'.

It would appear that there are three types of encoding

a) **Acoustic/phonetic encoding** or encoding for sound. This is when you hear in your head what someone has just said to you or you keep words in your head, in this case, the telephone number. Psychologists have found that it is really easy to get muddled up when the sounds are similar, for example if you try to remember a list of words that all sound the same such as bee, tree, three, he, me, see, wee, flee, tea, you will find it harder than a list of words that sound dissimilar.

b) **Visual encoding** is used to produce an image of what something or someone looks like.

c) **Semantic encoding** or encoding for meaning is where you process information by thinking about what it actually means rather than what it looks or sounds like. This seems to produce the best storage. In fact this method is so good that it is often used to remember lists of things. Take for example the colours of the spectrum. You probably know that they are red, orange, yellow, green, blue, indigo and violet. How can you remember what order they come in. Well the best way is to make up a rhyme from the first letters of each word, R O Y G B I V, and then make up a sentence which has meaning from those meaningless initials – Richard of York gave battle in vain. This method of semantic encoding is called using mnemonics.

Interestingly enough, many of the memory problems you may suffer from are due to failure of encoding – that is you do not pay attention to them. Suppose I said to you, I have the phone number of Mr. Bloggs the builder, and I read it out to you. You would probably think 'So what', and instantly forget it. However, supposing I said to you that I have the phone number of a stunningly beautiful actor/actress (take your pick), do you think you are more likely to remember it?

2 STORAGE

The second process is when you store the information. This requires you to retain the information in an understandable form so that you can then go on to the third process. With our phone number, we will more than likely have to keep saying it to ourselves as a way of storing it. This is probably because the numbers have little meaning and are not really of any great importance to us.

3 RETRIEVAL

Finally, you have to get the information back (retrieve it). This is done by either recognition, which involves matching a stored item with something in your environment, or by recalling it, that is bringing it back into conscious awareness.

Do you know, I was walking down the road the other day when I saw this bloke watching me as I walked along. It was horrible because I knew I knew him, but I couldn't work out how. I know I recognised him, but you know what it is like, you hope they won't talk to you because you don't want to admit that you cannot recall their name or where you met them before and I thought it might be something dodgy! As it turns out, he walked over to me and informed me that he was still waiting for my cheque. I immediately knew who he was – I had smashed my bike into his fence some time before and had said I'd pay for the damage!

Here, our 'lad' had no problems with recognition, but was unable to recall information about the person he had recognised.

Let us return to the telephone number I read out to you. When you tried to remember it, you would have had to recall it as you would not be matching it against any other numbers. However, the chances of you remembering it for any length of time are fairly remote (after all it was only Mr. Bloggs). On the other hand, you are unlikely to have problems remembering your own phone number no matter how long ago you moved into the house. This tends to indicate that there is more than one type of memory, memory which doesn't last for very long (short term memory – STM) and memory which lasts perhaps for ever (long term memory – LTM).

The first psychologists to notice this fact also discovered that people who sustained brain damage sometimes lost either their STM or their LTM. This indicated that there must be different types of memory store and they used this information to try to help them understand the component parts of memory and how they fit together.

Sensory memory

The first type of memory is known as **sensory memory**. This type of memory is necessary because if we don't retain an impression of whatever we have experienced, how can we decide whether or not we actually want to begin to process it adequately in order to understand it – or even decide to disregard it. Let me explain this further. Look around the room that you are in. There are lots of objects in the room but if I asked you to look for a pen you would need to be aware of all the other objects that are there before you could decide whether or not they were pens or whether they are likely to contain a pen.

It is called sensory memory because it refers to a 'fleeting' memory which is registered by the sensory receptors of sight (iconic memory) and sound (echoic memory). This information is stored within these receptors and not at a central location, lasts for seconds and is then gone. An example of echoic memory, which I am sure you will have experienced, is if you are watching TV or reading and someone speaks to you. Just as you are about to say 'What did you say?' you realise that you can 'play back' the words that are still echoing in your head.

Short term memory

Psychologists, including Atkinson and Shiffrin (1971), decided that information which stayed in consciousness after encoding was kept in short term memory whereas information that leaves conscious awareness but can later be recalled has been put into long term memory.

As I mentioned earlier, there has been evidence to support this idea from studies of both brain damaged people and people suffering from Korsakoff's syndrome (amnesia caused by alcohol abuse). These people can retain information in conscious awareness (STM) but have problems remembering information from the past (LTM).

It seems that some information from sensory memory is successfully passed on to the STM which allows us to store it for long enough to enable us to use it – for example, retaining the phone number long enough to dial it, although it may be forgotten soon after. It is also a memory store that allows us to have a conversation with another person. You can't remember the whole content of a conversation but if you can't remember what the person you are talking to has just said to you, how could you answer them? Therefore it seems that you need to retain that information for a short period of time.

We know that the capacity of STM is limited. In fact in 1956, George Miller gave the most famous account of the capacity of STM in his article, 'The magic number seven, plus or minus two'. Here he claims that we can retain between 5 and 9 pieces of information in STM. He also explained that we can increase the capacity of STM by chunking pieces of information together. If I asked you to remember the digits 0 2 0 7 9 4 6 1 4 3 2 individually, you would find that your STM memory was full, but if you put those letters together to form chunks, you would not have a problem remembering them – 0207 946 1432.

Another example of how we can increase this capacity is by chunking together information that would otherwise have no meaning. If I asked you to remember the letters T WA I B M B A B B C you may be able to remember them, but if I told you to remember TWA (Trans World Airlines) IBM (the computer company) BA (British Airways) and BBC (British Broadcasting Corporation) you would probably have no trouble. This organisation increases the storage capacity of STM by imposing units of meaning on chunks of otherwise unrelated numbers.

The duration of STM (how long the information is retained), according to Atkinson and Shiffrin (1971), is between 15 and 30 seconds. It can be easily disrupted, for example someone asking you a question while you are trying to keep something in your mind by saying it to yourself.

> Andrew was trying to work out why his bank statement said he was overdrawn. He was sure he'd put enough money in this month to cover all the things he had bought. Yes, OK, he had gone a bit mad when he went clothes shopping, but not that mad! He decided that the bank must have made a mistake. The trouble was that there were so many transactions that month, so he would have to add them all up. That way he could find out whether the bank had made a mistake or not.
>
> Right, he said to himself, I have used two chequebooks this month, so if I add up all the items in one, and then add them to the other, I should work out how much I have spent. He started to add them up and had just got to the end of the first one when he realised he had got the wrong second cheque book. He kept saying the amount to himself in his head while he looked for the right book when his mother called out, 'Andrew, that girl is on the phone again. Do you want to talk to her?'

Guess what he did. Yes, he completely forgot the amount he had totalled so far, because he was too busy thinking about the phone call and how he could tell this girl that he wasn't interested! This should give you some idea how fragile STM really is.

Long term memory

Some of the things we experience or learn as we grow up stay with us for very long periods and some for the whole of our lives. This information has gone into long term memory and seems to be fairly stable. No one has ever filled a long term memory, although sometimes it feels, say if you are revising, that you cannot store any more information. We believe that one cause of forgetting happens as a result of the memory trace no longer being available (having decayed), and this could be through lack of activation of information or through interference from other memories. This interference could be in the form of over-writing the memory or confusing it with other similar memories. The other cause of forgetting may be a result of not actually being able to get at the stored information, ie lack of accessibility. This is when you know you know something but cannot actually remember what it is you know.

Psychologists have constructed a number of models of memory which they have tried to use to explain how memory works. Obviously, you can't test a theory unless you have a theory in the first place, so you should think of a model as being no more than a theory. Psychologists then use various experiments to try to support the model, but if the results show that the model is not quite right they then have to modify their original design.

The multi-store model (Atkinson and Shiffrin, 1968)

Atkinson and Shiffrin proposed the first model of memory which was very simple and involved information passing into sensory memory, then into short term memory and finally into long term memory.

According to this model, incoming information is received by the sensory register and is either selected for further processing or is lost. If it is selected, it then goes into short term memory. Here it can be retained for a limited period of time before it is lost, unless we choose to transfer it to long term memory. The way this happens is that we have to say it over and over again to ourselves, which is called 'rehearsal'.

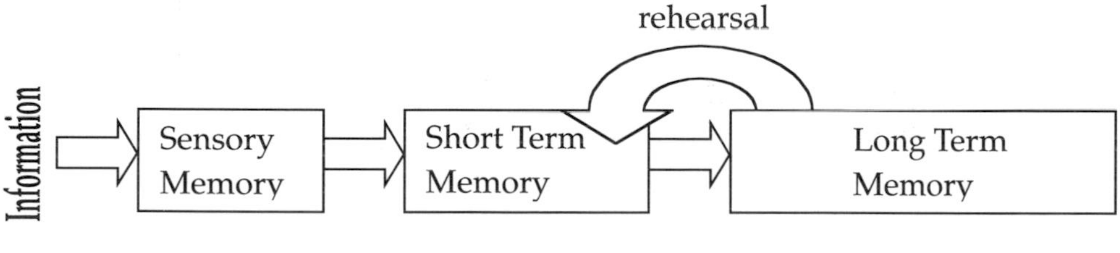

In the diagram, rehearsal is shown by the 'loop' between STM and LTM. According to this model, unrehearsed items are forgotten.

There is quite a lot of evidence to support the multi-store model and it is worth considering the evidence in order to decide whether the model is acceptable or just too simplistic.

The first kind of evidence comes from free recall experiments which are experiments where people are asked to remember lists of say 20 words, and then recall the words in any order that they like. Evidence has shown that subjects usually recall more items from the end of the list but they also recall quite a few from the beginning of a list.

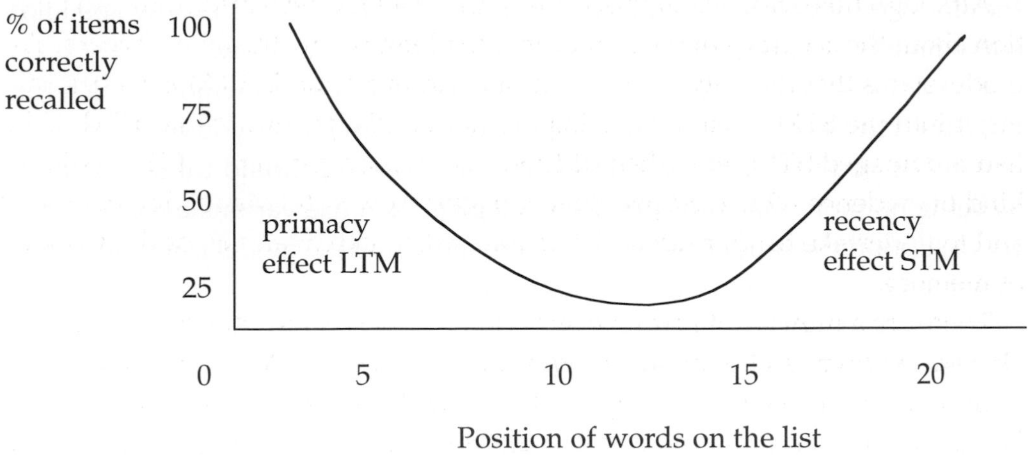

It is suggested that this is because the first words enter the STM where there is probably no other material, and so they are likely to be rehearsed and thus transferred to LTM (called the **primacy effect**). As more words are presented, the STM capacity fills up and so there is no chance to rehearse or transfer later words to LTM. Therefore, the items at the end of the list can only be retained in STM (the **recency effect**, Murdock 1962). It is believed that the reason why the words in the middle are usually lost is because they cannot be rehearsed sufficiently to transfer them into LTM.

> I remember, when I was studying at University, that I had a very similar experience (although not necessarily for the same reason) during some of my lectures. I remember the beginning and the end of most of the lectures I attended, but remembered very little of the information that I was given in the middle. This was either due to the primacy and recency effect or simply because I went to sleep.

There is further evidence for the multi-store model from people who have sustained brain damage. Patients have been found who have lost one part of their memory but the other is intact, ie they have either lost their STM or their LTM.

One piece of evidence comes from a person, known by his initials KF, who was studied by Shallice and Warrington (1970). KF was in his twenties when he had a motor cycle accident and as a result of this he suffered damage to the left parieto-occipital region of his brain which left him with a damaged STM. If he was given a list of numbers to learn he found he could sometimes recall two items, but often only one. His LTM was not damaged however, and he could remember things that he had 'stored' before his accident. The strange thing about him was that he seemed to be able to learn new information even though his STM was impaired.

Although this evidence supports the multi-store model it also leads to a question about the accuracy of the model as it challenges how the model works. The model states that the only way we can store information in LTM is by first taking it into the STM, then 'rehearsing' it, and finally passing it into LTM. If KF had a damaged STM, how then did the information get into LTM? This is the kind of evidence which led people to question how valid the model really was and to undertake further research into alternative explanations for the working of memory.

There are a number of further examples of amnesics who support the model. One was known as HM and the other a man called Clive Wearing. HM suffered with severe epilepsy from the age of 16. In fact his epilepsy was so bad that he had a number of seizures on a daily basis and this seriously impaired his quality of life. In 1953 he went into hospital for surgery to remove part of his temporal lobes as it was in his temporal lobes that the seizures originated. The surgery was a success as the seizures stopped immediately, but within hours of the surgery the medical staff discovered that HM could not recognise the medical staff and he could not find his bedroom in the hospital. It appeared that he was also unable to store any new information. Although the operation was a success, the cost to him was the loss of his ability to transfer any new information to his LTM, although his STM was seemingly intact. Interestingly though, he can remember his life up until a few years before the operation, but any new information is lost as soon as it is learned. Again this gives us evidence that STM and LTM are separate systems, although perhaps they are not as simple as was first hypothesised.

Clive Wearing was very different. He was the chorus master of the London Sinfonietta and although we cannot claim he gives much support for the multi-store model as both his long and short term store are gone, he illustrates how important our memories are to us and how they make us the people we are today with our past experiences and our future aspirations.

Clive Wearing was a brilliant musician with a wonderful career and a delightful young wife. One day he complained of a headache which was the beginning of a cruel and vicious illness. The cold sore virus (herpes simplex) had attacked part of his brain and caused irreversible damage. This resulted in the loss of both his STM and LTM. According to his wife, 'He lives in a blinkered moment in time with no past to anchor it to and no future to look ahead to'. He recognises his wife when she visits but will forget having seen her the minute she goes out of the door. If she walks back into the room again he cannot remember the previous encounter so he acts as if he has not seen her for years and he greets her with the same enthusiasm as he did only five minutes before.

His case is one of the most upsetting as he has lost all sense of who he is and where he is going. He has no recollection of his past and no idea of any future, so in effect his life has no longer any point.

As you should have realised by now, the multi-store model has a number of weaknesses. I am sure that you have experienced instances where something fairly meaningless has happened to you and you probably don't think about it again. Then suddenly, out of the blue, whatever it was springs to mind. That incident has been transferred to long term memory without you having repeated it over and over again to yourself. According to the model, this cannot happen.

The other problem with the model is the description of STM. Remember that STM is believed to have a limited capacity and is 'fragile' in that the information can be easily disrupted or lost. If it is simply a passive 'holding bay' for information which can be easily disrupted, this would indicate that the information is not processed in any way. But how do you decide what information to store long term and what information you can lose.

Imagine you are given a tube containing seven sweets. If you try to push another sweet into the end of the tube nearest you, a sweet falls out of the far end.

No matter what you do, you can't get more than 7 sweets in that tube. Now imagine information all around you as sweets! There are so many sweets that could enter into the tube that there is never a shortage (these sweets could be spoken or read words or numbers or they could be visual images such as faces or objects). BUT you can't 'see' the sweets unless they are in the tube.

How do you decide which ones to eat (i.e. store on a permanent basis). If they are rushing through the tube (STM) so quickly and are literally simply filling vacant spots, then this implies that you are passive in the process. The problem is you cannot be passive because if you were passive you wouldn't actually analyse the nature of the sweets enough to decide which sweets are worth eating and which ones to allow to fall out of the tube, ie you would not be able to decide which information to send into LTM. Therefore you *must* analyse these sweets (this information) to a certain extent.

This whole idea contradicts the multi-store model which states that the STM is a passive store where no information processing takes place. But as we have seen, you must process the information in order to decide whether you want to store it or not.

Carole was on a diet, but she was given a large box of sweets for her birthday. When she was given them, she decided that she would eat them slowly, a couple every day, in order not to make her diet pointless. For the first couple of days, she looked at each one before deciding whether she wanted to eat it or not. She looked for the soft centres, and noticed the shape and whether it was milk or plain chocolate. She could describe in detail which sweets she had eaten and what they were like. On the third day she felt really miserable. When she got in from college, she grabbed the box of chocolates and sat down in front of Neighbours and proceeded to eat her way through the box. She paid no attention to the type of chocolate and didn't even notice what each one tasted like. She was so fed up she just kept on eating until they were all gone, whereupon she felt sick!

If I asked Carole what the chocolates were like, do you think she could tell me about all the different types or would she only remember the ones she had deliberated over when she first got the box?

Carole would probably only remember the ones she ate on the first day. The reason is that she 'processed' far more information about them than the others. This would indicate that the information she has stored is the information which has received more processing. The information which received little processing was forgotten. As we have seen, Atkinson and Shiffrin's model would claim that the only way the information would have been stored in LTM was if it was rehearsed, or said over and over again. I am sure Carole did not say 'dark chocolate truffle' over and over again to herself!

It would make sense to conclude that perhaps rehearsal is not necessarily the process we use to transfer information from STM to LTM. It would seem likely that it is not simply repeating information to ourselves that decides whether it should be put into long term storage or not. Perhaps it is something to do with the amount of processing we give to pieces of information. Craik and Lockhart (1972) supported this theory with their 'model' of memory. They argued that it is not rehearsal as such that is important, but more important was what is done with the material during that rehearsal (ie how well it is processed) and it is this alone which will determine the duration of the memory. The methods we use for this processing are the ones we have already talked about when we talked about encoding, that is what it looks like, what it sounds like and what it means.

Craik and Lockhart claim that **iconic processing** (what something looks like) requires shallow processing. If you then consider what something sounds like, this requires more processing and if you then take into account what this thing actually means, you will have to process the information more deeply.

Here is an example of the way you can test this out:

Compose a list of about 21 words, for example house, egg, shoes. Divide the list into three so that you have 7 words in each list. For the first seven words, you should have a question which asks about the structure of the word e.g. is the word in capital letters or lower case. For the second seven words, find some words that rhyme and some that don't rhyme, and for the last seven words, ask something to do with the meaning of the word. Then put them in a random order on a sheet similar to the example given below:

Please answer the following questions and then complete the task at the bottom of the page:

			Answer
1	Is the word in capital letters or lower case?	EGG	
2	Does the word rhyme with spell?	Shoes	
3	Do people live in it?	House	
4	Do we wear them on our feet?	Gloves	
5	Is the word in capital letters?	Book	
6	Does the word rhyme with tree?	Knee	
7			
8			
9			

etc.

Please count backwards from 20 to 1.
Now turn over the page for the next instruction.

At the bottom of the page you should tell your subject to count backwards from 20 to 1 and then turn over, and on the back of the page you should ask them to recall as many of the words as they can. This process prevents them from continuing to rehearse the information so the words they remember will only be the ones they have transfered into LTM.

The first question asked the person to look at the physical features of the object and nothing more so this is an example of **iconic** or structural processing.

The second question asked the person what the sound of the word is like so this is an example of **phonetic** (also known as acoustic) encoding. This requires more processing than iconic but less than semantic.

The third is an example of **semantic** encoding, where you are actually asking the person to process the meaning of the word. This method uses the deepest level of processing of them all.

Give the list to a number of people, and then ask them to recall the words. Then count up the number of words remembered and look at the way they were processed; the chances are that the highest number recalled will be the ones that were semantically encoded. This will give evidence to support the levels of processing model, but the problem is that the theory is really more descriptive than explanatory and does not *really* explain why deep processing is so effective.

There is another problem – the only way we can test what has been stored is to look at what we can remember. If the only way we can test depth is to look at how many words we can remember, and if how many words we can remember is taken as a measure of depth, then what we are really saying is the only things which will be retrievable will be things that have been stored and the only things that have been stored will be things that are retrievable. The problem is that this gives us no idea of how well we processed the information we have retrieved, so if we accept the levels of processing model we *have* to conclude that the processing was semantic processing. However, further research has shown that it is the information *and its relevance* to the subject that will be more effective in deciding whether information is stored or not.

So far we have looked at how memory seems to be structured, but the structure we have talked about is very simplistic. The problem is that our memories are not simply units of information which remain in perfect form throughout our lives, documenting everything we experience and recalling it as necessary. In fact many of the things we experience are not stored and other things are stored but are not accurately stored.

It was a cold afternoon in late September and two women were standing talking outside their adjacent front gates. Both carried bags of shopping and one woman had a young girl standing by her side.

'I can't believe your Emily is going off to University. It only seemed like yesterday when she was playing in the front garden with our Paul,' said the other women to the girl's mother.

The young girl shuffled. God, she was bored and all she wanted to do was to go in the house and watch Neighbours.

'Come on mum, I'm cold, and I want to finish packing.'

'I remember the first day your mum and I took you to school,' said the other woman, totally ignoring her comments. 'You had a cream coloured coat on, and just as you were going into the school you slipped over on the ice and made all your coat dirty, and you really cried and cried. You refused to go in and you were clinging to your mum's hand and begging her to take you home. It only seems like yesterday.'

'No Elsie, that wasn't her first day at school. That was when we took the children to see Father Christmas, and she had asked me if she could wear her new coat so she would look smart when she went in to tell him what she wanted for

Christmas. Don't you remember that it was your Paul who pushed her over on the way into the shop,' said Emily's mother.

'No it wasn't,' said Emily. 'I remember that coat and falling over, but it was when I was on my way to Sophie's birthday party and I didn't want to go in because I had mud on my knees.'

I hope by now you will have realised that memory is not quite like a tape recorder, and many of the things we encounter in our environment are not actually remembered and the ones that are sometimes get muddled up with similar events. The next section we are going to look at, I feel, is perhaps the most interesting because it helps to explain how we use our memories in order to make sense of our environment rather than simply having a list of information that we draw on as and when necessary. Hopefully you will also understand the way our memories become distorted or positively inaccurate.

Schema theory

We are going to consider 'Schema theory' and this theory will help to explain many pieces of research, especially the work of Loftus and Palmer. But before we start I would just like you to consider the following.

If someone has lost their LTM but they can still talk, this is really a kind of contradiction because when did they learn to talk, write etc? Yes, it was a long time ago! Surely this implies that there must be different types of information stored in LTM and perhaps we don't lose all of it. Perhaps this information is organised into different sections, which would explain why some parts are remembered and some are forgotten.

Endel Tulving (1972) suggested that we have two different types of memory **episodic memory** which is a memory of episodes (or events in our lives) and **semantic memory** which is a memory of facts (such as trees lose their leaves in winter). Sometimes the experience of an episode such as going to the zoo, leads us to learn new facts. Often (even when we don't have a damaged memory) we remember the facts rather than the actual episode. These blocks of facts are called schemata. We seem to have schemata for all different types of events and situations, for example if I said to you what do you think you did on your fifth birthday, the majority of you would say you had a party and a cake and cards and presents – BUT you probably don't actually remember the event in itself.

So a schema is a packet of information. I always think of them as files in the drawer of a filing cabinet. You have schemas about school, work, holidays, clubs, picnics, parties, etc etc. You simply 'open the drawer of the filing cabinet in your head, take out the relevant file and look up the information' in a fraction of a second. In fact schema theory emphasises the fact that what we remember is influenced by what we already know.

Think of the idea of the fifth birthday. It is very unlikely that you remember your fifth birthday, but you will have no problem thinking what it was probably like. Therefore you make inferences about the situation using information about what happens at birthday parties, stored from past experiences.

Here is another idea which might explain still further how schema theory works and how your schema change over the course of your life.

If I asked you to imagine going to a restaurant and told you I wanted you to list 20 things that happened throughout the course of your time there, I am sure that you would include many of the same things as other people. They would be things like being seated, reading the menu, ordering the food, having drinks and paying the bill. In fact this was a study carried out in 1979 by Bower, Black and Turner when they asked 32 people to list the 20 most important events associated with having a meal at a restaurant. What they found was that 73% including the following six events in their list: sitting down, looking at menu, ordering, eating, paying bill and leaving the restaurant.

All the subjects of this piece of research named the same events as they had obviously had experience of restaurants and knew exactly what went on. Now imagine that you are a small child and the only 'restaurant' you have been to is MacDonalds. What sort of things would you describe if you were asked the same question? Then you visit a Harvester or Beefeater restaurant and your knowledge of restaurants would increase enormously, so you would realise that restaurants involve sitting down at a table and reading the menu and having the food brought to you rather than having to queue for it. Then you visit somewhere like the Savoy in London where things are different again.

You can see how, with an increase in experience and knowledge, the packet of information contained in your brain which stores information about a certain event will increase in size as you get older. You will then be able to use this stored knowledge to answer questions and interpret conversations without having to have all the details presented to you at the beginning of the conversation. You would understand what was meant by 'We went to the Harvester last night and the service was excellent,' without wondering what on earth the person was going on about.

The idea of schema theory was introduced by Bartlett in 1932 in order to explain how it is that when people remember stories they regularly leave out some details and introduce what he called 'rationalizations', by which he meant making the stories make sense.

He demonstrated this by asking people to remember a passage which came from another culture and didn't make much sense to them. He found that they *normalised* it into a much more familiar, westernised story, using prior stored knowledge, but didn't actually remember what they had read. The story he used was called 'The War of the Ghosts' and although I have read it many times, even now I cannot remember much about it as it is really quite obscure.

Bartlett's ideas are still widely accepted as they explain how the information we take in is affected by already existing schemas representing previous knowledge. If you think back to the example I gave you at the beginning of this section on memory, I mentioned Kit and the bear. Kit had a bear schema which included information about what bears look like (therefore enabling him to identify the bear) and what they do (eat people), therefore he could make his escape.

Schemas can also affect what we select to take in and how we actually interpret that information.

> Suppose you are walking along a corridor with lots of other people but you are looking in particular for your best friend. She is usually a very happy and smiley sort of person and great fun to be with. You also know that she had a French oral examination this morning and you really want to know how well she did because if she did do well she will be happy to come out with you this evening to the new club in town. Amazingly, you are so busy trying to see her in the approaching students that you don't notice the gorgeous male hunk walking towards you, smiling at you and trying to get eye contact, because just behind him is your best friend. You notice that she looks really miserable and quite pale and your immediate thought is that the exam went really badly and she won't want to come out tonight.

You have selected to take in information relating to your friend but actually missing other information. You interpret that information in the light of what you know about her. If you were also asked if there were any teachers in the corridor at the same time, you would probably say yes because although you couldn't remember you would refer to your 'default' value to fill in the gaps (that is – what is usually the case). You will never know about the gorgeous hunk though!

> Now imagine what answer you would give if someone said to you 'Did she look angry when you saw her in the corridor?' Although you thought she looked miserable rather than angry, you may wonder if you had misinterpreted her expression and that rather than looking miserable she actually looked angry. This would be reasonable because the exam did not go the way she wanted it to go. You would therefore answer 'Yes, I suppose she did.' When you met her later and had time to talk you would be more likely to say something like 'Was the exam really unfair'. This will be because you begin to think that she possibly was angry and the normal response to unfairness would be anger rather than misery.

Can you see how this one statement has changed your perception of how she felt after the exam. This should make you realise how fragile memories are and how information, introduced after the event, can actually distort a memory.

Let's briefly return to the analogy of the filing cabinet. If you accept that a schema is like a filing cabinet with lots of information in it, then when you read a new idea or theory there are a number of things you can do. You can either make room for it (accommodate it), you can throw out some of the old information which is not now relevant or has been updated, or you can fit the two together by modifying your old beliefs. Whatever you decide to do, the schema will have increased in size.

So how do schemas affect memories?

1. The schema guides the selection of what is encoded and stored in memory. You are unlikely to remember irrelevant details of events, eg what clothes you wore when you sat your GCSEs, assuming that it wasn't school uniform. The schema also provides a framework to store new information, like a file marked restaurant.
2. You abstract information from events. This means that you take out and store only *some* of the information from different events if there are a number of them and they are all very similar. Remember your fifth birthday? All you can remember is general information about birthdays – presents, cakes, parties etc. This also happens with conversations – you only remember the gist of them, not all the contents.

3 Because we have integrated lots of information into our schemas, they help us interpret different situations about which we have very limited knowledge. We may end up having to use inferences in the light of past knowledge and previous experience.
4 Memories can also be distorted to fit prior expectations and in order to make them consistent with your existing schema, they may actually be transformed. This is how eyewitness testimony gets blurred – you see what you expect to see.
5 Schemas may also aid retrieval. You can sometimes remember what happened by searching through the information you have already got stored in your schema, to see if you recognise what was required.

At this point we can return to the question 'Is memory like a tape recorder'? Of course the answer is no: it is far less accurate and I hope you are beginning to see why that is. It is interesting, though, that eyewitness testimony was considered to be one of the most important factors in court cases. Many suspects were found guilty as a result of their identification by witnesses and witness reports of events.

There have been lots of studies of eyewitness testimony such as the study by Adams and Nickerson (1979) where they asked their subjects to draw exactly what was represented on each side of a U.S. penny piece. Their subjects recalled, on average, only three out of eight critical features of the coin and these were often put in the wrong place. Do you remember what the coins that you handle every day actually look like?

One of the most prolific researchers on the phenomenon of eye witness testimony, and how our memory for witnessed events is really quite fragile, is Elizabeth Loftus. She was concerned not only with the fragility of memory, but also with the effects of stress on the ability of victims to recall facts.

Loftus and Burns (1982) showed their subjects a film of a hold-up and then tested their memory for details. The experimental group saw a violent version of the film where one of the members of a group of young boys is shot and collapses on the floor clutching his bleeding face. The control group saw the same film, but this scene was omitted. Instead their film changed to a scene inside the bank where the manager is explaining to staff and customers exactly what has happened.

Loftus and Burns found that subjects who saw the violent version had significantly less memory for details of events before the shooting. Most subjects failed to mention that one of the boys had a large number '17' on his jersey which was very obvious from the film. There were actually 16 items that subjects could have recalled, but those who had seen the violent version of the film recalled significantly less than the other group on 14 of those items.

Loftus was also interested in how you can actually change a witness's recollection of an incident by subtly introducing new information during questioning. She showed that it is possible to do this, which has considerable repercussions for the police. She concluded that it is possible for a memory representation of an event to be modified by subsequent information but stressed that some conditions make the original memory more resistant to distortion. If the misleading information is blatantly incorrect people are less likely to take it in and 'overwrite' previous information, so perhaps it is not so easy to change a memory for an important event after all.

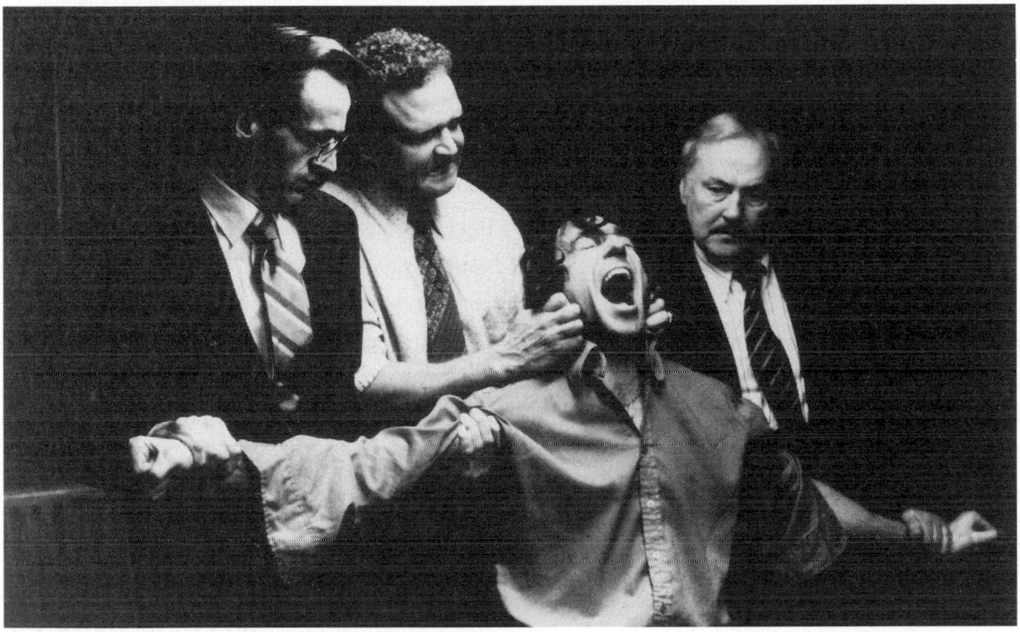

If we accept that stress affects memory, imagine how accurate any testimony would be if a 'witness' was subjected to pressure. This scene from the film – "In the Name of the Father" starring Daniel Day Lewis illustrates how someone could be "encouraged" to remember something which may later become part of his actual memory.

E.F. Loftus and J.J. Palmer (1974) Reconstruction of automobile destruction: An example of the interaction between language and memory.

Journal of Verbal Learning and Verbal Behaviour, 13, 585–89.

The purpose of these two studies was to investigate the effects of 'leading questions' on our ability to accurately remember events. The expectation was that the information subtly introduced after the event through leading questions – questions phrased in a particular way, would distort the original memory.

STUDY ONE

Method

Design: Laboratory experiment with independent subjects.

Subjects: 45 student subjects were divided into five groups with nine subjects in each group.

Apparatus: Seven film segments from the Evergreen Safety Council or the Seattle Police Department. Each segment lasted between five and 30 seconds. Four of the seven films were staged crashes, so the actual speed of the cars was known. There were also seven questionnaires, one for each film, containing the following instructions: 'Give an account of the accident you have just seen' and then answer the following questions.' The questions related to the accident. The independent variable was the wording of the critical question which asked, 'About how fast were the cars going when they hit/smashed/collided/bumped/contacted?' Each question just had one of the words, eg 'How fast were the cars going when they collided?' The dependent variable was the estimated speed.

Procedure: All the subjects were shown the seven film clips and then given a questionnaire. In order to counteract order effects, the groups were presented with a different ordering of films. Each group of subjects received one of the five critical questions in their questionnaires. The entire experiment lasted about an hour and a half.

Details of design used for the first study

	Group 1	Group 2	Group 3	Group 4	Group 5
No. of subjects	9	9	9	9	9
Order of films watched	1st film 2nd film 3rd film 4th film	2nd film 3rd film 4th film 5th film	3rd film 4th film 5th film 6th film	4th film 5th film 6th film 7th film	5th film 6th film 7th film 1st film
Critical word in question	hit	smashed	collided	bumped	contacted

Results

The average speed estimates in miles per hour for each of the verbs were as follows:

Smashed	40.8
Collided	39.3
Bumped	38.1
Hit	34.0
Contacted	31.8

The accuracy of subjects' speed estimates in miles per hour for the four staged crashes:

Film No.	Actual speed	Estimated speed
1	20	37.7
2	30	36.2
3	40	39.7
4	40	36.1

These results were significant at the $p<.05$ level and indicated that the phrasing of the question can have a considerable effect on the estimate of speed. The results also indicated that people are not very good at judging how fast a vehicle is actually travelling.

Discussion

There are two possible explanations of these findings. The first is due to response-bias factors where a subject is uncertain of the correct answer and the wording of the question influences the answer they give. The second is that the form of the question causes a change in the subject's memory representation of the accident. If the second explanation is the case, then further questioning may cause the subject to 'recall' information they would expect to see but that did not actually occur. The second experiment was intended to identify which explanation was correct.

STUDY TWO

Method

Design: Laboratory experiment with independent subjects.
Subjects: 150 student subjects were divided into three groups with 50 subjects in each group.
Apparatus: A film showing a multiple car accident which lasted less than 1 minute (the accident itself lasted less than four seconds). Three versions of the same questionnaire (Q. 1) asked the subjects to describe the accident in their own words, and then to answer some questions about the accident. The independent variable was again the wording of the questions. Two of the three questionnaires contained a critical question asking subjects 'About how fast were the cars going when they hit each other/smashed into each other?' The other questionnaire (given to the control group) did not ask subjects about vehicular speed. Another questionnaire (Q.2), asking 10 questions about the accident with one question placed in a random position in the list, asked 'Did you see any broken glass?' although there was none shown. The dependent variable was the answer to this critical question.
Procedure: All the subjects were shown the film clip and then given one of the three versions of Q.1. One week later, all the subjects returned and answered Q.2.

Results

Table 1 Mean estimate of speed (mph)

Smashed	10.46
Hit	8.00

Table 2 Responses to the question 'Did you see any broken glass?'

	Smashed	Hit	Control
Yes	16	7	6
No	34	43	44

Table 3 Probability of seeing broken glass according to speed estimate

	1–5mph	6–10mph	11–15mph	16–20mph
Smashed	.09	.27	.41	.62
Hit	.06	.09	.25	.50

These results were significant at the $p<.05$ level for Table 1 and indicated that the wording of the question can have a considerable effect on the estimate of speed. Table 2 shows that the verb used in the question affected the number of Yes responses when asked about broken glass ($p<.025$) although the differences between the control and the 'hit' condition were negligible. Table 3 shows that the probability of saying 'Yes' to the question about broken glass is not dependent on estimated speed alone, although it makes the likelihood of having seen it greater with an increase in speed estimate.

Discussion

The conclusion of the second study was that the verb not only affected the estimate of speed, but also the likelihood of subjects thinking they had seen broken glass. This can be explained by the fact that subjects took in information from the original scene, and then merged this with information given after the event. This produced a memory which contained some of the original information but this information would then be 'swayed' by the next piece of information they were exposed to. The final result was a mixture of both experiences together with extra information which they may have expected to see as a result of their distortion. This is illustrated in Table 3, which shows that the faster the estimated speed, the greater the chance of seeing broken glass regardless of what verb was used.

Evaluation

The study was well controlled and the variables were operationalised fairly, however the study lacked ecological validity because it was carried out in a laboratory and the real life experience of witnessing an accident would be far more arousing than simply watching the events on a television.

Also the subjects would have had an expectation that they had to remember something which may not be the case in real life. The subjects were all students and therefore not representative of the population and they may not have had any real incentive to remember the events whereas in real life this may not be the case.

Key words

Response-bias – the tendency to give a response in a certain direction according to the situation.

Critical question – the question which is the important one in the study. The answers to this question will be the ones which are analysed.

Ecological validity – whether the study is valid in the real world.

Key questions

1. What was the purpose of the Loftus and Palmer studies?
2. Give two criticisms of the study.
3. Why was a control group used in the second study?
4. What factors might influence your memory of an event?
5. Can you think of an alternative way of investigating the effects of eye witness testimony?

Perception

When information from the outside world reaches us, either by touch, sight, smell, taste or hearing, we need to make sense of what that information is in order to identify it. The information may vary in form, for example the 'things' we experience when we smell something are chemicals and the 'sounds' that we hear are actually waves of different frequencies. Each of our senses have a specific organ which contains receptors for taking in information, for example our eyes have receptor cells based at the back of the retina, which convert images into a type of electrochemical energy. This energy is transmitted via an internal 'wiring system', better known as neurones, to a specific part of the brain if you wonder where nerves feature here, nerves are simply a collection of neurones; so if you imagine a cable made up of lots of wires, this is what a nerve, made up of a collection of neurones, is like. This energy is then 'decoded' by the brain into something we understand.

The process we use to 'decode' or understand what we have just experienced is called perception. Let me give you an example.

If I was to present the following picture to you, and ask you to tell me what it is, you may find it difficult at first.

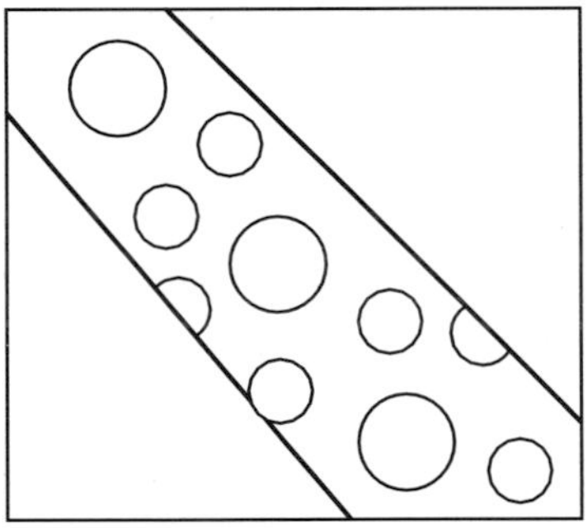

If I were to tell you that it was a giraffe going past a window, you would probably laugh, and realise that it could be a giraffe going past a window. However, what you actually see is a square with two vertical lines which are almost parallel, and a number of circles. What you have done is to use the information stored in your memory to help you identify what you have seen – you have perceived it as a giraffe.

Supposing you had never seen a giraffe before, you would have trouble understanding that my suggestion was a giraffe. You would not have had the relevant information stored in order to help you 'decode' the sensory input, and you would have simply identified it as what it is – lines and circles.

Now imagine that you had never seen a circle before. Although you would have seen the shape, you would not be able to name it but you would have been able to describe its properties, that is that it was a line that was curved and had no end. Again, what you would be trying to do is to make sense of what you have seen.

Most psychologists believe that we can't make sense of any stimulus on its own, and that we need to use stored information to help us interpret it. Let me give you another example. We sense the presence of a stimulus, in this case a noise. Our sense organs (ears) react to that external stimuli by detecting the sounds. What we actually perceive is music because we have interpreted that sensation as something we have heard before, which is called music.

Perhaps the best definition of perception is 'making sense of sensation'.

In vision, sensation refers to the reaction of the retina to light or stimulus and perception refers to our organisation, integration and recognition of these patterns from an upside down, blurred, double image which does not relate to the size of the object, into a clear, three-dimensional colourful image which is the right way up.

Research on the subject of perception has focused mainly on visual perception because it is estimated that 90% of the information we receive about the external world reaches us through our eyes. It would make sense, then, for vision to be the dominant sense and for the information we visually perceive to be so dominant that it can overrule the information taken in by other sense modalities.

'Oh my God, I've got to stay behind after school and go and see old Plunket,' wailed Juliet. 'What on earth have I done wrong this time. I gave in my maths on time – yeah OK, I didn't spend very long on it, and I didn't quite finish it, but I did give it in.'

'Well good luck,' said Rosie, 'I don't envy you. He must be the most ugly old man I have ever seen, and he really frightens me the way he stares at you with those little beady, piggy eyes. Rather you than me.'

'Thanks for that,' said Juliet.

Three thirty came and Juliet waited outside old Plunket's room. Suddenly the door opened and Plunket appeared to glower at Juliet. 'Come in.'

He was a big grizzly old man with little tufts of grey hair coming out of his nose and ears, and a mop of grey hair which was held in place by some sort of fixative. His teeth were 'interesting and formed a sort of asymmetrical array inside his thin narrow lips which were like a thin line which neither smiled nor frowned. Whenever he spoke he seemed to snarl. The worst part was his beady eyes which seemed to fix on you and make you feel that he was going to pounce any minute.

'Ah, yes, Juliet,' he said in a fairly quiet voice. 'I've been looking at your last homework and I'm quite pleased that at least you have made the effort at last. I wondered if extra lessons would be helpful because you are obviously having some problems understanding this part of the course. I am considering having an extra lesson at lunchtimes on Friday for people having problems, and I would like you to think about it. I think you would benefit by coming along because you obviously have some mathematical abilities and have the potential to do quite well.'

Juliet stood there, transfixed. Although she could hear what he was saying, she did not really take it in. Despite the fact that he was offering to help her, she could only just stop her teeth from chattering and her knees from knocking, and there was a horrible sick feeling in the pit of her stomach. All she could perceive was this beast of a man looking like he would pull a machete out of his desk drawer at any minute and chop off her head.

Here, although Juliet could hear the words that old Plunket was saying and could understand them, the visual information she was taking in overruled the information she actually heard. You can imagine that when she left the room in one piece, she would have to think about what happened and it would take her a little while to realise that he was not angry but simply trying to help.

This whole idea is illustrated by an experiment carried out some time ago by James Gibson (1933). He asked his subjects to put on some glasses which made straight edges appear curved. He then asked them to run their hands along a straight edge. The subjects all agreed that the straight edge felt as if it was curved, even though it was not. The evidence of the subjects' eyes was contradicting what they knew to be true.

Although Gibson's experiment indicates that visual information is very powerful, most psychologists argue that we need to have had some experience of the things we see in order to make sense of them. After all, if you had never seen a giraffe before you would have huge problems trying to work out exactly what the thing was walking past the window! The cue to recognising it might just have been its long neck and its height. This example should help to make it obvious that we use visual cues to help us understand and make sense of the large amount of information in our world and it should also be clear that many of these cues are learned.

We are now going to look at the types of cues we use in order to identify how far away things are from us. Depth perception is one of our major achievements because it is astonishing how we can turn a two dimensional retinal image into a three dimensional world. We must remember that many of the depth cues that are available are given by our movement or the movement of objects around us. For example, if we have been driving along a road, we know how far away something behind us actually is, because we know how long ago we passed it. However, sometimes we are stationary and the objects we are observing are also stationary, and yet we can still work out, very accurately, how far they are away from us.

The cues that we use can be divided into **monocular** and **binocular** cues. Monocular cues only require the use of one eye, although they can also be used easily when someone has two eyes open, and binocular cues are cues which need both eyes to be used together.

Monocular cues

Monocular cues are the cues that are used by artists to help give depth to a painting. They are also used if we only have one eye (but more of this later). Below are listed the monocular cues and examples of how they work.

Linear perspective

One of the most powerful monocular cues is linear perspective. This is where parallel lines pointing directly away from us seem to get closer together as they recede into the distance. An example of this is if you imagine railway tracks going off into the distance – they don't actually seem to be parallel.

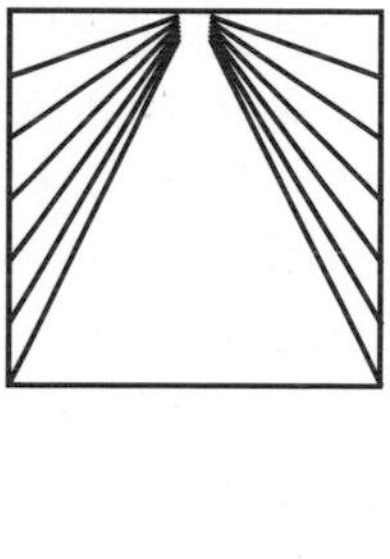

Linear perspective – parallel lines converge as they recede into the distance

Texture gradient

Most objects possess texture (eg carpets, pebbled beaches) and the texture of objects appears more dense the closer the object is to you.

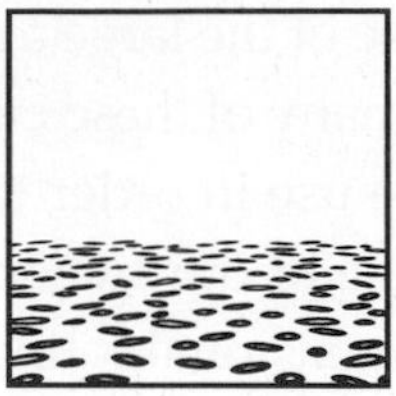

Texture gradient – the texture or gradient becomes finer as it gets further away

Interposition

Interposition is where a near object hides an object a little further away.

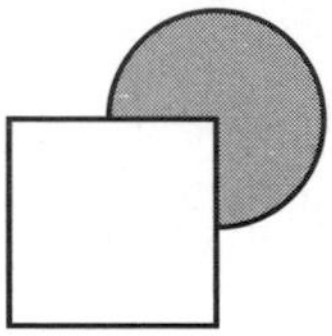

Overlap – if one object hides part of another, the complete object is closer

Many illusions are based on this depth cue, for example Kanizsa's (1976) illusory square is an example of how strong this can be.

Shading

If you look at an object in a picture and there is no shadow, that object appears flat. This is because you know that flat surfaces don't cast shadows. The minute that a shadow is present, that object has depth.

Motion parallax

If you are on a train, the objects near to you seem to rush past whereas the objects on the horizon stay still for much longer. This is because the images of the nearer objects rush over the retina, whereas the image of the distant ones do not move across the retina as fast and the brain compares the speed of movement of the two objects and interprets this as distance.

> Emily was looking out of the window of the car on the way home from holiday. 'Look mummy, there's the moon,' she said as she saw the moon in the sky. 'Is it the same moon that we saw on holiday?'
>
> 'Yes, darling,' said her mother.
>
> Emily continued to watch the moon out of the car window, and when it pulled into the driveway Emily leapt out of the car. 'Look, it's followed us all the way home.'

This happens because the moon is such a long way away that the retinal image does not appear to move, whereas objects very close to us move at a great speed.

Height in the horizontal plane

Objects that are a long way away from you are seen as being closer to the horizon. Therefore if one object appears to be lower than the other, we perceive that it is further away.

Height in the visual field – the closer to the horizon that the object is, the further away it is

The depth cue is so great that even without background we know where the objects are in relation to each other.

Relative size

Objects which are some distance away produce a small retinal image, whereas objects which are much closer produce a larger retinal image. The brain interprets this information in the light of what it knows about objects and uses this to tell how near to us or how far away objects that we are looking at really are.

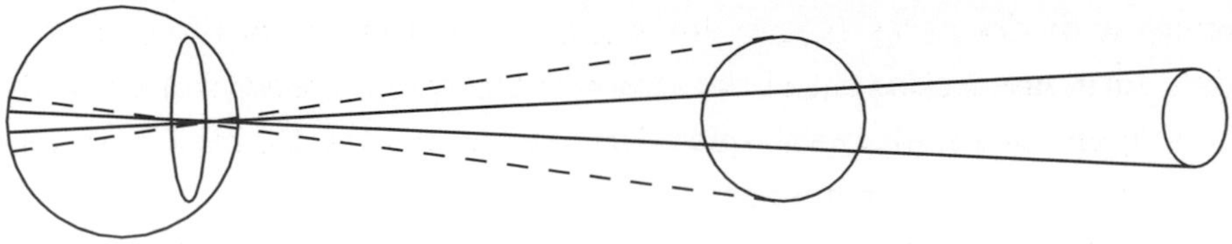

Binocular cues

If you have one eye you will not be able to use binocular cues as they involve both eyes being used together.

1 Convergence

This cue refers to the way the eyes need to turn inwards to a greater extent to focus on closer objects compared with those further away.
Note the difference of the angles when the eyes are looking at near and more distant images.

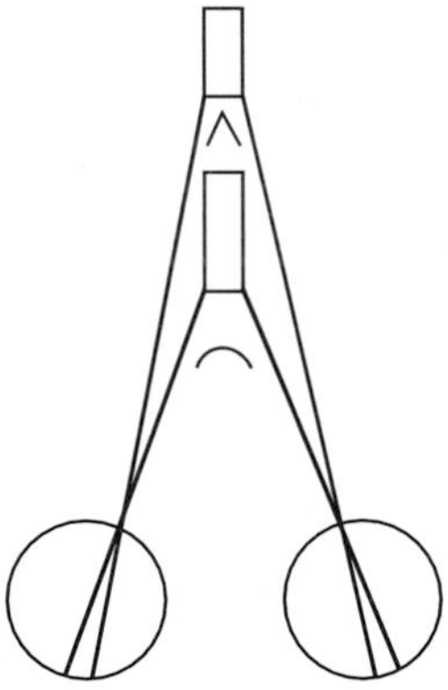

2 Accommodation

This refers to the way the lenses of the eyes change shape when we focus on objects at different distances. If we look at objects that are near to us then the lenses thicken, but they flatten for objects which are further away. The brain interprets this movement of the lenses to help give an idea of how near or far the objects are.

3 Stereopsis

Because your eyes are slightly apart, you actually see two very slightly different images at the same time, one from each eye. These two images are put together by the brain and this gives a very strong depth effect.

To see how different the images are, first of all close one eye. Then hold something like a pen or pencil vertically in front of you and line it up with the side of a window or door so it is actually 'sitting over' the line of the chosen object. Keeping your hand still, now open the eye that was closed and close the one that was open. You will see how far the pen has 'jumped' away from its original position.

You may have experienced this by wearing special glasses which give you a three dimensional effect at a cinema or a museum or looked at a stereoscope which contains two pictures which are almost identical, but when you look at them through a stereoscopic viewer the brain amalgamates the images into one three dimensional one. (In fact the 'magic eye' pictures work on this principle by overlaying one image made up of computer generated sets of dots with another. The reason some people can't see them is because one eye is not working as efficiently as the other.)

Visual constancies

Another aspect of perception which I feel is worth mentioning here is the matter of visual constancies. There are a number of 'visual constancies' which explain why our perception of objects seems to remain constant at all times even though there is a large variation in the image which appears on the retina. This will become clearer as you read on.

1 Shape constancy

Have you ever noticed that it doesn't seem to matter at what angle you look at a door, either open or shut, or half open, it always looks like a rectangle. Shape constancy refers to the fact that the shape of an object looks the same despite changes in orientation.

This is a really good illustration of perception: you do not actually 'see' what the retinal image looks like, rather you 'see' the object as you know it to be.

2 Colour constancy

This refers to the fact that the colour of an object looks the same even when the colour changes. An example of this may occur when you are at a club which has red lighting. Although it may make your friends faces look more red, you simply take into account the colour of the lighting and perceive their faces as the usual colour.

3 Size constancy

Size constancy involves objects looking the same size in spite of changes in the size of the retinal image. For example cars at the end of a car park do not look like toy cars even though the retinal image is very small. If you want to compare retinal images, first of all find an object like a tree or a car which you can see out of the window some distance away. Then hold your hand up and fit the image between your thumb and forefinger (as if you are holding it between them). Remember how far they are apart. Now do the same for a near object, and you will have a comparison in retinal sizes.

Here is a stunning example of how this works:

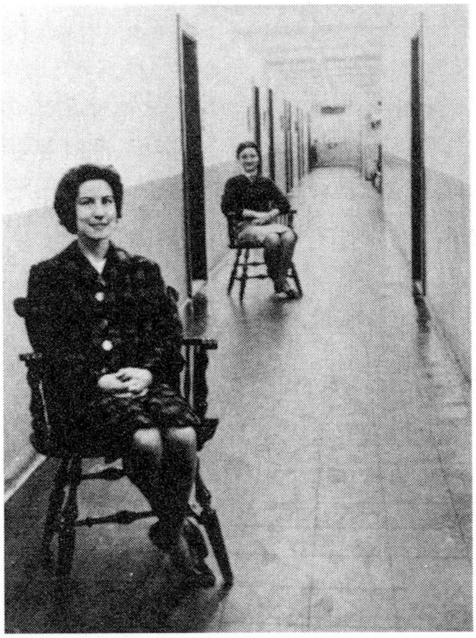

However, size constancy is not always found. Have you noticed if you look out of the window of a plane, or down from a very high building, that the scene below does not look real and that objects like cars look more like toys. This is because it is an unfamiliar experience for us. This should give you some idea about how experience helps us to perceive accurately.

If we accept that the relationship between size and distance is very strong, it would seem quite reasonable for it to work in reverse, that is perceived distance is influenced by familiar size.

A cunning piece of research by Ittelson (1951) illustrates how well this works. He showed participants playing cards through a peep hole into a long box that gave no indication of distance other than familiar size. There were actually three different size playing cards (normal, half and double size). They were attached to some wire and were put through the top of the box in exactly the same place, at a distance of 2.3 metres from the observer. When asked how far away the cards were from the observer, the half size playing card was estimated to be on average 4.6 metres away, whereas the double size card was thought to be 1.3 metres away.

Therefore familiar size had a large effect on distance judgements and, as the only way we know about familiar size is to have stored it in our memories, this must indicate to you that size constancy is learned.

Here is another example of size constancy which I am sure you will have experienced.

> You are away on holiday and you meet a whole crowd of really excellent people. You decide that you want to remember them, so you take a photo of them in front of a stunning view. When your holiday photos are developed you turn with excitement to the one of the group of people but to your dismay, the people look so tiny that you can hardly make out their features. They look much smaller against the background than you remember them to be when you were taking the photo, and you think to yourself it would have been better to have them closer.

When something moves away from us the size of the image cast on the retina diminishes rapidly but we know that they aren't really shrinking. Our visual systems compensate for this decrease in size making us see receding people and objects as larger than they really are, which makes them seem closer than they really are.

Richard Gregory (1977) thinks this is why certain visual illusions work.

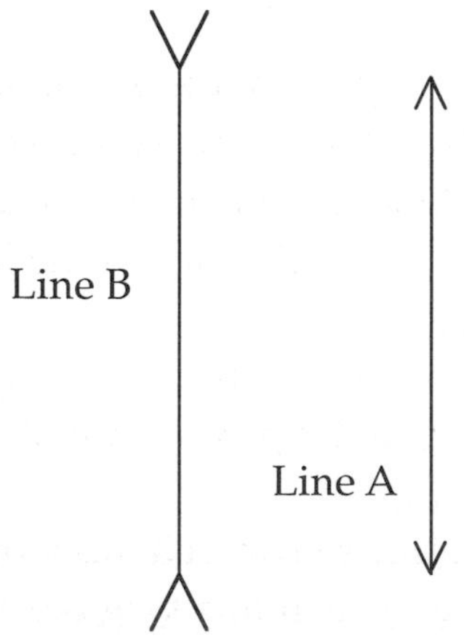

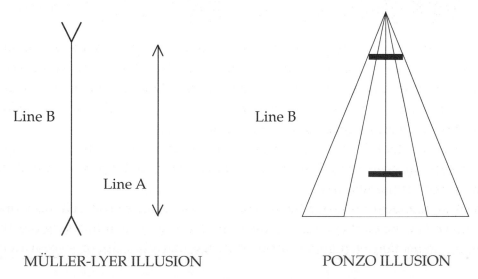

MÜLLER-LYER ILLUSION

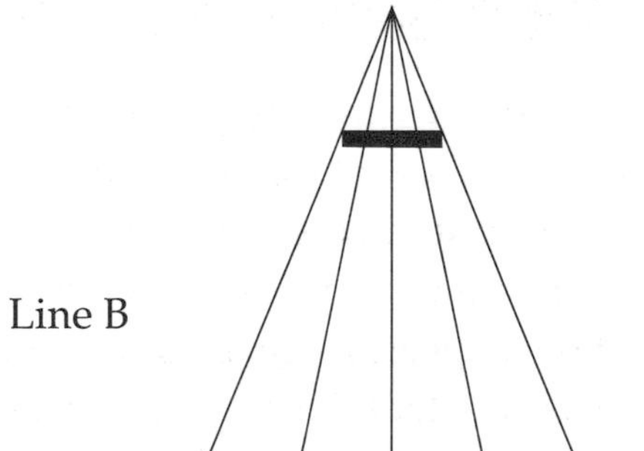

PONZO ILLUSION

He says that these illusions give up depth cues that line B is longer than line A in each case.

The Müller-Lyer illusion 'B' looks like the inside corner of a room. 'A' looks like the outside corner of a building which emerges towards us. We compensate for line 'B' because it looks further away than 'A'.

The Ponzo illusion suggests parallel lines receeding into the distance (like railway tracks) which leads us to think that line B is further away. So we compensate for the size of line B by making it look bigger to us.

However, as you will see later, other cultures are not always taken in by this because they live in a different environment with round houses rather than rectangular ones – this kind of cue is not available to them, as it has not been within their experience. Gregory concluded that experience therefore affects the unconscious cues we use to interpret visual stimuli, and that Europeans and Zulus have what are known as different learning sets (or learning experiences).

There is one more example of how perceived distance can affect size judgements and this is an 'everyday' illusion which we have probably all experienced at some time. Have you ever noticed how the moon looks much larger when it is close to the horizon than when it is right up high in the sky. Part of the reason is that the moon looks further away from us when it is near the horizon, because there are many depth cues present and we know that the horizon is a long way away. We therefore compensate for that distance by increasing the perceived size of the moon and so it looks quite large. When it is high up in the sky we have nothing to relate it to, and so although the retinal size of the moon is the same as it is at the horizon we perceive it as much smaller.

This was demonstrated by Kaufman and Rock (1962) when they asked their participants to look at the moon on the horizon through a small hole in a card, thus depriving them of the distance cues provided by the horizon. They reported seeing the image as very small, in fact much smaller than when they looked at it without the card. They also asked participants to look at the moon high in the sky through a sheet of clear plastic with an artificial horizon drawn on it. This resulted in them reporting an apparent increase in the size of the moon.

Motion perception

Motion perception is another example of how the brain intervenes in what we actually see. When we follow moving objects with our eyes, our eyes make small irregular jerky movements but we perceive a smooth continuous motion. We can therefore conclude that we interpret what we see and make sense of it in the light of what we know, rather than what we actually see because we know, for example, that cars do not actually jerk along roads (unless they are being driven by learner drivers).

Have you ever been sitting on a train in a station, and the train next door to you starts to pull away, but you feel that it is you that is moving rather than the train next door. Another example is going through a car wash – you feel that your car is moving backwards and forwards rather than the brushes either side of the car. There is also the example of the moon in the sky which has a thin layer of clouds across it which are moving along, but we think the clouds are stationary and the moon is the thing that is moving.

All of these relate to motion perception and stored information. We are much better at detecting motion when we see a moving object against a background which isn't moving. We also have the expectation that a car moves along the road, rather than the road moving and the car staying still.

This is why, when we look at real moving things, we find that if the largest object which surrounds a smaller object is the one that is moving, it makes the small object appear to move. Now think of this in relation to the train; the carriage we are in seems small in relation to the rest of the world, therefore we think that we are moving and the rest of the world is stationary.

I hope that the examples I have given you make you realise how our ability to perceive is so amazing and how it depends so much on our past experiences and stored information. If you accept this you will realise how the whole area relates to our memory and past memory representations, and why we need to understand memory in order to be able to comprehend perception.

Perceptual set

You will have realised that there are a number of cues which influence our perception, both external and internal. External are due to the nature of the object being seen, and internal which are directly related to stored knowledge. So far we have focused on the most basic factors, but we are now going to consider a few of the factors which are largely unconscious. These factors are known as 'perceptual set' and are defined by Allport (1955) as 'a perceptual bias or predisposition or readiness to perceive particular features of a stimulus'. They are, of course, influenced by past experience and learning.

The first of these is context, that is *where* you see something will influence your identification of that object. If you saw something that was a sort of golden orange colour and shiny, in the middle of a golf course, you would be very unlikely to identify it as a goldfish from a distance. Whereas, if you saw the same object in the middle of a tank of water in a hotel, you would have no problems identifying it from the far side of the lobby.

Your motivation will also affect your perception of an object. If you are trying to avoid someone in a blue Fiesta car, isn't it amazing how many blue Fiestas are on the road? In fact every third car seems to be a blue Fiesta! Gilchrist and Nesberg (1952) looked at the effects of deprivation on perception by using participants who were either very hungry or very thirsty, having gone without food or water for a number of hours. They were asked to rate the brightness of pictures of food or liquid and it was found that the longer they had been deprived, the brighter the pictures were rated.

Another of these predispositions is what is called expectancy bias. This is where you are meeting the man/woman of your dreams off the train and you misrecognise all sorts of people because you are so desperate to see the person you are meeting. This was investigated by Bruner and Goodman (1947) when they asked rich and poor children to estimate the sizes of coins. The poor children overestimated the size of every coin in comparison to the rich children, which could be explained by the fact that the money had a much greater value to the poor children. We mustn't forget that it may also have been due to the fact that the poor children had not had much experience of money handling.

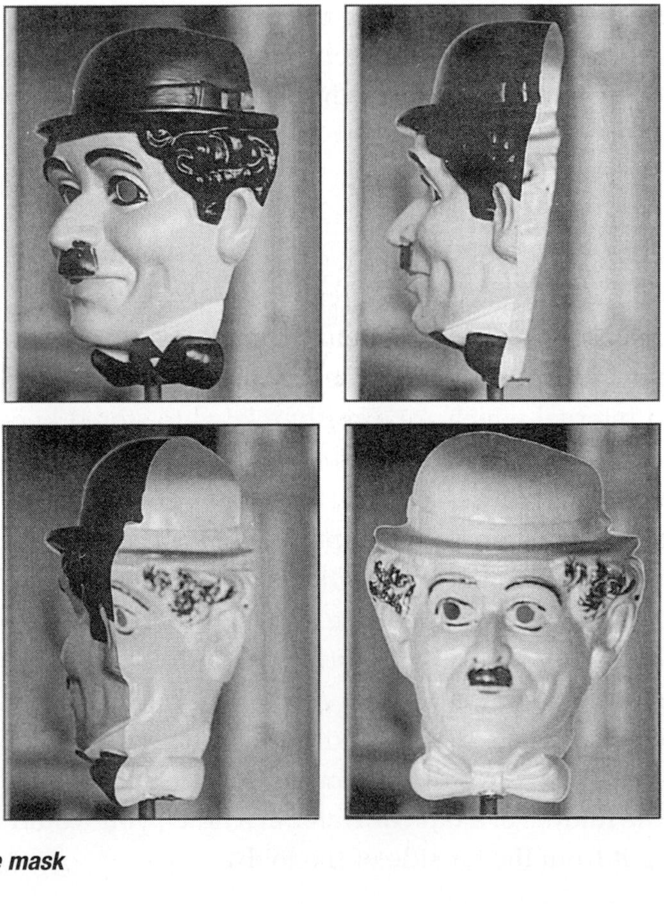

The rotating face mask

Another example is perhaps one of the most impressive ways of demonstrating expectancy – looking at the mask of a face. If we see it from the outside it is obviously convex (projecting outwards). If we rotate it very slowly so we are looking at the inside of the mask, the concave inside will suddenly seem to 'spring out' so it looks convex again. This is because we know that faces are convex, not concave, and so we perceive the image as it should be seen and not how it actually is.

Psychology and the nature-nurture argument

If we accept that perception requires the use of stored information, it would seem a reasonable argument to suggest that we have to learn how to perceive. But is this really the case? Perhaps we are born with the ability to perceive some things but not others. If this is so, what things are we able to perceive when we are born and how on earth could we find out (after all, you cannot question a newborn baby). Needless to say, some psychologists believe our abilities are innate and some believe that they are learned, and therefore a huge amount of research has been generated in investigating this area.

The ideal method used to investigate this area is to study humans who have no perceptual experience. If we are born with the ability to perceive, then our ability to process visual information and make sense of it should be no different to that of an adult. If, on the other hand, it depends on learning, it should be totally inadequate. Where do we find these inexperienced humans who can both communicate and who have had no perceptual experience. We could wrestle babies away from their mothers and bring them up with blindfolds on until they are old enough to talk, and then expose them to the visual world and see how they cope, but I think the mothers may possibly object. As a response to this problem, a number of alternative methods have been devised, some involving humans and others involving animals. However, it isn't necessary here to go into the studies in any detail, but simply to give you a general idea of the type of research and the findings.

One way of checking if babies can discriminate between different visual stimuli is to see if they have a preference for one picture over another. To investigate this, psychologists have looked at babies' eyes to see if they look more at one picture rather than another. The overall findings are that, even from a very early age, they prefer more complex pictures and pictures which resemble a human face (Ahrens 1954, Fantz , 1961).

One study which looked at very young babies (who had not had the chance to experience too much in the way of visual stimuli) was Bushnell and Sai (1987). They showed newborn babies their mother's face and the face of a female stranger, both of whom had the same level of contrast and the same hair colour. The babies, who had an average age of two days and five hours, showed a clear preference for their mothers. This also indicates that it is likely that infants have a preference for faces, especially familiar ones. Why do you think this may be? Well, if nothing else, perhaps babies are born with the ability to perceive familiar and unfamiliar faces as this would be a useful survival mechanism. This would indicate that should a stranger want to wander off with a baby, the baby would at least know that it was not its mother! The problem, even with this piece of research, was that the babies were still not experiencing visual stimuli for the first time, and therefore it may have been a preference for learned things which could have been associated with food and comfort.

The other area which has been investigated with regard to infant perception is depth perception, as it was reasoned that if babies are able to perceive depth at birth or very soon afterwards, the ability is likely to be innate. The most famous study was that done by Gibson and Walk (1966) using the visual cliff apparatus – a large step with a perspex cover over it.

They tested babies between the ages of six and 14 months and found that they would not crawl onto the deep side. Ah ha, they claimed, this indicates that depth perception is innate. The problem was that if you know anything about babies, you must realise that they can't crawl when they are born. In fact they can't crawl until they are about four months of age. Does this indicate that depth perception may have been learned?

Although this study is somewhat inadequate, other research has shown that other species who are able to move almost from birth, for example day old

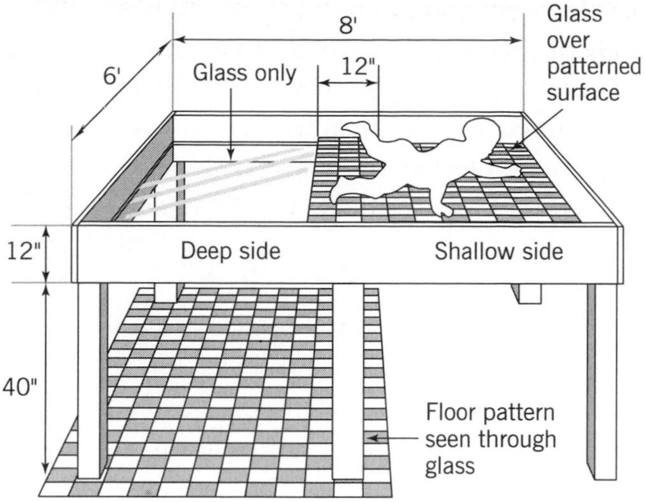

chicks, goat kids and lambs, would not go over to the deep side. If they were put on the deep side, they tended to freeze with fear. I have visions of researchers, sitting in fields, waiting for lambs to be born, and then running them into a laboratory and putting them on the deep side of the visual cliff. I would image the 'freeze' would be more likely to be the result of this!

I mentioned earlier that studies have been done on animals, and these are the kind of studies which would be impossible on humans. This involves keeping animals in the dark and then investigating how much they are able to visually discriminate after a given period of time, compared to animals reared in the light. If there were different visual abilities between the two groups, this would indicate that visual perception must be learned rather than innate.

The problem with the original studies which kept animals in the dark was that the animals' visual 'machinery' did not develop properly. Post mortem examination showed that the cells of the retina, and occasionally the optic nerve, had degenerated. Therefore other studies reared some animals in diffuse light, allowing the cells to develop, or kept them in a visually deprived or controlled environment where they had no experience of some stimuli, for example horizontal lines. Needless to say, the visual abilities of the two groups of animals were very different. Studies such as the ones by Blakemore and Cooper (1966) showed that if kittens were visually deprived of, say, experience of horizontal lines, they were perceptually inferior to non-deprived kittens. An example of their behaviour was that they did not put their paws out to land when they were put onto a table, and they did not chase a horizontal stick when it moved up and down, but were able to play with a vertical one. Although some of their abilities improved with normal visual experience, they were not as effective as normally reared kittens.

As I am sure you have realised, none of these studies mentioned are really adequate as methods of investigating whether perception is innate or learned. It would be far better to have a person who had grown up without sight, and who had then been granted sight at an adult age, to ask them what sense they made of their environment. One such study was done by Gregory and Wallace (1963) who investigated the case of S.B. He was 52 when he was given his sight after a corneal graft operation.

> 'When bandages were first removed from his eyes, so that he was no longer blind, he heard the voice of the surgeon. He turned to the voice, and saw nothing but a blur. He realised that this must be a face, because of the voice, but he could not see it. He did not suddenly see the world of objects as we do when we open our eyes.
>
> But within a few days he could use his eyes to good effect. He could walk along the hospital corridors without recourse to touch – he could even tell the time from a large wall clock, having all his life carried a pocket watch with no glass, so that he could feel the time from its hands. He would get up at dawn and watch from his window the cars and trucks pass by. He was delighted with his progress, which was extremely rapid'.
>
> When he left the hospital, we took him to London and showed him many things he never knew from touch, but he became curiously dispirited. At the zoo he was able to name most of the animals correctly, having stroked pet animals and enquired how other animals differed from the cats and dogs he knew by touch. He was also of course familiar with toys and models. He certainly used his previous knowledge from touch, and reports from sighted people to help him name objects by sight, which he did largely by seeking their characteristic features. But he found the world drab, and was upset by flaking paint and blemishes on things. He liked bright colours, but became depressed when the light faded. His depressions became marked, and general. He gradually gave up active living, and three years later he died.'

From this case study, it is obvious that S.B.'s perceptual abilities weren't as sophisticated as those of an adult with normal vision when he was first given his sight, and that he took some time to perceive objects with the same degree of accuracy as you and I. The problem is that he was not a naïve adult as he had developed other perceptual skills, such as feeling objects, and he combined what he could see with what he felt in order to perceive and therefore identify objects in front of him.

Cross-cultural studies

There is one final method that has been used to investigate the question of whether perceptual skills are innate or learned. This method has used what are known as cross-cultural studies. The idea here is to see whether people from different cultural groups perceive things in the same way. If they do, this would indicate that perception is a biological skill rather than something which is learned. It does make sense to look for comparisons when we think of the amount of cultural diversity there is on our planet, both in environment, lifestyle and beliefs. If perceptual skills are learned, then people from primitive tribes would not have the same learning experiences as white Europeans from developed cultures and would be unlikely to perceive in the same way as each other.

The other thing we need to consider before we look at cross-cultural studies is that many westerners are guilty of considering themselves to be educationally superior, culturally more advanced and basically 'normal'. This is called ethnocentrism, the belief that we are the 'centre of the universe', the prototype of normality, and therefore that anyone else should be judged by our standards. Unfortunately, much psychological research is guilty of this ethnocentrism as it was undertaken using white western subjects, many of whom were middle class, undergraduate, American, male students.

The method used to test members of different cultural groups is to use the same stimulus material in the form of pictures. After all, it would be an interesting experience for a selection of people from different cultures; such as a pygmy or a Bantu tribesman, to be flown to a psychologist's laboratory in order to look at a number of different visual stimuli. You can imagine how the very experience of flying might frighten them so much that they would have problems responding to anything else. Therefore the answer has to be to take the stimulus to the subjects.

I think my favourite example of a piece of research which actually took the subject to the stimulus was done by Turnbull (1961). Bambuti pygmies live in tropical rainforests of the Congo, where they are unable to see any distance in front of them due to the dense undergrowth. Consequently they have virtually no experience of looking at objects any distance away. Turnbull took one of the pygmies to an open plain and showed him a herd of buffalo a long way away. He identified the buffalo as insects and refused to believe that they were really buffalo. He became very distressed when he found that they appeared to increase in size in front of his eyes, as Turnbull took him closer to them. The only way the pygmy could deal with the situation was by telling himself that this was really due to witchcraft. (It's also worth bearing in mind ethical considerations here: perhaps this experience had long term effects detrimental effects on the poor old pygmy!)

One of the first studies where the stimulus was taken to the subjects was carried out by Rivers et al. (1901) on the Murray Islanders who live on a group of islands between New Guinea and Australia. They were found to be less influenced by the Müller-Lyer illusion than English people. The reason for this was that it was thought to be because they focused on the figure as a whole (including the arrowheads) rather than the shafts alone. Rivers believed this was due to something in their biological make-up which made them perceive things in a different way to the British.

Segall et al. (1963) undertook a large study which took a number of years to investigate the cultural differences in perception. His subjects were taken from many different cultural groups including Americans and Africans. He found amongst other things that Africans and Phillipinos were less likely to fall for the Müller-Lyer Illusion than the more westernised cultural groups.

Segall et al. concluded that there was a relationship between the physical environment inhabited by the subjects and their likelihood of being susceptible to visual illusions. As a result of this they came up with what is known as the 'carpentered world hypothesis'. According to Segall, we in the west live in a world full of right angles and straight lines whereas other cultural groups live in environments where there are no straight lines or right angles. Instead the dwellings tend to be round huts with little or no symmetry. The conclusion was that we were therefore using our cultural experience to help us to try and interpret an ambiguous figure by changing the way that it is perceived.

There is, however, considerable research which has disputed these findings, claiming that other cultures who live in very different environments show no differences in their assessment of visual illusions. One such piece of research was undertaken by Gregor and McPherson (1965). They found that there was less difference in the responses of two groups of Australian aborigines when shown the Müller-Lyer illusion, despite one group living in a relatively carpentered environment and the other living in primitive conditions, outdoors.

These findings may be explained by the fact that some cultures are more familiar with elements of western culture – namely pictures! If you had never seen a picture or photograph before, you would probably find it fairly amazing and difficult to understand. We find that hard to believe, but to give you an idea of how hard it might be, if you have never seen a technical drawing before you would find that really hard to interpret, whereas someone who either designs or works with technical drawings every day would have no problem understanding them.

From the above findings, we should realise that familiarity or lack of familiarity with an environment affects the way we interpret it, and similarly with drawings. If we return to the idea of depth cues and constancies we talked about earlier, we use these all the time to make sense of what we see. If we are not familiar with them, we will misinterpret the stimulus and this will give supportive evidence that perceptual abilities are learned. This whole idea was addressed in the article by Deregowski (1972) where he considers whether people from different cultures see and interpret pictures in the same way. Within the article, published in *Scientific American* in 1972, he looks at a number of pieces of research, both his own and that of others dating back to 1960. He comes to the conclusion that not only are pictures not interpreted in the same way by different cultures, but different cultures also produce different styles of picture.

Jan B. Deregowski (1972). Pictorial perception and culture.

Scientific American, 227, 82–88.

The intention of the article is to present the findings from a series of cross-cultural studies, both empirical and anecdotal, in order to answer the question: 'Do people from different cultures perceive pictures in the same way and if so, can we consider pictures to be a universal means of communication which go beyond language and culture?'

Method

Deregowski used a number of different sources of information in his article, including experiments, in order to gather evidence to answer his questions.

First source of evidence

Anecdotal reports from missionaries, explorers and anthropologists visiting remote cultures.

- **Robert Laws (missionary visiting Malawi, end of the nineteenth century):** Laws found that at first natives needed to have pictures of animals explained in order to understand them.
- **Mrs. Donald Fraser (missionary in Africa, 1920's):** She found that an African woman traced the outline of a profile of a head with her finger in order to understand it, but found it hard to understand why the head had only one eye. A further report attributed to Mrs. Fraser described how, when a picture of an elephant was projected onto a sheet, the people present jumped up shouting and the ones nearest the picture ran out, as they all feared the elephant was alive. The chief was reported to have crept behind the sheet to find out if the animal had a body and let out a great roar when he discovered that it was only the thickness of the sheet.

Second source of evidence

William Hudson tested South African Bantu workers plus other tribal and linguistic groups from different parts of Africa to see if they could identify the relative positions of objects in a series of pictures, using three pictorial depth cues. These depth cues were:

- **Familiar size** – The same object will be drawn smaller if it is supposed to be further away.
- **Overlap** – A nearer object may obscure part of an object that is further away.
- **Perspective** – parallel lines appear to converge as they reach the horizon.

(Hudson only included texture gradients in one of the pictures.)

A three dimensional perceiver would know the man is about to spear the antelope whereas a two dimensional perceiver would say he was about to spear the elephant.

The subjects were asked what the man was doing, and which object on the picture was closer to the man. Depending on the accuracy of the answer and the ability of the subject to interpret the depth cues, the subject would have been classified as either a two-dimensional or three-dimensional perceiver.

Results: The findings were that both children and adults from different educational and social levels found the depth cues in the pictures hard to interpret (although Hudson's original data showed that school children showed much higher rates of three-dimensional perception than adults).

Third source of evidence

In order to ensure that the results of the second source of evidence were not simply due to the nature of the drawings, a further study was carried out. Subjects were shown a drawing of two squares – one behind the other, connected by a single rod. They were then asked to make a model of what they saw using modelling clay and sticks. It was expected that the two-dimensional perceivers would build flat models, and three-dimensional perceivers would build cube-like models.

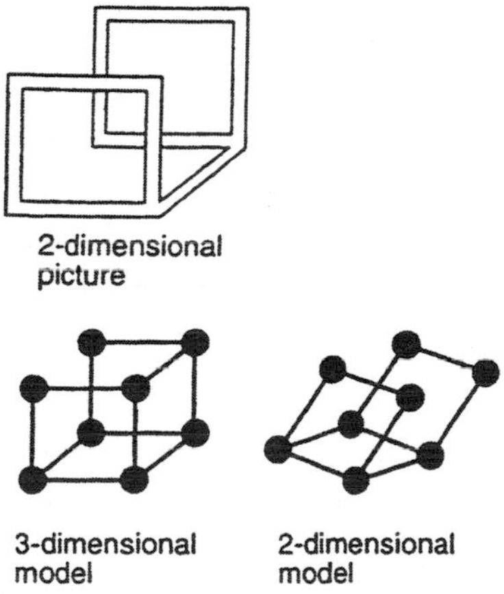

Subjects who found it hard to see depth in pictures generally made a flat model whereas most of the three-dimensional perceivers made a cube like model as expected.

Fourth source of evidence

A group of Zambian school children who had taken part in the previous study were categorised as either two or three dimensional perceivers. They were asked to copy a trident figure and an ambiguous figure of a trident (see over). Three dimensional perceivers are more confused by the impossible figure and would find it harder to copy.

In order to see the figure, the subjects had to lift a flap and then put it down again whilst they drew. It was expected that the three dimensional perceivers would have to hold the flap up for longer to try and make sense of the figure, so the time the flap was held up was timed by the researchers. The subjects also had to wait for ten seconds between lowering the flap and starting to draw. The results, as expected, were that the two dimensional perceivers spent approximately the same amount of time looking at the two figures, whereas the three dimensional perceivers spent much longer looking at the ambiguous figure.

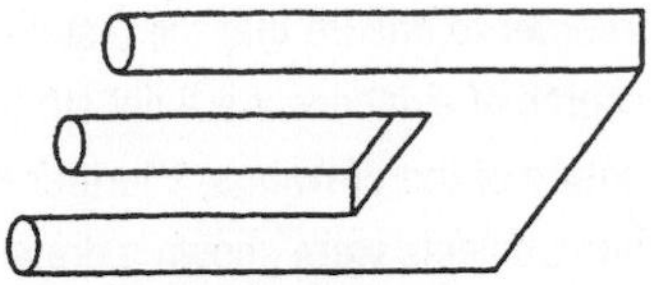

Illusory trident

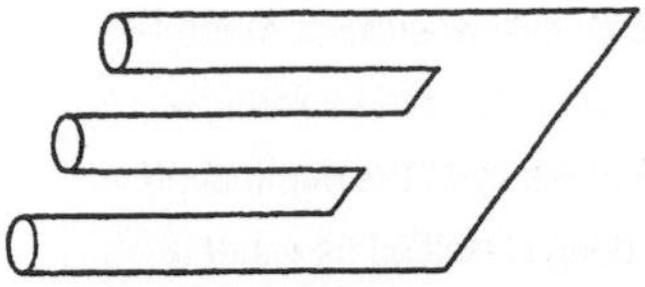

Control trident

Fifth source of evidence

It was found that people who had difficulty interpreting pictures containing perspective had a tendency to prefer pictures that showed all the details of an object, even though the details would not be able to be seen from the position of an observer, eg stripes on both sides of a zebra. Hudson showed African adults and children pictures of elephants. The first was an elephant seen from above and the second was a split drawing. All but one said they preferred the split drawing and the one who didn't said it was because the elephant was jumping around dangerously.

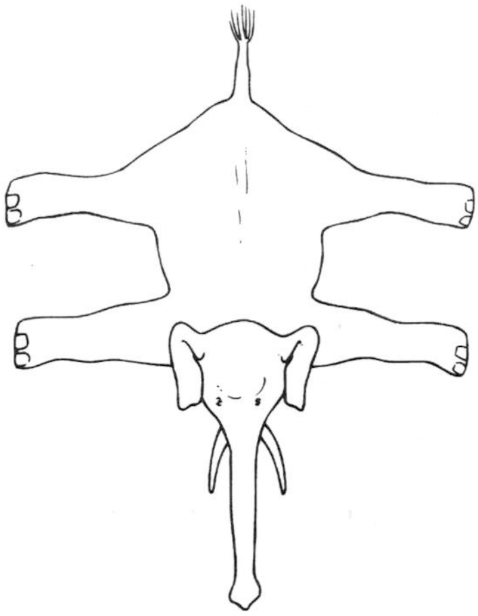

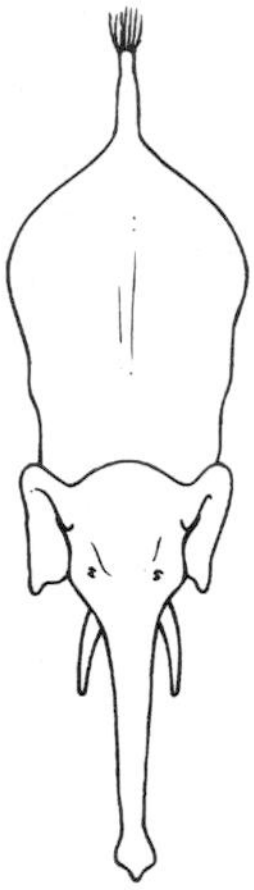

It is evident that certain cultures have a preference for this type of drawing, as demonstrated by the artistic styles of certain cultures eg Indians of the north-western coast of North America and rock art paintings of the caves of the Sahara. The problem is that this style is found in the drawings of children from all cultures, and some cultures will tolerate it whereas others discourage it. The reason for this is that it is not a photographic representation of an object and this is the style some cultures (notably in the west) find the most acceptable.

Discussion and evaluation

Although the article indicated that people from different cultures do not perceive and interpret pictures in the same way, much of the evidence is anecdotal and therefore possibly inaccurate. A number of evaluative points have been made about the findings ehich have looked at the nature of the materials and the way they are presented.

- The drawings used by Hudson were very simple and all but one lacked texture gradient. Unpublished research by Kingsley et al. found that by adding texture gradient to pictures the amount of three dimensional answers increased from 54 to 64%.

- They also lacked binocular disparity and motion parallax, which we use for depth cues in real life (although no picture contains these two cues).
- They were also presented on paper which was probably unfamiliar to some of the subjects and could have distracted them.
- They were also spoken to via an interpreter and this means that misinterpretation on both the subject and researchers part is a possibility.
- It has been suggested that the linear perspective in Hudson's pictures was too extreme. Parallel lines appear to converge at infinity, but the horizon of our visual field is rarely at infinity because there are trees, or hills or buildings in the way. Although we see lines appearing to come together, they don't visibly converge into a single point unless we can see them over a long distance on a flat surface such as a desert.

Perhaps the ability to see depth in drawings is due solely to experience, after all we are used to treating pictures as representations of real space whereas people from other cultures aren't. This should lead us to question whether our style of pictorial art is not actually correct but simply one we are used to. If this is the case, it becomes obvious that the tests used in the study were very ethnocentric. We, as westerners believe it is perfectly easy to extract information from the pictures we draw which implies that people from other cultures are inferior as they don't perceive our pictures in the same way as we do. However, who is to say what is correct – a picture which is similar to a photographic representation or a picture which is more diagrammatic, because both give information about the object being portrayed. We could argue that split drawings show more detail than perspective drawings, so really **they** are more accurate. Perhaps we are the ones who are sometimes unaware of the object's characteristics because we don't show them. In fact split drawings may be part of a developmental process from a culture rather than simply naïve art. The anthropologist Franz Boas proposed that split drawings developed from the desire to decorate flat oibjects by 'flattening' solid sculptures and that this form of art remained as the accepted from rather than some naïve effort. Another explanation came from Claude Lévi-Strauss who suggested that the style simply reflected the idea of torn apart or split personalities, which developed as a result of competitive stress within some cultures.

Key words

Ethnocentrism – refers to seeing ourselves and our culture as the norm and everyone else as being inferior if they do not match up to what we think is right.

Anecdotal evidence – an anecdote is a short narrative of an incident of private life which is unlikely to be totally accurate, therefore anecdotal evidence is evidence based on a story either heard from someone else, or recalled after the event.

Anthropologist – someone who is involved in the scientific study of human beings and their way of life.

Pictorial depth cues – cues such as used to help you understand perspective in a picture overlap and superimposition.

Ambiguous figure – a figure or drawing which is doubtful in nature as it has more than one possible meaning or interpretation.

Key questions

1. What question was Deregowski trying to answer by his article?
2. Describe what is wrong with using the descriptions given by the anthropologists and missionaries.
3. How did Hudson ensure that his materials were actually able to differentiate between 2D and 3D perceivers?
4. What advantage has split-style drawing over western style drawing?
5. Why was the study ethnocentric?

The Theory of Mind

As children grow up in a social world, it is important that they learn to understand that world including the social relationships which are a feature of their lives from birth. If they manage to master these aspects of growing up, they will be able to effectively deal with them in the future. The way they come to understand the world is initially through their social interactions with family members. It is here that most children learn what sort of behaviour is acceptable and what is not, although obviously this will vary from family to family. A fairly crude example of this would be that some children are very rude to their parents and this is ignored, whereas other children cannot open their mouths without being told off.

Jean Piaget argued that children, especially very young children, are very egocentric. To put it simply, they are centred on their own egos to the extent that they are unaware and unconcerned about others because they do not understand that others are not the same as they are and may have different perspectives and different feelings to themselves. To use terms that you may be familiar with, what we are talking about is the difference between selfishness and self-centredness. Self-centredness is being centred on self, where all your thoughts and feelings focus on you, what you want, what you need, what you feel. Self-centredness is not the same as selfishness. Selfishness is really where you know what effect you are having on others but you choose to ignore it and simply gratify yourself, so in some respects selfishness is much worse than self-centredness.

Have you ever noticed when you are waiting in the checkout queue in a supermarket, the horrible little child hanging about in front of you. Mother is there, trying to unpack a huge pile of food from the supermarket trolley with tiny baby suspended in the cot-like thing over the top of the trolley – crying! She is obviously fraught and wanting to escape and, the next thing you know, the small brat is whining, 'I want some sweeties'. (Why do they always leave sweets by the checkouts in a supermarket – I wonder!) This whining gets more and more insistent until, the next thing you know, he is having a full blown tantrum and lying on the floor, screaming and wailing and gnashing his teeth. Although you may feel like physically ejecting him from your vicinity, remember Piaget would argue that he has absolutely no idea how his mother feels and this is why he is behaving in this way.

Piaget would claim that this kind of egocentrism (or self-centredness) would continue until the child is leaving the pre-operational stage which he suggested was approximately seven years of age. However, there is considerable research that suggests that children are not quite as egotistical as Piaget insists and that many of the findings of Piaget were due to the methodology used (we will look at Piaget's theory in detail in the section on cognitive development). As a result of this, a number of researchers have looked again into the development of social awareness of children and begun to realise that investigating children in a laboratory or through a clinical interview is not the most ideal way.

The two white-coated psychologists waited, poised on the edges of their uncomfortable upright chairs. Both held clipboards and both wore glasses, perched on the ends of their noses. The door opened and a small boy was projected into the room by a long arm which did not seem to be attached to anything. The door closed.

'Ahhh,' said one of the psychologists. 'Child number four. Come in and sit down on that chair.' The chair was just too far away for the child to feel comfortable, and yet it wasn't far enough away for him to feel safe. The small boy had to climb up onto the chair by leaning forwards on to the seat and pulling himself up by holding onto the back of the chair. He managed to get one knee up on the seat and manoeuvred himself round so he was sitting facing the researchers.

'Now I have been primed that you descend from a relatively dysfunctional family which is celebrated for its impetuosity and predilection for aggressive and asinine behaviour. You understand that we intend to formulate a paradigm as a consequence of your attendance at this investigation, although of course, confidentiality is guaranteed. Now I would like you to play with those toys while I observe you.'

Poor little boy! I am not, of course, suggesting that all clinical trial situations are like the one above, but in any situation which is unfamiliar, small children are easily intimidated and may be terrified by the situation and may, therefore, give inaccurate answers.

I'm sure you will agree that the best idea would be to look at the child within their normal environment, and bearing in mind the family environment will have the most influence on a young child, it would make sense to carry out this kind of research in the child's own home. In fact, Hinde (1987) argued that unless we look at relationships in their social and cultural contexts, they will have little meaning as we will be unaware that some behaviours, which may appear unusual out of context, would actually have a great deal of meaning in the relevant environment.

Judy Dunn was very much aware of these factors and as a result of this conducted a series of studies in the 1980s looking at the social development of the child. These studies became known as the Cambridge Project and involved looking at 52 families who represented a range of income and social class backgrounds. The project also focused on the second child in the family and their pre-school development and was conducted as a longitudinal study where the researchers visited the families on a number of occasions over time.

The findings of the Cambridge project and other studies were that children as young as 18 months of age understood far more about relationships and morals than was previously believed. Dunn and Munn (1985) suggested that one of the ways they learn about how others react and what the consequences of their actions are is by teasing others. From as young as 16 months, children tease older siblings by taking or ruining something that belongs to them. This teasing extends to mother in their second year when they blatantly do something they know they are not allowed to do in front of their mother whilst looking at her and laughing. Although the child would probably start with little idea of how another person would react to such a situation, they would soon learn to predict and anticipate the responses of others by their actions. This would be one of the ways they would begin to work out how other people are feeling.

Other research has looked at how children comfort others, especially older or younger siblings and, in some instances, parents.

It was my daughter's fifth birthday and she was having a party. All her best friends were there in their best dresses and they had lots of glitter and pretty hair clips in their hair. As much as I didn't want to, I had to insist that Moonlight (yes, Moonlight!), the little girl who lived next door, came too. This obnoxious child was totally spoilt and had no friends, but her mother had sort of morally blackmailed me into inviting her, even though I knew my daughter loathed her. This revolting child arrived in some sort of over-the-top leopard-skin creation and high heeled shoes and I spent half the time trying to get the other children to let her join in with all the party games.

I had spent ages decorating the dining room table and it had a pretty pink and white tablecloth on it together with biscuits, cakes, jelly with sweets in it plus two tins of squirty cream. In the middle was the birthday cake which, as requested, looked like a 'My Little Pony' and was decorated with smarties and chocolate buttons.

My youngest daughter Emily was hanging around by the door. Hannah had begged me not to let Emily 'spoil' the party as she was only just two and that was 'too young'. Hannah insisted that she would just annoy everyone, so she had been bribed to stay in the kitchen with nice things to eat and a new toy. Finally it was time to light the candles on the cake and everyone gathered around. When the last one was lit, Moonlight seemed to jump up from nowhere and blew all the candles out and stood there with a self-satisfied grin on her ugly little face. Hannah just burst out crying.

Emily saw what had happened and ran in and hugged her sister, patting her on the back and saying 'Don't kye, Hannah, don't kye.'

Here little Emily, although she is only two, had an understanding of how her older sister felt. Not only did Hannah not want Moonlight there, but she also did the worst thing she could by blowing out the candles on the birthday cake. Emily's instant reaction was to go and comfort Hannah. Dunn, Kendrick and MacNamee (1981) had reports from mothers about this kind of comforting behaviour which was seen when the younger child was between fourteen and sixteen months of age.

This example of the comforting of one child by another is actually quite specific as the older child was crying, but in order for it to have happened the younger child would have to have had some understanding of how other people feel according to their behaviour.

Other examples of children's social awareness comes from researchers such as Stern (1977) who noticed that children as young as one can 'tune in' to the moods of others. We have all seen instances where a baby will cry if the mother cries, and laugh if the mother laughs (if not in real life, then on television). Stern called this ability 'affective tuning' and claims that it becomes more highly developed during the second and third years of the child's life. It seems that they are extremely interested in emotional states and ready and willing to learn about them, and, more to the point, that this is a normal developmental process which is generated by biologically hard-wired tendencies. By this I mean that children have an innate predisposition to learn about emotions and other people.

I suppose that you could argue that it is not solely related to the behaviour of children, because animals also seem to tune into moods. If you are frightened when you meet a dog, the dog seems to absorb that fear and respond by being more aggressive. Similarly if you are riding a horse that you are frightened of, the horse seems to absorb that fear and become even more stupid than it would be normally. The difference is that animals cannot rationalise their feelings and are unable to understand them, so they simply continue to function on instinct, whereas children have the developing ability to work out why not only they, but also others, feel like they do.

It is this working out which is directly related to how children develop what is known as an awareness of other people's minds.

Children initially have no clear sense of themselves and others as independent entities who do not feel the same about things. Although we have shown that very young children are aware that others exist and have emotions, they do not realise that others may not necessarily feel the same as they do. This is why the young child who teases an older sibling will keep doing it on and on, even though the older sibling goes from being amused to being angry. The younger child can't read the signs in the same way as say you or I would, and they don't know when to stop.

As the child starts to mature, the interactions they have teach them that you cannot predict what other people will do simply by observing the situation itself. If we return to the child in the supermarket, initially the child saw the bar of chocolate sitting there, waiting to be bought – a perfectly reasonable assumption to make. As that child matures, he will realise (we hope) that the other persons desires and beliefs also enter into the equation (I haven't enough money; it will rot your teeth/spoil your dinner etc). The child therefore develops various theories (not always correct) about other peoples' ideas, beliefs and desires and how they will affect someone else's behaviour. You will realise that gathering this amount of knowledge and using it effectively is a fairly sophisticated cognitive ability.

As I stated earlier, Piaget believed that babies are totally egocentric and that this egocentrism does not substantially diminish until they are about six or seven years old. However, the more recent research has shown that this ability to see things from other people's point of view can happen from as young as two or three although it is not fully developed until about the age of four or five. Once they can see things from the point of view of another person and understand that other people might do things that are different from what they would do, it enables them to begin to predict how other people will respond to different events. An example of this is if a child breaks something they will be able to predict that the person who owns it will probably be cross.

Understanding that people have independent minds of their own, that are not the same as that of the child, is called having a '**theory of mind**' and this ability seems to develop in most children between the ages of two and four. Having a theory of mind also allows the child to understand that other people may believe things that are not actually true. However, we must remember that although the child may have an understanding of other peoples' minds by the age of four, this is a fairly simplistic knowledge and it does not develop fully in terms of moral implications until the child reaches between six and nine years.

The way that researchers have investigated the theory of mind is by looking at children's abilities to understand false beliefs. One of the original studies was that undertaken by Heinz Wimmer and Josef Perner (1983) and involved a small boy and a bar of chocolate. The story required the children of different ages to attribute a false belief to another person and was acted out with dolls. The story went something like this.

Maxi puts his chocolate in a red cupboard and then goes to play outside. Unknown to Maxi, his mother moves the chocolate to a blue cupboard. Maxi then comes back from playing and wants to get his chocolate. A child who has observed this will be asked, 'Where will Maxi look for the chocolate when he comes back?'

Obviously the correct answer is the red cupboard, because that is where Maxi put it and where he believes it still is. If the child has an understanding of false beliefs, he will realise that Maxi will have a false belief as to where his chocolate will be found. If, on the other hand, the child does not understand that people can see things differently from the way that he sees it, he will answer that the chocolate is in the blue cupboard because that is where it really is.

Wimmer and Perner found that all children any younger than four years of age typically said that Maxi would look in the blue cupboard. This indicated that they could not take into account the fact that Maxi did not know that the chocolate has been moved.

Perner, Leekam and Wimmer (1987) decided to use a more simplistic methodology to investigate false beliefs in three year olds. The Maxi story required the children to follow a story, and the researchers decided that if they asked children questions which related to real life they may show that children would be able to succeed on the false belief task.

They showed three year old children a Smarties tube and asked the children what would be inside. The children obviously answered 'Smarties.' The researchers then opened the Smarties tube and took out a pencil. Then they closed the tube and asked the children what was in the tube (to make sure they remembered). Then they were asked what they thought was in the tube when they first saw it. They were then asked what their friend (who was waiting outside) would say if they were asked 'What do you think is in this tube?' Perner et al. found that the majority of children were unable to give the correct answer to the third question, and the only ones who could were the children who were nearly four years of age. Most of the evidence therefore indicates that children develop a theory of mind by the age of four.

Having given you an idea of how children discover the mind, and how important this is to their social functioning, we can imagine how awful it must be for a child who has no concept of other peoples' minds. If they are unaware that other people have thoughts and beliefs which are totally different from their own, they will be unable to predict what other people feel and how they will react to different situations. Imagine being unable to assess how someone is responding to you when you meet them. How would you feel if you were not sure whether they liked you or not, or whether they were angry, upset or bored with your company?

Under normal circumstances, having a theory of mind would help you in the following interaction.

> 'Do you like my new dress Miriam?' squeaked Edna as she wrestled with the buttons at the front of the vivid purple dress. 'I think it is soooo sexy, and I love the way the front shows off my cleavage.'
>
> Miriam grimaced. The buttons looked like they were on maximum tension, hanging on to both sides of the dress and trying to hold back the flow of excess flesh between them. One more inhalation of breath would result in the whole row just popping off and projecting across the other side of the room. As for the cleavage, it was more like two giant marshmallows trying to escape from the tight line of the bodice. If she bent over they would escape, projecting out and smothering the top of the dress. And why that colour? It would make someone with even the strongest constitution feel nauseous.
>
> 'Yes, it looks lovely!'

Now imagine the same situation but in this instance Miriam has no theory of mind. Her answer would have been something along the lines of, 'It looks absolutely awful. You look like a slapper. You are much too fat to wear it and the buttons look like they you are about to burst. And the colour makes me feel sick!'

What would Edna's response be like? She would either become extremely upset or be incredibly angry; but Miriam would have no concept of what her response would be because she had simply told Edna the truth.

There is one group of children who rarely seem to develop any sort of theory of mind – autistic children – and this is the next topic we will consider.

Autism

Autism is a rare condition, with only one to two cases in every 1000 (Frith, 1993). Four times as many boys as girls have autism and it is found in all socio-economic classes and across all racial and ethnic groups. It is considered one of the disorders of childhood and although there is a range in the severity of its symptoms, it produces severe disabilities in its sufferers which continue into adulthood. You may come across the disorder 'Asperger's syndrome' when reading about autism. (Asperger's syndrome, also known as 'high functioning autism,' is a pure form of autism without any other handicap whereas autism is associated with other problems.)

Leo Kanner, a psychiatrist at Harvard, first noticed the syndrome in 1943 while he was working with 11 disturbed children (a syndrome is a collection of symptoms which are characteristic of a particular problem or condition). The major characteristic of autism was that the children he described did not get involved in any, what we would consider to be, 'normal' contact with people. Instead they seemed to be completely self-absorbed and emotionally alone. Kanner called the syndrome '**early infantile autism**' because he claimed that 'there is from the start an extreme autistic aloneness that, whenever possible, disregards, ignores, shuts out anything that comes to the child from the outside' (Kanner, 1943). The word 'autism' comes from the Greek word *autos*, meaning self, so what Kanner was referring to when he described these children was an extreme desire to be alone, with one's self. This is obviously very different to the behaviour of most children who are happy to play alone for very short periods of time, but otherwise actively seek out the company of others. In fact Kanner believed that it was a normal biologically-driven inclination or predisposition, for children to want to relate to others and form relationships with them. He believed that autistic children '...have come into the world with innate inability to form the usual biologically provided affective contact with people' (Kanner, 1943).

Although Kanner considered this 'autistic aloneness' to be the most fundamental symptom, he also noticed that even from a very early age these children had shown problems in forming any sort of relationship with others which was not helped by the fact that they had limited language. They also showed an obsessive desire to keep everything in their world exactly the same day in and day out, becoming extremely distressed if anything changed.

Despite Kanner's identification of the syndrome as early as 1943, it was not accepted as an official diagnosis until 1980. The problem was that it was originally considered to be a kind of childhood schizophrenia which preceded adult schizophrenia. Although there were many similar symptoms such as social withdrawal and inappropriate feelings in certain situations, autistic children do not have hallucinations and delusions, and furthermore they do not grow up to be schizophrenic.

In the film 'Rain Man', Dustin Hoffman accurately portrayed the fear and discomfort of an autistic subjected to a change in routine

Autism begins in early childhood and can actually become evident in the first few weeks of life, although it is often not identified until the child is between 18 months and two years of age. In fact often parents only realise that something is wrong when the infant misses an important developmental marker, for example that they have not shown signs of using language, or any language they have used is odd in some way when they reach the age of two.

Kanner identified four major symptoms of autism and these remain the criteria for diagnosis today.

1 Inability to form relationships with other people

Autistic children do not seem to be able to form relationships with other people and seem to remain detached and aloof. Normal children may show signs of attachment as early as three months of age although this is usually to their mother, but in autistic children this early attachment is virtually absent. A normal child will smile or reach out to their mother to be picked up, craving some kind of interaction, and they will look at their mothers while they are being fed. Autistic children rarely initiate any sort of contact with their mother unless they are uncomfortable, either due to hunger or being wet. They may even actively avoid or reject parental affection and hate being picked up. They will often struggle or arch their backs to reduce the physical contact to a minimum. In fact they make few demands and are usually content to sit quietly in their playpens, unaware of the activities of others. However, they are not always totally detached from other people because by the age of two or three many of them do form some emotional attachment to either parents or other caregivers, although this may not be of the same quality as a normal child.

2 Lack of spontaneous play, especially pretend play

What does seem to be obvious with autistic children is that they rarely approach others and may look past or through people or turn their backs to them. Consequently they rarely initiate play, although they may respond to the play of others at times but usually for a limited period of time. They do not seem to use their imagination in play and instead become preoccupied and attached to inanimate objects or play in a repetitive or obsessive way with an object such as a toy or keys, passing them back from hand to hand or lining them up in meticulous order.

3 Serious abnormalities in the development of language and communication

Autistic children often have problems with language and 50% of autistics never learn to speak. If they do speak, their language is often odd and they may echo, with extreme accurateness, what another person said. This is called '**echolalia**.' Others who learn to speak may fail to learn to reverse pronouns so they say phrases that others have said to them. This means that an autistic child will often refer to itself as 'you' and to its mother as 'I' because that is how mother has spoken to it.

> Mother says to little Johnny, 'Would you like a drink? I am going to have one.'
> Little Johnny replies, 'Yes, you would like a drink. Is I going to have a biscuit too?'

Although this is an example of what I mean here, even this conversation would be unlikely to take place as the child is actually asking a question and is therefore continuing a conversation. More recent theories have indicated that the language problems found in autistic children are actually a totally independent disability which may be present alongside autism, but are not directly related

very upset if people do not behave in a predictable way. They have also been shown to become anxious if they are separated from their mother or caretaker, and react like a normal child on her return (Sigman et al., 1986). What seems to be the problem is their lack of ability to interpret emotional signals from other people and to thus make sense of them – this is linked with the theory of mind (Harris, 1988).

One explanation of why this situation has occurred is that they lack the ability to think about mental states (eg liking, reasoning, believing) both in themselves and in others, and this provides one account of why they have social difficulties. As these are essential components in order for them to develop a theory of other peoples minds, it would make sense to conclude that they are unlikely to have a theory of mind.

If we think back to the idea I suggested earlier, when I asked you to imagine what it must be like to be unable to work out what someone else was feeling or thinking, you might find this situation terrifying because you would have no idea and no ability to work out what they were going to do next. One way you could perhaps deal with this would be to simply withdraw from any sort of social contact. You would therefore be safe and the world would not be such a frightening place. This lack of theory of mind may therefore be a possible explanation as to why autistic children actively avoid any sort of social interaction.

Simon Baron-Cohen, together with Uta Frith and Alan Leslie, decided to investigate if this was in fact the case. If they discovered that *all* autistic children did in fact lack a theory of mind, then this could be identified as the core deficit in autism. The researchers also had to make sure that it was a deficit that *only* occurred in autistic children and was a totally separate phenomenon to other mental retardations, and so they compared autistic children with Down's syndrome children and normal children. The task they used was a slightly shorter and simplified version of the Wimmer and Perner Maxi doll study.

Simon Baron-Cohen, Alan M. Leslie and Uta Frith (1985) Does the autistic child have a 'theory of mind'?

Cognition 21, pp 37–46

The intention of this study was to find out if autistic children have a theory of mind. It was believed that a lack of theory of mind might be the core deficit in autism and so the researchers compared autistic children with other mentally retarded children and normal children. If autistic children were the only ones who lacked a theory of mind and it was common to *all* autistic children this could, therefore, be identified as the core deficit.

Method

Design: A quasi experiment where subjects were unable to be randomly allocated to each of the three conditions as they were already categorised by their individual characteristics. The independent variable was the type of child and the dependent variable was their ability to succeed at the Sally-Anne test.

Subjects: 20 autistic children, 14 Downs syndrome children and 27 normal children.

Apparatus: A table with a chair on one side for the subject and a chair on the other side for the researcher. On the table are two dolls, Sally with a basket in front of her and a marble, and Anne with a box in front of her.

Procedure: Each child was tested alone and was seated at a table, opposite the researcher and had to answer four questions. The child would be told that the first doll with the basket was called Sally and the second was called Anne who had a box.

- Q1 What are the dolls called? (Naming question). Sally then puts the marble in her basket and goes out of the room. Anne opens Sally's box and takes out the marble, putting it in her box, and then sits back down again. Then Sally returns.
- Q2 Where will Sally look for her marble? (Belief question) (Note: If the child says Sally will look for her marble in her basket, they will have realised that Sally has a false belief.)
- Q3 Where is the marble really? (Reality question).
- Q4 Where was the marble in the beginning? (Memory question).

These last two questions are intended to ensure that the child is actually aware of what is going on, and also has an accurate memory of where the marble was originally. If the child fails these two questions, then the assumption would be that the child is too handicapped to cope with the demands of the theory of mind test. The final part of the study involved the child being taken through the whole procedure again but the marble would be put in the experimenter's pocket rather than Anne's box to ensure that the original responses were not simply due to chance.

Type of Child	Mean Chronological Age	Mean Verbal Mental Age	Mean Non Verbal Mental Age
Autistic*	11 years 11 months	5 years 5 months	9 years 3 months
Downs	10 years 11 months	2 years 11 months	5 years 11 months
Normal	4 years 5 months	4 years 5 months**	4 years 5 months**

*The autistic children were a high functioning group (mean IQ = 82) as the intention was simply to test one deficit and not have that deficit confounded by other factors.

**These two mental ages were assumed to be the same as the children's chronological age.

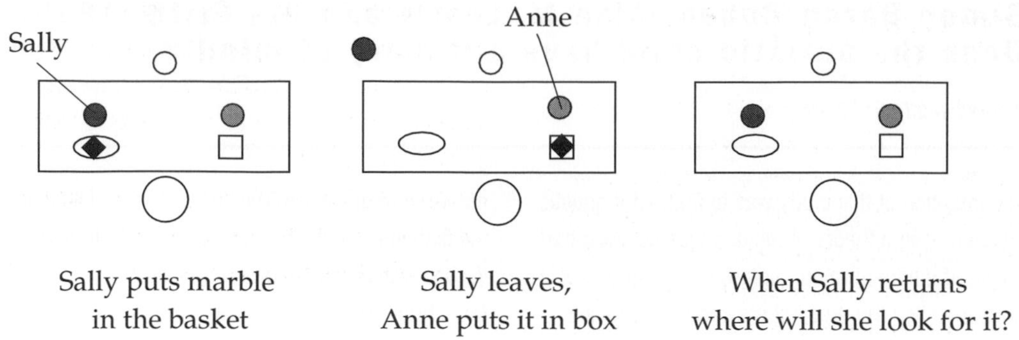
Sally
Anne
Sally puts marble in the basket
Sally leaves, Anne puts it in box
When Sally returns where will she look for it?

Results

	Percentage of correct responses				
	Naming?	**Reality?**	**Memory?**	**Belief?**	Actual no. giving correct answer
Autistic	100	100	100	20	4 out of 20
Downs	100	100	100	86	12 out of 14
Normal	100	100	100	85	23 out of 27

The difference in the performance of the autistic children compared to the other children was significantly different on the belief question, at a significance level of $p<.01$.

Discussion

All the children managed to answer the control questions correctly which gives evidence that they were aware of what was going on in the study and understood that the marble had been moved. The belief question was the only one which caused problems, *especially* for the autistic children. The interesting factor in these results was that some (4 out of 20 autistic children) could answer the belief question correctly and some of the other children were unable to do so. This indicates that although the results lean in the direction of supporting the experimental hypothesis, they are inconclusive because some of the autistic children do have a theory of mind. Therefore lacking a theory of mind cannot be a core deficit in autism.

Evaluation

The results may not simply be due to the fact that autistic children do not have a theory of mind; they may simply be due to the fact that the children were not interested in the study and simply 'switched off', after all the study does lack ecological validity. The study actually showed that autistic children could not attribute false beliefs to dolls (although later research using real people enacting the story also produced the same results). However, the study did indicate that other children with considerable cognitive deficits (the Down's syndrome children who had an average IQ of 64), do develop a theory of mind. Therefore we must conclude that perhaps the inability of the majority of autistic children studied to demonstrate that they have a theory of mind links in some way to the obvious social problems that they have. After all, unlike autistic children, children with Down's syndrome generally seem to take great delight in social interaction.

Key words

Quasi experiment – an experiment where subjects cannot be randomly allocated to a condition as they are already pre-categorised. In this study we are looking at the effect of people's mental condition on their ability to do a task. We cannot vary people's mental conditions – we simply have to assign people of different groups together. This cannot therefore be random, which is one of the most important aspects of true experiments.

Down's syndrome – a disorder which is caused by a chromosomal abnormality, in which there is mental deficiency and a broadening and flattening of the features.

Chronological age – the age that you are in years and months

Verbal age – this is gained by comparing a child's verbal ability with a control group of 'normal' children. If a child has a chronological age of eight, it may have a verbal age of five, because its verbal functioning will be at the level of most 'normal' five year olds.

Mental age – worked out by the same formula but involves other cognitive abilities such as mathematical and reasoning skills.

Key questions

1. Why were the autistic children compared with the other two groups?
2. Why were the ages of the children so different?
3. Do you think this age difference influenced the results?
4. What was the purpose of the memory question?
5. Was the experiment ecologically valid?

Language

The last area of cognition that we are going to consider is language and, as I mentioned at the beginning of this chapter, the key study in this topic area focuses on the nature-nurture debate. You will by now have realised that we are born with certain abilities, but these abilities 'improve' as we get older as a result of learning. The thing is that some of these abilities involve not only learning experiences but also require physical maturity in order for them to reach the level of skill we have as an adult. Let me give you a very simple example. Children cannot walk when they are first born although they are born with a reflex which allows them, if supported, to move their legs as if they can walk. The problem is that they cannot fully support their own weight on their legs (no, you are not allowed to go and dangle new born babies to see what happens – it is not good for them) and their necks are not strong enough to support their heads. They are unlikely to be able to walk before ten months of age at the earliest, and often they may be over a year old before they launch themselves into action without needing to hold onto things. By this stage their physical body will have developed sufficiently to allow them to master this skill.

The development of language follows a very similar route because a baby is born with the ability to make a noise as I am sure you know – it can cry! However, even if it was familiar with language and understood it, and knew the words it wanted to say, as soon as it was born it could not speak because its mouth is not the right shape.

When we are born our tongue is too big and our palate (the roof of our mouth) is too low. As we mature the relative sizes of these parts will change and soon we can make the first sounds which are called 'hard consonants'. These are sounds like mamamamam or dadadada or gagagaga. All children from all cultures make the same sounds, so it is a developmental process rather than luck! The problem with this is that when children say mama or dada, they aren't actually saying mummy and daddy, it is simply chance!

Our ability to learn language really is quite stunning and I think perhaps the best way to take in exactly *how* stunning is by looking at the stages children go through in language development. When we see how quickly we master the rules of language it would make sense to ask ourselves if we are perhaps 'hard-wired' or biologically programmed to learn language, or if it is simply something we are taught. My argument would be that we must have some innate predisposition to learn language as we seem to be able to do it so quickly and so accurately. In fact every child, no matter how intelligent, masters the rules of grammar and the learning of vocabulary in the first few years of life, despite the fact that children are not formally taught how to speak and do not have lessons in grammatical rules.

One of the studies which actually gives an indication of just how much our vocabulary increases over the first years of our lives and how much learning we undertake without realising, was a study done by Seashore and Eckerson (1940). They concluded that 19 year old college students had a vocabulary in the region of 150,000 (other samples have estimated as many as 250,000). This means that between the ages of 1 and 19 we have to learn on average 21 words a day!

Can you ever remember having to actually learn words, let alone having to learn that many throughout your life. This must give some indication that perhaps we are pre-primed to learn words without having to actually sit down with vocabulary lists. In fact a study undertaken by Carey (1978) looked at this learning process. His intention was to teach a single new colour word to 3–4 yr olds in a nursery class. He chose the colour olive green which was a colour less familiar to small children and decided that he would call it chromium. He wondered how many exposures to the word the children would need before they were able to use the word and understand what it meant. He found that eight of the 14 children chosen had begun to restructure their colour vocabulary with just two exposures to the word and with just one further exposure only one child seemed not to have learned anything about the new word. These findings give us some indication as to how quickly children can pick up new vocabulary. After all, we all know of how quickly small children pick up words we wish they hadn't overheard.

Imagine you had been given the dubious pleasure of looking after your little brother while your mum went out shopping. You really didn't want to and now here you are, fed up with looking at lego bricks and the Thomas the Tank engine video for the sixth time. The worst part was that your mum asked you to keep an eye on him and not let him get dirty before you took him to playschool later in the afternoon.

You have a master plan. You decide bribery with sweets is the answer so you take some money and walk him to the newsagents to get him some sweets. After you have decoded his squeals and abominations of the language, you come away with a bag containing revolting, brightly coloured things and when you get home you settle him in front of Thomas for the seventh time, together with the bag, and go and phone your best friend.

After you have been on the phone for about twenty minutes, having discussed every aspect of your life in graphic detail, you decide it would be a good idea to see how the little chap is doing. You walk through with the phone into the other room, still talking, when you see the most horrendous sight. 'OH ~#~#,' you scream, 'the little pig has got into a disgusting mess, there's chocolate and yuck everywhere – got to go, bye.'

The small child looks up at you, 'Oh ~#~# – dirty.' As you try to clean him up, all he keeps saying is 'Oh ~#~#, Oh ~#~#, Oh ~#~#.'

'Shhh, you mustn't say that,' you insist.

'Oh ~#~#, Oh ~#~#,' he continues.

'I've just told you, you mustn't say that. Mummy will be really cross,' you say more insistently.

'Oh ~#~#, Oh ~#~#,' he says even louder.

'For goodness sake – shut up,' you shriek.

'Oh ~#~#, Shut Up, Oh ~#~#, Shut up,' is his only answer.

In order to prevent this happening to you, we will consider the approximate timetable of language development in babies.

In the first two months babies make a sound (a cry) only in response to some sort of discomfort. The cry at first is the same for each sort of discomfort – wet nappies or empty tummies – but as they get older the cry has slightly different variations. In the second two months the baby begins to laugh and burble as a response to feelings of pleasure.

When they get to between three and four months they start babbling.

This is when babies keep repeating two-letter syllables. It occurs in every culture and deaf children babble too. It is interesting that babies use the same syllables throughout the world (eg gagagagagaga) even when those syllables are not used in the language. The sounds seem to emerge according to the physiological development of the child, that is as the child gets more control over the movement of the tongue. It is only when the child reaches about nine or ten months that the babbling seems to become related to the child's native language and some of the sounds, produced when the child was younger, are no longer heard. However, throughout the course of babbling, it occurs in sentence-like sequences with rising and falling intonations.

No one knows why babies start to babble. It may be because they enjoy the sounds they make and this is supported by the fact that they often babble while they are alone. Whatever the reason, it gives the babies practice at making basic units of words, although it cannot be described as a form of communication since the sounds don't stand for anything (they lack symbolic function) and, as we have already noted, the babies often babble when they are alone.

There is further evidence that although the babbling may have started simply because they found they could babble and it was a way of exercising the tongue and voice, they must derive some sort of pleasure from the experience. I suppose it must be similar to the way that when we first learn to whistle, we whistle (badly) all the time for a while. The evidence comes from the fact that most deaf babies seem to stop babbling at around nine months, and it is presumed that this is because they cannot get any sort of feedback by listening to themselves, so it serves no further function. Some children stop babbling when the first words appear while others continue to babble for a few more months.

Children seem to show their understanding of words from as early as seven or eight months when they respond to words, especially their names and names of common experiences, like drink and food or the command of 'no'. However, the first words can appear as early as ten months, although other children may not say their first words until they are over eighteen months (Harris et al., 1986).

Names of objects are usually the first words spoken and not surprisingly, perhaps, they tend to centre on things that are important to the baby such as food, animals, and toys. Babies tend to use one word as a general word to describe a whole series of vaguely similar things, eg wowo for dogs or other animals with four legs. These single words are called 'holophrases' and the utterance of the word, together with its context, allows the child to convey what it means. Many first words are action words that describe things that are happening: 'Da' when father appears, or 'up' to mean pick me up. Many of the words used might not sound like the adult version of the word, but the utterance of the word together with pointing, reaching and facial expression, generally get the meaning across.

Infants introduce one word at a time, extending their vocabulary gradually. However, most children can respond appropriately to a number of words before they can produce any. Interestingly, deaf children who are brought up in an environment of sign language, are seen to make their first signed words for objects at around eight months. The reason they do this when they are so young is because they *can* sign, whereas the mouth is not ready for speech for at least another two months.

When children have come to know about 50 words, they begin to adopt regular patterns of pronunciation which can lead to mistakes. The errors they make are typical of childhood speech where they may make mistakes in sounds by deleting parts of words, for example using the word poon for spoon. They may also regularise plurals because they know that by adding 's' to the end of a word, it will make it into more than one, such as sheeps for sheep, and mouses for mice. I think one of the nicest examples is that given by Hetherington and Parke (1986) when they described a child they knew who 'used the word "clothes" and insisted on calling one piece of clothing a "clo.".' It has also been shown that if the mother uses what are known as 'referential' words, the child's vocabulary is more referential; but if she uses more 'expressive' words, the child will use that type of vocabulary (Nelson, 1973). A referential word is a word which refers to an object, for example dog, house, table etc. An expressive word is a word which expresses a state such as happy, good, sad etc. Later research found that children who learn more object names tend to build up a vocabulary more quickly (Bates et al. 1988).

When the child is between 18 months and two years of age, they begin to make what are known as two word utterances. Obviously these 'sentences' will give the listener more information although they are sometimes quite unusual. The surprising aspect of two word utterances is that they already involve a simplistic type of grammar involving the use of what are called 'pivot words' which are words like 'more', 'gimme' and 'open', and 'open words' such as 'milk', 'teddy' and 'door'. The child puts these words together in the same order as adult speech. Roger Brown (1973) carried out a longitudinal study using naturalistic observation of his three children, and noticed that their two word sentences are like telegram messages. This kind of speech is known as telegraphic speech because it is like a telegram, that is a form of communication using the smallest number of words to convey meaning in the correct word order.

The rate of vocabulary growth seems to be very slow for a time after the first words have been uttered. This is quite strange if you come to think of how many words you need to learn each day to reach the 150,000 mentioned earlier. What happens to vocabulary growth to allow such a huge leap forward. Nelson (1973) undertook a longitudinal study of 18 children and noted that their first words were produced between the ages of nine and 15 months. She found that vocabulary growth was approximately one to two new words each week until the children reached a vocabulary of between 30 and 50 words which seemed to be when they were 17 to 19 months of age. It seemed that at this point there was suddenly a vocabulary explosion, when up to 8 new words were learned each week. This was believed to be because the children suddenly acquired an insight into the fact that words are just symbols. Prior to this time, they had only been able to use words in certain contexts. This was described by Martyn Barrett (1986) when he wrote about his son using the word duck. He first used the word when he knocked a yellow plastic duck off the edge of the bath into the water, but soon realised that the word duck did not simply have to be associated with that context. He started to decontextualise and then called every bird-like thing a duck (which was an overgeneralisation of the symbolic property of the actual word), until he finally realised that the word 'duck' applied to only one category of objects.

In the remaining years, until the child reaches the age of between six and seven, they will lean to master all the rules of grammar. This involves applying rules with increasing effectiveness although they are rules that have been deduced and inferred rather than rules that have been formally taught. All children make mistakes, but the mistakes they make are common such as over-generalisations, although they all seem to be part of the developmental pattern that all children go through. However, you never hear a child say 'lorry red' or 'drink gimme', they just 'seem' to know the grammatical rules of their language. If you remember that no matter what level a child's ultimate intelligence reaches, the vast majority of children master the complex rules of grammar with little or no problem and no formal teaching. This should really reinforce the idea that there must be some sort of pre-programming to allow this level of learning to take place. Perhaps we have a kind of language 'processing box', which once it starts to work allows us to extract the rules of grammar of our native language without any conscious effort on our part.

What we ought to consider is whether or not the 'processing box' works whether we share language with other people, or if it is enough for us simply to be put in front of a television or radio which emits the spoken word. It seems that children only develop language provided they are surrounded by it. Evidence has indicated that interaction between a child and other adults or children is essential for the child to learn language. We know this from studies of children who have been raised without language.

One study by Bard and Sachs (1977) looked at whether children simply pick up language from hearing it spoken around them. They studied a child called Jim whose parents were both deaf although he had normal hearing. The parents used sign language to each other but they did not use it with him. He listened to the radio and watched television so he heard spoken language regularly but he was unable to pick up the rules of grammar from simply passively experiencing language. His speech was seriously retarded and was not corrected until he started sessions with a speech therapist at the age of about three and a half. Fortunately, his speech from then on improved dramatically. This study provides us with evidence that we need to talk with other people in order for normal linguistic skills to develop.

It seems that adults alter their use of language when talking to young children by simplifying it – using baby talk. Have you ever noticed how even the hardest man suddenly goes into gooey babyspeak when looking at tiny infants. You probably do the same, although I am sure you would not admit it. It seems to be unconscious because if someone suggested what you were doing you would probably be embarrassed. Obviously, whatever the reason for doing it, it is easier for children to understand. It goes without saying that mothers and caretakers play a particularly important role in the child's language development and the kind of conversations they have with the babies seem to follow a pattern:

- They hold one way conversations (before the child has started to speak)

- They turn take with the baby, firstly with sounds, then with words, so that they respond to the baby's noise by making one back and then the baby will make the next noise. This is part of the socialisation process.
- They frequently interpret and often expand what the child says, for example if the child says 'my book' the mother might respond by saying 'yes, that's your red book over on the table.'
- They will describe objects surrounding the child and explain things in simple terms.
- They also answer questions with simple language, read stories and play games that use language.

As we mentioned earlier, the type of language the mother uses will have an effect on the type of language produced by the child. The context and frequency of a mother's conversations with her child can also affect language development.

In 1967 Lenneberg suggested that there was what he called a critical period for language development and language learning. By this he meant that learning would take place with ease during a certain period of time but after the critical period learning language would become much harder. He pointed out that the stages of linguistic development were both uniform and universal, which could only mean that children are somehow biologically prepared for language. He justified this critical period by suggesting that it was controlled by physical changes in the brain and maintained that up to puberty it was possible to learn language easily, but after puberty it would cause problems. It seems that there is no convincing evidence for the physical changes in the brain and there are many instances of adults who move abroad, learning new languages fluently with little effort.

One study which gives some support to Lenneberg's ideas was the case of Genie, a child who was found in Los Angeles in 1970. She was discovered at the age of 13 although she looked about eight. She had been kept in a small room from 20 months and punished if she made any noise. She was seriously deprived, confined to a small curtained room and strapped to a bed or a 'potty chair' so she could not walk around or interact with other people. In fact she was beaten if she made any noise and so she grew up in an environment of extreme social and physical deprivation. Her case was reported by Curtiss (1977) as she was an ideal subject for an in depth case study on late language development.

According to Lenneberg, Genie had passed the critical period and therefore should have tremendous problems learning language. However, she did learn a kind of primitive language, although her speech was never normal and she spoke in a kind of high pitched squeaky voice. She also lacked the ability to speak spontaneously and often had to deliberate about what she wanted to say.

She managed to learn some elements of sign language too, but as a case subject Genie was not ideal. It seems that she had some kind of brain damage but unfortunately it was impossible to work out whether this damage occurred from birth or whether it was a result of her early years of deprivation – so really it was a flawed study right from the start.

How do we acquire language?

We have already mentioned the question as to how we acquire language by considering that there might be some kind of 'processing box' inside us which allows us to extract the rules of grammar with no effort and perhaps it is this which is sufficient for us to learn language. We have also mentioned whether or not children need to have some kind of linguistic interaction with others. We should also consider that perhaps the learning of language is simply down to the child copying and being praised for making noises which sound like words.

There are really two main theories which suggest how children acquire language and we have now touched on both of them. The first theory suggests that language is simply learned in the same way as we learn other behaviours, that is we learn by operant conditioning. This theory was proposed by Skinner in 1957. Skinner is a behaviourist, and 'hard' behaviourists believe that *all* behaviours and abilities are learned. Skinner therefore suggested that if adults praise the child, reinforcing whatever it is doing, this will make it more likely for that behaviour to be repeated (remember the idea of a child learning to say ma ma and da da – the excitement that mummy and daddy demonstrate would be enough of a reinforcement to make it more likely to happen again).

The idea behind this kind of learning is that we learn by making an association between what we are doing and a positive result. The result, as we have already said, may be that the parent praises or laughs at the child. This means that the child is more likely to repeat the sound it has made and gradually it comes to shape the sounds into actual words. It may also be that the child get something as a result of what it says or does, for example if the child asks for a sweet and is given one this will be the reinforcement for that kind of vocalisation. This would continue while the child learns the rules of grammar, because they will receive approval for grammatical correctness, even if this is not directly obvious.

Critics of this theory argue that it is difficult to explain how children learn the sheer number of words, especially words which do not relate to anything physical. How does a child learn abstract words such as 'thinking', 'wondering', 'explicit' or 'positive', by operant conditioning? This theory also implies that children go through a gradual and lengthy process of trial and error learning but as we know, children learn language extremely quickly and these rules would not be mastered in as short a time as six years. The other aspect of language acquisition that is not explained by the theory is how we come to make up our own unique sentences and change the words which have been spoken as a statement into a question. Surely, we would only use language that we have heard before and yet we produce totally novel sentences every day of our lives. Also, parents prefer their child to speak the truth rather than lie, and they have been observed reinforcing ungrammatical truths, rather than grammatical lies (Slobin, 1975). Why then do children not grow up speaking ungrammatically when this kind of language was the language which was reinforced?

The other contender for the explanation of language acquisition is Noam Chomsky who put forward his opposing theory in 1965. Chomsky is a nativist and believes that we are biologically programmed to learn language. His argument suggests that parents do not pay close enough attention to children to provide the kind of systematic reinforcement that would be needed for this kind of learning. He agrees that language must be learned – because if you'd been born in Italy you would speak Italian **not** English – but he believes that we are in some way biologically programmed to learn language and that this biological programming explains how we manage to do it so successfully and so quickly.

Chomsky proposed that children have an innate 'processing box' which he calls a 'language acquisition device' (LAD) and this enables them to collect the information about grammatical rules and vocabulary from the world around them. He believes that the child acquires a 'deep and abstract theory' which lays behind the words of the language, irrelevant of whether the language is French, English or Chinese. This explains why any child can be brought up in any country and can effortlessly pick up the general grammatical principles of that language (what he termed the deep structure), even though the surface structure or actual words change.

To back up his theory, he states that children pick up rules about language too rapidly for it to have come from the child's experience. An example of this is their ability to reverse pronouns in a sentence depending on who is speaking.

> Mummy says to little Johnny, 'I am going shopping now. Would you like to come with me?'
>
> Little Johnny replies, 'Yes, I would like to come with you.'

The child refers to itself as 'I' and the person who it is talking to as 'you' very easily, yet the language the child hears from the other person has them the other way around.

He also argued that of all the noises children are subjected to, speech is the only one they pick up, and they master its complexities even though they are never formally taught grammar. They cannot acquire language simply by imitating parents either because when do parents speak to their offspring in two word sentences, but this is still a recognised stage in language development. However, perhaps parents do…

> Little Johnny is getting very bored waiting for Mummy because mummy has just had a phone call as they are about to go out of the door to the shops.
> 'Go away,' she says.
> 'No,' says little Johnny, whereupon he starts to shriek.
> 'Shut up,' yells mummy.

Having covered the development of language in children and considering the two main theories as to how this happens, this brings us on to another point. Are humans the only species with the capacity for language?

One way that this has been investigated is the attempt to teach language to other species. What better species than those closest to us on the philogenetic scale – primates. If we are biologically programmed to learn language (as suggested by Chomsky) and no other species has that ability then perhaps it is an innate ability. However, if other species can be taught to use language then it means that language is not only a human skill but also suggests that perhaps we do *learn* language after all, which would support Skinner's theory.

If I ask you whether or not animals communicate, your initial response is probably one along the lines of 'of course they do', and I would agree with you. But what we need to be aware of here is exactly what we mean by communication. Most other animals communicate with each other, by gesture, by smell, and even by sound, but is this language?

- The bee dances as a way of communicating to the other members of the hive where they can find pollen. If it dances in a sickle shape this would indicate a different direction from a figure of eight.
- Monkeys can indicate whether impending danger is in the sky or on the ground according to what kind of shriek they make.
- Dogs, foxes, cats etc communicate their territory by scent.
- Most animals and birds communicate threats to others of the same species by patterns of behaviour that are easily understood. The male stickleback, for example, uses the red underside of his belly as a way of demonstrating territorial aggression to other sticklebacks.

Therefore the first thing we need to consider is what is language

According to Banyard (1996) it is 'a small number of signals (sounds, letters, gestures) that by themselves are meaningless, but can be put together according to certain rules to make an infinite number of messages.' The key factors here are the rules that we use which are well defined. An example of one of the rules we use is the rule of syntax. This is the order of the words we use in a sentence, for example *subject – verb – object*:

> He hat the put on.
> The lorry green out of the garage rolled.

It is interesting that although we may think we know very little about English grammar, the sentences above are obviously wrong. On the other hand, communication is the way in which one animal or person transmits information to another and influences them, eg screeching to warn of impending danger.

As we know, language is important because it is necessary to help us socialise with others and we are creatures who need to be social. Even deaf and dumb people can use sign language, which has the same grammatical structure as spoken language and is able to transmit the same information. It is vital for the transmission of ideas, to help us understand the world, to organise our thoughts and as a useful tool in learning about our personalities from how other people react to us.

I mentioned at the beginning of the chapter that there is a school of thought that claims we cannot think without language. It is true that when we think it is like a form of sub-vocalisation, that is speaking to yourself in your head. We often reason and plan and work out things by thinking in words in our head. However, we do not always need to vocalise thought because we also use images. If you are interested in this topic area, one of the most interesting topics to read about is the Linguistic Relativity Hypothesis which was proposed by Edward Sapir and Benjamin Lee Whorf in (1941). Put in extremely simple terms, they claimed that language actually dictates how we think about things, and therefore if we don't have the words to describe something, we cannot actually perceive it or think about it. If, and only if this was true, it could explain why people seem to be far more advanced than animals in evolutionary terms.

In order to consider whether animals have the capacity for language we really need to consider what we mean by language. A number of researchers have described lists of features which seem to be the essence of language, for example Hockett (1959) listed 13 design features and Aitchison (1983) proposed that there were only ten which he considered were essential to make the difference between communication and language.

I have simply picked out some of the features which we could use as a guideline as to what we mean as 'language'. We must remember too that language and speech are not the same. After all a parrot can be taught to speak, but this does not mean that he understands what he is saying – this is why parrots have no problem saying rude words in front of Great Auntie Flossie!

- The function of speech is purely as a means of communication, is not a by-product of other behaviours and it uses the vocal and auditory channels. It is also a process whereby we usually take turns to speak with other people.
- Words have meanings or semanticity, that is they refer to things.
- Sentences are governed by grammatical rules (eg syntax), so the same few words can be organised in a different way to give different meanings to the sentence.
- Words do not resemble their meaning (they are arbitrary), that is the word cat for example does not sound like or even look like the animal we know to be a cat.
- Language can be passed on from one generation to the next.
- Language allows us to refer to things which are not actually present.
- Language can be used to generate novel utterances, that is utterances which have never been spoken before.
- Language allows us to talk about things which did not happen or could never happen, in other words to lie.

If you are happy with this outline of what we mean by language, it is obvious that many of these don't seem to appear in the communications of animals. There again, we need to consider whether this description of language is somewhat ethnocentric. It's a bit like the goalkeeper in a game of football, selecting a place to put the goalposts after the match has finished. Still, we have to accept that language needs to be defined and I suggest that we use the above outline for the time being.

This brings us back to the question 'Are humans the only species with the capacity for language?' Supposing we gave animals the tools to acquire language, would they then be able to develop the language skills of a human?

Primate studies

The first consideration was what animals should be used in language research. Since the 1930s, attempts have been made to raise chimps (and more recently gorillas) to communicate linguistically. As they are supposedly our closest relatives on the evolutionary scale, you can see that if they can learn language this would strengthen the nurture side of the nature-nurture debate – showing that innate predisposition is not necessary or exclusively human, ie anti-Chomsky.

The problem was that early attempts were unsuccessful, which is not surprising as the vocal equipment of apes is not equipped to deal with the range of sounds used in human language. Although they make lots of different sounds, these sounds are more like shrieks and are very unrefined. Also they are usually made when the chimps are either excited or frightened, and seem to relate to the situation they are in. The rest of the time they are silent, so we could interpret the sounds they do make as being a very primitive, situation-specific noise rather than anything else. In fact, I find it quite hard to imagine why the researchers believed that chimps could speak in the first place. However, Kellog and Kellog (1933) attempted to raise a chimp with their own child but she never managed to utter a word! Hayes and Hayes (1951) tried with Vicki who succeeded in saying the words 'up' and 'cup', 'mama' and 'papa', although these words were somewhat unclear. I think we ought to remember the desire of the researcher to get the results he wanted – possibly a case of serious experimenter bias.

Because the first studies were so unsuccessful, it was decided to try to give another method of communication to the primates to see if they could master the complexities of language. As they make gestures with their hands in the wild and in captivity it was thought that they would easily adapt to this form of communication. Therefore it was decided to teach some of them sign language and this is the basis of the next key study. Other studies involved giving the chimps small plastic shapes as a kind of symbolic language with the idea that if they managed to combine the shapes in a recognised and grammatical word order, this would indicate the use of language. Finally, work carried out by Rambaugh et al. in the 1980s used a 'lexical keyboard', which was a board that had 256 geometrical shapes drawn on it (like a keyboard) where each shape represented a word. Rambaugh taught bonobo chimps (small rare chimps with high levels of intelligence) to use the lexical keyboard by speaking words and pointing to the corresponding sign.

The studies that have been carried out using primates have been interesting although they are varied in their rates of success. We must always bear in mind that it was men who decided what criteria we should use when deciding what we mean by language. Perhaps the most important aspect we must not forget is that chimps have problems with language production but it doesn't mean they can't understand the spoken word, and maybe this is part of the process of language. The bonobo chimps demonstrated an impressive understanding of the spoken word and were able to carry out really complicated tasks with no difficulty, when given the verbal instructions. In fact one of the bonobos whose name was Kanzi not only had an impressive understanding of the spoken word, but also had a vocabulary of about 200 lexical words by the age of ten. Kanzi had learned these with no formal tuition, but instead picked them up from everyday life in the same way as a child learns language.

R. Allan Gardner and Beatrice T. Gardner (1969). Teaching Sign Language to a Chimpanzee

Science, Vol. 165, (3894), pp 664–72

The aim of the study was to investigate whether a chimp could be taught to use human sign language which contains all the features of spoken language.

Method

Design: Longitudinal case study which started in June 1966 and continued for 22 months.

Subject: Washoe (named after Washoe county – the location of the University of Nevada) was a wild caught infant female chimp aged between eight and 14 months at the beginning of the study.

Materials: The chimp was raised in a fully equipped house trailer and always had the constant company of a small team of companions while she was awake. The environment was rich in stimulation and with toys and games which promoted interaction and gave her as much freedom as a young child. Life also revolved around routines such as bathing, feeding and dressing, which are activities involving rituals that have been identified as important in children's language development. The teachers never spoke and only used American Sign Language whilst in her presence although they made other sounds, eg laughing and indicating joy or anger, and making noises with toys, eg drums. Every sound that was made had to be possible for the chimp to imitate. American Sign Language (ASL) has a grammatical structure so can be compared with spoken language. Some of the signs have no relationship to the objects they represent, whereas others are 'iconic', for example the sign for a toothbrush is where the index finger is used as if it is a brush to rub the front teeth. ASL users often use finger spelling to spell unusual words but it was not used by the researchers. It was chosen as a way of comparing Washoe's progress with deaf children learning ASL.

Procedure: Washoe was trained primarily by the use of operant conditioning techniques. She would happily imitate actions but not always when asked or in the appropriate situation. The trainers would tickle her as a reward (or reinforcement) for that behaviour. If she made a sign that wasn't totally accurate, the trainers would aim to get her to produce a better sign by shaping her fingers. However, she sometimes became angry, sometimes aggressive and would not take part any more.
Up to 16 months they kept full record of signing, but after that they introduced a system where they only recorded a new sign after thee different observers had seen it used in the correct context with no prompting. The sign was then said to be 'acquired' when it was used appropriately and spontaneously on 15 consecutive days. Careful observation was also made of the way that Washoe combined signs, as this is part of the development of grammatical understanding.

Results

Four signs appeared in the first seven months, nine during the next seven and 21 during the remaining time. By 22 months of age Washoe had a vocabulary of about 30 words that met the criteria. In the final month of the study, the smallest number of signs used in a single day was 23. Once she had about eight to ten signs in her vocabulary, she started to combine them, sometimes spontaneously rather than imitating researchers.

- The Gardners identified her random signing as a kind of **'manual babbling.'**
- She **transferred** signs from one context to

another, eg. 'open' from one specific door to a number of doors.

- She also **generalised** the sign for one specific object to different objects, eg 'dog' from one specific dog to all dogs.
- She also learned to **differentiate** new signs, eg she learned the sign for flower and used it to indicate smell. With 'shaping' of her behaviour, she later became able to differentiate between the sign for flower (all fingers and thumb put together as if tapered and then held to one then the other nostril) and smell (palm held before nose and moved up to nose as if to smell, several times).
- She showed **delayed imitation** by spontaneously producing a sign which she had learned before in a totally different context. She actually found a toothbrush in the bathroom of the Gardner's home and signed 'toothbrush' for the first time.

Examples of Washoe's utterances (each word represents a separate sign)
Washoe combined a number of signs although some of these were imitative and some were novel and many were understandable only because of the context in which they were produced.
Open food drink
Come gimme
Open door
Listen dog
Open flower (to open the gate to the flower garden)
Open key
Listen eat (alarm for mealtime)
Gimme tickle

Discussion

Although Washoe developed a number of basic abilities which indicated that perhaps she was beginning to develop what has been defined as 'language', she needed external reinforcers which children do not need. She displayed semanticity (knowing that the signs had meaning), generalisation, displacement and creativity but her ability to produce correct word order was limited. This may have been due to the fact that the Gardners did not reinforce word order, simply word production. Washoe did not manually babble early in the project which would have been the time that a baby would have babbled. Although many of the word combinations were spontaneous, many of them were inconsistent in their structure. Finally, as a human child gets older, the length of their sentences also increases and this did not happen with Washoe.

Evaluation

One of the biggest criticisms is that many of Washoe's 'utterances' were no more than imitations and video footage of the original study did indicate that this may have been the case. The findings may also have been subjected to experimenter bias, for example did the Gardners see Washoe's gesticulations as manual babbling because that is what they wanted to see? However, Washoe's vocabulary increased over the following two years and after four years of training she acquired 132 signs. The Gardners use of ASL has also been criticised as they only used a very simplified form, unlike real language.

The conclusion must be that although chimpanzees have been taught simple communication, it seems to lack the development shown by a human child and does not match the criteria specified by Aitchison (1983) and other theorists. However, the ethnocentricity of the original definition must not be forgotten.

Ethical implications as to the rights of primates have not been considered by this study. Is it acceptable to bring them up in an environment which is so totally different from their natural lifestyle? What happens to them after the study is finished? Is it acceptable to then remove the primate from the humanised environment it has grown up in, and relegate it to a primate organisation or other holding area?

Key words

Semanticity – having meaning, eg signs and words have meaning.
Generalisation – not specifically referring to one special item, but instead referring to lots of items without the special characters of any one member.
Displacement – to use a word or sign learned in one environment to refer to the object in a different environment.
Creativity – combining signs to produce novel utterances, eg psychologist being called a 'think doctor'.

Key questions

1. Why were the findings of this study important to help understand whether humans are the only species to have 'language'?
2. What are the strengths of this study?
3. What are the weaknesses of case studies?
4. Do you think it would be easy to interpret the signing of a chimp?
5. Can you think of another way to find out if language is innate only to humans?

3 Social psychology

One of the most important aspects of our lives are the relationships we form. These can have more effect on us than possibly anything else. Therefore one of the topics of interest to psychologists is how we interact in social situations and how we feel about these interactions. They also consider why we behave as we do in society and they try to explain why we don't always behave in the most logical of ways.

Humans are social creatures who need to interact with other people. In fact it has been shown by past research that one of the cruellest types of punishment is to keep someone in solitary confinement. This is not only because we like the company of others but it seems we are biologically programmed to be social creatures. If we are kept apart from others our brain manufactures people in the form of dreams or hallucinations in order for us to interact with them (many of the main psychology text books give information about sensory deprivation studies). You may argue that some people actually choose to live a life of social isolation, either by being anti-social or by living the life of a hermit. People who are anti-social will still have to have some social interaction with society in order to survive, but with regard to hermits I'm afraid I have no immediate answer!

You should have realised by now that if humans need to interact with each other, then this will guide their behaviour. If you need something enough, you will sometimes do things which go against what you actually feel or believe in order to get what you want. This is the basis of much of our social interactions – we need something from others, and will therefore do what is necessary to get it.

The topic of social psychology is divided into two sub areas. **Social interaction** is concerned with how we interact with each other and how our position in society will have a strong effect on the type of behaviour we demonstrate. It also takes into account the factors which affect this behaviour such as our past experiences and our perceived vulnerability. You always thought that the way you behave is entirely unique to you, but the trouble is that we all tend to follow certain patterns of behaviour and in some cases these patterns are entirely predictable. The two studies which focus on this area of psychology are the study by Milgram which investigates obedience and the study undertaken by Zimbardo who looked at how roles have such a dramatic influence on our behaviour.

Social cognition involves how we think and feel about current social experiences and how we try to make sense of them, much of which is affected by past memories. It also considers how we use stored information to predict the course of interactions and their possible outcomes. The two studies which relate to social cognition are the Piliavin study which looks at the factors which make us willing to help another person and the Tajfel Study which looked at how simply being put in a group will influence our negative feelings towards others who are not part of that group.

How does all this fit into real life? As a result of social relationships you should now be aware that we are often left trying to make sense of why people behave the way that they do. Consequently we spend huge amounts of time thinking about relationships and trying to work out why certain things happen. I would imagine part of the reason why people choose to study psychology is in order to understand their own and other people's behaviour – I know that was the case for me.

> On one particular day my best friend was absolutely foul to me. I was really hurt and spent some time trying to work out why she had been so horrible because it wasn't like her. It turned out that her boyfriend had dumped her that day and she was extremely upset and just couldn't bear to talk about it, so she snapped at me, almost as a way of making me leave her alone. The trouble was that I didn't know this at the time and I was concerned about the cause of her behaviour. Had she turned into a monster or was there another reason for her being so snappy?

This is really the basis of social understanding (or social cognition). What I have done here is to try to work out what made my best friend react like this. I was using my memory of what she was like normally, and I had to think about what I had seen and how I should interpret it. I also had to think if I had done anything wrong. I had to question my behaviour and to try to work out if I had been nasty to her or forgotten her birthday or given her some kind of just cause to be so horrible.

The one thing I have realised about social cognition is that we need to have answers to the questions we may pose because if we cannot come up with a reasonable answer it causes us anxiety. People hate anxiety. In fact we tend to do anything rather than allow ourselves to remain anxious for a long period of time. Just notice in the future, if you find yourself in a situation where you feel uncomfortable you will do something to change that situation. The problem is that we don't always behave in the most logical of ways and we don't always behave according to our feelings.

My best friend hates Joan. She thinks she is the most boring and opinionated person she has ever met. In fact, she has just spent half and hour telling me why she dislikes her so much. Suddenly, round the corner comes Joan.

'Hullo sweetie, how are you? We have missed you and were wondering when we would see you again,' says my friend in the most annoying way.

Why is she saying this when she hates Joan?

The obvious reason is that she is two faced. Well, yes she is, but there is a reason for her behaviour. Is it because she does not want to hurt Joan's feelings? Is it because she wants something from Joan or is it simply because she has been socialised to behave in a totally polite way and not to indicate how she feels? These are the areas that we will now look at in more detail.

Conformity and obedience

We are going to consider the topics of conformity and obedience although we will focus more on obedience. However, the two topics are very closely interlinked, and we often use one term when we really mean another. Let's begin by considering what we mean by conformity.

Do you remember when shell suits were all the fashion (apologies to those of you who may still wear them)? Everywhere you went you saw people wearing shell suits in bright colours, and the height of naffness was when you saw Mr and Mrs and kiddiewinks all dressed in matching shell suits. I even remember my children asking if they could have one each (but of course I said no!).

And do you remember the craze for Trolls, and Teenage Mutant Ninja turtles and Power Rangers, Transformers and My Little Ponies, BMX bikes and Sindy Dolls, and GameBoys and Sony Playstations? And now Pokemon.

Four wheel drive cars can be seen en masse in the more affluent rural areas. Mothers collect their small offspring from school in giant monsters that will never, in their mobile lives, experience the feeling of muddy tracks.

Fashion designers and toy manufacturers, in fact anyone in the retail trade, love conformity. Set up a craze, especially in the young, and everyone will go for it. In fact, it's an ideal way to sell huge quantities of merchandise once you have convinced people that it is the thing they have to have. The levels of conformity in consumerism are phenomenal. When you actually stand back from it and realise how easily we are convinced that having one of these items is the only way we can ensure peace of mind, you will realise what an important concept conformity is.

So how can we define conformity and why do we conform. Well conformity has been described as 'yielding to group pressure' (Crutchfield, 1962). However, this implies that other people put pressure on us to make us conform and this is not always the case. After all, how many people pressurised you into buying a shell suit? A better definition is given by Aronson (1976) who said it was a 'change in a person's behaviour or opinions as a result of real or imagined pressure from a person or group of people.' This would make more sense as he said it could be real *or* imagined pressure, and often the pressure is imagined. The group he was referring to would have to be a group that was important to the person at the time, irrelevant of their status. A group of school children do not have any status as such, but they would be very important to another school child.

We haven't looked yet at why we need to conform.

It was Roger's birthday. His mum had promised him a new pair of trainers and he was so excited because he would at last feel like he belonged to the group at school. All the other boys had designer label trainers with inflatable bits and bright coloured stripes and air cushioned soles. He had a pair of cheap old trainers from Tesco and all the boys had made fun of them. He so wanted to be part of the group and be accepted by them. Maybe when he got his new trainers, they would stop laughing at him in the playground.

On the morning of his birthday, he got up really early to open his presents. As he opened the box containing the trainers, he could feel his heart pounding with excitement. There they were, super deluxe 'Airy-Flash' trainers with inflatable areas all over them, flashing light bits in the heel and reflective stripes. As he put them on, he thought to himself, 'I'll be one of the gang now.'

Roger needed to conform to the norms of the group of boys he wanted to play with in order to be accepted by them. If he conformed, he would not feel anxious any more. It was a way of giving himself an identity as part of a group of people who were very important to him. No longer would he worry and feel unhappy. His anxiety would be gone.

There has been considerable research about conformity and probably one of the oldest studies looked at the answers people gave when asked to estimate the number of beans in a bottle (Jennes, 1932). Have you ever taken part on one of those competitions which are usually held at fetes or school charity events? If you have I am sure you will have looked at the previous people's estimates and based your judgement on them. This is more or less what happened in the Jenness study. First of all he asked the students to give their own estimates, and then he asked them to decide a group estimate and give that. Then finally he asked them alone again and discovered that they had stayed with the group norm answer.

Another well known was a study done by Sherif (1935) where he showed that subjects will accept the judgement of others as their own if the situation is ambiguous (has more than one interpretation or answer). He did this by getting subjects to look at a pinpoint of light in a dark room and say how much it moved. If you imagine a light in the sky, possibly a star, and you watch it for a while you may imagine that it is moving even if it isn't. This is because your eyes make very small movements when you are looking at an object. This effect is called the 'autokinetic effect'.

He found that when he asked them when they were on their own they gave varying answers as to how much the light moved. When he asked them when they were all together, their answers seemed to converge together so they ended with a sort of 'group norm' answer. Unlike Jenness's study, though, he did not ask them to come to this agreed answer. Even here the 'group norm' answer must have had quite a strong effect on them because when they were on their own they still stuck to it. It seemed to give them confidence in themselves when they were otherwise unsure, and this was why they stuck to the answers even after the original event.

Probably the most famous studies on conformity were undertaken by Asch (1951) when he created a situation where many of his subjects gave answers which were blatantly untrue, rather than contradict the people they were with. He did this by getting his subject to sit round a table with six stooges (confederates of the experimenter) so that the subject was the second to last. He then showed them a large card which had three lines of different lengths, labelled A, B and C, drawn on it and a card with a single line, and asked them to say which line length matched that on the original card.

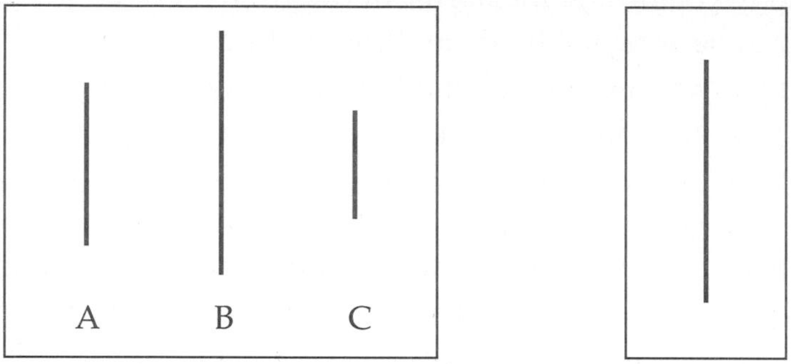

Examples of cards

In order to make sure that subjects were able to see the differences in line length, Asch tested a control group of 36 subjects a total of 20 times each when they were on their own. Asch found that in all the trials, there were only three occasions when mistakes were made.

With the experimental group, they took part in two trials where all the stooges gave the right answer before the first wrong answer was given. This must have lulled them into a false sense of security and made the next incorrect response seem all the more bizarre. The study continued with eleven more trials where the wrong answer was given, and four more where the correct answer was given. When the results were assessed, he found that in one out of every three trials where the wrong answer was given, the subject gave the same wrong answer as the stooges. This lead to an average level of conformity of 32% although 75% of subjects conformed to the wrong answer at least once.

Asch interviewed his subjects after the trials to try and find out why they conformed to an answer which was so blatantly wrong. Most of them said that they did not want to cause problems within the group and be seen as a trouble maker – they simply wanted to maintain a kind of 'group harmony'.

Asch also found that his subjects did not like giving wrong answers and when they did they felt very anxious. We all know that having some moral support makes it easier to tell the truth and Asch found that when there was just one other person present who did not go along with the majority, no matter how many others there were, it was sufficient to make the subject give the right answer. It didn't make any difference whether or not the dissenter gave another wrong answer, the fact that they disagreed with the majority seemed enough to give our subject the confidence he needed. It seems that if we have someone to share the responsibility with, it makes us more comfortable to stick up for what we know is right.

Imagine yourself in a situation where you are in class, and have all been asked to solve a maths problem which was written on the board. You know how to work it out (you asked your best mate to explain it to you last night, and your best mate is really good at maths), so you come to an answer that you *know* is correct. The teacher starts to ask each member of the class in turn what answer they have come up with and, to your amazement, most of the class has got the wrong answer. You start off thinking that they must all be really stupid if they really don't know what it is, and yet you are beginning to wonder if you are really right. You know you are going to have to state your point of view soon when suddenly one small 'nerd' with pebble glasses who is wearing an anorak (even though it's the summer), suddenly gives the same answer that you have come up with. Would this be enough to make you say what you believe, or would you not want to be associated with this totally uncool character?

Allen and Levine (1971) investigated this topic when they asked the question as to whether the type of person who went against the majority view had any effect on the subjects in studies such as the one done by Asch. They discovered that a dissenter who was wearing thick pebble glasses (obviously implying that he was extremely short sighted) was enough to encourage subjects to go against the majority.

I expect at this point you are thinking to yourself that you wouldn't ever feel so pressurised that you would give an answer which you absolutely know, without a shadow of a doubt, is an incorrect answer, especially if it was part of an experiment (this is part of the problem of using psychology students as subjects). You may feel that if you didn't know the other people, then it wouldn't matter if you didn't agree with them because you wouldn't see them again. You may even feel that if they were known to you, you would feel justified in turning around and saying to them that they are wrong. I agree with you in many ways because the nature of the situation would affect how I felt and whether I was prepared to go along with the crowd simply for a quiet life. On some occasions I might feel I would argue for the sake of it, and on others I wouldn't care that much. This is very much to do with individual differences between subjects. Each one of us has different pressures on us, and each one of us vary from day to day in how confident we feel depending on the situation we are in. However, some people feel confident most of the time, and it is these people, people with high self-esteem, who feel that they do not have to go along with the majority. They are confident enough in their judgement to go against the rest without feeling threatened or uncomfortable (Stang, 1973).

So why is it that we have to conform? Kelman (1953) outlined three processes which can explain social conformity.

1 Compliance

Where subjects go along with the crowd to prevent any in-group hostility or bad feeling and to maintain group harmony. However, they do not change their own private belief.

2 Internalisation

Where subjects come to internalise the view of the group, and see its view as the more valid one. They may be able to do this; for example, by convincing themselves that their eyesight is perhaps poor.

3 Identification

Where subjects actually seem to change their beliefs because they want to become more like their heroes. If they really want to become part of an in-group, they will start to identify with that group and take on the group's values and beliefs, even if they were different from their original values and beliefs. This can also happen if they want to become more like a person they respect or admire – they will change their attitudes to become more like them. This frequently happens with teenagers who want to become more like a peer group in order to be accepted, and suddenly seem to go against all the values and beliefs of their parents.

If we relate these back to the Sherif study and the Asch studies, we can perhaps begin to see what was happening for the subjects. In Sherif's study, the subjects stayed with the group norms, even after they were away from the group – so they had internalised the judgements. On the other hand, Asch's subjects were simply complying with the demands of the experimental situation but hadn't actually internalised the group's norms.

Obedience

Having looked at conformity, we are now going to look at obedience and we have considered both topics together because they both involve people renouncing (giving up) their personal responsibility in a given situation.

We give up our responsibility when we conform in order to be accepted by the group. We give up our responsibility to make decisions for ourself and go along with the decision of others as to how we should act and what we should do when we are being obedient. The reasons for this are not quite as simple.

There are a number of reasons why we are obedient.

First as a form of self preservation, especially if the authority figure who is telling us what to do has some kind of coercive power. By this I mean that if we don't do as we are told, we will be in trouble. In such situations we do not necessarily have to see the authority figure as being legitimate (although it helps) because no matter what we feel, we are looking after our own welfare.

This can be taken to extremes. If we were in the army, we may be court-martialled if we don't do as we are told. It may be to do with our parents, who will not actually have us shot (we hope) if we don't do as we are told, but the payoff is being grounded or having our allowance removed.

When I started teaching, I worked in a secondary school where part of the uniform consisted of an ugly brown blazer, made of a kind of synthetic material which would be very uncomfortable on hot days. The students were made to wear their blazer at all times, and were (supposedly) only allowed to take it off with the permission of the member of staff teaching them at the time. Then when they left that lesson, they had to put it back on again. On really hot summer days, the headmaster could decree that students did not have to wear their blazers, although often his idea of what was a hot summer day was not the same as the rest of us.

Part of my duties as a teacher was to tell students to put on their blazer. If it was a cold winter day and students had taken it off and put it in their bag so they could wear their coats in the playground, I had to tell them to go and get it and put it back on under their coat. This was more common for the 'girlies', who were more interested in what they were wearing. However, if it was a really hot day I used to feel quite sorry for them if the headmaster had not noticed how they were all falling about with heat exhaustion! BUT it was my job to tell them to put their blazers back on.

What made it really difficult was that I really didn't care whether they wore them or not! I was being obedient by telling them to do it. It made me feel somewhat uncomfortable, if not cruel, as I walked around in my strappy summer dress. But I had to do it as part of my teacher duties because if I ignored this stunning breach of school rules, I would have been in serious trouble. So like a dutiful member of staff, I screeched at small boys and girls, 'Put your blazer back on, NOW.'

The second reason is that we have been taught to be obedient and so it is more natural for us to be obedient than to go against the orders of an authority figure, especially one that is perceived as being a legitimate authority figure.

When we are really little, we are 'trained' from a very early age, both by our parents and by our schools to be obedient and we are also taught that these forms of authority are legitimate and have our best interests at heart. I am sure that we can all remember our parents saying to us, on many occasions, 'Do as you are told.' This will often have been backed up with threats if you are naughty, and praise if you were obedient. What happens is that we internalise the need for obedience and therefore become conditioned to obey voluntarily in most situations (we will talk more about the process of conditioning in the section on child development). This seems to become so natural within us that eventually disobeying becomes the difficult action, rather than obeying.

Once when I was teaching this topic, I decided to demonstrate how this works. I decided to pick on one particular male student who was sitting almost opposite my desk (my classrooms always have the tables set out in a semi-circle) and after the class had been running for about ten minutes, I shouted at him

'Go and stand outside the door.' He looked at me somewhat shocked and asked why. I simply answered in a very loud and angry voice, 'Just get out, do as you are told.' He reluctantly got up out of his chair and started walking towards the door, when I called him back.

He was actually quite shocked that he had obeyed, even though he had no idea why I had shouted at him and perceived the order as unfair (I had to do a good debriefing job on him!). He also said that he knew I couldn't really do anything to harm him, but teachers tell students to do things – that is just what they do, and so he did as he was told.

In instances like this, it is necessary for people to perceive that it is legitimate for the authority figure to order them to do something in order for them to obey.

What we must remember is that most of the time there is nothing wrong with being obedient. It is necessary to maintain social harmony, for without some form of obedience to an authority we would end up with a state of anarchy (which is a complete absence of law or government resulting in a total state of chaos and complete disorder, where everyone is out for themselves). On the

An example of anarchy where people hi-jacked a peaceful protest in London and ignored the normal rules of society by smashing up property

other hand, we also have to remember that blind obedience is also an undesirable state and can result in acts of destruction and damage to others.

This really brings us around to why obedience was studied. It was suggested that the type of person who is seemingly 'blindly obedient' must be very different from the rest of the population. Examples often cited are the instances of the Holocaust and the Vietnam war, where innocent civilians were slaughtered as a result of orders given by authority figures. However, research has suggested that the people who committed these atrocities, were completely normal and not, as was suggested, some kind of amoral monsters.

Eichmann was perhaps one of the worst offenders in the Second World War. He was responsible for arranging the transportation of six million Jews to their deaths. In 1961, after having escaped and lived in Buenos Aires, he was caught and sent to trial for his part in the killing of millions of Jews. While the case was being prepared, he was interrogated for a total of 275 hours as it was believed he must have been some kind of monster to have allowed this genocide to happen. Captain Avner W. Less, who interrogated Eichmann for the duration of the 275 hours, wrote:

> 'My first reaction when the prisoner finally stood facing us in the khaki shirt and trousers and open sandals was one of disappointment. I no longer know what I had expected – probably the sort of Nazi you see in the movies: tall, blonde, with piercing blue eyes and brutal features expressive of domineering arrogance. Whereas this rather thin, balding man not much taller than myself looked utterly ordinary.'
>
> *(Von Lang and Sibyll (eds.) 1983 in R. Brown (1986) p.3)*

He was described as an average man of middle class origins and normal middle class upbringing, and a man without identifiable criminal tendencies. In fact half a dozen psychiatrists examined him and found him sane. His family background was quite normal and he had good relationships with his parents, wife and children. He also had no strong anti-Jewish sentiments, having supported the idea before the war that the Jews should have a separate territory. He also had a Jewish mistress which was not an accepted state of affairs for an SS officer, as well as having a Jewish half cousin for whom he arranged protection. He also never committed an overt act of killing but was totally insistent on the obedience and adherence to duty of his fellow officers. In fact Hannah Arendt (1965), who reported on the trial of Eichmann, concluded that he was simply a commonplace bureaucrat like any other, who obeyed orders given to him without question.

He was found guilty and was executed by hanging in Jerusalem. As part of his defence, he unsurprisingly denied responsibility for the deaths and said it was simply because he was ambitious that he felt it was his duty, though a somewhat distasteful duty, to obey the Führer's orders.

The other frequently cited evidence of how obedience to authority can be destructive was the case of Lieutenant William Calley's part in the My Lai massacre during the Vietnam War in 1970. Calley was the commander of a platoon of American soldiers when he received orders to round up all the inhabitants of a village called My Lai. He was told that there were Vietcong in the village, and that the soldiers should round up all the members of the village and 'waste them' (shoot them dead). The inhabitants were mainly women, old men and children and yet they were all wiped out.

After the event, there were questions about the nature of the 'massacre' although Calley said that orders had been received from a superior and it was his duty as a soldier to obey. It seemed that there was some doubt as to whether the orders sent were that explicit, and consequently Calley was held to be 'guilty', but was only given a minor sentence.

Again the nature of the man who was at fault was questioned. How could a 'normal' person agree to order their men to shoot obviously innocent children? However, he had shown no criminal tendencies before My Lai and after his sentence he continued to live quietly as an average American civilian. In 1972 a survey was carried out in America to gauge the reaction of the public to Calley's trial. The results were that 51% of the sample said they would follow the same orders by killing the inhabitants of the village if that is what they had been ordered to do, because the orders were coming from a legitimate authority.

Whether we agree with Eichmann's or Calley's actions, the reasons why they were obedient are perhaps easier to understand. Imagine that you were in Eichmann's position and knew that if you did not obey orders, you may stand the chance of being shot or being demoted. I am sure that most of you would still refuse to go ahead and send so many millions to their deaths. But what if everyone else was behaving in the same way. You would not only look at the obedience aspect, but you might consider the behaviour of others and conform to group norms. Also, if you are not directly 'doing' the killing, would it make it easier?

With the soldiers in Calley's platoon, they were all taking part, so perhaps they were diffusing the responsibility amongst themselves ('they are all doing it so I can share the responsibility with them'). Also the fact that the other soldiers were going along with it made it seem the right way to behave and so each soldier was conforming to what they thought was the group norm. They also wanted to avoid rejection and having the mickey taken out of them by not joining in, which was yet another reason to go along with the situation.

It should be evident that there is more than one simple reason why people are obedient and often the reasons involve conformity too. It seems that if there is a group other factors occur which influence our behaviour, but with Eichmann these factors were nowhere near as relevant as the other people involved were not present all the time to exert the same type of social influence, and yet Eichmann blindly followed orders.

This is why Milgram became so interested in the fact that perhaps there was something unique about certain members of the German nation, who were prepared to commit what could be seen as mass murders during the Holocaust. If this was the case, perhaps other members of society like William Calley shared the same characteristics. On the other hand, perhaps their unquestioning obedience to authority may simply have demonstrated what most ordinary people would do when subjected to extraordinary social influences.

In order to test this hypothesis, Milgram designed an experiment in 1963 whereby members of the public would be told to administer electric shocks to another person as part of a learning experiment. The experiment involved putting subjects in a situation where they had no previous experience to use as a guideline as to how to behave. They were also pressurised into administering higher and higher levels of electric shock in their role of teacher, until 65% of the generally normal, American, civilian subjects had seemingly *killed* the learner, even though they were not in any sort of danger.

S. Milgram (1963). Behavioural Study of Obedience

Journal of Abnormal & Social Psychology. 67. 371–378

The aim of the study was to investigate what level of obedience would be shown when subjects were told by an authority figure to administer electric shocks to another person.

Method

Prior to the commencement of the study, Milgram questioned a number of psychology students, adults and psychiatrists as to how many people would give people fatal electric shocks as part of a psychology experiment and the estimate from all groups was 0% and 3% of subjects (mean 1.2%).

Design Laboratory experiment with independent subjects also using observation to collect data.

Subjects 40 males between the ages of 20 and 50 who came from the New Haven area of America and came from a range of occupations. They were recruited by newspaper article and direct mail advertising which asked for volunteers to take part in a study of memory and learning at Yale University. They were to be paid $4.50 for simply turning up at the University.

Apparatus Two rooms were used within Yale University. One room contained what looked like an electric shock generator which had a row of thirty switches which ranged from 15 to 450 volts in 15 volt increments. There were also descriptions about the type of shocks, eg slight shock, strong shock, intense shock, danger: severe shock and finally the last switches were marked XXX. In the other room was a chair with restraining straps where the learner was to receive the shocks via his wrist. There was also a tape recording of responses which were played according to which switch was depressed, ensuring that all subjects heard the same responses in the same order from the learner. The dependent variable was the level of shock the teacher gave the learner.

Experimenter The experimenter was a 31 year old 'stern' biology teacher who wore a grey lab coat.

Learner The learner was a 47 year old accountant who appeared mild mannered and likeable.

Procedure The subjects 'drew lots' to see who was to be teacher or learner although the situation was rigged and the subject was always the teacher. The teacher was told that the subject had to learn word pairs such as 'fat neck', 'blue box' and 'nice day'. The teacher had to read out the first word of the word pair and another four words, one of which was correct and the subject had to choose the correct word. If the subject got the answer wrong, the teacher was told to give the subject shocks of increasing intensity, although there were actually no shocks given. As they administered the 'shocks', the tape recording gave pre-recorded responses at each level to ensure that all subjects experienced the same feedback from the 'subject'.
Meanwhile the experimenter used four verbal 'prods' to pressurise the subject to continue with the experiment. If the subject disobeyed all four prods then the experiment was ended.

Prods used by experimenter

Prod 1: Please continue/Please go on
Prod 2: The experiment requires that you continue
Prod 3: It is absolutely essential that you continue
Prod 4: You have no other choice, you *must* go on.

Further prods used by the experimenter if the subject questioned the welfare of the learner

Although the shocks may be painful, there is no permanent tissue damage, so please go on.

Whether the learner likes it or not, you must go on until he has learned all the words correctly. So please go on.

Examples of responses given by learner

Groan – I can't stand the pain, get me out of here. I told you I had heart trouble. My heart's starting to bother me now. Get me out of here, please. I've had enough. I won't be in the experiment any more. I absolutely refuse to answer any more. Get me out of here. You can't hold me here. I told you I refuse to answer. I'm no longer part of this experiment. At 300 volts the victim kicks on the wall and ceases to give answers to the teacher's questions.

At the end of the study, the teacher was introduced to the learner and thoroughly debriefed about the nature and purpose of the experiment.

Results

Observed results Subjects became very anxious, especially when the shock levels were higher. They sweated, trembled, stuttered in their speech, bit their lips, groaned, dug their fingernails into their hands or appeared almost to be crying. Many laughed, not in amusement but as a nervous reaction. Three subjects had violent convulsions.

Statistical results All 40 subjects gave shocks up to 300v.

Discussion

The level of obedience was totally unexpected. Milgram suggested a number of reasons to explain the results:

- The fact that the study was carried out in a prestigious university influenced subjects as to the worthiness of the study and the competence of the experimenter.
- The subject believed that the learner had also volunteered and that the allocation of roles was due to chance.
- The subject has agreed to an implicit social contract by agreeing to take part and being paid for his participation and he therefore felt obliged to continue.
- The subjects were told that the shocks were not harmful.
- The situation was entirely new for the subject so he had no past experience to guide his behaviour.
- There was no obvious point at which the subjects could stop administering shocks, because each shock was only a small amount more than the previous shock. The subjects who did withdraw from the study did so when the 'natural break' occurred – when the subject ceased to reply.

Later work by Milgram indicated high levels of conformity, even when the study was conducted

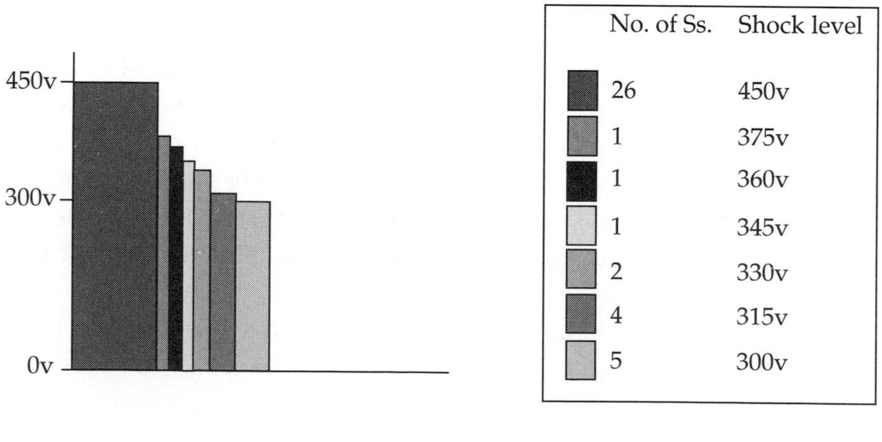

in a downtown office block with the experimenter being seemingly just a member of the public.

Milgram (1973) explained the findings by saying that people have two distinct states of consciousness which develop as a result of living in a hierarchical society. These are the 'autonomous' and the 'agentic states'. When a person is in an autonomous state, they act according to their own values and conscience, but when they act as an agent for another person (the agentic state) they suppress their own values, no longer feeling that responsibility. It seems to be the period when we switch from the autonomous to agentic state that causes the most discomfort. He also pointed out that because we are strongly socialised to be obedient, disobeying becomes more difficult than obeying.

Evaluation

Ethics Milgram's study has been one of the most highly criticised studies in the whole of psychological research and provoked an investigation after it was published, during which time Milgram's membership of the American Psychological Association was suspended. Milgram justified his work by saying that he had not anticipated his results and that subjects were not forced to remain in the laboratory as a number of subjects chose to leave after the 300 volt level.

He also thoroughly debriefed his subjects at the end of the study introducing them to the learner and telling the 'obedient' ones that their behaviour was normal. All subjects received a report on the findings of this and subsequent studies and 92% responded to a questionnaire regarding their feelings about having taken part. Less than 2% said they were sorry to have taken part whilst 84% said they were glad to have been involved. This may simply have been a way of reducing their cognitive dissonance *(see key words)* at taking part and having administered high levels of electric shocks to another human being. To claim that they had learned something of personal significance from the study would have reduced that dissonance.

Ecological validity Although the original study took part in a laboratory, this was essential to convince subjects that it was a valid piece of research. However, it has been claimed that they were not really deceived by the study and did not really believe that they were administering electric shocks to another person; therefore it lacked ecological validity. Milgram asked his subjects whether they believed they were administering real shocks in the questionnaire they completed a year after the study. Only 2.4% claimed to be 'certain' the learner was not receiving shocks.

Key words

Group norms – behaviour considered normal for the group.

Ambiguous – something which has more than one meaning or interpretation.

Prods – verbal encouragements or orders.

Autonomous state – acting according to your own values and beliefs.

Agentic state – acting as an agent for someone else, shelving responsibility.

Hierarchical society – a society where there are different strata of people. In a hierarchical society there are people who do menial tasks and others who have responsible positions.

Compliance – the majority influences the minority (the majority has power and can use rewards and sanctions).

Conversion how a minority influences a majority to internalise a change in beliefs.

Cognitive dissonance a state of discomfort or anxiety, caused by holding two opposing attitudes or beliefs about a situation, eg I smoke *and* smoking is bad for me; or I am giving electric shocks and I shouldn't be giving another person electric shocks for something as silly as a memory test.

Key questions

1. What was the purpose of the Milgram study?
2. Why was it considered to be so unethical?
3. How were the subjects recruited?
4. What was wrong with this type of recruitment?
5. Give two examples of how we are taught to be obedient.

Postscript

Milgram was shocked at the level of obedience found in his 1963 'baseline' study. As a result of this, different aspects of the experiment were manipulated in a series of 18 follow up studies, to try to find out exactly what it was that caused such a high level of obedience. These studies were reported by him in 1984 in his book 'Obedience to Authority'. Further studies were also carried out by other researchers, who looked at the levels of obedience in different areas of the world. However, many of these studies could not be directly compared as there were a number of methodological differences. For example, in all of Milgram's studies the learner was male, whereas this was not always the case in subsequent studies. Below you will find a short summary of a selection of the later research.

Varying the proximity of teacher and learner affected the levels of obedience. The original study involved having teacher and learner in different rooms, but when they were about 1ft 6 inches apart in the same room, the obedience level fell to 40 per cent. I find this quite surprising because with a wall between them the impact of giving shocks may have reduced, and yet in this case it would have been obvious what was happening. One question comes to mind here and that is: was the learner a good actor?

To increase the proximity still further, the teacher in one set of experiments had to force the learners hand onto the electrode plate in order to ensure he actually got a shock. In this case the obedience level was 30 per cent, which is almost a third of participants. Surely they must have felt immensely uncomfortable in this situation, but still one third of them were obedient.

The proximity of the experimenter also influenced obedience because it was found that when he gave instructions over a telephone the level dropped to 20.5 per cent. If he actually allowed the subject to have a free choice of shock level and gave the subject no orders, only 2.5 per cent of subjects continued until the end (which was more or less what was predicted by the original questionnaires).

What about the location of the study – would this have influenced obedience? It would seem likely that, carrying out such a study at Yale, one of the most respected American universities, people would have felt that the study was completely 'above board' and acceptable with nothing dodgy going on. In order to check this out, the study was replicated in a tatty, downtown office block and it was found that the obedience levels dropped a little but were still 48 per cent.

When the researcher gave up his grey laboratory coat and simply looked like a member of the public (he did not wear a white coat as he may have looked like a medic), the level of obedience fell to 20 per cent. This indicates that 'uniform' must have some influence on obedience levels. After all, you would be more likely to do as you are told by a policeman than if the person doing the telling was simply a civilian. This was backed up by research done by Bickman (1974) when he varied the outfits of researchers when they approached members of the public in New York and asked them to either pick up a paper bag, give money to a stranger or move away from a bus stop. When they were dressed as a civilian, 40 per cent of the public obeyed, whereas when they were dressed in a guard's uniform which was similar to that of a policemen, 80 per cent obeyed.

Giving the subject support from two others (who were actually confederates of Milgram) affected obedience levels. One confederate refused to continue after 150 volts and the second refused after 210 volts and also moved away. The level of obedience for this version was 10 per cent with the rest of the subjects claiming that they had not realised they could refuse to continue. This also relates back to the Asch experiments where one dissenter was sufficient to prevent the subject from feeling he had to conform.

Another version involved two teachers, one of whom was a confederate of Milgram. The confederate had to throw the switches whilst the subject simply read the words. In this variation, 92.5 per cent of subjects continued to the end. Obviously they felt they were shifting responsibility to the person actually administering the shocks.

The amount of feedback given by the victim also affected obedience with 100 per cent of subjects carrying on to the highest voltage when there was no sound from the victim throughout. They probably did not believe it was really an experiment. With other studies, it was noticed that some subjects actually went against the experimenter when they thought they weren't being watched, by pressing a lower levels shock button than they should have done.

Although Milgram only included 40 female subjects in his study, gender seemed to make little difference with obedience levels of 65 per cent. However, a study by Kilham & Mann, (1974) conducted in Australia required female students to shock a female learner. The obedience level in this study was 16 per cent but this can't really be compared to Milgram's studies as Milgram's learner was always male.

Cross-cultural studies indicated similar levels of obedience with two thirds of subjects, on average, going the whole way. Mantell (1971) repeated Milgram's study in Germany and found 85 per cent obedience. In Holland, Meeus and Raaijmakers (1986), using a sample from the general population, found 92 per cent obedience. Similar studies in Jordan produced an obedience level of 80 per cent and 50 per cent in Australia.

I wonder if these levels of obedience would be found today when it is almost more the norm to question the demands of an authority figure than to blindly accept them. I think this has become increasingly evident to me, working within education. Students are trained to question and evaluate information, whereas when I was at school we would not have dreamt of questioning the authority of a teacher (mind you, my headmistress was like a small, female Hitler, complete with moustache!). Even younger pupils are willing to challenge and question the authority of teachers, which is sometimes really annoying, but may well lead to a much lower chance of blindly following orders without evaluating whether they are in fact fair or not.

Before we finish this topic, I would just like to tell you about a couple of other studies which addressed some of the criticisms surrounding the methodology of Milgram.

The first study was addressing the question, did the subjects really believe that they were shocking the subjects or did they think it was an unrealistic set-up? Sheridan & King (1972) set up an experiment to get over this criticism by asking people to help train a puppy to learn a discrimination task by giving it stronger and stronger electric shocks every time it made a mistake. Horrific though it seems, the puppy did actually get electric shocks although they were quite small ones but the subjects did not realise this. They were in a position where they could not only see what was happening but could also hear the puppy squeal every time a shock was administered.

In order to make it look like the puppy had died, the researchers released an odourless anaesthetic into the puppy's cage. This made it fall asleep. Subjects obviously did not approve of the procedure, and complained to the researchers but they were told that they must continue to give shocks because the puppies lack of response was an incorrect response and therefore needed punishing. This aspect of the experiment was very similar to the Milgram study.

Seventy five percent of subjects continued to give the unconscious puppy the maximum electric shock possible. This study indicates that perhaps the subjects in Milgrams' experiments did believe they were administering electric shocks to the learner after all!

Hofling et al. carried out the second study in 1966. Its intention was to look at obedience in the workplace rather than within a laboratory, which as we know lacks ecological validity. The idea behind it was to see how many nurses would be prepared to directly contravene hospital regulations when told to do so by a doctor on the telephone.

Hospitals require that any doctors who wish to prescribe drugs for their patients have to sign the drug chart and until that is done the patient cannot have the drug. It is the nurse's duty not to exceed the maximum daily dose and the nurse also has to be sure that the doctor prescribing the drug is a real doctor. Obviously we can't have bogus doctors walking in off the street, prescribing any sort of drug for patients. It doesn't really bear thinking about.

In the Hofling et al. study, the nurse was given instructions over the telephone to administer double the maximum daily dose of a drug to a patient and that the doctor, 'Dr. Smith', would come to the ward in ten minutes, when he would see the patient and sign the drug chart. The boxes of the drug were clearly labelled and stated that the normal dose of the drug was 5mg and that the maximum daily dose was 10mg. The drug was actually a placebo of glucose.

Twenty one out of 22 nurses did as they were told! A further 22 were interviewed about the situation and 21 of them claimed that they would not have given the drug without the correct authorisation. The huge discrepancy between what people think and what they actually do is very interesting.

When questioned later, the nurses said that many doctors regularly gave orders by telephone and became very annoyed if they weren't obeyed. It was the unequal power relationship between the two which meant that the nurses felt they had to do as they were asked, or life would become very difficult for them. This indicates how an imbalance of power *can* lead to someone putting someone else's life at risk rather than disobeying a direct order.

Altruism

The definition of altruism is when you do something for someone else without gaining anything for yourself. But do you think we ever do anything to help another person without getting something back for ourselves? I know that I am very sceptical about this whole idea and have had a number of interesting (and often heated) discussions with students in the past when they say that I have obviously lost my faith in human nature. I don't believe I have, because I feel that we are all very similar in the things that motivate and guide us. If you think about it honestly, how many times have you actually done something for another person without thinking that it *might* be to your benefit in the future?

You go and have tea with your grandma who is a bit crotchety and smells of moth balls when you would rather go out with your mates.

You wash up and clean the house while your mum is out.

You help your friend with their homework.

You help to decorate a friend's bedroom/house.

You collect money for a charity.

You help your teacher on open evenings at college.

You volunteer to stay behind at work to finish something, even though you aren't getting paid for it.

All these activities are possible acts of altruism, but even though it may appear at first glance that they are being done for someone else, all of them have ulterior motives.

Grandma may appreciate the visit so much that:

- she may donate you a small amount of money when you leave or leave you a huge amount in her will
- maybe it will stop your mum from moaning at you for never visiting (the pay-off here is lack of moaning) or
- just possibly it might make you feel good because you have brought some joy into her life in which case you are rewarding yourself.

Mother won't nag you and will probably let you stay out for longer or give you extra pocket money.

Your friend may help you in the future when you are stuck with your homework.

He/she may help you at some time in the future.

You no longer feel guilty about all the charity boxes you didn't contribute to in the past (and if you are a student it will look good on an UCAS statement or C.V. for an interview).

Your help on open evenings is rewarded by a better reference from your college.

Your boss bears you in mind for promotion or finishing the tasks will make life easier for you the next day.

This should give you some idea as to how acts of human altruism are often really selfish acts.

Research into animal behaviour has also shown that apparent acts of altruism are also basically extremely selfish. If we think of the example of the rabbit who thumps his feet to warn all other rabbits of impending danger, surely it appears that this rabbit is putting itself at risk for the sake of the rest of the group. What we must remember is that this animal is a collection of genes rather than simply a rabbit and it is more important for the genes to go forth into the next generation than the rabbit. Now think about how quickly rabbits breed. The majority of the rabbits in the group are probably related to our seemingly altruistic rabbit, and therefore carry the same genes as he does. So if he lays down his life for his kin he is allowing their genes to go forth into future generations. As they are shared genes, he will, in effect, also be 'going forth'.

Returning to human altruism, we cannot be quite so objective, because many seemingly altruistic acts have no relationship to genes although they still have a selfish element. An example of this is where adoptive parents are as protective of their children as biological parents – what would it cost them in terms of pain and misery if they weren't protective. After all, the 'cost' of adoption in terms of time, emotion and organisation means that they have a vested interest in the welfare of that adopted child. However, other evidence shows that kin selection does operate in human beings. Burnstein, Crandall and Kitayama (1994) discovered that people claimed that they would help others most closely related to them if the situation was life threatening, but also said that if it was less serious they would help anyone. Sime (1983) interviewed a number of survivors from a holiday resort fire and discovered that they had searched for their family members rather than their friends, before leaving the building.

Let's return to having tea with Grandma. There are two ways we can be rewarded for giving up our time. One is extrinsically (or externally), that is we get praised and shown gratitude either verbally or by being left her entire fortune. The other is intrinsically (or internally) by having a degree of self satisfaction or, in effect, rewarding ourselves.

At this point, you may have started to think that perhaps altruism does not exist and that is quite a reasonable belief. There are, however, others who strongly believe that altruism does exist, such as Daniel Batson (1991). He agrees that often people help for selfish reasons, but suggests that at other times they are willing to do something for someone else with no apparent gain for themselves, but this is usually because we feel empathy for the person in need of help. This means that we identify with the person and can almost feel the pain and heartache that they are feeling.

Julie had had a rotten six months. Her parents had just split up and she had been sent to stay with her aunt who lived near the college while her parents sorted out the house. Her aunt had three very young children who always seemed to be having tantrums and so the only place she could study was in the college library. She missed her home and her parents and she missed having her own room with her own computer. In fact her aunt did not have a computer in the house and the college computers always seemed to be booked weeks in advance.

She had worked so hard on her Psychology coursework. She had spent hours in the library doing research, collecting and analyzing the data. Each part had been painstakingly completed despite the fact that she found it really difficult as she was dyslexic. But she had finally succeeded in writing it up by hand, and finishing it on time.

It was raining as Julie crossed the playground to the Psychology Department office, clutching the work. Suddenly a huge gust of wind blew the work out of her hand and scattered the sheets all over the floor. The beautifully presented work was progressively becoming damp and sodden and the ink began to run with the rain. Julie just stood there, looking absolutely gutted as the sheets blew away...

If Batson is correct, we would probably run to help Julie, despite the rain, as we could all imagine how devastated she must feel to see all that work reduced to an unreadable mess.

Obviously these differing opinions are what provoke research into specific areas but an even bigger provocation was an event which occurred in America in 1964.

This event involved a 28 year old woman called Kitty Genovese, who was attacked on three separate occasions within a 35 minute period by a man carrying a knife, although it was not until the third attack that he actually succeeded in killing her. What made it worse was that 38 people actually saw the killer from the windows of their homes, but none of them reported the incident to the police. No one was prepared to come forward and help, either by intervening or by telephoning the police until, finally, one man got a neighbour to call after phoning a friend in a different county for advice.

The incident was reported in the New York Times in March, 1964 and contained the following condensed extracts:

> 'Twice the sound of their voices and the sudden glow of their bedroom lights interrupted him and frightened him off. Each time he returned, sought her out and stabbed her again. Not one person telephoned the police during the assault; one witness called after the woman was dead.'
>
> Kitty Genovese 'was returning home from her job as manager of a bar in Hollis. She parked her red Fiat in a lot adjacent to the Kew Gardens Long Island Rail Road Station … She turned off the lights of her car, locked the door and started to walk the 100 feet to the entrance of her apartment … She got as far as a street light in front of a bookstore before the man grabbed her. She

screamed. Lights went on in the 10 storey apartment house ... Windows slid open and voices punctured the early-morning stillness.

Miss Genovese screamed: 'Oh, my God, he stabbed me! Please help me! Please help me!'

From one of the upper windows in the apartment house, a man called down: 'Let that girl alone!'

The assailant looked up at him, shrugged and walked down Austin Street toward a white sedan parked a short distance away. Miss Genovese struggled to her feet.

Lights went out. The killer returned to Miss Genovese, now trying to make her way around the side of the building by the parking lot to get to her apartment. The assailant grabbed her again. 'I'm dying!' she shrieked.

'I'm dying!'

Windows opened again, and lights went on in many apartments. The assailant got into his car and drove away. Miss Genovese staggered to her feet...

The assailant returned. By then, Miss Genovese had crawled to the back of the building where the freshly painted brown doors to the apartment house held out hope of safety. The killer tried the first door; she wasn't there. At the second door ... he saw her slumped on the floor at the foot of the stairs. He stabbed her a third time – fatally.

... the police received their first call from a man who was a neighbour of Miss Genovese. In two minutes they were at the scene ... The man explained ... 'I didn't want to get involved.'

I don't know if you found this as shocking as I did when I first heard about it, but then I thought about the incident. How many times have you heard a child screaming in the street and simply assumed that the child is playing? How many times have you rationalised the situation to yourself and decided that you should not get involved?

In fact if you think about many of the instances of criminal activities that go on in our world, it makes you realise that it is probably almost normal not to get involved. The case of two year old Jamie Bulger being abducted by the two ten year old boys was seen as being so horrendous. But imagine how you would have seen the situation if two ten year old boys were marching a small child out of a shopping centre. You would think that they were perhaps the child's older brothers rather than murderers. You would justify your lack of involvement by seeing the situation as nothing untoward.

Imagine that you saw a mother having a go at a small child, possibly even smacking it for something you consider totally unjustifiable (as far as you know). Although you may think it looks a really unpleasant situation, would you go up to the mother and stick up for the small child? If not, why not?

Now imagine you are walking down a road with terraced houses on either side. You turn the corner into a similar road when you see a man holding on to a woman's arm and shouting at her while she screams back at him and looks as if she is pulling away. Would you feel that you could 'interfere' in this situation?

Now imagine that you are out walking on a warm summer afternoon. You turn around a bend in the path and ahead of you, you see a man holding on to a woman's arm and shouting at her while she screams back at him and looks as if she is pulling away. Would this justify your getting involved?

Each one of these events would necessitate us becoming involved firstly in what may be seen as an ambiguous situation. We would have to make attributions about the nature of the situation and decide who was to blame (if anyone) or whether or not the person actually needs help.

This is the basis of what is known as 'attribution theory', which is a theory which helps to explain how people attribute causes to their own and other people's behaviour. Although we are really concerned with altruistic behaviour, attribution theory is relevant here because it is part of the basis on which we decide to intervene or not intervene in different situations. If we believe that it is someone's fault that they have got themselves into a situation, then we may be less likely to help than if we attribute the situation to an accident. For example, if a man was drunk and therefore fell over in the snow, we would perhaps be less likely to help him up than if it was a little old lady. We would make the attribution that it was his own fault that he fell over, and he shouldn't have drunk so much, whereas being old isn't the little old lady's fault.

We would also be aware of what might happen if we got our interpretation wrong in the situations mentioned above. The mother would be furious and tell us to mind our own business. The man and woman might do the same. The cost of getting involved might far outweigh the benefits and so we would decide not to risk it.

In fact research has shown that people are less likely to get involved in a situation involving two people if they think that the subject knows the attacker. Shotland and Straw (1976) staged a fight between a man and a woman in front of two groups of male subjects. In the first condition the couple pretended they did not know each other, with the woman shouting 'I don't even know you' and in the second condition the woman shouted 'I don't even know why I married you.' The results were that three times as many subjects went to the woman's assistance when they thought the couple did not know each other.

It is considerations such as these, together with the Kitty Genovese incident, which resulted in researchers becoming interested in looking into altruism and whether or not it really exists. I am sure from what we have said so far that you will realise there are a number of things which will affect the likelihood of someone helping another person. We have already touched on these above, but let us now put them into some kind of framework:

1 The nature of the situation

If you were in a dark street in the middle of the night, you would be less likely to go to the aid of someone lying in the gutter than if you were in the middle of a street on a summer's day and found someone who had seemingly collapsed.

If there were lots of other people around would that make you more or less likely to help? If everyone else was ignoring the situation would you feel it wasn't critical?

2 The nature of the potential or actual helper

If you were a doctor would this make you more willing to help than if you had no medical training? If there were people watching and you didn't think you were very competent would this affect whether or not you intervened?

3 The cost of helping

If you were on your way to an interview for a job that you really wanted, would this make you more or less likely to stop and help?

4 The nature of the victim

If the person who had collapsed was drunk would this make you more or less likely to help than if the person was sober?

The nature of the situation

We also tend to consider what action, if any, other people present at the scene are taking, and this will affect whether or not we see the situation as one which requires our intervention. Latané and Darley (1968) were social psychologists, teaching in New York at the time of the Kitty Genovese incident. They were also interested in whether the presence of other people affected helping behaviour. Using the Kitty Genovese incident as a stimulus, they decided to look at the idea of the 'unresponsive bystander'. They thought that it was *because* there were so many witnesses to her murder that she wasn't helped.

Latané and Darley asked male college students to sit in a waiting room to fill in a questionnaire. They believed that they were about to take part in a study of people's attitudes toward the problems of urban life and the questionnaire was to be completed before the study started. The researchers had the subjects either alone or in groups of three. The researchers arranged for smoke to pour through a small ventilation grille in the wall whilst the subjects sat completing their questionnaires, and secretly watched their behaviour over the next six minutes.

You would expect that the moment smoke came through the vent they would feel very uncomfortable and start to become concerned that the building was on fire. When they were on their own, this was what happened with 50% of cases reporting the smoke within two minutes of it starting and 75% of subjects within the six minute period. However, what happened with the subjects waiting together was quite different. Only 12% of these subjects reported the smoke within two minutes and only 38% reported the smoke within the six minute time limit, which meant that the other 62% carried on working for the full six minutes, even though the room was completely full of smoke.

The subjects were later questioned as to how they had felt about the situation and why they had behaved as they did. The ones who were waiting together had looked to each other for guidance as to how to behave. What they had found was that because none of them knew what to do, and no one had moved, they had redefined the situation as one which was harmless. They had decided the smoke was harmless, otherwise why had the other subjects not run away? Latané and Darley called this redefinition 'pluralistic ignorance', and this situation can only occur when the subjects are not actually aware of all the facts of a situation.

Another possible explanation of why the effects occurred was that none of the subjects wanted to look like a wimp in front of the others, after all if you are the only one running to get help it is not exactly good for your 'hard' image is it?

Latané and Rodin (1969) decided to investigate the 'macho' ingredient by having subjects wait outside a room. They suddenly heard a female researcher cry out for help after apparently falling in the next room. Obviously it wouldn't affect the 'street cred' of our potential helpers this time, but again the subjects appeared again to be suffering from some kind of problem. This time 70% of subjects waiting on their own went to help the woman but only 40% of the subjects waiting with other people actually bothered to help. This was an improvement but still suggested the presence of others was having a considerable influence. Subjects again showed that they had redefined the situation as not being serious. They had also been influenced by each other's apparent calmness, producing another situation of pluralistic ignorance.

Another factor which influences whether others are prepared to help or not is when 'diffusion of responsibility' occurs. Diffusion of responsibility is where the responsibility for the situation is actually spread or diffused amongst the people present. This means that the person's lack of action is actually not so bad because everyone else isn't doing anything to help either, so all are equally to blame.

Let me give you an example of how this works

> Okay Class 4B, I know that some of you wrote those obscenities on the board. I want the culprits to own up or the whole class will stay in after school tonight.

Doesn't feel so bad when you are part of the group, does it? You have shared the responsibility amongst all of you, rather than just one single person taking the blame.

Darley and Latané (1968) thought that if there were lots of people present this would perhaps decrease the likelihood of helping behaviour. They decided to investigate this by again manipulating the size of a group, although in this case none of the group could see each other yet all were apparently aware of exactly what was happening.

They recruited their subjects from a group of students and told them that they were to take part in a discussion group where college students were to talk about the kinds of personal problems they were experiencing. They were told that the way they would be assured of anonymity was to stay in separate cubicles and talk over a kind of intercom. It was also explained that this was to ensure that they could talk openly without embarrassment.

At the beginning of the discussion students were led to believe that they were taking part in the discussion with either five other students, three other students or one other student. They were also told that they would each have a chance to speak for two minutes and that the other members of the group would then have a turn each to make a comment on what the student had just said. The reason for this was in fact because there was only one subject per group, and all the other 'subjects' were actually prerecorded voices.

Suddenly one of the other 'members' of the discussion group sounded like they were having a seizure, crying out:

> 'I – er – um – I think I – I need – er – if – if could – er – er somebody er – er – er – er – er – er – er – give me a little – er – give me a little help here because – er – I – er – I'm – er –er – h – h – having a – a – a real problem – er – right now and I – er – if somebody could help me out it would – it would – er – er

– s- s- sure be – sure be good … because – er – there – er – er – a cause I – er – I – uh – I've got a – a one of the – er – sei – er – er things coming on and – and – and I could really – er – use some help so if somebody would – er – give me a little h – help – uh – er – er – er – er – c – could somebody – er – er – help – er – uh – uh – uh (choking sounds) … I'm gonna die – er – er – I'm … gonna die – er – help – er – er – seizure –er (chokes, then quiet)'

(Darley and Latané, 1968, p. 379).

Darley and Latané noted the number of subjects who actually left their cubicle to find out what was happening to the victim or to find someone to help.

- When they believed they were the only ones present, 85 per cent helped within 60 seconds, and by two and a half minutes everyone had sought assistance.
- When they thought there was one other person besides themselves, the speed of response was slower and only 62 per cent helped within 60 seconds. Even after the full six minutes allowed by the researchers, only about 84 per cent finally helped.
- When the subjects thought there were four other students besides themselves and the seizure victim, only 31 per cent helped in the first 60 seconds and after six minutes only 62 per cent had tried to help.

The conclusion was that the likelihood of people helping in an emergency situation will go down as the number of people who witness the situation goes up. This is the bystander effect, where the responsibility is diffused amongst the people present and the more people there are, the less responsibility each one takes. But is this really diffusion of responsibility?

We should note here that Piliavin et al. (1981) said that we should clarify what is meant by diffusion of responsibility. Diffusion is where everyone knows what is going on but all the people present share the responsibility for the event. He claims that it is often confused with dissolution of responsibility which is where we know there are other witnesses but their behaviour cannot be observed, and so we can rationalise that someone else will have done something. This is probably what happened in the Darley and Latané 1968 study above.

Other research looking at the effects of being assessed either as an individual or as part of a crowd has confirmed these findings. The first research was undertaken by Ringelmann (1913) when he discovered that a group of men pulling on a rope exerted less individual effort than when they did it on their own. This lack of effort made when we are part of a group is known as 'social loafing', which is another way of stating that when a number of people are performing an action an individual will put less effort into it than if acting alone.

It seems, however, that social loafing only occurs when people feel that their individual performances can't be evaluated. If they are in a situation where it could be assessed, this phenomenon doesn't occur.

When I was at school, I was absolutely useless at French. I am sure part of this was due to the fact that I was terrified of my French teacher who told me on more than one occasion that my French accent was so pathetic that I was a disgrace to the class! (Actually she used far stronger words.) Lessons were either class based, where we had to take turns in reading from French textbooks, or were held in the language laboratory (a new invention at the time) where we sat in little booths, wearing earphones and repeating what came over the headphones into a microphone. I hated the classroom lessons. I had to make a noise and she would correct, on average, every second word.

When we were in the language laboratory, I would breathe a sigh of relief. I thought that all our answers mingled together and the teacher simply listened to a chorus of small schoolgirls reciting French sentences. Therefore I mouthed the words (just in case she could see me through the front of the booth which was made of glass) although I was too frightened to actually make any noise in case it could be heard. What I didn't realise was that she could tune in, at any time, to each and every one of us, and listen to and comment on our pronunciation!

You can imagine my horror when, half way through the second lesson, this loud voice boomed through the earphones saying 'I haven't heard one noise from you yet girl. You have wasted a whole lesson sitting there pretending to speak. You can stay behind after class and do all the exercises again and I will make sure that you actually have a tongue.'

You can imagine how I felt. I had to speak French (well try to) for half an hour, on my own. I never ever mimed again!

What I was trying to do was a bit of social loafing. The minute I realised my performance could be evaluated, I couldn't do it any more.

Psychologists have examined how this works, by asking college students to shout either on their own or seemingly as part of a group of five others. Williams, Harkins and Latané (1981) asked the students to shout, supposedly to look at the effects of sensory feedback on noise production in groups. They had to wear earphones and were blindfolded so they had no idea whether they were the only ones making the noise or not but they were told that they would be shouting alone and then shouting as part of a group of six. The researchers found that they did not shout as loudly when they thought they were part of a group. They were then asked to go through the procedure again, but were told that there would be a microphone in front of them this time which would measure how loud they were shouting. When this happened there was no difference in the level of shouting showing that when they thought their performance could be assessed, social loafing did not occur.

The nature of the potential or actual helper

As we mentioned earlier, the type of person who is on hand to help will have to make the decision as to whether they are competent or confident enough to help. There are a number of factors which will decide whether or not they will intervene.

According to Eagly and Crowley (1986) in their review of more than 170 studies, if you are a male and the situation requires some kind of heroic deed, you are more likely to help than if you are female. This is especially evident in Western cultures where men are socialised to be chivalrous and heroic. Although there are only a few studies looking at gender differences in situations requiring more caring and nurturing, or involving a longer time commitment, women in such situations are more willing to help. This is supported by the fact that the majority of carers of elderly parents in the UK are women.

If we return to the idea of social loafing, Karau and Williams (1993) found in a review of more than 150 studies that men are far more likely to loaf than women. According to Eagly (1987), the reason for this is probably because women tend to care more about the other members of a group whereas men tend to be more individualistic and concentrate more on their own performance than the performance of the group as a whole.

Perceived competence also plays a part. If you think you are experienced at dealing with a situation you will be far more willing to intervene than if you feel you don't really know what you are doing. In fact Huston et al. (1981) investigated what sort of people helped in an emergency situation and discovered that people who are most likely to assist would be those who have the relevant skills such as first aid knowledge or life-saving skills. This is even more likely to be the case if you are being watched. If you think that someone is there, assessing your performance (even if they aren't), you will be far less likely to help if you don't feel very competent, but if you feel confident in your ability you won't mind being observed. Baron and Byrne (1991) found that this was the case with swimmers who were trained in lifesaving skills.

The cost of helping

Have you ever been in a car and witnessed an accident? Did you stop and offer to be a witness and if not why not?

> I was driving home one evening from college when I saw two little boys some way ahead of me, taking the bollards away from a huge hole in the pavement. My instant thought was to stop and tell them to put them back, but I was late for picking my daughter up from school and so I drove past and did nothing. All that evening I worried about the hole, imagining little old ladies walking down the road and falling down the hole and breaking their legs and ending up in hospital and having operations that went wrong and then never being able to walk again.

I really wished I had stopped, but the cost of stopping was too great because I was so frightened something would happen to my daughter if I left her standing outside school. What I was actually doing here was weighing up the costs and benefits of helping. The cost was that I would have been late to get my daughter and the benefit was that I wouldn't have had to worry all evening. However, I wouldn't know if the little old ladies had fallen down the hole, but I would know if anything happened to my daughter, so I decided that the cost of helping in this instance was too great and I passed by.

The same situation tends to happen when it comes to accidents. I have often heard people say they have seen some kind of accident on their way to work. When I have asked them if they have agreed to be a witness, they all tend to say they hadn't stopped because it would have taken time and they would have had to fill in lengthy forms or even go to court. It seems that everyone weighs up the cost of helping, often unconsciously, and usually instantaneously, and this will have a huge influence on whether they are willing to get involved.

This cost/benefit analysis is known as 'Social Exchange Theory' and was proposed by Thibaut and Kelley in 1959. This theory can be used to interpret studies of bystander intervention. What it is stating is that we may decide to help if there is some kind of profit in the situation for us. We calculate this profit by looking at the rewards minus the cost of helping.

Rewards could be things like feeling good about ourselves, not worrying, striking up a new relationship, gaining some kind of money (remember grandma's will?). Costs could be things like being late to an appointment, looking a complete idiot in front of other people, getting dirty, catching something, being in danger, especially if the person is drunk or the area is one with a high crime rate. Remember here too that women may perceive themselves as being in greater danger than a man even though they are in the same situation – this may also help to explain some of the differences in helping behaviours between the genders.

So, according to Exchange theory, we only get involved in some kind of prosocial behaviour as the likelihood of 'making' a profit increases. Where there is too much to lose and very little to gain we would decide not to help. Basically this points to the fact that acts may look altruistic but are not really altruistic after all.

The example I gave earlier mentioned the fact that I did not help because I was short of time. It seems that time seems to be one of the main reasons for not helping and this was demonstrated in a study by Darley and Batson (1973). The subjects in the study were students at a theological seminary who were training to be ministers of the church. They were split into two groups having been told individually that they had to give two talks. The first group had to give a talk in a nearby building on the Good Samaritan, followed by a second talk in another building on jobs they had most enjoyed. The other group had to give the talks in the reverse order.

I am sure, at this point, that we would expect theological students to be altruistic. We would probably expect them to be even more altruistic if they had just given a talk on the good Samaritan. When the subjects left the first building they were told that they were either ahead of time, on time or behind time. On the way to the second building they passed a confederate of the researchers, lying in a doorway groaning. The single most relevant factor in deciding whether or not they would assist the poor confederate was how they were doing for time, with 63% of those ahead of time helping, help from 45% of those on time and only 10% of the students behind time offering to help. The strange thing was that the talk they had just given had no bearing on whether they stopped to help or not, so it appears that the cost of being late was higher than the feeling of guilt for 'passing by on the other side of the street'.

The nature of the victim

If you saw a really unpleasant looking, smelly, dirty old tramp trip over something in front of you, would you immediately rush up to him and try to help him up? What about the fact that it might be a little frail old lady, who smelt of lavender and had a walking stick in her hand – would that make a difference? It seems that the nature of the victim has a huge effect on whether or not we are willing to act in an altruistic way.

First of all, as you know, we have to make attributions about the type of situation we are in. We have to decide, on the basis of the available information, whether or not the person really needs help. Kelly (1973) devised the Causal Schemata Model, which is one of several models that help to explain how we frequently make attributions about a situation (and why these attributions are often wrong). Let me explain how this model works with an example.

> Ruth is walking down the road when she comes across a man lying in the gutter. He stinks of alcohol and he is holding a paper bag containing what is left of a broken bottle. Her initial thought is what a state for a drunk to get into and she passes by on the other side of the road.
>
> What she doesn't know is that he is a priest who is extremely fond of his elderly mother. He also suffers with high cholesterol levels and has been told that he has to take things easy as he has a weak heart. It is his mother's eightieth birthday and he decided that he would buy her a bottle of her favourite spirit as a birthday present. He was just on his way to the off licence to get the bottle when he was stopped by a parishioner who seemed to have a crush on him. Consequently he was late and was extremely concerned that the off licence would close, so he had hurried all the way there and was now on his way to buy her a card. Because he had become so anxious, and because he had put his heart under such pressure when running, he had had a heart attack and had fallen down, in the gutter, and the bottle had smashed as he hit the ground.
>
> What a mistake for Ruth to make!

What is happening here is that we are actually using stored information which has come from our schemas in order to make sense of the situation. We know that usually if someone has collapsed and smells of alcohol it is the alcohol that is responsible. We also tend to think that if we found someone in this condition, it would be their own fault because they shouldn't have drunk so much. We will therefore take the supposedly obvious explanation for the situation without considering other possible causes. We seem to use what is known as the 'discounting principle' which means that we discount other possible explanations in favour of what *to us*, is a more familiar explanation. In fact what we are using is a kind of 'causal shorthand' (Fiske and Taylor, 1991) to explain behaviour quickly.

Darley and Latané (1970) illustrated how this happens with a study looking at how many people would be willing to give money to someone in the street, and whether the person's reason for asking affected the amount of giving. In the first condition the actor asked for some money for no reason, and in this case 34% of people gave money. I suppose they figured that there must have been a good reason for him to ask in the first place! In the second condition he said it was to make a telephone call and this resulted in 64% of people giving money. In the third condition the man said his wallet had been stolen (a more worthy cause?) and in this condition 70% of people helped. It seems that the perceived nature of the victim's need influenced helping behaviour.

Research has shown that the nature of the victim has a large effect on whether or not we are prepared to help. The key study for this section was undertaken by Piliavin et al. (1969) when they decided to investigate, using a naturalistic experiment, whether the nature of the victim affected helping behaviour. They also chose to reduce the ambiguity of the situation to a minimum so that pluralistic ignorance should not enter the equation. The results indicated that the nature of the victim had a large effect on whether or not people were willing to help with people being more willing to help a lame victim (90% within 70 seconds) than a man who was drunk (20% within 70 seconds).

The researchers extended their studies to look at this phenomenon further and found that if the lame collapsing man had blood oozing from his mouth, this reduced the help he received (60% within 70 seconds). Why do you think this is? I would imagine that you might think first of all that there is something very seriously wrong and that you would be incompetent to help. It may also be that he may have some infectious illness, and we are all aware of the dangers of contact with infected blood for illnesses like Hepatitis and HIV. The costs of helping here would perhaps be too high.

This is reasonable, but there are other instances which are not so clear cut. An example is the research undertaken by Piliavin et al. (1975) when he manipulated the appearance of the subject further by giving them an ugly facial birthmark. The help he received was 61%. The person cannot then been seen as being responsible for his appearance. He certainly isn't drunk and he isn't bleeding, so why has helping reduced so dramatically? Gross (1992) suggested that we perceive that the cost of helping someone who is very different to ourselves is much higher than if they are the same, and that 'different-ness' can be either in their lifestyle or their appearance. He also suggests that the greater their distress or disfigurement, the more disapproving we tend to be.

We also help less if we believe that the victim's distress is seen as a result of their undesirable behaviour such as abusing alcohol (even though the attribution may be incorrect). If we believe that they had control over the cause of their distress, then we tend to feel angry with them rather than sympathetic and often decide that they can jolly well get themselves out of the situation! Weiner (1988, cited in Weiner, 1992) asked people to rate ten conditions, some of which may cause intense emotional feelings in many people. The conditions were Alzheimer's disease, blindness, cancer, heart disease, paraplegia, what was called 'Vietnam War Syndrome' (post traumatic stress disorder), AIDS, drug additions, obesity and child abusers. The last four were seen as being responsible for their conditions and were subsequently rated as less likeable and less likely to receive help, both financially and in terms of personal assistance, than the other six.

If we accept that we are likely to help people who are seen as being like us rather than very different, what effect does this have on racial differences? The Piliavin et al. (1969) study showed that there was no evidence of black people helping black people and white people helping white people when the victim was lame. However, when the victim was drunk, the instances of same race helping were much higher than cross racial helping. Piliavin et al. (1981) suggested that this was because people don't like to project a public image of any kind of prejudice. After all, it isn't politically correct to help *only* people of the same race as you! Therefore they were willing to help in the lame condition even if they internally felt some kind of prejudice, but when the costs of helping were perceived as higher (in the drunk condition) they could not justify their intervention to themselves.

In some ways I find this whole idea of costs and rewards as somewhat strange. I know it happens and yet I find it hard to understand how we can weigh up all the pros and cons unconsciously, in such a short time. But it does seem to happen although the costs and rewards are different for each of us, and our feelings of identification with other people are also very different and based on our past experiences. After all, I may be able to remember what it was like to be a student (in my dim and distant past), but I would find it very hard to identify with the problems of being a vicar – never having been one! At the end of the day, it is our individuality which makes us likely to help or not help, but as to whether altruism actually exists or not, I would like to think it does.

I.M. Piliavin, J.A. Rodin and J. Piliavin (1969) Good samaritanism: An underground phenomenon?

Journal of Personality and Social Psychology, 13, 289–99.

The aim of the study was to look at bystander intervention in a natural setting and to see if the type of victim – lame (carrying a cane) or drunk, or their racial identity, influenced helping behaviour. The intervention of a model was also used to see if this would influence helping behaviour.

Method

Design Field experiment using participant observation.

Subjects Anyone of approximately 4450 people travelling on the New York 8th Avenue, Independent Subway between 11 am and 3 pm between April and June, 1968. The racial mix of travellers was about 55% white and 45% black. The mean number of people in the critical area where the incident took place was 8.5, with the compartment carrying a mean of 43 altogether.

Victims The victims were all males, aged between 26 and 35, three were white, one black. All were dressed in the same outfits. In 38 trials the victim smelled of alcohol and carried a bottle in a brown paper bag. In 65 trials he carried a cane and appeared to be sober (students did not like playing the role of the drunk victim – hence the difference in numbers of trials).

Models The models were all males, aged between 24 and 29 and all white. They stood either in the critical area or adjacent area and helped either early (70 seconds after collapse) or late (150 seconds after collapse).

Apparatus The study took part in the carriages of two trains in the New York subway. These trains were chosen because there was a period between two stops of $7^1/_2$ minutes which was enough time for the procedure to be followed. The layout of the carriages was as follows:

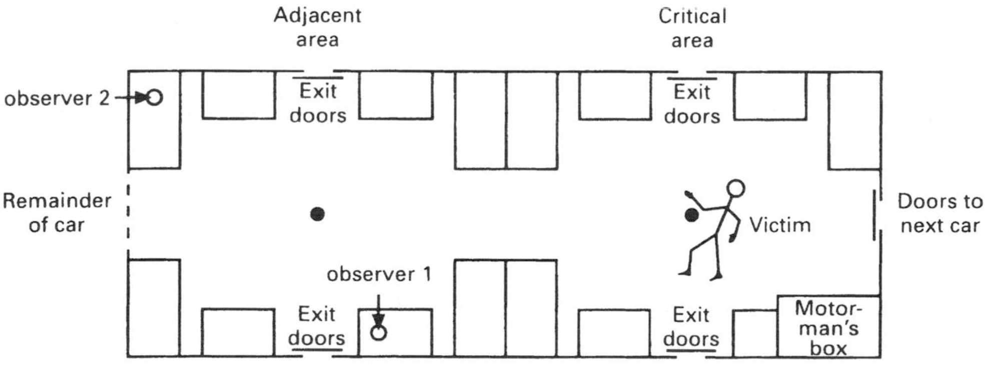

Procedure Groups of four students, two males and two females, got on the train, entering the carriage through different doors. There were four different teams who always worked together and between them carried out 103 trials. Sometimes they used carriages in the middle, sometimes the front and sometimes the rear of the train. However, they always used the end of a compartment as the critical area. The females sat in the adjacent area and recorded data as discretely as possible. Both the 'victim' and the model would be standing, with the male victim located next to a pole in the critical area. Seventy seconds after the train started moving, the victim staggered forward and collapsed on the floor, and lay, looking up at the ceiling. If no one helped, the model would come to the assistance of the 'collapsed victim'. When the train reached the next stop, the team would get off. They would then wait until everyone left the area before going to the other platform to get on the next train back again.

Data The race, sex and time it took helpers to give the victim assistance. Also where the helper had been in relation to the victim and whether or not they had finally decided to help: before or after the model had gone to the victim's assistance.

Results

- One of the main findings was that the spontaneous help occurred before the model had a chance to act in 93% of trials. This meant there were insufficient trials for the model effect to be studied.
- In 60% of the 81 trials (the total of lame and drunk conditions with no model) where the model received spontaneous help, it came from **more than one helper**.
- However, the help was offered to the lame person significantly **more quickly** for the cane than drunk condition (a median of 5 seconds rather than 109 seconds for the drunk trials).
- 90% of the spontaneous first helpers **were males** (although the breakdown of gender in the critical area was 60% males and 40% females).
- There was a very slight (non significant) **tendency to same race helping** but this was slightly more evident **in the drunk condition** than the lame condition.
- No one left the compartment in any of the trials but in 21 of the total of 103 trials, 34 people left the critical area, with more leaving in the drunk trials.
- There appeared to be **no evidence of diffusion of responsibility**, with larger groups helping faster than smaller groups.

Discussion

The findings that the lame victims were helped on every trial, unlike the drunk victims, could be explained by the attributions made by the observers who may have seen the drunk as being responsible for his own condition. Perhaps the reason why help was offered to the lame person

Lame condition with no model

	No of trials	No of times helped	Overall % of helping
White victim	54	54	100%
Black victim	8	8	100%

Lame condition with model

	No of trials	No of times helped	Overall % of helping
White victim	3	3	100%
Black victim	0	n/a	n/a

Total No. of Lame trials = 65 — Spontaneous help received on 62 trials. Model induced help on three trials. Therefore helped on every trial.

Drunk condition with no model

	No of trials	No of times helped	Overall % of helping
White victim	11	11	100%
Black victim	11	8	73%

Drunk condition with model

	No of trials	No of times helped	Overall % of helping
White victim	13	10	77%
Black victim	3	2	73%

Total No. of Drunk trials = 38 Spontaneous help received on 19 trials. Model induced help on 12 trials. Not helped on seven trials of which three were white drunks and four were black drunks.

more quickly was because they were not seen as being 'to blame'. However it is interesting to note that in the drunk trials 50 per cent of people were helped spontaneously (19 out of 38 cases), which is still surprisingly high. An explanation for this relatively high percentage of helping behaviour may have been due to the enclosed environment where the study was conducted and the fact that it was extremely hard to diffuse responsibility.

The fact that first helpers were males in 90 per cent of cases could be explained partially by the comments made by women at the scene. 'I wish I could help him – I'm not strong enough' perhaps relates to the competence of the potential helper. However, it is more likely that women would feel more anxious about the situation and fear becoming involved, especially with the drunk victim, who may then attack them. Therefore the cost of helping for women in this instance was perceived as being too high.

The tendency to same race helping was insignificant and related to the racial breakdown of travellers (55 per cent white and 45 per cent black people on average travelled the subway). The situation in the drunk condition might have related to feelings of fear and blame which are more easily handled if the person is perceived as coming from the same group as the potential helper.

With regard to potential helpers leaving the critical area, it is interesting to note that more people left when the victim was drunk. It was also noted that if people did not help within the first 70 seconds, this proved an even greater encouragement for people to leave the scene.

Perhaps the reason why diffusion of responsibility was not evident was because there were more **potential** helpers present than in laboratory experiments. All past research had involved the use of only one subject with the rest being stooges of the experimenter. Therefore there was only one potential helper and that potential helper may have been looking to everyone else to guide them as to what they should do. Bearing in mind that all the other people 'taking part' did nothing as part of the study, perhaps the phenomenon of pluralistic ignorance could explain the results of past research in this area. In this subway study, there were large numbers of potential helpers and this may have resulted in more helping behaviour rather than less, and as the group size increased, the potential number of helpers increased.

Evaluation

One of the biggest problems which makes the results slightly invalid was the difference in numbers of drunk and lame victims (65 compared with 38 trials). There were also far more trials involving white victims rather than black (81 compared with 22 trials) bearing in mind that the racial breakdown of travellers was 55% to 45%.

There are ethical considerations which need to be taken into account. The researchers involved participants who were unaware that they were taking part in psychological research and therefore did not give their informed consent, and they were not debriefed at the end of the study.

We may question whether travellers on the trains saw more than one trial, but should conclude that this is unlikely as the trails were carried out over a period of two months between 11 a.m. and 3 p.m.

There were also different groups of students carrying out the trials, and even if they had been seen, it would be unlikely that the same group would be seen again (although it must have looked somewhat suspicious).

Were the students able to see all that was going on during the trials? It would seem likely bearing in mind there were on average 43 travellers in the whole compartment and we are only focusing on the critical area and the adjacent area.

The final evaluation relates to ecological validity. Surely this field study had far higher levels of ecological validity than past research which had been undertaken in laboratory situations, often involving bizarre circumstances!

Key words

Ambiguous situation – a situation which is not easily understood and could have a number of possible explanations.

Intrinsic reward – the kind of reward that comes from within, eg feeling good about ourselves.

Extrinsic reward – the kind of reward that comes from outside us, eg praise from other people, promotion, payment.

Pluralistic ignorance – people are not actually aware of all the facts of a situation, perhaps because the situation is ambiguous, and therefore they look to each other to define what they should be doing. This may result in them redefining the situation in accordance with other people's supposed interpretation, even if this goes against what they first thought.

Diffusion of responsibility – people are aware of all the facts but share the responsibility for the event amongst all the observers.

Dissolution of responsibility – people know there are other witnesses to an event although it is impossible to see what they are doing, so they rationalise that someone else will have responded and this allows them to remove, or dissolve, their responsibility to act.

Empathy – empathy involves imagining yourself in someone else's position and experiencing their feelings as if they are your own.

Social loafing – when a number of people are performing an action, an individual will put less effort into it than if acting alone.

Key questions

1. What was the main purpose of the Piliavin et al. study?
2. What was the purpose of the model coming to the aid of the collapsed student?
3. Why were there different teams of students?
4. Was the study ethical?
5. What was the difference between this study and previous studies of altruistic behaviour?

Postscript

You may now be able to understand what was going on for the people who witnessed the murder of Kitty Genovese, although it does not make the event less horrific. Banyard (1996) points out that perhaps we should question the interests of the psychologists in this case. Yes, bystander behaviour is an interesting and important aspect of the murder of Miss Genovese, but wouldn't it be as relevant to look at the reasons 'why women are violently and sexually attacked by men regardless of the presence or absence of bystanders' (Banyard, 1966, p. 15).

Banyard continues by giving a description of the background of the man charged with the murder, one 'Winston Moselely who had murdered three other women, raped at least four more and attempted rape on other women' (Banyard, 1966, p.15). What was it about him that made him enjoy the act of hurting and raping women? Was there something in his childhood which may have influenced his behaviour and should we not try to identify this in order to try and prevent it happening again. However, this aspect of the event seemed less socially relevant in the 1960s than the response by the people of New York. I wonder if it would be the same now?

Roles

We have considered so far the social influence that can be exerted by one person onto another in the form of obedience to authority. We have mentioned too that conformity also affects others' behaviour because they will adjust their behaviour in order to fit in with the desired person or group in order to be accepted by that group.

Another area of our lives which is affected by social influence is the fact that when we take on a role it will affect our behaviour. Your behaviour is influenced by the role you are expected to adopt and the status this gives you in relation to others. In fact, a role does not exist unless it involves some kind of interaction with others. You can't be a nurse unless you have a patient, or a teacher unless you have a student.

A role is usually defined as 'the behaviours expected of a person occupying a certain position in a group.' These behaviours are expected by people seeing you in that position – you would be considered very strange if you dressed in a nurse's uniform and then went out and started directing the traffic.

Think of the roles you have to undertake and the fact that each of those roles requires a slightly different type of behaviour. You would not act with your grandparents in the same way as you would with a group of friends, so the two roles are completely different and involve different norms of behaviour. One important psychological effect of taking on a role is that your individual identity may be replaced by a group or role identity which could offer you a different status and also perhaps an anonymity. I have reused the example from the previous section when I was talking about obedience.

> I have taken on the job of teacher at a school. The students are really good and work hard but I have been given the job of reorganising a classroom and moving books from one side of the school to the other. One of the other teachers may have suggested using students to help. It is a really hot day and the last thing anyone wants to do is to move boxes and books about but I decide to use my authority to get a flock of small boys to carry all the things I need moved. I therefore take no notice of the sweat dripping from their brows as they labour under huge piles of books, and of course I must insist they keep their blazers on. The role I am playing dictates that I can exert my authority in this way (although as an individual I would find this morally wrong), so I am going against the usual constraints upon my behaviour.

Can you see how playing a role can lead to lack of individuality, or as it is known, 'deindividuation'? I stopped being me and instead became a teacher, which in turn may have affected my own personal social, moral or societal constraints on my behaviour. This sounds a little extreme, especially using this example, but let me take the analogy one stage further by relating another of the experiences I have had.

> I trained as a nurse many years ago. I remember my first experience of walking onto a ward in nurse's uniform, feeling extremely anxious and not being sure of what I was going to be asked to do. From one of the beds at the side of the ward, an old gentleman with a huge shock of white hair and a big white beard was looking in my direction. Suddenly he called 'Nurse'. I looked behind me to see who he was calling when I realised that it was me… I was so frightened, but I went over to his bed to see what he wanted, and I found myself slipping into a 'nurse' role which I had never officially played before. If I had been in my civvies, I think I would have been terrified, but the uniform I was wearing offered me an element of anonymity. (At least if I made a mistake, I looked like everyone else!) As it turned out, he only wanted a drink, so I was safe.

In fact you should realise that roles can affect behaviour but it is possible to make the roles even more overwhelming. If you take the individuality from a person by putting them in a uniform (deindividuate them), it may well make them even less constrained by their individual feelings because they are now feeling less obvious. In this example, I wasn't constrained by my feelings because I felt as if I, as an individual person, was hidden by the uniform I was wearing. I think this effect may have been even more obvious because the uniform consisted of a huge white starched apron, a starched dress with a stiff white collar held on with cufflinks, black tights and shoes, and a hat that looked like a fairy cake!

So let's now look at how the idea of deindividuation developed and what an enormous effect roles can have on all types of behaviour in the real world.

Past theories and research

One of the topics which inspired the theory of deindividuation was that of 'mob psychology'. This was an idea proposed by Le Bon (1895) when he suggested that crowds were dangerous and he suggested that when a crowd gathered it would behave in a primitive and totally irrational way. He maintained that the members of the crowd would become over aroused and therefore the normal social constraints which controlled their behaviour as individuals, would no longer apply. He actually called this social contagion the law of mental unity.

It is very interesting that he should develop this theory around the time when the Government was trying to justify the suppression of demonstrations, and in fact there is very little evidence for this process actually occurring. However, you and I know that crowds can behave in a totally different way to individuals.

You have decided that you want a cup of coffee, or even a drink (cola of course) and so you decide to go into a pub. Although you have actually gone into the pub, you are actually quite self-conscious, so you are quiet and will probably sit somewhere where you can view what is going on, rather than having your back to the crowd.

In this instance you are behaving according to your own code of behaviour, but there is a certain amount of social influence as to how you conduct yourself. You would feel ostentatious if you started laughing out loud to yourself, or if you put your feet on another chair, or even talked to yourself. Now picture the same situation with a friend.

This crowd of Croatian football fans feel confident in their behaviour because there are so many of them. Would one of them be happy standing singing with arms raised and no shirts on if they were alone?

completely anonymous they were more willing to steal money and sweets than the identifiable children.

Another study which is perhaps more familiar to us investigated whether the uniform of a sports team increased the aggressiveness shown by that team. Rehm, Steinleitner and Lilli (1987) randomly assigned fifth graders in German schools to five-a-side teams. In each game one of the teams wore the uniform of orange shirts while the other team wore their normal clothes. It was found that the teams dressed in orange were significantly more aggressive than the teams in their everyday outfits. Perhaps this was due to the fact that they felt they were less obvious, although one could argue that another explanation would be that they felt more unified as a team and therefore more committed to win.

Diener (1979, 1980) suggested that when we are in a group, we focus our attention on the group rather than on ourselves. We may become increasingly aroused and are therefore taking in what is going on around us so we become more impulsive and less self aware.

Imagine you are in a crowd at a football match and all your friends are maniacal 'Shadwell' supporters. You have never seen the team play before, in fact you aren't even a football supporter, but you become infected with the crowd's enthusiasm.

> *You find that the people directly around you are all singing the Shadwell anthem which is a song you know well. You can't sing but suddenly you find yourself singing along with everyone else, totally unaware that you sound like a foghorn!*

Not only do we become less self aware, but when aroused we are less capable of rational thinking. If we thought rationally about our behaviour, nothing would persuade us to sing in front of our friends at a high volume. Another example you may be familiar with is when we have to do an examination: we are often highly aroused and sometimes this makes it harder to think clearly. On the other hand, if we focus inwards on ourselves, we are in touch with our own moral standards and codes of behaviour and are capable of more rational thought.

Diener (1979) suggested that this high level of arousal may lead to the following outcomes:

1. Our normal restraints against impulsive behaviour become severely weakened as we are less able to monitor our own behaviour (self-monitor) due to the high level of arousal.
2. We will have a heightened sensitivity to any sort of emotional state and respond in a different way than usual to any sort of situational cue.
3. We have a much lower level of concern about whether others approve of our actions.
4. We find it much harder to rationally plan subsequent behaviour and events.

Interestingly, however, the story of deindividuation is not quite that simple. A study undertaken by Zimbardo in 1970 found that when women were more likely to give higher voltage electric shocks to another woman when they were deindividuated (by wearing bulky lab coats and hoods, and not being referred to by name) than when they were identifiable (wearing normal clothes and being referred to by name). However, another study by Johnson and Downing (1979) showed that the nature of the uniform itself seemed to affect the level of shocks rather than the deindividuation. They suggested that the outfit worn by the women in the Zimbardo study was very like the outfits worn by the Ku Klux Klan and that this may have affected the levels of aggression shown by the participants. They therefore replicated the study but had another group dressed as nurses, and they found that although the nurses were wearing identical uniforms and therefore lacked individuality, they actually gave fewer and less severe shocks. So this gives us some indication that the role is interacting with the means of deindividuation.

These examples of research should therefore help to explain how prisons manage to deindividuate their inmates. Their identity is removed because they wear uniforms and have their hair cut in a similar way. Members of the police and also prison officers are also deindividuated because they wear uniforms which hide their individual identity. This gives them anonymity when they deal with others, but it also makes them anonymous to a crowd where they may be perceived as being less human and therefore targets of aggression.

We have also established that this deindividuation process *together with* membership of a crowd are likely to affect the types of behaviour demonstrated and this may result in an increase in aggression. We have also shown that the role played by the people wearing uniforms will affect the way that they behave.

All of this theory has a direct relationship to one of the most famous pieces of social psychological research. This research was undertaken by Haney, Banks and Zimbardo (1973) and was known as the prison simulation experiment. This research looked at how the pathology of power affected the behaviour of 'normal' American students who were playing a role and who were deindividuated by the uniform they were wearing.

C. Haney, C. Banks and P. Zimbardo (1973). A study of prisoners and guards in a simulated prison

Naval Research Reviews 30 (9), pp 4–17

The purpose of the study was to investigate the effects of an environment on a group of students, and to see if the roles they were randomly assigned to play would significantly influence their behaviour.

Method

Subjects 22 male subjects were selected from a group of 75 who answered a newspaper advertisement asking for volunteers to take part in a study of prison life in return for a payment of $15 a day for up to two weeks. The volunteers completed a questionnaire and were interviewed to screen them for stability, maturity and lack of anti-social tendencies. They were randomly allocated to the role of 'prisoner' or 'guard'. They did not know each other as these friendships may have affected the study, or may have resulted in the break up of existing friendships. Two standby prisoners were not called and one guard dropped out before the start of the study which left ten prisoners and eleven guards.

Apparatus A basement corridor in Stanford University was converted into a mock prison containing three small cells (6' x 9') with black painted steel barred doors and no furniture besides a bed with mattress, sheet and pillow. The rest of the accommodation consisted of an unlit broom cupboard used as a solitary confinement area, a recreation 'yard' which had an observation window, and several rooms nearby for the guards. Prisoners wore loose fitting smocks with identification numbers, a nylon stocking on their heads to cover their hair, no underwear, rubber sandals and a lock and chain around the ankle. They were issued washing gear and bed linen but were not allowed any personal possessions. Guards wore khaki uniforms, reflective sunglasses and carried a baton and whistle.

Procedure Before the study actually started, the 'prisoners' signed a consent document which specified that some of their human rights would be suspended and they were told that they must remain in the prison for the duration of the study, but they were given no further information. The guards were given no specific instructions as to how to behave, but were told they could not use physical violence although they were expected to 'maintain a reasonable degree of order' within the prison. Prisoners were arrested from their homes by the police, the day before the study was due to start. They were taken to the local police department and charged with suspicion of burglary or armed robbery, finger printed and driven blindfolded to the mock prison. They were then stripped, deloused (with a harmless deodorant), photographed and given a prisoner's uniform, read the rules of the prison and were assigned three to a cell. From this moment onwards, they were referred to by number only. To increase the feeling of powerlessness they were only allowed supervised toilet visits and received three tasteless meals a day. During the rest of the time they were given work assignments or rested and had to attend two roll calls a day.

Results

The experiment had to be stopped after six days principally because of the pathological reactions of the subjects. The results were recorded by observation but were backed up by video and audio tape, observations, dialogue, self report questionnaires and interviews. The guards became absorbed in what has been described as the 'Pathology of Power' where they enjoyed the power they felt they had been given. This was demonstrated by the fact that they were willing to work extra time with no extra pay. The prisoners became extremely negative, either shown as depression or as excessive obedience. Half the prisoners were seen to demonstrate symptoms of depression by crying, or being angry and very anxious. Monitored conversations showed that they talked about the prison as if it was real.

Discussion

The study showed that the behaviour of the 'normal' students, who had been randomly allocated to each condition, was affected by the roles they had been assigned, to the extent where they seemed to believe in their allocated positions. Five of the remaining prisoners were asked if they would be willing to give up their payments in order to be released. Three of them agreed but chose to return to their cells and await a mock parole board's decision as to whether this was acceptable rather than simply walking out. The responses of the prisoners were believed to be due to their loss of personal identity (remember their clothing), their dependency on the guards and subsequent emasculation and the fact that they had 'learned they were helpless'. The guards on the other hand had shown considerable enjoyment of the power they had assumed. They had redefined many of the normal activities of the prisoners as 'rights' such as going to the toilet and eating and refused to let them watch films or read which had been part of the original plan. Many of them were disappointed at the termination of the study.

Evaluation

Lack of ecological validity The study lacked ecological validity because it was not a prison, and the people involved were not prisoners or guards. Prisons are not situated in the basement of universities and they usually contain some element of physical violence, racism and homosexuality, whereas Zimbardo's did not. In fact what was happening in this study was that the subjects were playing the role of what they *thought* prison life was like. This in itself makes the study valid and whether that role was accurate or not is not really that important. The study set out to show that an environment results in behaviour rather than the nature of the people involved and this is exactly what happened. The people were randomly assigned to their roles and undertook them to the extreme.

This was illustrated by the fact that both the guards and the prisoners continued their behaviours, even when they thought they were not being observed.

Ethical problems The study produced strong ethical objections. However it was given firm approval beforehand from the Office of Naval Research, the Psychology Department at Stanford and the University Committee of Human Experimentation. The subjects all signed informed consent documents although how much information they were actually given was a different matter. They were, for example, not informed that they would be arrested in public and the extreme responses of the subjects had not been predicted. Finally the subjects were debriefed and assessed weeks, months and years afterwards to try and ensure no long term lasting effects.

Key words

Deindividuation – a mental state where you no longer feel that you are an individual but have been taken over by the group you are with, or the situation you are in, resulting in a loss of conscience, personal values etc.

Social contagion – a situation where the attitudes and beliefs of the group you are in affects the way that you think and behave. This relates to mob psychology, were you take on the values and beliefs of the group and forsake your own values and beliefs.

Autonomous – acting independently.

Emasculation – putting a man in a situation where he no longer feels masculine.

Key questions

1. What was the purpose of the Zimbardo study?
2. Give two criticisms of the nature of the study.
3. What argument can you use to justify the **validity** of the study?
4. Why does uniform affect the behaviour of individuals?
5. Can you think of an alternative way of investigating the effects of roles on behaviour?

Postscript

What we must remember is that there are instances of deindividuation which do not produce anti-social behaviour; in fact the behaviour that deindividuation can produce could be described as liberating.

Chrissie is having a party and you are there advising her what sort of music to have and what drinks to provide. You have a discussion about how the furniture should be arranged and whether you should make a room for dancing. Both of you have had all afternoon to get the place ready and you are now dressed up and ready with Chrissie for the first guests to arrive. The music is playing and you are really excited. Chrissie says she is so nervous as to how the party is going to go. Is it going to be good? Will many people turn up?

Two hours later, the party is going reasonably well but people are still a little stand-offish and not mixing as well as you hoped they would. There seem to be small groups of people in different places, and the atmosphere definitely leaves something to be desired. Suddenly all the lights go out. There is a power cut. A couple of lighters light up, but there is lots of giggling and people actually start talking to each other. They are no longer so self-aware and feel much more confident to talk to each other.

The lights are out for about half an hour. Although there is no music, it doesn't seem to matter because everyone is talking and joking and seem to be enjoying themselves. Suddenly the power comes back on again. Within a very short space of time, the magical atmosphere has diminished. People have become self-aware and identifiable again.

This process was described in an experiment done in 1973 by Gergen et al., known as the Black Room Experiment. Gergen had two groups of subjects who spent an hour together. One group of subjects were in a completely darkened room and the other group in a normally lit room. In the dark room, the subjects were far more friendly, chatting to total strangers, exploring the room and some even began to discuss far more serious matters. Even more amazing was that 90% of the subjects actually became involved intentionally in physical contact with each other, 50% hugging each other and 80% admitting to being sexually aroused. In contrast to this, the control subjects talked politely in the light for the whole hour.

Ethnocentrism or In group/out group Preferences

The idea of ethnocentrism was introduced in the section dealing with perception. If you remember, it is the belief that the group we belong to are the 'norm' and everyone else has to be judged by our standards which, of course, are the best. It's almost like being egocentric about your group, so I suppose you could say ethnocentrism is group egocentrism.

Ethnocentrism seems to occur the minute people are divided into groups. It doesn't matter what that group is, or on what basis it was formed but what happens is that we perceive the group we belong to as being superior to other groups and we develop an 'in-group bias' (we are biased in favour of the group we are in with). This bias is demonstrated by consistently rating the abilities and characteristics of the group we belong to as much higher than other people, even when this is not the case.

Ethnocentricity is linked to the process of stereotyping which involves grouping people – other than us – on the basis (usually) of some superficial physical characteristic such as colour, and then attributing the same characteristics to all the group members. In this section we are going to focus on ethnocentricity rather than stereotyping, although often the results are the same because they may both lead to a kind of discrimination.

All of us have opinions and ideas about the groups we belong to and we usually have ideas about the nature of other groups we come into contact with, even when these opinions are not always rational.

'Hello Harry, how's it going?'

'Don't ask,' snapped Harry as he entered the door to the saloon bar of the Pig and Gusset on Friday evening.

'Sorry I spoke,' said Gerald, turning towards the bar, 'do you want a drink?'

'Yes, a whisky would be appreciated. In fact a double would be even better. I feel like I need it.'

Gerald ordered the drinks from the middle aged barmaid, whilst thinking that it was typical Harry should ask for a double. 'So what's the matter Harry old son? Who's stepped on your toes?'

'B***** women drivers. They shouldn't be allowed on the road.'

'Why, what's happened?'

'This stupid woman slammed her brakes on in front of me – no warning, and I went into the back of her. The road was clear, stupid woman, but she just braked for no reason. Probably looking in a shop window or something stupid – and what makes it worse is that I'm seen as the one to blame because I went into her and I just happened to be driving the boss's new Jag.'

'Why were you driving it?' asked Gerald.

'Well, he's away in Munich at the moment, and all the boys had been out to the local for lunch. Most of the lunch time was spent talking about cars and when we got back to the office, his keys were just sort of on his desk and I thought it would be good to just try it out, so I sort of borrowed it briefly.'

The barmaid, who had picked up on this conversation, handed Harry his drink, which he knocked back in one. Her eyebrows raised slightly.

'So basically, you're up queer street?'

'You could say that. Stupid cow – if she hadn't been on the road, it would have been fine.'

'But not all women drivers are that useless,' said Gerald unconvincingly.

'Oh come on – it's obvious.'

'How many women drivers do you actually know?' interrupted the barmaid.

'What's that got to do with it?' snapped Harry.

'Do you know *any* women drivers personally?' she insisted.

'Well, um, no, but everyone knows that women can't drive.'

At that point, the barmaid picked up a pint of lager which was sitting on the bar, and kind of accidentally tripped, flinging the lager in his direction. She knew lots of women drivers and she also knew they were the best!

Here both Harry and the barmaid have very strong feelings about women drivers and, in fact, so have I. Harry believes they are all useless whereas us women think they are far safer than men – but both of these ideas are really very subjective attitudes which are not necessarily based on fact because you get good and bad drivers regardless of their sex (although *I still believe* that on the whole, women are safer and it would be hard to convince me otherwise).

I am sure if I asked *you* what you think about women drivers and whether you think they are better than men, you will probably have an opinion about them. I would also guess that if you are male, your opinion may be less than complimentary, but if you are female your opinion would probably go along the lines of believing that they are far safer than male drivers. What about your opinions regarding people from the North of England, or people from the Southern Counties? Your opinions would probably be more positive towards the group you belong to. We can even narrow the groups down still further.

'What set are you in for maths Mel?' said Natalie.

'In set one,' said Melanie smugly. 'How about you?'

'I'm in set four,' said Natalie.

'Oh, that's the thickies group isn't it – and you're in with them?' Melanie sounded even more smug than before.

Natalie became very defensive. 'The people in my group are not thick. We just can't be bothered with subjects as boring and meaningless as maths and so we don't see any point in wasting our energy trying to do a load of boring old sums. We are far more interested in other things and we have some really good and interesting discussions about the world and stuff. Anyway, the people in my set are a lot nicer than people in other sets,' she emphasised.

What is happening here is that Natalie is defending her group. If you believe the group you belong to is full of people who are really not very nice people or are 'intellectually challenged', then being part of that group will give people the impression that you too are like them. Therefore what we have to do is to believe our group is more worthy and worthwhile because that will reflect on us and make us too seem more worthy and worthwhile. This in turn will give us a much better self-image and help us develop our self-esteem. If we have a positive self-image and high self-esteem, we will feel good about ourselves and this will result in a kind of self-fulfilling prophecy whereby we live up to our own expectations of ourselves.

'What do you do for a livin', mate?'

'I'm an entrance technician.'

'What does that mean? It sounds very complicated.'

'Well, I have to decide who can and can't be admitted to one of the local establishments in the evening.'

'What establishment?'
'A night club.'
'A night club?'
'Yes.'
'Oh, you mean you're a bouncer?'

Or even:

'What do you do for a livin', mate?'
'I'm an Estate Manager.'
'What does that mean, it sounds very high flying?'
'Well, I have to maintain the estate and make sure that everything is running well, and sort out if the buildings need repairs and that the grounds are well kept.'
"What estate?"
"Well, it's really a college."
"A college?"
"Yes."
"Oh, you mean you're a caretaker?"

This is often demonstrated by the way jobs that were once described accurately are nowadays often given fancy titles to try and increase the person's self-esteem. The self-fulfilling prophecy rule works well here. If someone is told they are stupid they tend to perform according to the expectations the person has for them. If I said to you, you are so thick that you will never understand the rest of this book, you would either just think 'Oh well, what's the point,' or you would get really angry and prove me wrong. The problem is, most times people just give up. If, on the other hand, I told you that you were actually really clever, but you just needed a little bit of extra support at the beginning, you would feel so much better about yourself and you would probably try harder and consequently end up achieving more. If I told you your job was just a general dogsbody job and that anyone could do it because it didn't take many brains, you would probably have no pride in what you do. But if I give your job a fancy title and make you feel really important (even if you're not really), you would have far more pride in your work and consequently do what you do have to do so much better.

According to Tajfel (1982), the process of trying to give ourselves some kind of positive self-identity seems to explain why people have what are known as in-group preferences. If we are assigned to a group, any group, either by birth or by colour or by gender or by design, we immediately seem to feel a kind of innate automatic preference for that group over any other group and somehow elevate the group to a higher status than any other groups. This in-group bias, then, is simply a tactic to increase our self-esteem and even if the reasons why the groups have been formed are minimal, if our group wins over the other group it will strengthen our feelings of pride in belonging to the winning group and increase our self-esteem still further.

There is another reason why it is very beneficial for groups to have a positive social identity.

I was thinking the other day of a group of people who came from a very close-knit community, both in their work and their living conditions, and who were poorly treated by their bosses and the government in the early 1970's. That group were the coal miners who had grievances regarding the import of cheap coal, leading to the subsequent closure of many of the pits in the UK. I remember them specifically because I was at university at the time, and we welcomed groups of miners to stay in our university lodgings while they were engaged in blockading the ports to prevent the import of foreign coal. Many evenings were spent sitting around candles in the kitchens of our flats, discussing Marxist politics and feeling we could help change the course of future policies – the optimism of youth!

The miners felt underprivileged and ignored, and rightly so, but in order to give themselves the impetus to fight their cause they had developed a kind of group pride which spurred them on to fight the necessary battles. We, being impressionable young students from a somewhat leftwing university, were more than willing to join in (and it was good fun).

If a group believes it is less worthy than other groups, it will be much more likely to accept any discrimination and disadvantage shown towards it without complaint, because it will believe that the discrimination is probably justified. This will result in the group being very unwilling to fight for its cause. By raising the self esteem of the group, it will realise that the system *is* unjust and will therefore be less willing to allow society to continue to discriminate against it. This recognition of the injustice being shown towards it will be a sufficient trigger for the members of the group to demonstrate their anger and possibly their aggression. This also has implications because if the group is convinced that it has no worth and no value it is going to be far more placid and less willing to become involved in any sort of dispute.

So far we have seen the purpose of in-group identity and ethnocentrism. It also appears that part of the process can involve some kind of conflict between the two groups – certainly this was the case with the miners. Harry also had

Robbie Fowler of Liverpool pulls up his shirt in celebration of a goal. The T shirt underneath says "500 Liverpool DOCKERS sacked since Sept 1995." This display was judged to have raised the profile of the strike and, in doing so, increased the dockers' self-esteem.

some kind of conflict between himself and the woman driver. Sherif (1966) suggested that inter-group conflict arises because of a conflict in interests. If two groups of people want to achieve the same goal this is going to lead to hostility between the groups.

The Robbers Cave Study

Probably one of the most famous pieces of research looking at ethnocentrism was a field study conducted by Sherif in (1956). This involved taking 22 white, middle class boys aged between 11 and 12, who were considered well adjusted, and dividing them into two groups who were roughly matched in terms of sporting ability, camping experience and general popularity. Their parents were told that they were going to a three week summer camp to see how well they would work alongside other boys when put into different teams. The parents were also told that they would not be allowed to be visited during that time, but would be able to go home if they wanted to. It was intended that the data for the study would be collected by participant observers.

The first step was the creation of the 'groups' which took place over the first week. At first, neither set of boys knew of the existence of the other set. They were taken to their respective campsites which were located on a 200 acre, densely wooded area in Robbers Cave State Park, Oklahoma. The campsites had swimming facilities and boating alongside the cabins where they were to stay for the three week period. This first week was spent doing a variety of activities where the boys worked together such as pitching tents and cooking and they took part in a treasure hunt.

During this week the two groups seemed to develop different groups norms, one group being more 'tough' than the other group where two boys went home early as they were homesick. They were given caps and t-shirts and gave themselves the names of the 'Eagles' and the 'Rattlers' (the Rattlers being the tougher group).

At the end of the first week they became aware of each other's existence by finding litter left by the other group or overhearing voices. Sherif noticed that already the groups started to refer to the other group as 'them' and their group as 'us'. This was the beginning of part two of the experiment. The groups were told that they were going to take part in a 'Grand Tournament' which involved ten different sporting events and they were shown the prizes for winning which included a trophy, medals and pen knives which they all found very attractive. The tournament was also to include in the final scores points which would be awarded for other activities such as how tidy the cabins were kept. These scores were displayed on big scoreboards in what now became a joint mess hall where hostility that developed between the two groups of boys was much greater than anticipated, and the results that occurred in such a short space of time were stunning. But we have to remember that the extreme results of Sherif were produced by not only the two groups, but the perceived unequal status of the groups. There was a conflict of interests between the boys and they perceived inequalities in their situations some of which were true. The Eagles believed the Rattlers were physically bigger although they weren't but they did have two more members in their group. The groups even believed that one group was getting better and more plentiful food than the other group, which consequently increased this feeling of inequality.

Secondly, the findings of the Sherif study have been mentioned over and over again as the way to remove ethnocentrism and prejudice. Equal status contact and the pursuit of common goals with the support of the people in charge worked for the children at Robbers Cave. The trouble is, it is not that easy in the real world where there is a much greater history involved in the divisions between the two groups which may have been present for decades or even centuries. To add to the situation there may also be other pressures from external forces which will help to maintain the segregation, such as pressure from other members of the family or from society, laws which prevent equal status contact, living environments being separated, job discrimination and so on.

This situation was demonstrated by Gerard and Miller (1975) when they undertook a longitudinal study in California after schools stopped the process of ethnic segregation. Originally, the ethnic groups were separated by going to a different schools but when groups such as white, black and Hispanic-American attended the same school, therefore having equal status contact, the students continued to 'hang-out' in ethnic groups. What we have to remember here is that the schools may have removed the ethnic boundaries but they were not able to remove them from other areas of the children's lives, such as at home or in the areas where they lived.

Was Sherif right though? Do we need conflict for ethnocentrism to occur? We showed at the beginning of this section that conflict is not essential but that discrimination can occur without any conflict of interests between the groups. Tajfel claims that simply being in a group and being aware of the existence of another group is sufficient for the development of some kind of prejudice and, consequently, discrimination in favour of the in-group and against the out-group. In order to do this, he divided groups up on a totally arbitrary basis and discovered that even if they did not know who else was in their group, ethnocentric feelings seemed to occur and resulted in the group members favouring each other to the detriment of the other group. This indicates that the whole concept of group mentality goes way beyond any sort of conflict or perceived inequality.

H. Tajfel. (1970) Experiments in intergroup discrimination.

Scientific American, 223, 96–102

The intention of the study was to illustrate that simply by putting people into groups would lead to them showing in-group preferences and out-group discrimination. It was believed that this would happen even when group members had no idea who the other members of their group were, so could not be attributed to any personal interest or negative attitudes that may have existed before the study.

STUDY ONE

Method

Design Laboratory experiment with independent subjects.

Subjects 64 schoolboys aged between 14 and 15 from a state school in Bristol who came to the laboratory in groups of 8. The boys from each group knew each other because they were from the same house in the same form at school.

Apparatus A screen was used to flash 40 pictures of clusters of dots. There were also booklets containing a number of matrices which were used for the boys to allocate rewards and penalties to members of their own group or other groups (never to themselves). The booklets contained 18 pages and on each page there was one matrix.

This is an example of a matrix where the numbers represented money. The subject would be required to allocate the amount in the top box to one person and the amount in the bottom box to someone else, for example:

If a boy was allocating money to two members of his group, he may go for the choices marked 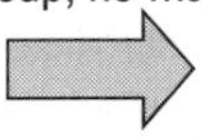 as they are more or less equal.

If he was asked to allocate money from the top row to a member of his group and money from the bottom row to a member of another group he may choose 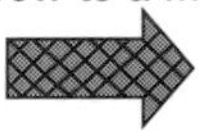

If he was asked to allocate money from the top row to a member of the other group and money from the bottom row to a member of his group, he may choose 

Variables The independent variable was type of allocation they were asked to make (whether to their own group or another group) and the dependent variable was the choices they made (either being fair or showing discrimination towards their group by giving them less or more rewards).

Procedure The boys were brought into a laboratory and told that the study was about visual judgements and they were then asked to estimate the number of dots in each cluster that was shown on the screen. In order to be categorised the boys had to participate in two conditions. The first condition involved the boys being told that people consistently overestimated or underestimated the number of dots. In the second condition, they were told that some people are always more accurate than others.

18	17	16	15	14	13	12	11	10	9	8	7	6	5
5	6	7	8	9	10	11	12	13	14	15	16	17	18

fact, if the study had been conducted using females as subjects, it is more likely that the idea of fairness would have been demonstrated to a greater extent than it was. The groups themselves were also meaningless, whereas in real life group membership is based far more on something specific. Finally, the subjects may have simply been conforming to demand characteristics. They may have worked out what the researchers were looking for and this would be supported by the fact that the matrices were fairly transparent – you could work out what they were trying to show by comparing the numbers in the upper and lower rows.

Key words

Self-esteem – Your image of yourself is your self-concept. If you think well of yourself you have high self-esteem, and if you don't think much of yourself you have low self-esteem. It is therefore the evaluative part of your self-concept.

In-group – This is the group that you feel you belong to.

Outgroup – This is the group you don't feel you belong to.

Transparent matrices – This means that the purpose of the matrices is obvious and that you can easily work out the purpose of each choice.

Demand characteristics – These are the characteristics of a study which suggest to the subject the way that they are supposed to act.

Key questions

1. What was the main aim of Tajfel's study?
2. Give two criticisms of the study.
3. In what way would the type of subjects influence the results?
4. Were the studies ethical?
5. If you were asked to allocate money to members of your own or other groups, what rewards would you choose?

Children's development

4

In this chapter we are going to look at the subject of children's development. If we accept the fact that much of what happens to us as children shapes what we become as adults, it is obvious how important it is to understand what goes on in childhood.

The four studies we will look at address different aspects of children's development. The first section looks in greater detail at the general development of cognition than the Baron-Cohen study in the chapter on Cognitive psychology. If you remember, the Baron-Cohen study focused on how children understand that others do not always see the world in the same way as they do. Here we will focus on the theory of Piaget who believed that all children go through specific and age related stages of development which seem to build on each other. Don't forget what we mean by cognition is the higher order thinking and reasoning capabilities, rather than simply instinctive and innate processes.

The second section looks at different theories about how children actually learn, and focuses specifically on how they learn to be aggressive. The topic of aggression is in itself quite controversial, with some theorists claiming that we are born with an innate capacity for aggression, and others arguing that we are basically placid but that we learn how to be aggressive in order to survive. If we accept that perhaps we do have an innate capacity, but it is shaped by learning, we can understand why research has focused on the area of aggression and *how* it has been learned.

The third section looks at the influences on early socialisation and the development of relationships. So often we hear about adults who have problems with relationships which seem to stem from their early experiences. Imagine a child who is not wanted by its parents either because it was unplanned or because it is a restriction on their lives. How would that child feel about itself? Imagine a child who has never felt the unconditional love of a parent? The child will grow up feeling it has little value, after all, if no one loved you as a child, perhaps you weren't worth loving. The problem here is that we also learn how to have

A really good example of the differences in thinking between a younger and older child can be illustrated by something I remember reading in a book some time ago. The book explained how a small child described a sentence as 'a big word with holes in it,' which I think sums up the difference quite nicely.

This is very different from how adults used to think of children a few hundred years ago. In the seventeenth century it was believed that children were born with minds like a *tabula rasa*, or blank slate, and therefore everything they knew had been learned. Thus it would make sense that the things they learned were the same as the things adults knew, so their thinking would be the same as that of an adult. It was therefore believed that children were simply miniature adults and had all the same cognitive and reasoning skills as adults. This was why many children were punished for behaviours which to us would seem quite normal and why they were expected to understand the behaviour of the adults in their lives without question or explanation.

Nowadays we consider childhood to be a special time for learning, demonstrated by a strong focus on nursery schools and educational toys. We also no longer believe that children think in the same way as adults and much of this knowledge is thanks to a man called Jean Piaget (1896–1980). He developed not only one of the most comprehensive theories of children's development, but also one of the most influential theories of our time. Piaget's theory focuses on the idea that development is maturational (to do with the increasing maturity of the child), age related and universal across cultures.

Piaget's theory

Jean Piaget was not actually a psychologist, which is quite surprising when you consider how important he is in the world of developmental psychology. In fact he was born in Switzerland and published his first article on a rare type of albino sparrow in a journal of natural history in 1907, when he was aged 10. Initially trained as a biologist and zoologist, Piaget became interested in the relationship between biology and psychology in the early 1920s. He was especially interested in how animals adapt to their environment and extended this to humans when he went to work in Paris for Alfred Binet. Binet was responsible for developing the first intelligence tests for the French Education Department as a way of testing children to identify those who had learning difficulties. The last chapter looks at the development of intelligence tests in much more detail.

The idea behind the intelligence tests was to compare children on what was believed to be a fixed ability – their innate intelligence. We would expect that Piaget would have been interested in the number of correct answers children gave to questions, but what he started to notice was that they seemed to give the same wrong answers and these wrong answers depended on their age. It was almost as if the children went through different stages of reasoning according to what age they were, with younger children producing similar errors in reasoning to each other. These errors would then differ from the errors of slightly older children.

This led him to formulate a theory that intelligence must be a kind of biological adaptation which allowed the child to develop more efficient interactions between themselves and the world in which they live. When they were very little they did not need to interact in a very complex way because their needs would be taken care of by mother and father. Once they were able to interact (and operate) in the world by doing things and making things happen, they needed to develop a greater understanding of how things work. This would require more complicated thought processes and so the child would develop these as necessary.

Piaget realised that the development of mental abilities was not simply the result of the child maturing. If you stuck a small child in a box with nothing to play with or test out he would not learn anything about the nature of the world. He would also not learn simply by sitting in a chair passively, watching the world go by outside a window. It was necessary for him to get in amongst things, try them out and play with them in order to realise how they work.

Piaget believed a child's knowledge and understanding had to come through their interaction with the environment and could *only* be developed through their own activity. He also believed that they would be self-motivated to discover the world – almost to the point that if you put a child in a room with lots and lots of stimulating and interesting toys and games and objects, they would find out for themselves about the properties of those objects and universal rules that apply to them. Teachers would therefore be seen as facilitators rather than directors of the child's education. This means that they should provide the help the child asks for, and should make the environment as stimulating as possible by providing the facilities required to allow the child to learn for itself, rather than directing the child to learn. When I was at school the regime was pre-Piaget and we passively sat in rows at desks, did the tasks the teachers set and learned things like the times tables which didn't really mean much, but had to be repeated on command. By the time my children went to school the whole system was very different. The children worked in groups at circular desks on projects, where they had to find out the information from a vast array of resources and the teacher took a different role of supporting and providing help as it was wanted. Maths was taught by using games and looking for patterns in the way numbers go together rather than simply learning once two is two, two twos are four and so on.

He also used the term schemata, (singular = schema, which we have already come across in the section on memory) to refer to all the cognitive structures or inter-related and organised groups of memories, thoughts, actions and knowledge that represented everything that the baby or child knew about objects or actions. He said that these schemata develop from the child's own interactions with the environment and that any new experiences the child had, would lead to new schemata being developed. The way the schemata develop and become more complex involves organising their past experiences and adapting them to any new information they come across.

Piaget claimed that adaptation has two components: *assimilation* and *accommodation*. He saw assimilation as the process of fitting new information and experiences into existing schemas, while accommodation is the process of changing the existing schemas when new information cannot be assimilated.

Let me give you an example. If you had been to a kind of restaurant before, but that restaurant had only been somewhere like MacDonalds where you don't have a waiter or a menu to order from while you sit at the table, the first time you went to a Harvester you would be experiencing new information which could be fitted into your current 'restaurant' schema. If on the other hand you had no idea that you could buy food ready cooked and eat it on someone else's property because you had only ever eaten at home, you could not assimilate the new experience in the light of anything you already knew about, so you would have to set up a new schema in order to accommodate the new information.

Piaget used these concepts to help explain the different kinds of thinking that happen during different stages in a child's development. One way to think of a stage is that it is a time of relative stability when a child will think in a similar way across a wide range of situations or problems. Remember Little Johnny and Nigel? What happened for them was that their thinking and understanding was challenged by a new experience which gave them new information they could not fit into their old schemas, so they had to reorganise them in order to make sense of the new information. This process of accommodation resulted in their ability to understand a process at a new advanced level or stage.

Piaget identified four major stages in the development of a child's thought and claimed that all children progress through these stages in this fixed order and cannot miss one out – although not everyone reaches the final stage. He also suggested ages for each stage, although he was aware that the ages were averages rather than actual ages and he also said that children move through the stages at slightly different speeds, dependent on their experiences.

The stages are listed below and we will look at each one in some detail:

1 The sensorimotor stage (0 to 2 years)
2 The pre-operational stage (2 to 7 years)
3 The concrete operational stage (7 to 11 years)
4 The formal operational stage (11+ years)

His belief was that children are internally driven to find out about their world, and so if you give them a stimulating and well equipped environment they will explore the environment themselves and find out about the properties of the objects within that environment with little or no guidance. I'm sure you realise that this was a bit fanciful because if you put a group of young children together in a well equipped room with no guidance, I think they will do all sorts of things other than learning, not least squabbling about who has what.

The sensorimotor stage (birth to two years)

When a baby is very young, the only knowledge it has about the world is based on what it can experience and what it can do, both of which are somewhat limited. Babies are born with reflexes such as sucking and grasping and they can also move their limbs, kicking and waving their arms. This restricted repertoire of movement limits what they can actually do although each one of these actions results in some kind of sensual experience. They can also see, hear, taste, touch and smell the world around them and they begin to put together very primitive schema about the world. This is why the stage is called the sensorimotor stage because it is to do with the child's sensual experiences and their motor movements.

During this stage we see one of the biggest leaps in development because they go from being a helpless incontinent blob, with limited reflex behaviours, to becoming able to completely turn the world of their parents upside down by exerting their will, arguing and forming strong bonds. They will be able to speak, they may well be potty trained, they will be able to throw things around, and understand that when people leave the room they haven't vanished off the face of the earth. They will also be able to solve simple problems, like finding the things that you don't want them to find, and to interact on their environment to such an extent that granny might even dread them crossing the threshold. They will also begin to understand and show concern for others in their world, and will have developed their own little personalities.

What happens is that biological maturation has a huge part to play here. When they are born they are unable to sit up or to make words, but the growth and development of the body makes each achievement possible. The child

Piaget found that children under the age of five always seemed to pick out the view of what they could see from their own position and seemed to be unaware that the doll would see something different. He also found that between the ages of five and seven they knew there would be a difference but they weren't sure what it was. Then when they reached seven years they seemed to be able to cope with the 'in front' and 'behind' perspectives but not the 'left right' perspectives. By the age of between eight and nine, they would be able to choose the right pictures for all the positions around the table.

According to Piaget, this clearly demonstrated that children were unable to see things from someone else's point of view until they were at least seven years old.

2 Conservation

Do you remember when I talked about Little Johnny and Nigel. They did not understand that even though their mother had not put any more Cola in the glass, it looked as if there was more because the glass was taller and thinner? This is a demonstration of lack of conservation. The pre-operational child is unable to 'conserve' because they don't understand that the basic properties of matter are not changed by superficial changes in their appearance. The Cola looked like there was more and this proved to be even more confusing when it was returned to the original glass.

This situation deals with conservation of volume and is probably the best known example of a conservation experiment (although studies have also been carried out on conservation of number and weight). In fact Piaget demonstrated this in exactly the same way with three beakers, two short beakers and one tall one. Both short beakers had the same amount of liquid in them and the tall one was empty. He then poured the liquid from one of the short beakers into the tall beaker and discovered that pre-operational children thought this changed the amount of water in the tall thin one.

When investigating number, Piaget used two rows of counters equally spaced, and asked the child if there was the same number of counters in each row. The child would dutifully say 'Yes'. Piaget would then spread the second row of counters out and ask the child again if there was the same number of counters. At this point the child would say 'No.'

The conservation of weight would be tested using plasticine. Two balls of plasticine of equal size would be shown to the child and the child would be asked if there was the same amount in each. The child would say "Yes". Then one of the balls would be rolled into a sausage shape and the child would again be asked if there was the same amount of plasticine in each ball at which point the child would say 'No.'

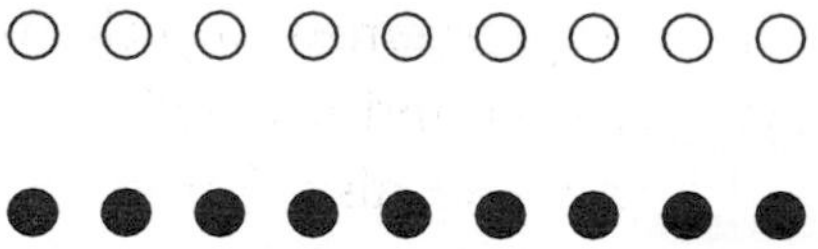

Pre-transformation

The second row of counters are now spread out and a child without the ability to conserve will see the black array as one which contains more counters.

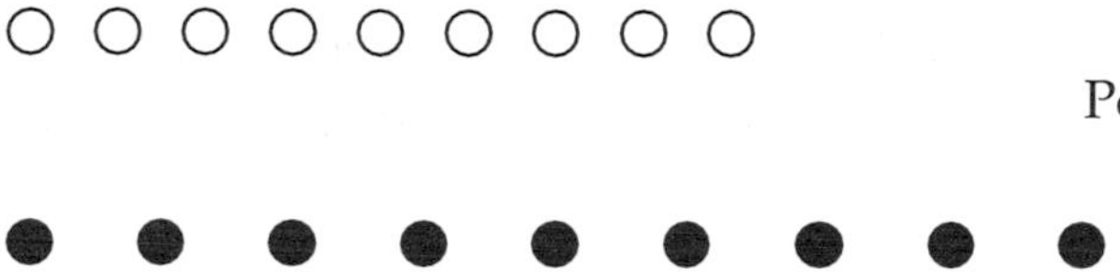

Post-transformation

3 Irreversibility

Piaget also demonstrated another limitation in pre-operational children's thought by these experiments. If we use the liquid experiment as an example, when the water from the tall thin beaker was then poured back into the short beaker, the child would be quite satisfied that there was again the same amount of water in both of them. The problem was that the child couldn't really understand why this was and was unable to work it out. Therefore they would be unable to 'reverse' the operation in their heads.

Reversibility is the ability to reverse the logic of a train of thought. According to Piaget a three year old girl would be unable to do this. An example is the following conversation:

Adult: Do you have an older brother?
Child: Yes.
Adult: Does he have a younger sister?
Child: No.

4 Centration

This refers to the way a child will focus or centre attention on only one aspect of a task and ignore all the other aspects. This is when they rely on their intuitions about what they can see rather than what they can reason. An example would be to put three sticks of equal length on the table in front of a child. The child would then be asked if the three sticks are the same length or if one was longer than the others. The centre stick would then be moved slightly so they are no longer in line. It is very likely that the child would then say that the sticks are no longer the same length (in fact the centre stick will possibly be seen as either longer or shorter) because they will tend to focus on only one end of the stick, not the other.

5 Seriation

Piaget maintained that pre-operational children were unable to put things in order of sequence, for example size or height.

These are the main limitations to pre-operational thought according to Piaget, although he identified other weaknesses in their ability to reason. For example, children up to the age of four often develop what Piaget called pre-concepts which are kind of generalised rules. An example of this is when a child knows that as daddy owns a blue car therefore all blue cars must be daddy's car.

> I remember a friend of mine who had a very interesting private life. She had had a number of relationships with various men, and had finally decided to live with one of them, when she discovered she was pregnant. The couple were reasonably happy, although her partner was still somewhat insecure about her past. The baby was born and they seemed to become much closer. When the child was nearly three years old, they were out shopping. Her partner was looking in a shop window and she walked slowly on ahead so he could catch up. The small child was toddling around in the shopping centre in front of her when suddenly one of her past 'relationships' walked towards her and on recognising her, broke into a smile, walked towards her and kissed her on the cheek. The little child ran up to the man and said in a very loud voice 'Daddy, Daddy.'
>
> I will leave you to imagine the rest...

Here what was happening was the small child held the pre-concept that daddy was a man, this was also a man, therefore he must be a daddy too! You can see the logic in the reasoning, and also the limitations.

Piaget also said that children of this age show animism which is giving life-like qualities to inanimate things. I remember my mother saying to me when I was little that if we had peas for dinner, I was not to leave any or they would be lonely. I remember using that technique for my children when they were little. I also hated picking flowers in case I hurt them, and I used to always put things in pairs in case they too became lonely.

Here is an example of a child attributing life to an inanimate object when talking about the sun:

> Piaget: Does the sun move?
> Child: Yes, when one walks, it follows. When one turns around it turns around too. Doesn't it ever follow you too?
> Piaget: Why does it move?
> Child: Because when one walks it goes too.
> Piaget: Why does it go?
> Child: To hear what we say.
> Piaget: Is it alive?
> Child: Of course, otherwise it wouldn't follow us, it couldn't shine.
>
> *(Piaget, 1960, p.215).*

The concrete operational stage (seven to eleven years)

In this stage children cease to be egocentric and acquire 'cognitive operations' which are much more complex mental schemata which enable the child to come to logical conclusions about the world.

They are now able to put items in order, such as height order, whereas they were unable to do this before. They would also be able to put a sequence of pictures in the right order because they could logically work out which one comes before the next.

However, they still have problems with abstract concepts and principles and tend to see rules as black and white.

> Have you ever played Monopoly when you knew you didn't have much time or when someone was going to be out because they had run out of money, and you hand them an extra wad of notes in order for them to stay in the game. I also remember making it so that any money collected for fines would go into a kitty and whenever anyone landed on free parking they would get all the fines. I remember my oldest daughter, who was about eight at the time, having hysterics because that was not right. The rules said you can't do that so why were we doing it because it couldn't be done. She got herself in such a state that she went off sulking and didn't play at all.

This was a good example of the logic of a concrete operational child.

Formal operational stage (eleven+ years)

The final stage of development involves the ability to not only reason logically, but also to deal with abstract concepts. Piaget referred to these abilities as the 'logic of combinations' where the child may need to deal with the mental manipulation of several factors at the same time.

> Do you remember questions in maths such as 'A train left London station at 2 pm on the third day of the week and arrived in Aberdeen at 3 am the following day. If the train was travelling for half the journey at 40 miles per hour and the rest of the time at 60 miles per hour and the driver needed to stop to pick up passengers for 15 minutes half way through the journey, how many miles was it to Aberdeen and what percentage of the journey was spent picking up passengers, and when he got there, was the sun shining?'

These sorts of questions are unlikely to be given to a child of less than eleven, because according to Piaget they would be unable to deal with all the elements involved in the question.

Also, they no longer see rules as being black and white, but understand that rules can be changed if everyone agrees – so Monopoly games become far less traumatic!

Criticisms of Piaget's theory

There has been a great deal of criticism of Piaget's theory, much of which is based on the idea that children are far more competent than Piaget reckoned. It has been suggested that the language and methodology used by Piaget in his questioning was responsible for many of the supposed inabilities of the children. However Piaget's work has been replicated by many researchers and what seems to be the case for most subsequent research is that although he was inaccurate in the ages he suggested children enter the different stages, the types of answers the children gave seemed to be related to their age.

This suggests that there *do* seem to be developmental stages that children go through, and that these stages do seem to be cumulative. We must use the suggested ages as guidelines only. For example, a child of five may be able to conserve liquid quantity whereas a child of eight may be unable to, but their progress through the stages will be similar. It also appears that when children are faced with a difficult or stressful situation, they can return to an earlier stage of reasoning (which Piaget said would not occur). This has been seen to happen with the birth of a new baby in a family, when the older child who had been showing a good rate of cognitive progression, suddenly regresses to a more babyish level. The thing is that we can never be sure whether this is simply a defence mechanism and a way of them gaining attention, or whether they do actually forget what they knew.

We are going to deal with some of the specific criticisms of Piagetian theory, beginning with his ideas about lack of object permanence. Later research has indicated that it is not a lack of object permanence that stops a small child from looking for a hidden object in the sensori motor stage – but it is more likely a memory problem. If a child is shown an object and then it is hidden they may attempt to see where it has gone but forget where they last saw it and then give up looking. It may also be the case that they really don't care where it went. Bower (1971) demonstrated this idea of 'fragile memory' by looking at the searching behaviour of babies as young as 20 days when a ball was hidden. By assessing their facial expressions, he discovered that even the youngest babies showed surprise when a ball was hidden from view and no surprise on its return. If they realised that the ball hadn't vanished off the face of the earth, it would make sense that its return into view would not cause them any surprise, whereas if they thought it had really vanished they would be amazed by its magical reappearance. This indicates that babies of all ages show object permanence when the period between hiding and reappearance is short. Bower also demonstrated that the older babies had the same response when the ball was hidden for longer which indicates that they perhaps had a better ability to store the information that the ball still existed, whereas the youngest babies may have been unable to remember for an extended period of time that the ball was there originally. On the other hand, it may be the case that the babies really don't care where the object went! If the object that hides is actually mother, the child will look for her (say, behind a sofa) whereas the same child may not bother if the object that disappears is an inanimate object.

Another criticism involves Piaget's claims about the extent of egocentricity in young children. One of the biggest critics of Piaget's methodology was Margaret Donaldson in her book 'Children's Minds'. She cites a study by Hughes (1975) which illustrates that children, when given a task that was more familiar to them, were far less egocentric than Piaget suggested. Hughes arranged an experiment designed to test whether children could see something from someone else's perspective but used objects which were far more familiar to the children. If you think about it, unless you lived in the Alps, you wouldn't be very familiar with mountain scenery and would therefore find it hard to imagine what these large models in front of you were actually supposed to represent.

I think the most amusing memory I have of this study was watching the behaviour of a small boy who had been videoed while being shown the three mountains before he was asked the questions. The 'mountains' which looked about two feet tall, were made out of papier maché and had been painted to look like grass and snow. The little boy was wondering around, looking at them and suddenly focussed on a hole in the base of one of the mountains. He pointed the hole out to the researcher and asked whether a mouse lived in the hole. He was so interested in the hole that the rest of the task became irrelevant, and no matter what the researcher asked he kept going back to the idea of the 'mouse hole'. This should give you some idea how the task itself was meaningless or beyond the comprehension of most children.

Hughes set up an arrangement of partitions on a table in the form of a cross (see facing page), and put a policeman doll in a position so that it could 'see' behind some partitions but not others. The children were told that the policeman was looking for a boy doll and asked them to put the doll in a position where the policeman could not see him. Obviously this was much more familiar to the children, and Hughes found that 90% of children between the ages of three and a half and five had no trouble doing so.

Further experiments have shown that children have no problems seeing what familiar dolls such as 'Sesame Street' characters can see when they are positioned in different positions to themselves. This supports the idea that a child can give a better idea of what they can do when they are familiar with the materials used.

Another aspect of Piaget's task which may have been confusing for the children was the fact that they were not only being asked to interpret what someone else could see but also to interpret photographs which may have made the

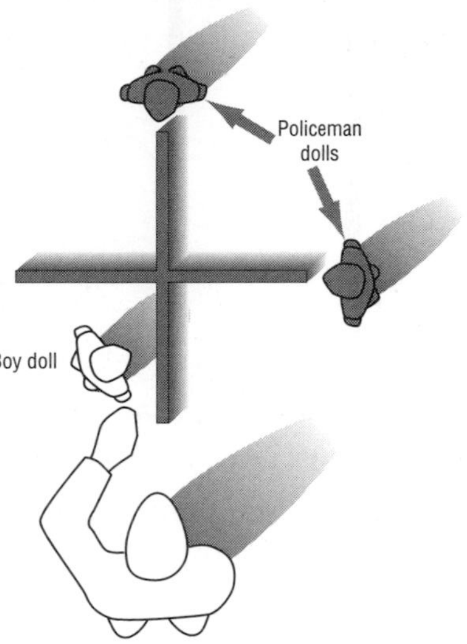

task twice as difficult. Donaldson (1978) said the tasks given by Piaget tested what she described as 'disembedded' thinking, by which she meant thinking out of context. When children were asked to do things which were more familiar to them, they were able to complete the task as they could relate to it (after all, snow covered mountains are not as familiar as dolls to most children).

Another study investigated children's ability to conserve numbers by presenting a different version of the study using counters and again showed that young children can think quite logically in situations they understand. In an experiment carried out by McGarrigle and Donaldson (1974), the children were again shown the two rows of counters on a table and asked if there was the same amount in each row. Then, instead of the experimenter changing the layout, a 'naughty teddy' appeared and made the change while the experimenter looked in the other direction. This resulted in the children realising that although the counters looked different, there were still the same number on the table.

I think that children at the 'pre-operational' stage (ie under seven or so) may not have quite the same understanding of the questions as the adult experimenter but the trouble is there is no way of knowing that the child really understands the questions in the same way as the experimenter intended. Further research has suggested that children quite often become confused with the word 'longest', thinking it means highest. Although this may initially seem quite strange, you could argue that if something is longer than something else, and you stand them both on their ends, the longest one would be higher than the other one. Therefore centration tasks which asked children to say which stick was longest may be interpreted as which stick is highest on the table? Children might look at the sticks like this.

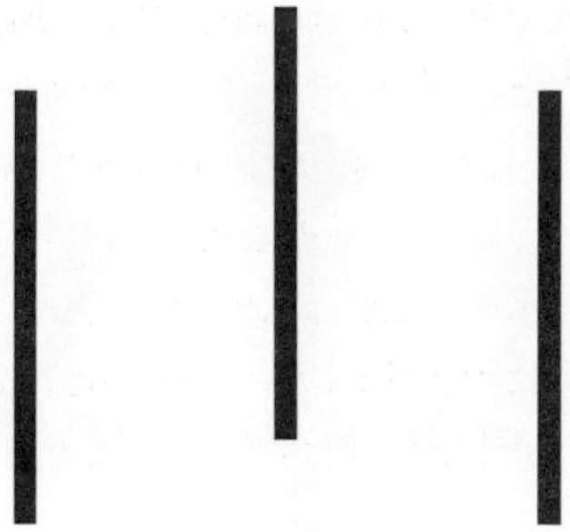

They may be quite correct in thinking that the middle stick looks highest, and if it is the highest it must be longer than the other two.

If we go back to the conservation of number experiment (with the counters) there are a number of suggestions which might explain this result. Perhaps Piaget unconsciously hinted to the children what sort of answer he wanted when he changed the layout of the counters. Perhaps they thought that he wanted them to say that it *looked like* there was a different amount of counters. The other possibility is that they actually thought the first answer they had given was wrong.

Ruth had been out clubbing but she was due to come home by midnight as she had exams the next week. She had made sure that she caught the last bus, even though it meant leaving all her mates and that gorgeous man who had bought her a couple of drinks. When she got home her blasted parents were in bed with the lights out. She was really fed up because she thought she could have come in later and they would never have known.

The next morning her mother was in the kitchen when she came downstairs. 'What time did you get in last night?' she said.

Ruth replied 'Midnight, as promised.'

'*What time* did you get in last night?' she said again.

You can imagine what Ruth was thinking – why did she ask me again? – She obviously didn't believe me the first time and she's giving me the chance to tell her – but I did come in at twelve.

If someone asks you the same question twice, you might think it is because you got the answer wrong the first time.

"What are two and two?"

"Five."

"What are two and two?"

"Sorry – four."

This is exactly what Piaget did. He asked the children after presenting them with the two rows of counters, 'Are there the same number of counters in each row?' He would then widen the spaces between the counters and ask the child again, 'Are there the same number of counters in each row?' Rose and Blank (1974) suggested that the child was actually demonstrating a very sophisticated social strategy by interpreting that the reason the second question was being asked was because they may have given an incorrect answer to the first question.

They suggested dropping the pre-transformation question (the question asked before the change in appearance had been made). They believed that if the child was simply shown the two rows evenly spaced and then one row was changed, if they were then asked if there were the same amount of counters in each row, this would give a much better set of answers. This is the basis of the following key study.

J. Samuel and P. Bryant (1984). Asking only one question in the conservation experiment.

Journal of Child Psychology and Psychiatry, 25, 315–18.

The aim of the study was to investigate whether the methodology used in Piaget's conservation experiments was the reason why children in the pre-operational stage were unable to conserve number, mass and volume (liquid).

Method

Design Laboratory experiment using independent subjects doing repeated measures (all subjects performed in all conditions).

Subjects The subjects consisted of four groups of 63 boys and girls. The first group had mean age of 5 years 3 months, the second 6 years 3 months, the third 7 years 3 months and the final group 8 years 3 months. Each age group was then further subdivided into three more groups consisting of 21 children.

Apparatus The apparatus used was the same apparatus as used in the Piagetian experiments. It consisted of two balls of playdough of equal size, two rows of counters and three beakers of liquid, two beakers being the same size and the third being taller and thinner.

Variables The independent variable was the methodology used with each group of children and the dependent variable was whether or not they could 'conserve'.

Procedure

Each age group was subdivided into three.

The standard group was tested using the standard Piagetian task which involved asking a pre and post transformation question.

Counters spread in two identical rows – 'Is there the same number of counters in each row?'

Counters in second row are then spread out and the child is asked 'Is there the same number of counters in each row?'

The one judgement group was tested using only the post transformation question.

Counters spread in two identical rows.

Counters in second row are then spread out and the child is asked "Is there the same number of counters in each row?"

The fixed array group was tested by being shown the two rows of counters only once, after one of the rows had already been spread out so they did not witness the transformation.

The procedure was the same for the mass and liquid experiments, with the mass (playdough) involving flattening one piece of playdough, and the liquid condition involving tipping the liquid from one beaker into another of a different size.

Each child had four attempts at the tests of number mass and volume. However, the group that they were allocated to (standard, one judgement or fixed array) did not vary.

Controls

To ensure that the children really understood, there were four trials in each situation.

The order in which the children undertook the tasks systematically varied to prevent order effects (eg first child – number, mass, volume; second child – mass, liquid number; third child – liquid number; mass and so on).

Results

Correct answers were recorded, and after being subjected to a number of statistical analyses, it was concluded that children were significantly more able to conserve in the one judgement condition than the other two conditions. It was also found that the older children were significantly more likely to be able to conserve than the younger children and that the number task produced the least errors for the one judgement task and the fixed array task. Interestingly enough, the results also show that the fixed array task produced more errors in all conditions.

Age	Standard Condition	One judgement	Fixed array
5 years	8.5	7.3	8.6
6 years	5.7	4.3	6.4
7 years	3.2	2.6	4.9
8 years	1.7	1.3	3.3

Mean number of errors made by children for all three tests
(Maximum number of errors = 12)

This table shows that the number of errors in the one judgement condition were lower than the other two in every case. It also indicates that the number of errors made by the children as they got older decreased in every condition.

Test	Standard Condition	One judgement	Fixed array
Mass	1.5	1.2	1.7
Number	1.5	1.0	1.5
Volume	1.8	1.6	2.5

Mean number of errors made by children for all ages
(Maximum number of errors = 4 as there were four age groups)

This table shows that the mean number of errors in the 'number' test were lower than the mean number of errors in the mass and volume tests in the one judgement and fixed array condition.

Discussion

These results suggest that Piaget's methodology may well have produced some of the results he achieved, but they also support the idea that cognitive development is age related because the older children were more able to conserve than the younger children. It seems that as children get older the more they understand that simply by changing the appearance of something doesn't mean the quantity changes. This was shown by the fact that the children who only saw the fixed array were less able to appreciate this because they could not carry over previous information into the new situation. In fact adults may well have the same problem because if you show an adult two glasses of different sizes containing liquid and ask them if there is the same amount of liquid in each, it is very likely they would either say 'Possibly' or 'No', but they could not be certain.

Evaluation

The study itself was well designed and accounted for many of the extraneous variables which could have interfered with the results. The possibility that the answers were given by chance was covered by the children having to have four attempts at each conservation test, and order effects were accounted for by varying the order of tasks given. One criticism of the number test was that the children may have simply counted the number of counters used and this may have accounted for the level of accuracy with the number task. All the children used as subjects would have been capable of counting to six and it would also take a very short space of time to add up the number on the table. Children often get nervous in laboratory settings and they also have a limited attention span which may have resulted in their answers being instantaneous rather than considered. On the other hand, the number of trials should also have prevented these factors from influencing the results. However, as with all research, we can never be absolutely certain that subjects are not simply responding to even the most carefully designed experimental situation.

Key words

Conservation – understanding that a change in shape or form does not necessarily mean a change in quantity.

Preoperational stage – the Piagetian stage between the ages of two and seven when children are more egocentric and have no understanding of logical rules.

Pre-transformation – before the objects were transformed into a different position

Post-transformation – after the objects had been moved into a different position

Standard group – group of children who were asked a pre-transformation and then a post-transformation question.

One judgement group – the group who were asked only one post transformation question but witnessed both conditions.

Fixed array condition – the group who only saw the objects after they had been moved or changed.

Key questions

1 What was the aim of the study?
2 Why was a control group used in the study?
3 Why was the order of task varied between subjects?
4 Give two criticisms of the study.
5 Can you think of an alternative way of investigating conservation which may have been more true to life?

Is aggression innate or learned?

This next section is going to consider two topics which are quite closely linked together. The first topic looks at the theories of aggression, and the second topic is going to look at how children learn. The reason these two topics are put together is because of the argument that many of our behaviours are innate and don't need to be learned, for example aggressive behaviour. However, there are other researchers who claim that we learn aggressive behaviour. In order for you to be in a position to understand both sides of the argument, we will briefly consider learning theory.

Aggression

It makes sense to think that aggressive behaviour is innate because how many parents actually teach their children to be aggressive, especially the boys, and yet both boys and girls demonstrate aggressive behaviour from an early age. Can you honestly say to me that you have never hit another person when you were a child? Has anyone ever taught you to get so angry that you have had to throw something or punch the wall, or scream and shout? So if no one actually taught you to do it, it is likely that perhaps you did not actually learn these behaviours but they came from inside you – an innate tendency.

On the other hand if I asked you to take time out for a moment and list a dozen different ways of killing someone, I am sure you wouldn't have too much problem in coming up with twelve or even more gruesome suggestions – here's mine!

- Hanging
- Electrocuting
- Cutting the throat
- Stabbing
- Poisoning
- Injecting with bleach
- Hacking up with a chainsaw
- Burying alive
- Drowning
- Suffocating
- Shooting
- Beheading

So how do I know these? Now to make it even worse, imagine I have told you to disembowel someone. In your mind can you picture what you would have to do and what their innards look like? I am sure you can conjure up a totally gruesome picture which is very messy and bloody and probably quite lifelike. But how do you know all these things? How come you can imagine all these horrific pictures without too much trouble? I trust none of you have ever done any of these things, and I know I certainly haven't, so how is it that we have no problems knowing what and how to do it? Your answer is probably something along the lines of 'I've seen it on the telly,' or 'I've seen it at the cinema.' Yes, you have learned by observing and have stored that information to be used if and when necessary.

To start with, we will very briefly consider the debate as to whether aggression is innate or learned.

Here Mike Tyson demonstrates aggression. Is his aggression innate or learned?

What is aggression? Aronson et al. (1997) describe aggression as:

> 'an intentional action aimed at doing harm or causing pain. The action might be physical or verbal; it might succeed in its goal or not. It is still aggression.'
>
> *(Aronson et al. 1997, p.437)*

Aggression can also be instrumental, which means it is used as a way of getting something, or it may be simply what is known as hostile aggression which is the result of anger. Whatever sort of aggression is shown, it may either be the result of an instinctive drive or it may be that we are usually naturally happy and good creatures who have to cope with restrictions from society, and these end up causing us huge amounts of frustration which manifest themselves in aggressive acts.

These views are echoed by two philosophers: Hobbes in his 'Leviathan', written in 1651, and Rousseau's 1762 image of the noble savage. Hobbes claimed that we are naturally brutal savages and it is only society's laws that ensure we control our natural instinct to be aggressive. Freud (1930) continued this theoretical idea when he claimed that humans are born with two instinctive forces *Eros*, the life force and *Thanatos*, the death force. Rousseau on the other hand, believed that we are benign by nature and society's constraints force us to become aggressive and depraved. His ideas were backed up by Dollard et al.'s (1939) frustration-aggression hypothesis which we will look at later in the chapter.

Lorenz (1950) proposed that aggression is innate and builds up within all species, both humans and animals, until something happens to trigger its release – and that this build-up is inevitable. The trigger is usually something specific to each species, for example the baring of teeth in a dog or a cat arching its back and spitting.

> The club was really throbbing and the music was so loud that everyone seemed to be into the dance. The air was thick with cigarette smoke and the smell of alcohol, and as the temperature got higher and higher the sweat was evident on the dancers' faces. More and more people seemed to pack the dance floor and the atmosphere felt like it was explosive.
>
> Dave was really going for it. His body seemed to have a life of its own and he wanted to dance all night. There were too many people though, and he kept bumping into them. The alcohol had really got to him and he felt like he was going to explode. He suddenly caught sight of this bloke staring at him and he felt really angry. 'Wot you lookin' at?' he threatened. The bloke just sneered back at him. Next thing, Dave was across the floor laying into the bloke and trying to get him onto the ground.

Here the trigger was the stare which was perceived as threatening, but it could be something much more simple than that, for example someone driving into your parking space in a car park just as you are about to back into it.

Lorenz claimed that these aggressive energies continually build up inside us, just like a tank filling with liquid as a result of a constantly dripping tap. Obviously the tank will overflow unless the liquid is allowed to drain off from time to time. Therefore Lorenz believed that it was necessary for society to

provide opportunities for this level of aggression to be released in a harmless way, such as playing football or national service.

Unfortunately, there is virtually no evidence to back up the idea that allowing a safe method of discharge actually reduces aggression. It may almost appear to work the other way, with people who practise aggressive sports or boxing actually becoming more aggressive. You can probably imagine that if someone is trained to fight, and they are better at it than the average person, then it will come easy to them to use it as a means of settling any sort of dispute – a sort of automatic response.

There is some evidence to back up this idea that when we allow our innate aggressive tendencies to be discharged in a 'harmless' way, they actually increase. Subjects who were given the chance to give electric shocks to another person, with no repercussions, demonstrated more aggressive behaviour rather than less (Buss, 1966). Also Loew (1967) reported on the fact that subjects who were allowed free range to express their anger became more wound up. I am sure you can imagine how this would happen.

Think of a situation where you feel angry with someone and you shout at them. Their response will affect whether you get more or less angry, because if they shout back it will make you even more aroused. If they don't respond but just stand there in front of you it makes you really furious because you don't seem to be able to get through to them.

Julie is really quite upset with Kate. Not only has she borrowed her best top, but she has actually ruined it by shrinking it in the wash. Instead of saying something, Kate simply put it in a carrier bag and left it on the seat of her car, not even having the courage to own up to what she did. Now was her chance as Kate walked into the pub.

'I can't believe you ruined the top I lent you. Why didn't you say something?'
Kate shrugged and sat down.
'Don't you have anything to say?' Julie is getting really wound up now.
'No.'
'But I lent it to you, and you have wrecked it and you don't even care.'
Kate ignored Julie's raving and turned to talk to one of the others at the table.
'You selfish * * * * *. I want it replaced. I'm never lending anything to you again.'
No answer.
'I want it replaced.'
Still no answer.
Julie grabs Kate's shoulder and screams 'Look here you ***** *****, I want it replaced.'
'Oh do be quiet,' says Kate.

You can feel how Julie's disappointment finally becomes replaced with anger which gets more intense. This contradicts Lorenz idea that if you release the aggression it dissipates, because here it is building up.

What we must remember is that Lorenz's ideas came from his study of animals and birds and related to behaviours known as fixed action patterns. These are patterns of behaviour where aggressive responses appear automatically to the behaviour of another member of the same species. I mentioned an example earlier of dogs baring their teeth, but it could also be a ritual 'dance' to demonstrate the weapons the animal has at its disposal for aggression (teeth, horns, spurs on cockerels etc.). Most of these responses are ritualised so that, at the end of the day, neither member actually dies. Think of dogs rolling over on their backs when another dog, or you as its master, acts aggressively towards it. According to Lorenz, humans are somewhat more complex and do not have these appeasement responses which is why, when they fight, it is generally far more serious and someone will get hurt. I can't imagine a muscular rugby player rolling over on his back when someone threatens him! However I believe that aggression is somewhat more complex than Lorenz believes, because occasionally the Julies of this world will shrug their shoulders and simply walk away.

Another explanation for aggressive behaviour focuses on biological factors (which may not be innate) such as hormone levels, chromosomes and abnormalities in the physiological structure of the brain, but the physiological aspect will be discussed in more detail in Chapter 6. It has often been noted that high levels of the hormone testosterone result in aggressive behaviours (which helps to explain why men are more aggressive than women). To back up this argument, Maccoby and Jacklin (1974) concluded that boys are consistently more aggressive than girls after undertaking dozens of laboratory experiments and field studies, amongst different social classes in various cultures. It is also the case that men are far more frequently charged with violent offences than women, whereas women are usually charged with offences against property. It has been found that testosterone levels are actually higher in both male and female prisoners who have been convicted of violent crimes compared with prisoners who have been convicted of non-violent offences (Dabbs et al. 1995).

Olweus (1980) found that boys who had higher levels of testosterone were more impatient and irritable. They were also aware that they were more likely to respond aggressively to being provoked or threatened (however, we can never be absolutely sure whether the testosterone levels shown in the boys were the cause of the aggressive behaviours or simply raised as a response to the environment in which they lived.)

Another explanation for aggression which indicates that it takes more than a sign stimuli to produce an aggressive response, is Dollard et al.'s (1939) frustration-aggression hypothesis. Dollard suggests that if we feel frustrated in our efforts to achieve some kind of goal or to get what we want, we are more likely to become aggressive.

The only present Neil wanted for Christmas was a Dreamcast games unit but he knew his parents couldn't afford to buy him one. His dad was out of work an although his mum would love to get him one, there was no way she could help. He tried to hide his disappointment when his parents asked him to choose something 'a little bit cheaper' for his Christmas present. Neil's dad knew how disappointed his son was and when he saw an announcement in the local newspaper that there was to be one Dreamcast unit at a quarter of the listed price in a sale to be held at the local electrical superstore, he decided he **had** to get it.

The morning of the sale arrived and he was up bright and early to drive to the shop. The car battery was flat. He ran to his bicycle – it had a puncture. The only option was to use his daughter's small pink girly bike and hope no one saw him. He stopped at the cash machine on the way and it ate his card, so he had to cycle back home and pick up his other card to pay for the machine. When he finally reached the shop, he could not believe his eyes when he discoverd that there was already a huge queue but he said to himself that they may not be there for the Dreamcast, after all there were lots of other bargains. He waited getting more and more anxious but finally the doors opened and he was carried inside with the rush of people, No one had bought it yet – he could see it on the shelf. He tried to push his way through the crowd but there were people all around him. It felt like to took him an eternity to cross the shop floor. Finally he was in front of it and was just reching out to get it, when a mountain of a woman, with a mouth to match, carrying about six different types of electrical items, leaned forward and took it from under his nose. He exploded in frustrated anger...

I empathise with these sentiments. It's like queueing to get into the cinema and they sell out of tickets to the people in front of you. You can see how frustration can lead to the expression of anger, much of which is not directly related to the situation itself. Neil's dad was so cheesed off by the time he got to the shop, that it would have taken very little to trigger the explosion. However, according to this theory, if we have all our needs met and can achieve the goals we aim for, we are unlikely to act aggressively – which suggests that we, as a species, are naturally non-aggressive.

There is a small problem with this argument, and that is that we don't always act in the same way if we are frustrated. I know of people who simply walk away from a situation if they can't get what they want and seem to be unharrassed by it. Actually I find this quite hard to accept and always imagine that they are just hiding what they feel and will go berserk later. However, Seligman (1975) pointed out that continual frustration may lead to us becoming totally passive because we have learned that we are helpless. He calls this state a state of 'learned helplessness'.

Just to clarify what learned helplessness is, I always think of the media pictures of the hundreds of tiny Romanian orphans, lying in their cots or sitting rocking, with no one to see to them. You can imagine how horrific it was for them because they could cry and cry and yet no one would come and sort out what they wanted. In the end, they learned that they were helpless, and no matter what they did it would not make any difference to their lives. Imagine living with that knowledge and how it must affect you as you get older. In fact people who have 'learned helplessness' have a much higher chance of suffering from depression in later life.

Although so far we have looked at innate or biological theories of aggression, Bandura (1977) suggested that aggression is actually something we learn to demonstrate because it seems to pay. An example of this is a child who has become a very aggressive bully at school because he has learned that he will get what he wants – sweets, money, status with the other children. But where has he learned to be aggressive? The vast majority of parents wouldn't dream of teaching their children to be aggressive and the few that do will be the ones who use aggression in their everyday lives (wife-beaters and child abusers). Bandura claims that they will have learned by seeing others behaving aggressively during their childhood or adolescence, through their own experience of being bullied, or through observation of the media. The likelihood of them imitating the behaviour will increase if they see the person being rewarded (reinforced) for their aggression – perhaps by getting what they want, and so they will be more likely to do it again.

Perhaps hostile aggression is innate, whereas instrumental aggression may be learned.

Conditioning

The next topic we are going to look at before we get on to the key study is how children learn. I have already mentioned that they learn by observation but that is not the whole of the story. After all, we do not observe everything we learn to do. We can't observe how to talk, study or write essays. Also, we can teach animals how to do things, but I have never seen a human demonstrating to a dog how to beg, although I have seen a human trying to demonstrate to a flock of small ducklings how to fly by running up the garden, flapping their arms as if they were wings – it didn't work! Therefore there must be some other mechanism by which we learn. This is known as conditioning.

Imagine that you live in a huge house, with four floors. In fact it is so big that in order for you to hear whether or not dinner is ready, the butler has to sound a huge gong which vibrates throughout the whole house. As you grow up, you always associate that sound with food, and it seems the minute you hear it you can feel your mouth watering in anticipation of the scrummy meal which awaits you.

When you leave home you move into a flat and here you are responsible for feeding yourself. One day you are walking down the road past some antique shops when you hear the sound of a gong being hit. It instantly makes you think of dinner and you can feel your mouth watering so you have to go off to the nearest cake shop to get some food.

What you haven't realised is that you have become conditioned to associate the sound of a gong with food. Although you know that a gong does not indicate food when you are away from home, you cannot help the reflex response of your mouth watering when you hear the gong being hit.

This whole process is known as classical conditioning, and was described by Pavlov in 1927 after he discovered that it was possible to teach dogs to salivate to the sound of a bell, rather than food. The thing was, that the dogs did not consciously salivate to the sound of the bell in the first place, and you did not consciously make your mouth water to the sound of the gong. The salivation (or mouth watering) was a reflex response which occurred to an unusual stimulus.

The way it happened with Pavlov was that he discovered that the dogs he was using for experiments started to drool before they were actually given any food. In fact they drooled when the keeper approached the cage, or when they saw the bucket the food was carried in, or even the white coats of the keepers. Pavlov was actually interested in the digestion of dogs and was undertaking research which involved collecting dogs saliva in a tube attached to the outside of its check. He decided to investigate this further, and wondered if he could teach the dog to salivate to the sound of a bell, which, as we have said, was a stimulus that under normal circumstances would not produce salivation.

For a while, Pavlov arranged for a bell to ring every time the dogs were fed. They learned to associate the sound of the bell with the fact that dinner was on

Food (unconditioned stimulus) = Slobbering (unconditioned response)

BEFORE LEARNING

Food (unconditioned stimulus)
+
Bell (conditioned stimulus)
= Slobbering (conditioned response)

THE LEARNING PROCESS

Bell (conditioned stimulus) = Slobbering (conditioned response)

LEARNING HAVING TAKEN PLACE

its way, and soon they were slobbering the minute the bell was rung. He had taught them to make the association between a stimulus (the bell) which does not normally suggest food, and a reflex response (slobbering).

The process of classical conditioning is often referred to by a series of simple equations but what you must remember is that classical conditioning involves *training* someone to produce a **reflex** response to something.

So what have a load of slobbering dogs got to do with anything you may well ask? The most important part of this concept is that it *is* possible to teach someone to respond with a reflex action to a certain stimulus. If we accept the idea that perhaps aggression is innate, and is a reflex response to certain stimuli, then we can see how some people can *learn* to be aggressive in specific situations. It also helps to explain how people develop phobias.

Probably the best known example of how a phobia can develop is the case of Little Albert reported by Watson and Rayner (1920). Poor Little Albert was a 'stolid and unemotional' child who was healthy and happy. When he was nine months old, Watson and Rayner tested his response to a number of different things to find out if he was frightened of anything such as white rats, rabbits and masks (fear can be considered a reflex response). They discovered that the only thing that frightened him was a hammer hitting a steel bar, directly behind his head – how surprising! Every time they showed him a white rat, they struck the steel bar, which was the conditioning process. After they had done this seven times over the next seven weeks, Albert showed fear and extreme distress every time a white rat was shown to him. In fact this phobia had become so strong that he seemed to generalise the response to any furry creature, hair and Santa Claus's beard! At this point his mother decided it was time to remove her son, so if you meet a little old man who is about eighty years of age and he is frightened of furry things and called Albert, it may be him!

Although this seems somewhat amusing, as I am sure you will have realised this experiment was extremely unethical. It is essential to safeguard the welfare of participants and ensure that they leave the experimental situation in the same state that they entered. This was hardly the case with Little Albert although part of the reason was that his mother decided to remove him before Watson and Rayner could desensitise him. I also wonder if the researchers sought informed consent from Little Albert's mother, because I would have though that most mothers would have been very unhappy to have their child subjected to such a traumatic experience!

You will probably have realised at this point, that there are only so many reflexes to retrain. It is possible to learn other things that have nothing to do with reflexes, such as teaching dogs to beg.

Many years ago, I used to have an old English sheepdog called Josephine. When she was little, I decided to teach her to shake hands. I went about this by saying 'Shake hands' to her, and holding her front paw and making her shake hands with me. Every time I did it, I would give her a doggie chocolate as a reward. She soon learned that by shaking hand, she would be rewarded, but the trouble was when she had come in from the muddy garden, she would walk up to me and hit me with her front paw, leaving dirty marks all over whatever it was that I was wearing.

What I had done was to use the process of conditioning to train her to something which was not a reflex response. She had learned that she would get something if she did something and this meant she was far more likely to do it. This process is called 'operant conditioning', and involves increasing the likelihood a behaviour will happen again by rewarding that behaviour. Now think about how it works. I paired her behaviour of giving a paw with a doggie choc (a reinforcement) until in the end I could forget the reinforcement because the behaviour would happen anyway.

The difference between this and Pavlov's theory about how we learn is that Pavlov's learned responses would be *automatically* triggered by a stimuli without any sort of conscious awareness. B. F. Skinner pointed out that there was a difference between 'automatic responses' (where the response or action happens without conscious thought), and 'operants 'where initially responses happen as a result of voluntary choice. Josephine could have chosen not to shake hands when the process of training started, although after a while the response becomes almost automatic.

Skinner (1938) described teaching rats how to press levers to gain food and explained how he would allow the release of a food pellet every time the rat approached the lever. Next time the rat would have to get just a little bit closer in order to get the food pellet. This would continue until the rat stepped on the lever, possibly by chance, and this released the food pellet. Finally, the rat would only get the pellet when pressing the lever. The rat learned by having its behaviour reinforced. Skinner shaped the rat's behaviour until the rat learned what was required. Sooner or later, the rat would not have to make the conscious decision 'Mmmm, now I'm hungry, I think I will go and press the lever.' He would simply go and do it without having to think through the process. He would have made an automatic association between the two behaviours.

We, as humans, also make automatic associations, which we had to learn originally. In fact you are doing exactly that now. You are reading without thinking about what each letter sounds like or each word means. You actually learned reading by a process of operant conditioning because each time you read a word

Room 3: This room was next to an observation room with a one way mirror so that observers could monitor the behaviour of the children. It contained a number of toys which were always placed in exactly the same position for each of the subjects. They toys were either considered aggressive or non-aggressive: see below for examples.
Non-aggressive toys: Dolls, bears, crayons and cars and plastic farm animals.
Aggressive toys: A three foot high Bobo doll, a mallet and peg board and dart guns.

Subjects

36 boys and 36 girls from Stanford University Nursery School, aged between 37 and 69 months (mean age 52 months). In order to prevent subject variables from influencing the results (children in one condition being more aggressive than children in another) the children were rated for aggression before being allocated into their groups. This was done by both the experimenter and the teacher (who knew the children prior to the study). The children were rated on a five point scale for previous displays of physical and verbal aggression, aggression towards objects and their ability to control their behaviour when they were angry (aggressive inhibition). The results of the two raters were considered to be reliable because they significantly correlated with each other.

The control group (24 subjects)

12 boys and 12 girls who would see no role model

The two experimental groups were then subdivided

Aggressive Model Observers (24 subjects)

six female and six male to see a female role model
six female and six male to see a male role model

Non-Aggressive Model Observers (24 subjects)

six female and six male to see a female role model
six female and six male to see a male role model
There were four hypotheses:

1. That subjects who saw an aggressive model would reproduce aggressive acts resembling the acts of the model.
2. That subjects who saw the subdued, non-aggressive model would show less aggression than a group who had no role model, indicating that the subdued non-aggressive model would actually have an inhibitory effect on the subjects behaviour
3. That subjects would be more likely to imitate the behaviour of a same-sex model rather than a model of the opposite sex. (This is based on the idea that children believe their parents have a preference for sex-appropriate models of behaviour and discourage sex-inappropriate imitative responses.)
4. That boys are more likely to imitate aggression than girls and this will be even more likely, if they observe an aggressive male model.

Procedure

Part 1 (Duration approximately 10 minutes)

The children in the aggressive and non-aggressive conditions were tested alone and were taken into the first room where they were seated at the table and encouraged to play with the potato prints and stickers. The model was then escorted into the opposite corner of the room and told that the tinker toys set, mallet and Bobo were for them to play with. Then the experimenter left the room.

Aggressive condition The model started by playing with the tinker toys, but after a minute turned to the Bobo doll and started to act aggressively towards it.
Aggressive acts: Laid Bobo on its side, sat on it and punched it on the nose (all as one continuous action), hit it on the head with the mallet, threw it in the air and kicked it around the room.
Aggressive phrases: Kick him, pow, sock him on the nose, hit him down, throw him in the air.
Non-aggressive phrases: He keeps coming back for more, he sure is a tough fella.

Non-aggressive condition The model assembled the tinker toys in a quiet, subdued way and ignored the Bobo doll.

Part 2

All the children, including the control group, were then taken into room 2 where they were subjected to mild aggression arousal.

Part 3 (duration approximately 20 minutes)

The experimenter then took the child to room 3 and stayed with them (but discreetly worked in a corner of the room) as some of the children would have refused to stay in the room on their own.

Two observers scored the subjects' behaviour at five second intervals which gave 240 observations for each subject and the level of inter-observer reliability was highly significant.

Three measures of direct imitation were recorded:

- Imitation of aggressive acts
- Imitation of aggressive phrases
- Imitation of non-aggressive phrases

Two measures of indirect imitation were recorded:

- The subject hit other things with the mallet (remember the subject only saw the model hit Bobo with the mallet).
- Subject laid Bobo on its side and sat on it but was not aggressive towards it.

Four further types of aggressive behaviour which were not imitations of the adult role model:

- Striking, slapping or pushing the doll aggressively.
- Behaving aggressively to any other objects.
- Producing novel hostile remarks aimed at Bobo or other objects eg 'Cut him'.
- Shooting darts or aiming the gun and pretending to shoot various objects in the room.

Results

(The results have been broken down to make them easier to digest, but at the end of this section you will find the whole table for the mean aggression scores for all subjects.)

1 Children who saw an aggressive model reproduced more aggressive acts resembling the acts of the model (physical aggression, verbal aggression and non-aggressive verbal responses) than all the other children.

	Aggressive role model	Non-aggressive Role model	Control group
Imitative physical and verbal aggression	83.6	5.6	5.6

Simplified table showing mean totals of imitative physical and verbal aggression demonstrated by both male and female subjects to male and female role models, compared to other groups.

Children who saw the aggressive role model usually showed more partial imitation of the role model or non-imitative physical and verbal aggression than those who saw the non-aggressive or no model (but the results were not always significant).

	Aggressive role model	Non-aggressive Role model	Control group
Mallet aggression	80.2	26.4	26.6
Punches Bobo	53.6	40.5	27.4
Non-imitative aggression	82.6	57.0	30.7
Aggressive gun play	29.5	30.7	18.0

Simplified table showing mean totals of partial imitation or non-imitative physical aggression demonstrated by both male and female subjects to male and female role models, compared to other groups.

2 Subjects who saw the subdued, non-aggressive role model showed low levels of aggression although they were not always significantly lower than the group that had no role model. So it could not be concluded that the subdued non-aggressive model would actually have an inhibitory effect on the subjects' behaviour

3 Subjects who saw the same-sex role model only imitated their behaviour in some categories. For example boys imitated male role models more than girls for physical and verbal imitative aggression, non-imitative aggression and gun play.

Girls would imitate female models more than boys for verbal imitative aggression and non-imitative aggression only (not significant).

	Female model	Male model
Imitative physical aggression		
Female subjects	5.5	7.2
Male subjects	12.4	25.8
Imitative verbal aggression		
Female subjects	13.7	4.3
Male subjects	2.0	12.7
Non imitative aggression		
Female subjects	21.3	8.4
Male subjects	16.2	36.7
Aggressive gun play		
Female subjects	1.8	7.3
Male subjects	4.5	15.9

Table showing mean total of aggressive behaviours and the gender of the role model

4 Finally, overall the male subjects were generally far more aggressive than the female subjects (even when they had no aggressive role model) except when they saw an aggressive female role model.

Discussion

It appears that although the children who saw the aggressive models were far more aggressive than the other two groups, the gender of the role model had a large impact on their behaviour. The female role model seemed to cause confusion in the children, because she was not behaving in a way that they would expect for a female role model. They made comments like 'Who is that lady? That's not the way for a lady to behave. You should have seen what that girl did in there. She was just acting like a man. I never saw a girl act like that before. She was punching and fighting but not swearing.' (p.581.) The male role model's aggressive behaviour on the other hand was more likely to be seen as normal. The children made comments like 'Al's a good socker, he beat up Bobo. I want to sock like Al' and so on.

It also appears that the subjects who saw the non-aggressive models were more inhibited and unresponsive than the other children, which suggests that children can learn to control anti-social behaviour when they are in the presence of such models.

At the end of the day, although the study strongly supports the idea that aggression can be

Response Category	Experimental groups				
	Aggressive		Non-aggressive		Control groups
	F model	M model	F model	M model	
Imitative physical aggression					
Female subjects	5.5	7.2	2.5	0.0	1.2
Male subjects	12.4	25.8	0.2	1.5	2.0
Imitative verbal aggression					
Female subjects	13.7	2.0	0.3	0.0	0.7
Male subjects	4.3	12.7	1.1	0.0	1.7
Mallet aggression					
Female subjects	17.2	18.7	0.5	0.5	13.1
Male subjects	15.5	28.8	18.7	6.7	13.5
Punches Bobo doll					
Female subjects	6.3	16.5	5.8	4.3	11.7
Male subjects	18.9	11.9	15.6	14.8	15.7
Non-imitative aggression					
Female subjects	21.3	8.4	7.2	1.4	6.1
Male subjects	16.2	36.7	26.1	22.3	24.6
Aggressive gun play					
Female subjects	1.8	4.5	2.6	2.5	3.7
Male subjects	7.3	15.9	8.9	16.7	14.3

Table showing mean totals of behaviour for all conditions

learned by observation, it doesn't help to answer the question as to whether that aggression is primarily innate.

Evaluation

This study gives us a number of areas to consider. The study could simply be said to be looking at how children learn to be aggressive to an inflatable doll. The fact that the object of aggression was not human may have had an effect on the results. We cannot be sure that the behaviour of the children was not due to the experimental situation because they may simply have realised what was expected of them (demand characteristics). The situation also lacked ecological validity because how often is a child given a table with toys and asked to play while an adult beats up a large inflatable doll in the other corner of the room! It is likely that the child may even have become quite concerned to see such behaviour. Finally, how could we be sure that the models behaviour was the same from child to child. It is extremely likely that their behaviour would vary in one way or the other, and this too may have influenced the results.

Ethically, the question as to whether the children who experienced the anti-social role model became distressed in any way should be considered. There is also the problem of whether or not the children suffered any long term consequences as a result of the study. Although it is unlikely, we can never be certain. This is one of the major problems with any sort of study which involves looking at the origins of aggressive behaviour.

aggression in children who lived in communities where television had only just become available with children who already had access to television. They found that aggressive behaviour in the children aged six to eleven increased during the two years after television had been introduced, but was no different for the children who already had access to television. This indicates that watching violence leads to increases in aggressive behaviour.

Huesmann and Eron (1984) conducted a 20 year follow-up study of 400 children who had had considerable access to television violence when they were eight years old. They discovered that there was an association between their viewing habits and later levels of violent crime, including wife beating and child abuse, irrespective of what sort of socio-economic background they came from.

Finally, what we must remember is that many of the studies which find a relationship between watching violence on television and violent behaviour are simply finding a 'relationship' and nothing more. Relationships between two things do not necessarily indicate cause and effect because there may be something else which has not been considered. Take for example the case of a small boy who watches lots of violent television. He may not always watch it, although he may sit in front of it. He may, however, see his dad regularly beating his mum, and this may have a far greater effect on him than television alone. He may also have high levels of autonomic arousal (which make him feel very uptight all the time), and this may result in him 'discharging' his energy by beating up his baby brother rather than imitating what he has seen on telly.

We can never be sure what is the ultimate cause of aggressive behaviour. It seems like there are lots of possible answers but it is useful to at least know that we do learn from observation – *and* that we can learn good behaviours as well as bad.

Maternal deprivation

When you listen to the news and there is an item on about some criminal who has recently been committed to trial, have you noticed how the reporters tend to always relate back to their childhood. They focus on things like coming from 'deprived backgrounds' or being part of a 'single parent family' or having been 'abused as a child'. Although few of us have idyllic childhoods, and many of us come from single parent families, we don't all turn into raving psychopaths – do we?

Carole: Do you know, if a child doesn't have a mother, it will turn into a weirdo and won't be able to form relationships with other people. It may even become a psychopath.

Alex: Where on earth did you get that rubbish from?

Carole: I read it in a book.

Alex: And how old is the book?

Carole: Dunno. It was an old Penguin book called 'Childcare and the Growth of Love' by a man called John Bowlby. I found it propping up the bottom of a bookshelf at my gran's.

Alex: Well you should have left it there!

Carole found a book which was published in 1953 and had been commissioned by the World Health Organisation as a way of looking into what is needed for the large number of children who, as a result of the Second World War, had become orphaned or separated from their parents and had therefore been taken into care. Bowlby had produced a report which drew not only on his own research but also took into account the findings of other researchers, suggesting that if a child was deprived of its mother this would cause deep, long lasting psychological problems for the child which would mean that they would be unable to form meaningful relationships with other people in later life.

Before we look at Bowlby and the evidence he used towards forming his theories, just think for a moment. I'm sure you must realise that there are things that happen to us in our childhood which will have an effect on how we turn out as adults. Deprivation and neglect, experiencing family violence and learning from the behaviour of others are all likely to affect how we develop into an adult. Whether we really believe that 'mother' is the key to our development, and lack of 'mother' is going to turn us into someone unable to function emotionally, is another matter.

I am going to tell you about Bowlby's 'Childcare and the Growth of Love' and its contents. I will then give you an idea where his ideas came from and then look at some of the other research which has contradicted what he had to say. I must admit, I find Bowlby's book actually quite amusing because all it seems to do is list study after study which supports his idea that a child needs its mother and if it suffers any separation it is absolutely stuffed! Unfortunately, many of the studies are not actually named but simply talked about in general terms, which means that you cannot check them or read any more about them. The worst part is that it actually makes me wonder if perhaps he was not always as honest as he could have been about all this past information. I have also quoted from the book quite a lot because it will give you an idea how extreme some of the ideas really are.

The other thing to remember is that Bowlby wrote the book in 1951 and I wonder how much influence the war had on his ideas. Women had found a new kind of freedom – in effect they had been running the country while their men were away fighting. This was the first time that women had demonstrated their abilities by showing a much greater equality with men, farming, working in factories, mending vehicles and so on. Pity the men on their return. Perhaps they felt superfluous to requirements and therefore unnecessary and Bowlby's book was a move to put women back into the homes, in their rightful places!

Isn't she a lucky girl? This 1950's picture was intended to show women what they were missing by going out to work.

The purpose behind Bowlby's study was to look at how the mental health of the children who had been orphaned or separated from families, and therefore needed institutional care or foster homes, may be affected. It was not intended to look at refugees, who would bring with them even more complex problems such as cultural and language difficulties, so the report focused on children who were in their native countries. Institutional care of the time focused on children's physical needs but not on their emotional needs, and so the intention of the report was to try to identify the best kind of upbringing for these disadvantaged children.

I wonder if Bowlby was the best person to carry out such a study because before he even started this study, he stated that he believed that mothers and babies had evolved a biological need for each other. If they were separated from each other during the first five years of the child's life, this would result in emotional and social repercussions for the infant. In fact, Bowlby was strongly influenced by the teachings of Freud (who we will look at in the final section) and his work involved him in the psychoanalysis of people with emotional and social problems. He actually believed that children are genetically programmed to bond with a specific 'other' person during the first months of life and claimed that 'mother love in infancy and childhood is as important for mental health as are vitamins and proteins for physical health' (Bowlby, 1951). It therefore seems quite obvious that he would suggest having no mother would cause problems for a child's mental welfare. He does accept that sometimes the relationship between a mother and child is not always perfect, and that there are rejecting mothers (but this would be caused by the mother having suffered maternal deprivation in her childhood and, as a result, being unable to form a relationship with her baby).

To give you some idea how convinced Bowlby was about the importance of mother, he states:

> 'What is believed to be essential for mental health is that an infant and young child should experience a warm, intimate and continuous relationship with his mother (or permanent mother-substitute – one person who steadily 'mothers' him) in which both find satisfaction and enjoyment.'
>
> *(Bowlby, 1953, p.1)*

In the book, he gives example after example of children who have been separated or have experienced what he calls 'grossly disturbed relationships with their mothers in their early years.' He gives a number of typical features which would be found such as the following list:

- superficial relationships
- no real feeling – no capacity to care for people or to make true friends
- an inaccessibility, exasperating to those trying to help
- no emotional response to situations where it is normal – a curious lack of concern
- deceit and evasion, often pointless; stealing; lack of concentration at school.

(Bowlby, 1953, p. 37)

He also insisted that a baby can only form an attachment to its mother during the first two years of life as this was the 'critical period'. By this he was suggesting that if the child did not 'attach' during this time, it would lose the ability to do so and this would result in serious long term consequences for the child. (Although this sounds a bit extreme, Bowlby based many of his ideas on the work of ethologists who had looked at animal behaviours.) Therefore, the first two years of life were most important although the risk of suffering damage due to lack of maternal care was 'still serious, though much less so than earlier.'

The final conclusion to Bowlby's beliefs was that children who had been deprived of a mother over the first five years of life would have their social development affected and would be extremely likely to become juvenile delinquents. They may even develop what Bowlby described as 'affectionless psychopathy'. Affectionless psychopaths have a disorder whereby they can't form personal relationships with others and are unaware or (more likely) indifferent to other peoples' feelings, which would have come from lack of the primary relationship with their mothers. They are amoral, often very manipulative and frequently commit antisocial acts such as using violence or demonstrating some kind of perverted behaviour. Most serial killers are psychopaths, as they experience no guilt about their behaviour which allows them to go on killing.

What we need to consider is where did all these ideas come from because although Bowlby might have been somewhat extreme he was not stupid, and he used documented evidence as a way of developing his ideas. As I mentioned earlier, studies of animal behaviour, especially work carried out by Lorenz, heavily influenced his thinking.

The influence of Lorenz

Lorenz was an ethologist. Ethologists study behaviours where they naturally occur because they believe that this is the only way the behaviour has meaning. Imagine a fox and dog digging holes – the behaviour is the same for both, but the reasons are very different. The fox is digging a new home and the dog is burying something but you wouldn't know this unless you watched them in their own natural environments.

Lorenz was interested in the way that young ducks and geese follow their parents around from very soon after they have hatched and seem to avoid any other creatures, even other ducks or geese.

> I used to breed strange bantam chickens and wildfowl in my garden. I actually had quite a large garden because I had taken over (with the owners permission) a plot of land which was overgrown with brambles. I have always loved birds and this seemed like a good idea at the time. My poor, long suffering husband built all sorts of runs and also a huge pond and I duly filled the garden up with various breeds of fowl. The chickens did well but the ducks didn't seem to get the hang of sitting on their eggs and used to deposit them in odd places and then leave them.

I then had a brilliant idea – buy an incubator! When the first of a batch of eight duck eggs were due to hatch, I stood over them in amazement as these soggy, wobbly things sort of fell out of the shells onto the wire mesh. I must have spent most of the next day gazing in amazement as they dried and turned into little sweet ducklings. I transferred them to a box under a lamp and did an excellent impersonation of mother duck as they became stronger. The weird thing was that whenever I moved from one side of the box to the other, they all seemed to gravitate to that side too. When I let them out, they kept following me. I didn't realise at the time that this was perfectly normal and they saw me as mother. It just got to be a pain in the neck when they were finally loose in the garden and every time I went to go indoors they all trooped into the kitchen. I ended up running inside every time, immediately shutting the door before the first one arrived. In the meantime, I fulfilled my duties as far as possible, but I had huge problems trying to teach them to fly!

So why did this happen? Lorenz found through laboratory experiments that young geese had an innate tendency to follow a large moving object if they encountered it soon after hatching. If they object was removed before they had been following it for ten minutes they seemed to give up on it and then ignore it. But if they were allowed to follow it for more than ten minutes then they seemed to become extremely attached to it and they wouldn't follow anything else.

Lorenz called this process 'imprinting'. Imprinting is a rapid attachment which is formed as a result of a special kind of innate learning. This makes sense in evolutionary terms – in the natural environment the only large creature that is likely to stay around for a whole ten minutes is most likely to be the mother. Therefore this time gap is perhaps a safety factor.

Lorenz had the same problem as me! Here we see him being followed by a band of ducklings who have imprinted on him.

Lorenz carried out another experiment with a set of ducklings, in which he kept them together and didn't let them see any large moving objects. After 25 hours he found that they seemed to have completely lost the ability to imprint. As a result of this, he concluded that there was a 'critical period' during a young bird's development when it had to imprint. This idea of a critical period was the reason why Bowlby believed that young children had to form attachments within a certain time. Other 'critical periods' have been identified in children's development when it has been suggested that things have to happen or else they never will, for example the belief that children will not learn a language unless they have done so by the time they reach puberty. (In fact, the term 'critical period' is now often referred to as 'sensitive period' because research has shown that it is often possible for children to achieve goals even outside the supposed critical period although they find it much harder.)

Another study Bowlby cited to back up his claims involved identical twins. He explained that if you look at one twin brought up in a foster home and one in its natural home, you would get a very good idea of the effects of upbringing on those children. When we talked about experiments, you may remember that if you compare two children who come from different parents, obviously the differences between them may be something to do with their genes rather than the experiences they have. One child may be sickly and weak while another child may be bonny and healthy. If you look at their parents, it would seem likely that they have inherited their parents' physical characteristics rather than their appearance being caused by their life experiences. (The problem is, maybe their parents are as they are because of their life experiences.) The book then points out that at the time of writing there were no human twin studies of the problem but there was a very interesting study being done by a psychologist on twin goat kids!

Bowlby continues by saying that one kid

> 'is separated from its mother for a brief spell each day and the other not. Except for the daily experimental period of 40 minutes, both kids live with and feed from their mother. During the experimental period the lights are periodically extinguished, which is known to create anxiety in goats, and this produces very different behaviour in the twins. The one which is with its mother is at ease and moves about freely; the isolated one is "psychologically frozen" and remains cowed in one corner. In one of the first experiments the isolated kid discontinued suckling from its mother, and the experimenters being unaware of this and so unable to help, it died after a few days (*sic*). This is ample demonstration of the adverse effects of maternal deprivation on the young of mammals, and disposes finally of the argument that all the observed effects are due to heredity.'
>
> *(Bowlby, 1953 p. 25)*

So there you go!

Although we can argue that these two examples of 'evidence' come from animal studies, (and as you know, we differ slightly from geese and goats), there are studies involving human children which also influenced Bowlby! Research undertaken by Goldfarb, a New York psychologist, in 1943 was cited by Bowlby as strong evidence for the effects of maternal deprivation. Goldfarb matched a group of 15 children who had gone from their natural mothers to institutional care, where they all stayed until they were about three years old, with another group who had gone direct from mother to foster home. Apparently Goldfarb 'took great care to see that the two groups were of similar heredity' and they had all been given up by their mothers 'usually within the first nine months of life'. My initial thoughts are that even though Bowlby believed the study was well designed, there are a number of aspects which seem to lack real scientific rigour and we are given no clue as to why the children were given up by their mothers in the first place.

However, the children who were in the institution obviously had a very different experience to children raised in a home environment. According to Bowlby, the institutions were very clean but lacked 'the elementary essential of mental hygiene.' Although he does not state what exactly he means by this, he went on to state, presumably quoting from Goldfarb's report,

> 'Babies below the age of nine months were each kept in their own little cubicles to prevent the spread of epidemic infection. Their only contacts with adults occurred during these few hurried moments when they were dressed, changed or fed by nurses.'
>
> *(Bowlby, 1953, p.43)*

Between the ages of nine months and one year, the poor children were then grouped with about 15 or 20 other children and looked after by one nurse. You can imagine how little attention they got, and how fraught the poor nurse must have been. Things didn't improve much in the next two years either. Apparently they lived, according to Goldfarb in 'almost complete social isolation during the first year of their life.'

Bearing in mind what you know about learned helplessness, do you think these children were suffering only from maternal deprivation? I think that they were probably so lonely and miserable, and learning how helpless they were, that this must have affected their social development. As we have mentioned before, children who learn helplessness realise they can't control their environment and so they give up trying and consequently become passive and withdrawn. They were also totally unstimulated as they would have little to play with or watch and it is extremely likely that any long term effects would be due to their physical situation rather than purely lack of mother.

Sure enough, when they were tested some years later, when they were between the ages of ten and fourteen, the group who had been in the institution gained lower scores in tests of intelligence, abstract thought, social maturity, ability to keep rules (obviously potential juvenile delinquents), making friends and all but three showed 'backwardness of speech'!

There are countless other studies cited by Bowlby, all of which point to the fact that maternal deprivation seems to be the key feature in children's lack of emotional development. The only other study I will mention here is one that Bowlby conducted in 1946 when he was looking at juvenile delinquency. He had a child guidance clinic in London for disturbed teenagers and his subjects were selected from the people attending the clinic, which was hardly a representative sample of the population as a whole.

He compared a group of 44 emotionally disturbed teenagers, who had been reported as thieves, with a control group who were similar in number, age and gender and who were also emotionally disturbed, but who did not steal. Bowlby noticed that 14 of the thieves were 'affectionless characters' but none of the control group fitted this category. In fact, 17 of the thieves had been completely separated from their mothers or established foster mothers, for at least six months, if not more, during the first five years of their lives, whereas only two of the control group had experienced that type of separation. I suppose we could ask why, if 17 had been completely separated, only 14 developed 'affectionless characters'? What happened to the other three? Also, what made the two members of the control group 'normal'?

Unfortunately Bowlby didn't answer these questions. He simply concluded,

> 'there can be no doubting that for the affectionless thief, nurture, not nature, is to blame … There is a very strong case indeed for believing that prolonged separation of a child from his mother (or mother substitute) during the first five years of life stands foremost among the causes of delinquent character development.'

Perhaps we should simply put the results down to the methodology. As I said, he had a pre-selected sample. Bowlby chose delinquents as his subjects and used retrospective evidence, that is evidence which is remembered. As we know, our memories are not always as accurate as we would like them to be and they can become distorted with time. Perhaps there were incomplete records of the childrens' childhoods and perhaps the children just felt really angry and upset about their experiences as little ones. They may well have had distorted memories about these events, and we have no idea what else happened to them in the intervening years. Think of the other things which could have affected them – peer groups, institutions, poor fostering, physical deprivation, lower levels of intelligence and so on. Also, this study did not consider how many children were separated and *didn't* suffer from the same effects.

Before we go on to look at the research which disputes Bowlby, I would like to mention one study which was carried out after Bowlby's report. Again it was a study of animal behaviour but in this instance it involved primates, rhesus monkeys to be precise. I remember being so upset when I saw a video showing tiny monkeys who had been separated from their mothers, and who were kept in cages where they clung to a towelling mother substitute while feeding from a wire 'mother'. The idea behind the study was to look at why we form attachments. The obvious answer to this is that it must have something to do with survival. How could we survive if we didn't have some kind of caregiver to feed and protect us, especially as we are so helpless when we are born? But why is it that we seem to form such a strong attachment to one person, usually mother? Is there something biological there, or is it simply that we know when we are on to a good thing, and form attachments with the person who is most likely to do the best for us? We also know that sometimes mother is not the best caregiver around, and yet the attachment of the child to mother is still very strong.

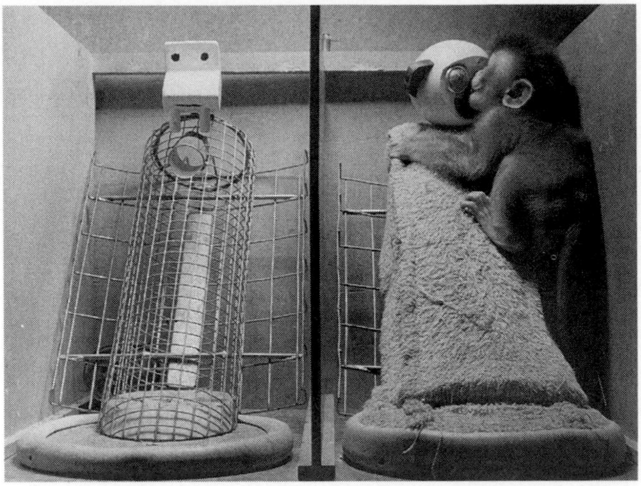

The tiny rhesus monkey clings to the towelling mother even though the wire mother is the one who provides the food.

The primate study looked into what was called 'cupboard love theory'. This theory suggests that we do attach to the person who feeds us. If this is the case, Bowlby's theory that mother is the most important person factor in children's development would collapse in a heap because it would suggest that any old 'feeder' would do. Harlow and Zimmerman (1959) put newborn rhesus monkeys in cages with these two mothers, with the expectation that the one with the food would become the surrogate mother for the tiny monkey. However, the towelling one became the mother substitute and the tiny monkeys ran to cling to it whenever they were frightened. Food seemed to be an irrelevancy in this case, and suggested that the nurturing factor is probably more important in the formation of attachments.

The whole reason why I wanted to mention this study was because the after effects of the study were far more important. Three years later, Harlow reported on the monkeys who had now grown up. Although they had appeared physically normal and were fit and healthy, it seemed that they had not developed emotionally. They were much more timid than the other monkeys and didn't know how to act when put in a cage with other monkeys who had been raised normally. It was heartbreaking seeing these little monkeys cringing in the corner of the cage and being absolutely terrified when the other monkeys came closer to them. They had no idea how to behave and were obviously a prime target for bullying. They couldn't relate to the other monkeys at all and showed some very disturbed behaviours. Obviously they had no idea how to relate to other monkeys sexually, and any females who did successfully mate, were inadequate mothers who were unable to care for their babies.

The conclusion Harlow made as a result of this study was that their behaviour was due to maternal deprivation and he claimed that if the baby monkeys weren't allowed to form a relationship with their mother within the first six months they would never form one. This, for them, was the critical period. When you think about it, they weren't just suffering from maternal deprivation but also social deprivation. They had learned neither how to behave with others not what the appropriate social skills were. Further studies raised monkeys in isolation, but allowed them 20 minutes a day in a playroom with three other monkeys. These poor little souls grew up to be quite normal because they had learned how to interact with others. We must use this evidence to accept that perhaps it is not mother after all who is the most important person. It is also not the 'feeder' because someone can shove food down your throat with no devotion at all. It must therefore be social deprivation rather than anything else that is really the key to emotional development. So perhaps it is the nature of relationships that seems to be the most important factor. This may explain why some children still crave their mums, even when the nature of the relationship is very poor and mother doesn't really seem to care about them – perhaps she is the best they can get.

Henry clung to his mother's skirt and she tried to brush him off as if he was some irritating little fly hanging on for dear life. She caught sight of herself in the mirrors along the wall in the supermarket and adjusted her hair. 'Mmmm, not bad,' she thought as she turned as far as possible to see her profile. On her way to the checkout, she spied an attractive man in his early thirties, and gently manipulated her way in his general direction. Henry dragged behind. She tried to remove him with a well aimed shove from her snakeskin high heeled boots, but missed. She couldn't do it again without it becoming obvious and then she'd have one of the old dears in the supermarket wittering on about child cruelty.

Henry fell off. She launched forward, hoping to leave him behind for the few minutes it might take her to gently bump into her target. 'That should be long enough,' she thought, 'then I can go and find him again after I've been asked for a date.' She had already worked out that if they did go out together, she could leave Henry in his bedroom when she went. He should be alright there till the morning, even if she didn't come home. After all, she'd done it before. He even survived until the afternoon of the next day, although he was quite hungry and had wet himself. Still that could be cleared up.

Suddenly there was an almighty crash from the other side of the shop and a huge scream and a child started to cry, large inconsolable sobs. 'Oh damn,' she said to herself as she guessed what had happened. Next minute Henry was running towards her, covered in tomato ketchup, and made a huge lunge for her crying 'Mummy, mummy.' Her cover was blown. Tomato ketchup and white miniskirts don't go too well together. The man walked away.

Poor little Henry. His only caregiver was pretty hopeless, but she was all he had. What do you think he would be like when he grew up? Do you think he would be a secure, self confident little boy, who valued his own worth, or would he be insecure with low self-esteem? What about his role model for caring relationships? This should give you some idea how the nature of our early relationships give us a 'prototype' for our future. We learn patterns of behaviour, and he would be learning a very poor pattern. If Henry was to have a loving and caring father or even grandparents who he spent lots of time with they would teach him the other side of relationships. But if his mum was all he had, his prognosis would be pretty poor.

At this point, I am sure that you realise 'mother' is perhaps not the key person after all, but that it is essential for children to have a good relationship with *someone*. What we will look at next is evidence which supports the idea that it is the nature of the child's relationships which seems to be most important, no matter who that relationship is formed with. It has been shown on numerous occasions that children who are looked after by people who are sensitive and responsive to their needs form much more secure attachments with their caregivers. This leads to them being rated as more popular by their peers, showing leadership qualities, showing more initiative, being less aggressive and having higher self-esteem than children with insecure attachments.

The child with a rejecting carer, like Henry, will end up with a poor self image that suggests they are unacceptable and unworthy. This would come from the idea that if they had been better, nicer or more intelligent they would not have been rejected. Children with carers who are inconsistent will also have a negative self-image and will probably be attention-seeking in their behaviour as a way of getting some kind of recognition. This ties in with children with behaviour problems, who are always naughty as a way of gaining attention from parents.

Michael Rutter

Michael Rutter is probably one of the most well known critics of Bowlby, although he points out that Bowlby's writings are often misinterpreted. The idea that mother and mother alone should provide 24 hour care for her child, and any less than this would not be good enough, was never actually suggested by Bowlby although many people believed this was what he was saying. In fact Bowlby mellowed in later years and agreed that 'mother' may not be the most important person in some relationships after all because children who formed a strong relationship with someone (be they father, nanny or whoever) often matured with no long term problems. However, citing evidence from people such as Schaffer and Emmerson (1964) and Schaffer (1971), Rutter makes the point that it is the nature of the relationship which is the most important factor. He also goes on to say that a child does not necessarily need one caregiver, although it seems that the attachments may be stronger if there are less rather than more. This would make sense, because if a child is with lots of different people who are all attentive, it is hard to like one of them more than the others. Think about it – if you have lots of friends, you don't have enough time to spend with all of them, and so often you don't have a special friend because you don't get to know one more than all the rest.

Perhaps the most important argument that Rutter makes is that many children who have lost their mothers as a result of death do not suffer the long term effects suggested by Bowlby. He says that it is more likely to be the type of arguments and bad feelings going on in families which will affect the child. If the child is part of a family where the parents are separating or divorcing, the arguments and atmospheres will frighten the children. They will probably not really understand what all the arguments are about, and may end up thinking that it is their fault that the parents have split up. It is very common for young children, who do not have the situation explained to them because they are too young, to try and make sense of it for themselves. Perhaps one parent has been unfaithful but they are unlikely to go into details in front of small children. The child may then attribute the break up to the fact that they were naughty or didn't work hard enough at school.

Rutter (1970) studied boys between the ages of nine and twelve and looked into their backgrounds. Several had been separated from their mothers when they were little but seemed to have adjusted well and appeared to have overcome the earlier problems. However, as they became older some of them again seemed to be quite disturbed, and Rutter wondered what it was that had caused the differences in the two groups who had supposedly had the same early experiences.

The children who showed long term effects seemed to have a different pattern of reasons for the earlier disruption. The reasons their families broke up seemed to be reasons the child found hard to understand, such as psychiatric illness or acrimonious divorces. The children who did not suffer later problems had reasons that were more concrete such as physical illnesses or even death, problems with housing or even parental holidays. None of these involved a disturbance of the social relationships involved, so again we return to the fact that it is the relationship that is important, rather than mother herself.

Rutter (1981) also pointed out that we should be aware that there are different types of 'carer-deprivation' which the child may experience, and these types will also influence the way the child handles the situation.

- Deprivation is where you have had something which you later have taken away from you which is obviously going to cause pain, but may be overcome.
- Privation is when you never had it in the first place so it is likely that you will suffer from lack of any emotional experiences.
- Distortion is where there is stress caused by emotional upheavals such as divorce or mental illness and this is likely to result in more long term effects.
- Disruption is where there may be separation caused by an event but later the original situation will be reinstated (mother going into hospital but later coming home and family returning to normal). It may also mean that the original family situation may be superseded by another family situation (mother dies and father remarries). The most important factor is that even if the disruption seemed really horrific at the time, if the new situation is good, it will result in minimal, if any, long term effects.

If we now accept that it is the quality of the child's relationships and the nature of any break up which is going to cause problems for the child, we can probably also accept that the relationship does not even have to be with an adult. After all, how many times have you paired up with your brother or sister when your parents give you a hard time. It seems to make it more bearable if you have someone to support you in times of adversity, even if both of you are children.

Anna Freud and Sophie Dann (1951) showed that as long as you have an attachment figure, it doesn't have to be an adult. They studied six German-Jewish orphans who were rescued from a concentration camp when the second world war ended. They were all orphans having lost their parents when they were a few months old. But they had been kept together through the war, and were cared for by camp inmates who were never around for very long. You can imagine the kind of experiences they must have had, and how frightened they must have been. The war ended when they were three and they were flown to a place called Bulldogs Bank in the Lake District where they were kept until five out of the six of them were adopted.

When they first arrived, they were virtually inseparable and totally dependent on each other. They were also resistant to forming relationships with the adults at the institution so if anyone was going to be disturbed and have problems in later years, then this group should have been the worst. However, over time they began to relate to the centre's adult caregivers, and formed attachments to them. Although they had all experienced maternal deprivation none of them turned into criminals, and most of them married and had children of their own. To say they had come through the experience unscathed would be too much to hope for. Many of them still had fragments of memories which would come to them from time to time, causing nightmares or irrational fears of places like hospitals or institutions but it is evident that their early experiences influenced their behaviour in later life.

It does seem that these six children's relationships with each other helped them to cope with most of their early experiences, and it certainly seems likely that they were better off with each other, even if they were all children, than if they had been put into some kind of home where the quality of relationships was very poor and uncaring. We mustn't forget that we **do** learn from early experiences and, as we have seen, one of the most important things we learn is about how to have relationships with other people. The thing is that we also learn from later experiences. In fact lots of the studies which were carried out over a number of years failed to show any consistency in the long term effects, probably because they didn't take into account that other things besides the first few years can have an effect on children.

We also have to bear in mind that the age of the child when they first experienced the separation will be quite relevant. If you take a baby who is a month old, not only will it not realise what time of day it is, it will also likely have little preference for who actually looks after it, as long as it is taken care of. On the other hand, a two year old will know exactly what is going on. It would make sense to suggest that children who are old enough to know what is going on, and who have suffered long term emotional deprivation, will probably develop some long term consequences unless those deprivations are addressed.

However, if a child is put into a loving home, even if it is not the biological home, and made to feel of value and importance, it would therefore seem likely that they will develop into a well balanced adult with high self esteem. On the other hand, if they are not made to feel of value, they are likely to become attention seeking and manipulative as a way of making themselves feel better. They will not have learned appropriate behaviours and may become too familiar with people in charge rather than associating with their peers, because they don't know how to form 'normal' relationships. This may also spin off into

J. Hodges and B. Tizard (1989) Social and family relationships of ex-institutional adolescents.

Journal of Child Psychology and Psychiatry, 30, 77–97

The aim of the study was to investigate whether children who had been placed in institutions before they were four months old, and who remained there until the age of two, would experience long term problems in their social relationships as suggested by Bowlby.

Sixty five children were assessed initially at the age of two having been in the institution for over a year. They were assessed again at the age of four, then 51 of them when they were aged eight. The final part of the study was intended to assess the remaining children now aged 16, who were still in contact with the researchers, to look for long term effects of their early experiences.

Design

The study was part of a longitudinal investigation, and formed a kind of quasi experiment where children who were already categorised by circumstances were compared with each other.

Subjects

All the children in the groups were aged 16.
Adopted children: 23 (17 boys and 6 girls)
(Note: 31 of these 34 children participated in this part of the study and are referred to as ex-institutionalised)
Restored children: 11 (6 boys and 5 girls)
Institutionalised children: 5 (3 boys and 2 girls) who were interviewed but do not feature in the results.

Control group 1: Children who had continually been with their families were matched for sex, whether a one or two parent family, occupation of main breadwinner and position in family with the adopted and restored groups. (Note that 30% of these control families included families who had problems rearing their children.)

Control group 2: In order to assess the information obtained from the schools, a second group who had continually been with their families was used comprising friends who were the same age and sex.

Procedure

The data was collected using a number of different methods.

1. Interview with subjects (recorded).
2. Interview with one or both parents or care workers (recorded).
3. The parent or care worker completed a questionnaire about the subjects behaviour.
4. The subject completed a questionnaire on 'social difficulty' which looked at how well they got on in social relationships.
5. Teachers were asked to complete a postal questionnaire containing the Rutter 'B' scale which screened for any sort of psychiatric disorder.
6. The teachers also completed two questionnaires, one about how the subject got on with their teachers and peers and the same questionnaire about their same-sex classmate.

Results

The results included data on a number of areas:

Attachment to parents

- Adopted adolescents were just as attached to their parents as the control group.
- Restored adolescents were less attached to their parents than adopted group and control group.

Relationships with siblings

- Ex-institutionalised adolescents, especially the restored group had more problems with siblings than the control group.

Showing affection

- Control group was the most affectionate towards their parents, then the adopted group, and the restored group were considerably less affectionate.

Confiding and supporting

- No difference in both confiding in parents and support from parents between ex-institutionalised adolescents and controls, although restored mothers felt less certain that their children were willing to turn to them for advice.

Disagreements over control and discipline

- Fewer disagreements between the control group and their families than all the ex-institutionalised adolescents. Of the ex-institutionalised, the restored group had the most disagreements.
- Disagreements about staying out, homework, helping round the house and pocket money was much less in adoptive families.

Peer relationships These were judged from the point of view of the adolescent, their mothers and their teacher).

- Ex-institutionalised adolescents had poor peer relations than controls and were said to be less choosy about who they were friendly with.
- Ex-institutionalised adolescents compared to controls, said they were less likely to belong to a group or crowd of friends.
- Ex-institutionalised adolescents were less likely to confide in peers than controls
- Teachers said the ex-institutionalised were more often argumentative, less popular and more likely to bully others than the controls.

Special friends

- According to mothers, ex-institutionalised adolescents were less likely to have a special friend than comparisons.

Over-friendly behaviour

- According to parents, ex-institutionalised adolescents were less likely to be selective when choosing their friends and would make friends with anyone.

Relationships to teachers

- Teachers believed the ex-institutionalised were more attention seeking compared with control group 1 but not control group 2.
- The restored group were seen by teachers as being more aggressive.

In summary, all the ex-institutionalised children showed differences in peer and adult relationships outside the home compared with control groups. However, the most relevant finding was that the restored group had worse family relationships than the other groups, were less attached to mother, showed less affection to both mother and father, identified less with parents and had problems getting on with siblings.

Discussion

The causes of the problems experienced by the ex-institutionalised children could be put down to the number of caregivers they had while they were in institutions and the fact that they were unable to form any long term bonds in what are considered the most critical years. However, this explanation is possibly too simplistic as the results were not the same for all children.

All the ex-institutionalised children seemed to have problems with later relationships, but the results indicate that the restored group came off worse within their families, possibly due to a sense of betrayal and desertion – after all, they must have questioned why they were 'sent away' when they were tiny. The study doesn't explain the reasons why the adolescents were taken into institutions to start with and this may have had some kind of effect on the long-term consequences to the adolescents. We also don't know why some children were restored while others were adopted and whether this actually had anything to do with the nature of the child (Hodges and Tizard state that there were no evidence of differences in the children).

The study did indicate that there were a number of differences between the groups of children, but it also showed that maternal deprivation does not always lead to long-term irreversible effects because many of the adopted children showed no effects of their early experiences. However, others did and two of the adoptive placements had failed.

In this study the adoptive parents were very different from the restored parents because they wanted the child whereas the restored parents were often indifferent. The adoptive parents also made a lot of effort to make the relationship work, had more resources and were accepting of a high level of dependency from the adopted child at the beginning of the relationship in comparison with the restored parents. This may well have been the explanation for many of the differences that appeared between the groups. Also, four of the restored group had demonstrated emotional or behavioural problems and spent time in residential units, although three of those had been returned to their families.

Evaluation

Longitudinal studies suffer with subject attrition. The original study had 65 subjects and yet in this final part there were only 39. Some of the children from each group were unavailable or unwilling to take part in this follow up study – why was this? This should make us question whether this final sample was actually representative of the original group.

There were problems with the methodology because questionnaires are only as accurate as the answers given. Although they were given to both the children and their caregivers there is no guarantee that they were really objective. One explanation for the reports made by teachers would be that they had little knowledge or understanding of their early experiences of the children, and therefore saw any sort of unusual behaviour as being unacceptable rather than understandable and would thus judge it more harshly.

The control group included 30% who had family problems and these may have confounded the results in some way. This was because of a lack of families willing to take part in the study.
Finally, the study ended when the children were 16 and therefore did not indicate what happened to them when they reached adulthood or whether the earlier problems resolved themselves with age.

Key words

Longitudinal study – a study carried out over a long period of time, often years.
Subject attrition – the loss of subjects which often occurs in a longitudinal study. This may be caused by subjects moving away or no longer wanting to take part for whatever reason. Remember the ethics of any research allow for subjects having the right to withdraw at any time.
Peers – friends
Siblings – brothers and sisters

Key questions

1. What was the purpose of the control groups?
2. Why is subject attrition a problem in longitudinal studies?
3. Give reasons why the restored group had the most problems getting on with family members?
4. Why do you think the ex-institutionalised adolescents were more attention-seeking with adults?
5. Do you think the results of early institutionalisation can be overcome and why?

The weird and wonderful world of Sigmund Freud

One evening, when I was talking to prospective students about the topics that were covered in the college course, I happened to mention Freud. One student had brought a friend with him to look around. I realised that the friend was obviously studying something to do with psychology at another institution because I overheard him say, 'Yeah, I know who Freud is. He's the one that reckons we all want to have sex with our mothers. He must've been havin' a larf – I don't fancy mine at all!'

I must admit, I found it very hard to bite my tongue because although I think that Freud certainly had some very strange ideas, his original motives were actually very honourable. He was the first person to bring to the public attention the fact that we are actually influenced by things we are not always aware of and if for no other reason he must be thanked for that.

Sigmund Freud (1856–1939)

feelings, accompanied by a related set of behaviour patterns' (Berne, 1964) seem to correspond to the id, the superego and the ego. If someone makes you feel small and useless, it is probably their parent that is interacting with your child, neither of which are rational. Have you ever felt like that with another person – it is usually so irrational because you tell yourself that they are no better than you, but you end up going into this kind of 'role' and it affects the way you feel and consequently how you respond.

If you try to reason with someone or offer some kind of support but they respond in a stupid, childlike way, then you are probably using your adult and they are responding with their child. The best and most desired way to interact with another person is adult to adult and Berne's strategy is to try to get people to identify the way they interact with others as a way of dealing with the problems they face in their lives.

Here is an example of two interactions, the first as adult/adult:

> 'Do you know where my calculator is?'
> 'Where did you have it last?'

And the second, parent/child:

> 'Do you know where my calculator is?'
> 'You always blame me for everything.'

Berne's theories have been used as a basis for counselling therapy which focuses specifically on interpersonal relationships.

Freud's developmental theory

Freud's theory is called a psychodynamic theory because he claimed that there are psychological forces (*psycho*) that move or drive us forwards (*dynamic*) to do things – these forces are innate. As we have mentioned, the forces he is talking about are instincts and Freud identified two instinctive driving forces. The first is known as Eros, the life instinct, whose main active component is the sexual drive or libido. The second is Thanatos, the death instinct, and its main active component is aggression both to ourselves and to others. Freud initially ignored the aggressive instinct, but found it hard to explain the dreadful loss of life and carnage of the First World War, and so he later incorporated Thanatos as a representation of our innate destructiveness and aggression.

Freud believed that the development of a child's personality is based on these biological drives and the drives evolve through a number of biologically determined stages. He believed that the strongest drive was the libido or sexual instinct and he maintained that babies and young children are capable of sexual pleasure. I think the word 'sexual' is too strong here, and that we should substitute it for 'sensual' because he was referring to physical pleasure from any area of the body rather than simply the genitals, which is what we as adults tend to think of as sexual pleasure. In fact we are wrong, because even sexual pleasure can come from other areas of the body besides genital stimulation!

Oral stage (0–15 months)

The first stage is the oral stage because the main area of sensitivity and pleasure are the lips and mouth. The baby gets great pleasure in two ways from putting things in its mouth, even when it isn't feeding. One way is by sucking and swallowing and the other is from biting and chewing. According to Freud, if the child's desires are satisfied and they are not left to cry for hours on end without food, and they are weaned at the right time, they will be fine. If however they are weaned at the wrong time, they will become '**orally fixated**' which means as adults they will have an excessive interest in oral gratification. They will either become compulsive eaters, drinkers or smokers, or constantly chew things like gum, pens and fingernails. If they get excessive amounts of pleasure from sucking and swallowing, they will become too trusting and gullible and easily fooled whereas if they enjoyed biting and chewing more they would become sarcastic and verbally aggressive. In fact Freud believed that they even become incapable of personal love for other people, with a tendency to treat people as objects to be used to fulfil their needs.

The evidence to support this stage is somewhat sparse! Kline and Storey (1977) found evidence for two different types of oral characters. The first group showed a cluster of traits which could be called oral optimism; sociability, dependability and a relaxed nature. The other group showed a different cluster called oral pessimism; independence, verbal aggression, envy, hostility, ambition and impatience. What we have to remember here is that we can never be sure whether they were a result of their oral experiences or something completely different!

Anal stage (1 to 3 years)

In this second stage, the sensitive area shifts from the mouth to the anus. Apparently the child now derives great pleasure from either expelling or retaining faeces. Although this seems somewhat weird, many children do have a fascination with their poos and often, when they first manage to go in a potty, will express interest and pleasure in what they have done. In fact some children seem to develop a fascination with poos in general!

When my children were little and I was into the round of things like playschool with friends who had children of the same age, I had a friend called Alison whose daughter developed a very strong fascination with her bodily functions when she began to use the potty. Every time she went, she used to stand up and point proudly at the offending item saying things like, "I did that, aren't I a clever girl." Of course we all praised her, as you do.

The thing was, her preoccupation with bowel habits broadened to not only other people, but also animals (at this point, I began to wonder how broadminded one should be). Whenever they came to visit, she used to spend all her time watching my Old English sheepdog either in the garden or out of the window. I think part of the reason for her interest was because the dog went through a kind of ritual whenever she wanted to defecate. She would walk round and round and round in circles for quite a while until she was ready, and then would produce the offending item. The minute the dog had finished her business, Anna, the little girl in question, would want to rush out and look at what she had done.

Anna was one of these children who went on and on asking questions, the classic being 'WHY?' to just about everything you said to her. On this particular day, the question 'Why?' had been flogged to death already when she noticed Josephine starting her ritual poo-dance. Then the inevitable question came, "Why is the doggie doing that?" My instant thought was "Go away," but I thought I had better give her a reasonable answer because if I didn't I had visions of her doing the same, walking round and round her potty for about five minutes before she sat down!

"Making a nest Anna," I replied. To be honest I wasn't quite sure why she did it either, and this was the first acceptable thought that came into my head. From that minute onwards, the ritual became known as making a nest and as is normal in language development, Anna generalised (or overextended) the name to anyone pooing, animals and humans alike and we found it quite amusing but really disregarded it as being something she would grow out of.

About a month or so after the nesting event, my daughter and Anna started Nursery School together. We went to pick them up at lunchtime and as we walked into the school the teacher approached us and turning to my friend said, "Mrs. Jenkins, Anna has been saying something very strange this morning, She keeps saying she wants to make a nest."

During this stage, as we have already mentioned, the child is potty trained whereas before they could go where they liked, discreetly protected by the gentle comfort of freshly washed nappies! Now the child learns that in order to get praise from its parents it has to behave in a certain way. No longer can it 'do as it pleases'. This may well be the first type of condition that will have been put on its behaviour and it learns that there is a huge significance to defecating.

Therefore, if the parents are very strict and over-anxious about its bowel habits, the child will become almost too worried and frightened about going, and therefore will become an 'anal retentive'. Here the child will associate the normal functioning with messiness and dirt and may become preoccupied with orderliness and cleanliness as a reaction. Freud claims that this trait will continue as it gets older and it will become an adult who, instead of holding onto its faeces, will hold on to its possessions instead – in effect, a miser or a hoarder, or a collector of some kind.

On the other hand, if the parents are extremely laid back and perhaps over lenient about the child's ability to use the potty, the child will drop them anywhere so to speak! This child will become an 'anal expulsive', who will grow up to be over-generous, untidy and completely indifferent to material possessions.

Again, these collections of traits are often found together and provide some support for his analysis, but the explanations he gives as to why they cluster together have received very little support.

Phallic stage (3 to 5 years)

Freud claims that the area of sensuality shifts from the anus to the genitals when the child reaches the age of about three. This is the time when children play with their 'bits' and become inquisitive as to the differences between little boys and little girls. One of my earliest memories was one little girl at nursery school saying something to me about how clever little boys were, they way they could wee up in the air. This provoked a deputation of small girls to watch this stunning feat at the next opportunity! It is also quite normal to see small boys with their hands tucked down the front of their trousers at this age, and I suppose you could say that this lends support to Freud's ideas. The thing is, fascination and comfort (which is the main reason why most little boys hold onto their 'bits') are not necessarily the same as sexual interest.

It is during this stage that Freud believes that the awareness of sex differences form the basis of what he calls the 'Oedipus complex'. He claimed that girls feel inferior to or jealous of boys because they have a penis, and that boys believe that because girls don't have a penis, they must have been castrated. During this stage, children also have intense emotions, usually directed at the parent of the opposite sex. (I have to say that the only time I have ever envied boys having a penis has been when I have been out walking, on a cold day, and have wanted to wee! I have also asked a number of males if they believed that girls were really castrated boys, and they have all said that the thought never entered their heads – although Freud would say that they were repressing their memories so of course they would not be able to recollect the idea.)

Before we talk about the Oedipus Complex, I think it might be useful to explain who Oedipus was to those of you who are not into Greek mythology. Oedipus was the mythical son of the King of Thebes, but an oracle prophesied that Oedipus would kill his father and in order to prevent this happening his father ordered him to be put to death. He was rescued by a shepherd and brought up, unaware of his identity. One day, when he was on the road to Thebes, he quarrelled with a man and accidentally killed him, not realising that this man was his father. He was made King of Thebes as a result of an act of bravery against a mythical creature called the Sphinx, and subsequently married Jocasta, not realising that she was his mother. When he found out who she was, he gouged out his eyes.

As a result of this relationship between Oedipus and his mother, Freud coined the term 'Oedipus complex' to describe the situation which occurs when boys develop a short of intense attachment to their mothers.

It often occurs that little boys become quite clingy to their mothers at this age, and often girls to their fathers, but we will stick with small boys for the moment. Freud believed that this attachment becomes increasingly intense and causes the boys to regard their fathers as a rival, especially as Father sleeps with mother and has the closeness and familiarity with her that the boy would like. However, the boy also sees his father as a powerful and threatening figure who has the ultimate power to deal with this rivalry – namely to castrate him (after all think of the girls!). The small boy is caught at this point between desire for his mother and fear of his father's power.

What we must remember here is that the boy does not have real sexual feelings that we know about as adults. Most of his feelings are unconscious and therefore cause a kind of internal conflict or anxiety which the small boy has to deal with. Anxiety is an unpleasant state and we strive for much of our lives to find ways to reduce our feelings of anxiety, no matter how they are caused. Therefore Freud claims that the boy deals with it by using a defensive process

Oedipus and his mother, Jocasta, in Pasolini's 'Oedipus Rex'.

called sex role identification. The boy will start to identify with his father and repress any further feelings he has for his mother into his unconscious. He will begin to spend more time with his father, wanting to be like daddy, and this in turn will reduce any further chance of being castrated as his father will no longer see him as a rival. Through this process he will internalise his father's moral standards and this is the core of the child's superego.

So what about girls? The 'Electra Complex' is the supposed female equivalent which occurs in girls between the ages of three to six and is manifest by the excessive attachment of little girls to their fathers and corresponding hostility to their mothers. The term 'Electra complex' also comes from Greek mythology. Electra, the daughter of the Greek leader Agamenmon, was famous for the devotion and loyalty to her father until he was murdered by her mother and her mother's lover. In order to avenge the death of her beloved father, Electra with her younger brother's help, murdered the mother she detested and also the lover.

The problem was that Freud hadn't clearly worked out the female side of this developmental process, probably because he found women puzzling throughout his life. The course of the Electra Complex goes something like this: the girl will be very close to her mother when she is little until she discovers that she doesn't have a penis. This makes her feel inferior and she will blame her mother for allowing her to be castrated. She does realise that one way she can feel equal to men is by producing a baby (and this is all at three plus years of age!) and so she sees her father as a potential impregnator to allow her to have a child of her own as a substitute for the missing penis. She will therefore transfer her affections from the mother to the father.

Why this happens is the main problem with the Electra Complex. Boys renounce their feelings for their mother because of the fear of castration by father, but this can't be the case with girls who had already been 'castrated' by their mothers. Freud suggested that males do feel that their penis is the thing that they value most in the world but the thing that girls value is loss of love. If the girl continues with her desire to have a relationship with her father she is likely to lose the love of her mother, so she will renounce her feelings for her father and do her best to make her mother love her by being a good girl. The problem is, the fear on the girl's part, would be far less (according to Freud) than the boys fear and this led him to suggest that girls will have a much less developed superego.

Latency stage (around 5 years to puberty)

The sexual drives seem to be removed from consciousness during the latency stage although they are still there. According to Freud the child has repressed its memories of the earlier sexual impulses by a phenomenon called 'infantile amnesia'. The child redirects the drives into intellectual development and social activities as it learns about the world beyond the family. The friendships it makes tend to be with children of the same sex, which helps the child deal with any possible sexual thoughts. The problem with this idea is that children from other cultures where sexual activity through childhood is seen as acceptable show interest in sexual matters throughout childhood.

Genital stage (puberty onwards)

With puberty, there is a re-emergence of the earlier drives and the centre of attention is again the genitals, although this time an adult expression of sexuality is shown through relationships with members of the opposite sex.

Freud's developmental theory has been challenged and criticised by many researchers who claim that the theory is untestable. There is evidence from cross-cultural studies that children who are brought up with extended families show no problems with morals or sex role development. If Freud was right, having a father (if you are a boy) is a prerequisite to developing morals, superego, appropriate sex role behaviour etc. What happens to orphans and boys from single parent families? He also claimed that the first five years of life are the most critical but this implies that the next 80 odd are actually irrelevant.

Now we have been through the stages, you may wonder why these stages are so relevant? Freud believed that if an adult suffers from any kind of neurosis, it can be traced back to their progression through the stages of development. The poor old adult will either have unresolved problems due to lack of gratification or, on the other hand, will have achieved excessive gratification – both being a result of the parental treatment they received. What then happens is that the child will become fixated at one of these stages either because they have enjoyed it too much, or because they have been deprived of what they really wanted. If they enjoyed it too much, they won't want to leave the stage they are in. If they have been deprived, they want to stay in the stage for a bit longer in order to achieve the level of gratification or satisfaction that they desire. Obviously this put a tremendous amount of pressure on mothers who were frightened of over- or under-feeding, or who over- or under-stressed the importance of potty training. The problem was, Freud gave no guidelines as to what the 'right' amount actually was!

The other possibility could be that something has happened to them during their lives that they have found distressing. For example, they may have had an experience they found unacceptable or very hurtful (such as rejection by a parent, or even sexual abuse) or they have done something very wicked or unpleasant (hurt or abused or murdered someone else). It may not be that enormous, because even having unpleasant or unacceptable thoughts can be tremendously upsetting to some people because they feel disgusted that they could even contemplate such horrendous ideas (remember Anna O). Whatever the cause, their ego will have stepped in and dealt with the situation either by projecting the feelings onto something else more acceptable (such as developing a phobia about a related object), or by repressing the memory into the unconscious in order to protect the person. This may then result in the person developing an anxiety or panic attacks when they experience a situation which reminds them of the thing they are trying to forget. The situation may also affect their behaviour, for example they may become obsessive about certain things but not understand why. Only if that feeling is brought into conscious awareness can the person deal with the situation.

I once heard a true story about a man called Maurice. Maurice had been referred to a psychiatrist as he was suffering from 'obsessive compulsive' behaviour. Obsessive compulsive behaviour means that you have intrusive thoughts which are the obsessions and the compulsion to keep doing certain things. Most people have small compulsions like going and checking if you have shut the door or turned off the gas but Maurice's compulsion was getting the better of him.

'Well Maurice, tell me what seems to be the matter,' said the psychiatrist.

'I can't seem to get out of the house in the morning, I have to keep going back to the bathroom to make sure that the towel is hung straight on the door.'

'Why?'

'I don't know, I just hang it up there, over the hook behind the door. I make sure it is straight and both sides are of equal length, and then I close the door very carefully before I go out.'

'Mmmmm,' hummed the psychiatrist.

'I seem to get as far as the bottom of the stairs and I suddenly need to go back and check if it is still there, so I open the door again, and hang it up again on the hook. It's getting so silly that I do it for anything up to two hours, up and down, back and forward. I get so worried it's slipped that I just have to go and look again.'

'Has it ever slipped?'

'No, but it might, so I have to go and check.'

The psychiatrist looked perplexed. After several hours of therapy with Maurice, he discovered that this whole activity was actually nothing really to do with the towel as such. Maurice was about 45 and lived with his ageing mother, who was a bossy old bag and wouldn't let him do anything. In fact he felt totally trapped living with her and secretly wished she would simply drop dead (although he would never have admitted it). One night, while he lay in his bed with his hot water bottle, teddy bear and cocoa, he started to daydream. Apparently he had imagined that she had gone to the bathroom and tried to push the door open, but the towel had fallen off the back of the door and was stopping the door from opening. She pushed and shoved and pushed harder until the door flew open unexpectedly and she fell through the door head first, bashing her head on the loo (which was opposite the door), cracked her skull and died. Of course this was too awful to contemplate and he felt absolutely mortified that he could think of such a dreadful event, so rather than live with the guilt his ego had pushed the memory out of his conscious awareness and he therefore had no idea why he had this bizarre behaviour. Once he had admitted it to the therapist, the obsession and compulsive behaviour seemed to subside.

So here you can see how the unconscious can affect our behaviour.

Perhaps you can now understand the basis of psychoanalysis, which developed from Freud's theories and involved gaining access to this unconscious part of the mind in order to resolve repressed conflicts. It is done by using techniques such as hypnosis, the analysis of dreams and free association – talking about anything that comes into the head. All of them require the patient to be relaxed enough to be able to speak openly and honestly to the therapist. The problem is, who knows whether they are being honest or not. Perhaps the reason why psychoanalysis is so popular is simply that the client actually enjoys the undivided attention of the therapist, and it's also quite fashionable to have a therapist.

Does it work? Although psychoanalysis has been used throughout this century, psychoanalysts have been reluctant to investigate whether they really did help people with their treatment (and the only people who would be able to judge the effectiveness of psychoanalysis are psychoanalysts as no one else would understand what they were getting at and how they operated). Eysenck (1950s) reviewed 24 studies on the effectiveness of psychoanalysis and concluded that the 'improvement' rate for psychoanalysis was 44 per cent, for mixed therapies was 64 per cent and for spontaneous remission was 66 per cent. So psychoanalytic treatment was actually worse than no treatment at all.

The key study is relevant here because it is one of only six accounts of individual patients out of 133 cases mentioned in Freud's collected works. Four were personally analysed by Freud (Dora who had had advances made to her by a friend of her fathers, the obsessional 'Rat Man' whose main fear was being eaten alive by rats, an unnamed female homosexual aged eighteen and 'Wolf Man' who was petrified of wolves). The others are the case of Judge Schreber, who Freud never saw, and Little Hans, the focus of our key study.

It is the report of a little boy who was the only child Freud ever had any dealings with; it formed the basis of much of Freud's ideas about child development. He was the five year old child of a friend of Freud's who had developed a phobia towards horses, but Freud reinterpreted this fear of horses and claimed that it was really a fear of his father (something to do with castration). Most of the diagnosis and treatment was carried out by letter between Freud and the boy's father, Freud only ever meeting the small boy on one occasion.

S. Freud (1909) Analysis of a phobia in a five-year-old boy.

In The Pelican Freud Library (1977), Vol 8, Case Histories 1, pp. 169–306.

The aim of this case study is to document the case of Little Hans who was suffering from anxiety which led to a phobia. It was also used by Freud to support his ideas about the origins of phobias and the fact that they are often influenced by unconscious forces. He also used it to support his ideas on psychosexual development and the Oedipus complex, and the effectiveness of psychoanalytic therapy.

Design

This case study was actually conducted by Little Hans' father, a friend and supporter of Freud who only met the boy on one occasion. The father reported on the boy's behaviour via correspondence (including his own interpretations) and Freud gave directions as to how to deal with the situation based on his interpretations of the father's reports. Freud believed that the reason the analysis could progress using this kind of method was because the father and son had a very special and close relationship with each other.

Introduction

In the introduction which formed the background to the study, Freud talked about Little Hans and the origins of the case study. He acknowledged that Hans was not a normal child and had a predisposition to neurosis so he realised that it might not necessarily be valid to generalise from him to all children. He also said that the argument that children are untrustworthy was unfair. Adults are untrustworthy because they are prejudiced and this might influence what they say. Children on the other hand may lie but they lie for a reason and this reason may well be one of the most important things to consider.

Hans was described as being a cheerful and straightforward child but when he became 'ill' (by this Freud meant that he developed his phobia) it was obvious that there was a difference in what he said and what he actually thought. Freud suggested that this was because of things that were going on in his unconscious of which he was unaware. In order to put this right, Freud decided that Hans' behaviour had to be interpreted and he had to be told why he was thinking and acting as he was. Freud was emphatic that this was not putting suggestions into the boy's mind but was only a way of helping him understand what already existed.

The first information which Freud thought was interesting was Hans' interest in his 'widdler' (penis) when he was three years old. He thought everyone had a widdler, males and females alike, and the only things that didn't have widdlers were inanimate objects. He even thought his baby sister Hanna, who arrived 'by stork' when he was three and a half, hadn't grown hers yet. (Small children around this time were told that storks brought babies rather than explaining where they really came from.) In fact Hans liked playing with his widdler, which is quite normal for small boys, but his mother told him that if he carried on playing with himself she would call the doctor to cut it off. He obviously found this somewhat disturbing but was still sexually curious, so he tried to see other people's widdlers and liked showing his off. He even said to his parents that he wanted to see theirs and Freud explained that this was probably because he wanted to see how theirs compared to his. Hans thought his mother must have a widdler 'like a horse' and presumably thought that as he got bigger his would grow too. In fact, much of the focus of his dreams and fantasies during this time was widdlers and what they do.

Hans wanted his father 'out of the way' so he could have his mother to himself and sleep with her. This idea had come from spending lots of time with her when his father was away one summer. He had become apprehensive and nervous about things and had been comforted by his mother who cuddled him in bed. He enjoyed her attention and probably resented having to 'share her' on his father's return. In fact Freud believed that he attempted to seduce his mother when he was four and a half by asking her why she wouldn't put her finger on his penis when she was putting talcum powder on him after a bath. She answered that it was not proper, but according to Freud he had 'found an incidental channel of discharge' for his sexual feelings towards her and this resulted in his 'masturbating every evening, and in that way obtaining gratification.'

Freud claimed that Hans feared that another baby might come (more competition?) but suppressed his anxiety which surfaced in another form – in a fear of the bath. Hans had said he was worried about drowning in the big bath having previously been bathed in a baby bath. Freud suggests this fear comes from being frightened that if he was naughty his mother wouldn't love him anymore and therefore might let him drown. Hans also expressed jealousy towards his sister and he asked Hans the following question. 'When you were watching Mummy giving Hanna her bath, perhaps you wished she would let go of her so that Hanna should fall in?' Hans answered yes to this question which confirmed Freud's idea that this was evidence of his death wish towards Hanna.

Case history

Hans' father wrote to Freud describing the fact that Hans had developed an irrational fear that a horse would bite him in the street, and that the fear was in some way connected with his having been frightened by a large penis. Father believed that this was the onset of the illness, and that there was a motive for being ill – he wanted to stay with his mother and never be separated from her, which was the result of a dream where his mother had gone away. This irrational fear probably developed from two events, overhearing a father say to his child 'Don't put your finger to the white horse or it will bite you,' and seeing a horse pulling a carriage fall down and flay about in the road. It affected Hans sufficiently to make him fear that a horse would come into the room. Freud suggested that there was a connection between putting a finger towards the horse that may actually be bitten and the event when his mother wouldn't touch his penis with her finger after giving him a bath. This connection had something to do with Hans' knowledge that his parents thought masturbation was not a very good behaviour to indulge in. In fact, Hans' father said to him 'If you don't put your hand to your widdler any more, this nonsense of yours will soon get better'.

Freud also suggested that Hans' desire to see his mother's widdler was increasing. At this point, his father told him that women didn't have widdlers. Hans may have made the association between his mother's threat to castrate him if he didn't stop playing with his bits and her lack of widdler. Perhaps she was in fact a castrated man who had played with hers too much in the past and had suffered the consequences!

Freud began to make the connection between Hans' father and Hans' fear of horses, and started to think that the fear was simply of father which had been projected onto horses. This happened as a result of a daydream of Hans about two giraffes: a big one and a crumpled one. Hans took the crumpled one away from the big one and after a while the big one stopped calling out for it. This fantasy was recognised by father as a re-enactment of what happened in the morning when Hans climbed into bed with his parents. Often his father objected and Freud believed that he was represented by the big giraffe who was calling because Hans had taken the little giraffe (mother) away. There was also some discussion about whether the long neck of the giraffe represented a penis but this was denied by Hans.

At this point, Freud saw Hans and asked him about his fear of horses. He suggested that the horse must represent his father because Hans must be frightened of his father because he was jealous of him and felt hostile towards him. The reason why Freud made this analogy was because Hans mentioned the black on horses, mouths and the things in front of their eyes (blinkers). Hans father had a black moustache and wore glasses. Hans explained that he was also afraid of horses biting him, as well as carts and buses which was interpreted as having some kind of analogy with pregnancy. He then told Freud about seeing the bus horse fall down and kick about with its feet which terrified him because he thought the horse was dead and this led him to think that all horses would fall down. Hans' father suggested that when Hans saw the horse fall down he must have wished that his father would fall down and die in the same way. According to Freud, Hans' behaviour towards his father after this 'confession' became much less fearful and he was much more boisterous and overbearing. He did, however, still retain his fear of horses.

Hans then developed a preoccupation with his bowels and 'lumf' (German for faeces). He had been in the habit of accompanying his mother or the maid to the toilet until he was forbidden to do so. Father again recognised another analogy between a heavily loaded cart and a body loaded with faeces. Then Hans started to talk about Hanna and father concluded that the reason for the train of thought was because he thought his sister was lumf and was born in the same way as we produce lumf. This lead on to the analogy between loaded carts and pregnancy, horses falling over and giving birth. He then described an imaginary friend called Lodi who was called after 'saffalodi', a German sausage. This time father pointed out that the sausage looked like 'lumf'.

The final fantasies Hans produced at the end of his conflicts focused around plumbers and being a parent himself. The first involved a plumber who 'took away my behind with a pair of pincers and then gave me another, and then the same with my widdler.' Hans' father immediately interpreted this as the fact that they were replaced with bigger ones like his, which meant that Hans wanted to be like him. The second fantasy was that he was the father of his own children (his mother was now his wife) and his father was their grandfather. This was then the final piece of evidence that showed that the Oedipus conflict was the cause of Hans' problems, and that once he had acknowledged his desires towards his mother his problems would be resolved.

Freud's discussion

The discussion focuses on the fact that this study offers support for Freud's theory of sexuality. Support for the Oedipus complex:

- Hans was sexually aroused by his mother.
- He was jealous of his father's relationship with his mother and frightened of him (castration fear), symbolised by a fear of fingers being bitten by horses.
- He fantasised about taking mother from father (giraffe fantasy).
- He tried to seduce his mother by asking her to touch his widdler.
- He finally admitted he wanted to marry his mother
- Resolution came with wanting to be like his father (the plumber removing his widdler and behind and giving him a bigger one).

Discussion

Little Hans was the only child studied by Freud and Freud had already formulated his 'Oedipus' complex, before he met him, supporting the idea that the report was extremely biased. Hans was probably quite normal, but became 'phobic' about horses because of a traumatic event which may well have frightened any small boy. It is quite likely that his fear of horses was absolutely nothing to do with his father but that this idea was introduced and stuck in Hans' memory.

Freud believed that phobias are a result of hidden conflicts found in the unconscious mind and, as such, interpreted everything on that basis. His questioning of Hans can therefore be understood as a way of getting at the unconscious mind and trying to resolve what he saw as a potential cause of trouble for the boy as he got older. Hans agreement with many of the interpretations offered to him indicated to his father and Freud that they were correct in their beliefs about the origin of his phobia and the Oedipus complex. Hans' final fantasies about wanting to marry and have children with his mother was the final confirmation they needed.

Another way we could interpret the findings is that the boy' was suffering from what Bowlby called 'separation anxiety'. Hans' mother frequently made alarming threats to Hans to make him behave, such as beating him with a carpet beater. His fear of castration was founded on firm ground – after all his mother had threatened him when he wouldn't stop fiddling. She also threatened to leave the family which would have made him quite insecure, and consequently he may have become very possessive and clingy. Hans was actually kept away from his mother when Hanna was born, and this must have made the situation worse. Because he was frightened that she might leave him, he would have felt very angry and unhappy that she was the cause, so it would make sense that these feelings were directed towards her. However, it is not right to be fearful or angry with your mother, so he may have projected those feelings onto something else – horses. This idea is illustrated in the following conversation when Hans talked about a fantasy he had that he had taken a horse out of the stable:

Father: You took it out of the stables?
Hans: I took it out because I wanted to whip it.
Father: Which would you really like to beat – Mummy, Hanna or me?
Hans: Mummy.
Father: Why?
Hans: I should just like to beat her.
Father: When did you ever see someone beating their Mummy?
Hans: I've never seen anyone do it, never in all my life.
Father: And yet you'd just like to do it?
Hans: With a carpet beater.

Evaluation

We must remember that this case study was intended to support the Oedipus complex which replaced Freud's earlier 'Seduction theory'. The change from believing that the parent was responsible for child sexual abuse to suggesting that it was a fantasy in the mind of a child was, however, responsible for the resistance of society to acknowledge how widespread such abuse really was. Even if there was some overt physical evidence of abuse, such as a pregnancy, the child would be blamed. In this respect, it would have been better if Freud had stuck to his original ideas. Most of the evaluative points about the study are methodological:

- One of the biggest weaknesses of case studies is that contact with the subject over time may well lead to extreme subjectivity. This case study was even more subjective because the child was being 'treated' by his father (emotional involvement) who was a strong Freud supporter (biased) and his mother had been treated by Freud before her marriage (it would be interesting to know why she was treated).
- On the one hand, Freud suggested that children's memories were in fact quite accurate, but the next minute he was making some fairly stunning leaps by reinterpreting what Hans said to give it a different meaning! Perhaps Hans' memory was originally quite accurate but the likelihood of his father (and Freud) introducing new

interpretations may have affected his subsequent memory of events or clouded their interpretation. In fact the whole study brings new meaning to the idea of leading questions, for example the question asked by Hans' father 'When the horse fell down did you think of your daddy?'

- Perhaps some of the interpretations were because the father was preoccupied with matters sexual or physical. After all, father was the one who suggested that a German sausage looked like a lumf. In fact, Hans' mother and father divorced and both remarried somewhere between the time when Hans was 6 and 19 and he had gone to stay with father while his sister went with mother. Perhaps the relationship between father and mother was somewhat strained during the time when Hans became phobic and in fact father was projecting his own preoccupations onto Hans.
- Psychoanalysts claim that they cannot be judged by anyone except a psychoanalyst because no one else would understand the procedures and would therefore be biased in some way. In effect, they are making their beliefs and profession unquestionable, so perhaps we should simply accept that the case history of Little Hans is true, because until we are psychoanalysts ourselves, we can't judge it!

Whether you think this case study was good or bad, Hans actually came out of it seemingly unscathed, although we cannot be sure that he wouldn't have been fine anyway. When he was 19, Hans met Freud and told him that he was well and that he had no troubles or inhibitions. He also claimed he had no memory of the discussions with his father or Freud which took place during his childhood and that he got on well with both parents despite their break-up, but actually missed his younger sister. However, we can never be sure whether or not this was because he was repressing the memory or not.

Key words

Case study – a detailed report usually but not always undertaken by a doctor or psychiatrist to document and try to understand the problem of a client. The problems focused on in most case studies are rare and unusual phenomena.

Neurosis – a high level of anxiety where the person is worried or concerned about either specific things or things in general.

Oedipus complex – part of the theory of child development where boys want to posess their mothers and are jealous of their fathers, but renounce their mother and identify with father because they fear castration.

Seduction theory – Freud's original theory whereby he suggested that his patients had been victims of incest as children.

Psychoanalyst – a therapist who uses the techniques of psychoanalysis to try and get at the underlying unconscious motives and feelings in order to help someone deal with their problems.

Repressed memories – memories that have been pushed into the unconscious because they cause too much pain or anxiety to be retained in conscious awareness.

Key questions

1. Can you think of the strengths of a case study over a snapshot study?
2. Why was the data used in this case study so unscientific?
3. Does this study actually support the idea of the Oedipus complex?
4. Why do you think the birth of Hanna upset Hans, and was his reaction normal?
5. Do you think that we have unconscious motivations for some of our behaviours?

Physiological psychology

5

I suppose in many ways it is very easy to forget the physical basis of all human behaviour – our bodies. Our bodies are the most amazing organisms, which are so complicated that it is likely we will never understand absolutely everything there is to know about them. They have also been the basis of many heated debates that focus on whether our bodies are all there is to us, or whether we also have a spirit (or soul). Just think – if our bodies are all there is to us, then when we die, we must cease to exist. If, on the other hand, we also have a spirit, when we die does our spirit die too or does it go on existing? This is known as the 'mind-body' problem and really questions the basis of consciousness and existence itself. Logic says to me that we are simply what goes on in our bodies and so when our body dies, our spirit must die too – but my experiences when I was nursing almost contradict what I have just said.

One of the duties of a nurse is to 'lay out' patients who may die when they are on duty. What this means is that it is a nurse's duty to wash and care for the person's body, put a clean nightdress or pyjamas on that person, brush their hair and make them look at peace. When this was done the person's partner could come and visit and say goodbye to that person if they wanted to, and the image they would have would be one of peace and order. Obviously this is not the same as the responsibilities held by undertakers, but it was the first step towards preparing the body for burial or cremation. It sounds a bit gruesome but I will never forget the night sister, in charge of a number of wards, who was with me when I laid out my first body. She said to me that it was an honour to do it, because it was the last thing that anyone would ever do for that person – and when you look at it like that, she was right. From that moment onwards, it never worried me.

All I can say is that when a person dies, it is as if they have gone away. Their body is like an empty shell. I can't actually decide if it is because this thing we call a soul or a spirit has left their body, or if it is simply because all the activity within the body had stopped. I think the reason I have chosen to accept that our spirit or soul is actually part of our body, and not some non-connected spiritual being which has floated away like it does in cartoon films, is because I can't understand how this can be, and I like to understand things in order to be able to accept them!

In some respects it is a shame that I can't accept the separateness of the body and mind. If I could, I could go along with the idea that the body is really a space ship for me, and I am inside it, looking out of my eyes in order to see where I want my body to go. Another interpretation is the idea of the 'Numbskulls' who were in 'The Beezer' comic. There were lots of little men living in a person's skull and directing all of the person's activities. This idea was soon dispelled when I went to a lecture and someone said to me, yes but how do these little men work there must be little men inside their heads and so on and so on, until in the end it becomes totally ridiculous (not that it wasn't already!).

If you are a biologist, you will have thought about how our bodies work and you will be familiar with the information in the next section which I've made very basic. However, for those of you who have spent your time trying to ignore biology, I hope that this simplistic overview of the physiology of the nervous system does not put you off. You need to have some understanding of the structure of the nervous system because psychology also involves an understanding of physiology. Once I have done this, we can begin to look at the interaction between what goes on physically and our subsequent behaviour as the topics in this section look at that interaction.

The first study looks at the topic of emotions and whether or not they are simply a result of our physical response to a situation. The question is whether or not our physical response can be interpreted in different ways. The second study looks at sleep and dreaming and investigates the pattern of sleep and whether the rapid eye movements we make when we are asleep have any relationship to dreaming. The third study considers the fact that the brain is made of two symmetrical halves which are joined by connections. The study looks at what happens to the person when those connections are severed by surgery to try to reduce the effects of epilepsy and whether this is really going to cause the person permanent problems. The final study looks at whether the actual structure of the brain is responsible for abnormal behaviour by investigating how it functions in convicted murderers.

The physiology of the nervous system

I personally find the nervous system absolutely fascinating because it is so complex and each component is so tiny and yet it seems our abilities are limitless. With all the technological knowledge in the world, we have not yet been able to mimic much more than the most basic of human abilities. Humans can make assumptions that are correct on the basis of very little information; computers are far more likely to make errors. They cannot use information that is not clear whereas we process the past, the present and what we know about the future, at the same time. That is not saying that we don't make errors, we just make far less.

Actually the analogy between humans and computers is not only relevant because of the way we both process information, it is also the case that we both use electricity. We don't, obviously, have to plug ourselves in to the mains but we do actually work by a system of electrochemical changes and these are caused by external stimuli and also by changes in our bodies.

The structure of the nervous system

The nervous system consists of the central nervous system (CNS) which is the brain and spinal cord. This is the central control for all the activities of the body, where information received is processed and there is co-ordination of actions and reactions both conscious and unconscious. The other part is the peripheral nervous system (PNS) which consists of a network of neurones which are located around the whole of the body and are responsible for carrying information from the world to the CNS and from the CNS back to the different parts of the body.

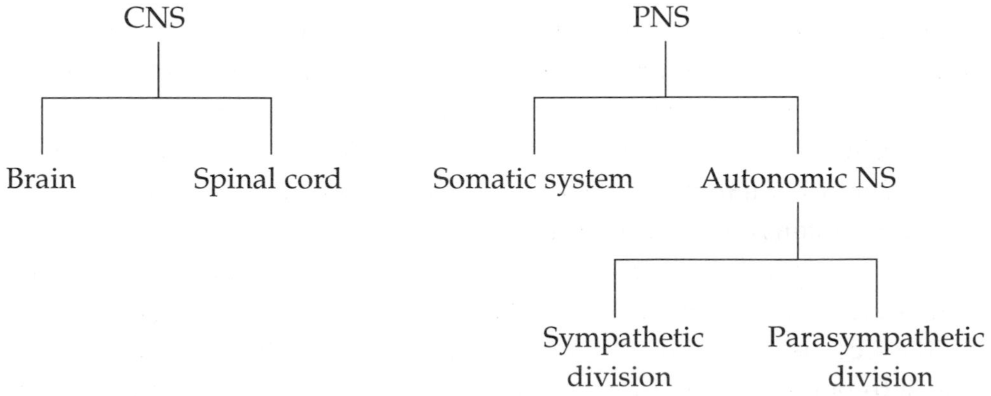

The nervous system

The PNS can also be subdivided into the somatic nervous system and the autonomic nervous system (ANS).

The somatic part is the part that is generally conscious of the responses it is making, for example the sensory nerves of the somatic system carry information about external stimulation from the different receptors to the CNS. The information is 'decoded', and then messages are carried back from the CNS to the muscles of the body where action is then taken in response. Therefore, the somatic part of the nervous system is responsible for all the muscles we use in making voluntary movements, as well as involuntary adjustments in posture and balance.

The nerves of the ANS run to and from the internal organs and are affected generally by information from inside the body (although occasionally they may respond to external information) which require the regulation of, say, breathing, heart rate and digestion. It is called the autonomic nervous system because many of the activities it controls are automatic and self-regulating – such as our rate of respiration and heart rate – and these continue whether a person is asleep or unconscious.

The ANS can be further subdivided:

- The sympathetic division is the mechanism that speeds bodily systems up and prepares the organism for activity so it has an excitatory function. It is the fight/flight mechanism which prepares the body for a response by, for example, speeding up the heart, dilating the arteries of the essential organs and constricting the arteries of the less essential organs such as the skin and digestive organs. We need more blood to the vital organs in order for us to survive, whereas we don't need to digest things if we are running away (that can be done later).
- The parasympathetic division is responsible for returning the body to normal by slowing it down again and allowing bodily functions to return to their original state – so it is inhibitory.

In order for this to happen, neuronal fibres from both the sympathetic and parasympathetic divisions supply most organs and the normal state of the body is maintained by a balance between these two systems.

But what are these things called neurones? How do they work? In order to begin my explanation, I will start by looking at the workings of the nervous system and consider how we take in sensory information from the outside world.

Information from the outside world comes through sensory receptors which are 'devices' used to convert information, for example light, pressure or chemicals, into nerve signals. Receptors usually only convert one kind of information, which means that we have different types of receptors to do specific jobs. This is why you can't see with your ears or smell with your eyes.

The different types of receptor cells fall into the sense categories:

- The retina of the eye takes in light and gives us vision.
- The cochlea of the ear takes in sound of different wavelengths giving us the ability to hear.
- The receptors on the tongue and in the nasal membranes take in chemical stimuli and give us taste and smell.
- The receptors in the skin receive pressure or give us contact with surfaces of different temperatures and these give us the sense of touch or temperature.

Some areas are more sensitive than others and this is because these areas either have more receptors or they have less dead skin. It is necessary for us to have areas that are less sensitive because we would find it very hard to walk if the soles of our feet were as sensitive as, say, the tips of our fingers.

Receptors are found at the end of what are called sensory neurones which are the cells of the nervous system and are the things responsible for carrying messages from one part of the body to another. In our bodies three types of neurone: sensory neurones, motor neurones and inter-neurones. There are between 10 and 12 billion neurones in the nervous system which will give you an idea of how tiny they are. A nerve is actually a bundle of neurones (like a telephone cable) which are held together by glial cells. Glial cells are smaller cells than neurones and provide the neurones with nutrients and structural support.

The three different types of neurones all have different functions:

- **Sensory neurones** transmit impulses received by receptors to the central nervous system.
- **Interneurones** receive the signals from the sensory neurons and send impulses to other interneurons or to motor neurons. They are found only in the brain or the spinal cord.
- **Motor neurones** carry outgoing signals from the brain or spinal cord to the effector organs such as the muscles or the heart and lungs.

All these neurones form connections with each other in order to carry information around the body by way of impulses or 'electric messages'. Some of these impulses are messages to do something, and in other cases they are messages to remain inactive. In order to understand how this works, we need to briefly consider the structure of a neurone.

As we have already mentioned, a neurone is a cell of the nervous system but the thing that sets these cells apart from other cells are their shape. From the central body of the neurone come lots of small, thin fibres called dendrites. Some are very short and others extend for long distances with lots of branches to them. Consequently the shape of a neurone can vary enormously, and it is their shape which dictates both the number of excitatory or inhibitory connections they make with other neurones and how each one will contribute to the overall functioning

electrical conduction – for example potassium chloride stopped any sort of reaction.

Further research on the neurones of squid (which are about .5 mm in diameter, hundreds of times larger than the largest mammalian axon) have resulted in the discovery that they contain a balance of chemicals consisting mainly of potassium and protein although sodium and chloride are also present. The extracellular fluid, which is found on the outside of the neurone in a body, consists of sodium, chloride and potassium. To put it very simply, all chemicals have positive or negative electrical charges and if we consider the electrical charges of the chemicals involved, and their respective quantities, we will see that there is a difference in the charge between the inside and the outside of the cell whereby the inside of the cell has a total negative charge and the outside of the cell has a total positive charge.

This difference in charge is called the 'membrane potential' and is about 70 mV (a millivolt is a thousandth of a volt). It is the cell's resting potential because this is what the charge is when the cell is inactive. The conventional description of a 'membrane potential' is really the measure of charge inside the cell – not the difference in the positive and negative charges between the two.

As you can see from the following diagram, the mix of chemicals found inside the neurone have a negative charge in total, whereas the chemicals on the outside of the cell have a total positive charge.

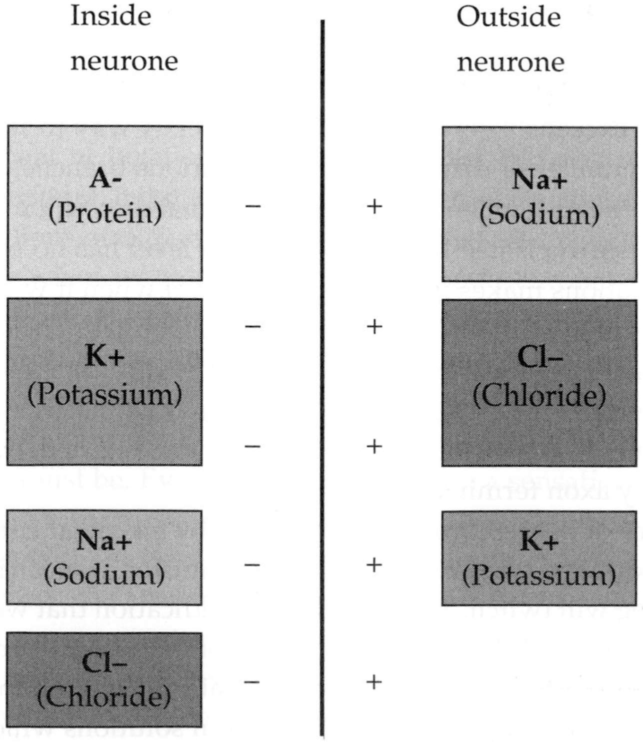

When some kind of stimulus is applied to the axon, the electrical potential (the charge) across the membrane of the cell is reduced at the point where this stimulation happens. If the reduction in potential is large enough it changes the permeability of the cell membrane by allowing what is called a sodium gate to open at that place. The sodium gate can be thought of as a disc which spins on a central axis, allowing chemicals to enter the cell from the outside and allowing chemicals from the inside to escape.

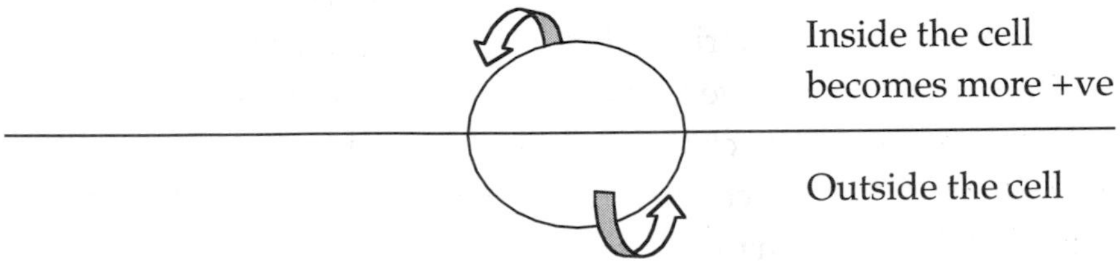

This allows sodium to enter the cell which results in a change in the electrical charge of the cells, so the inside becomes more positive and the outside becomes more negative. This process is known as depolarisation. Once this has happened, the sodium gates suddenly reverse back again restoring the permeability of the membrane at that point to where it was originally. The whole process takes about 2 milliseconds.

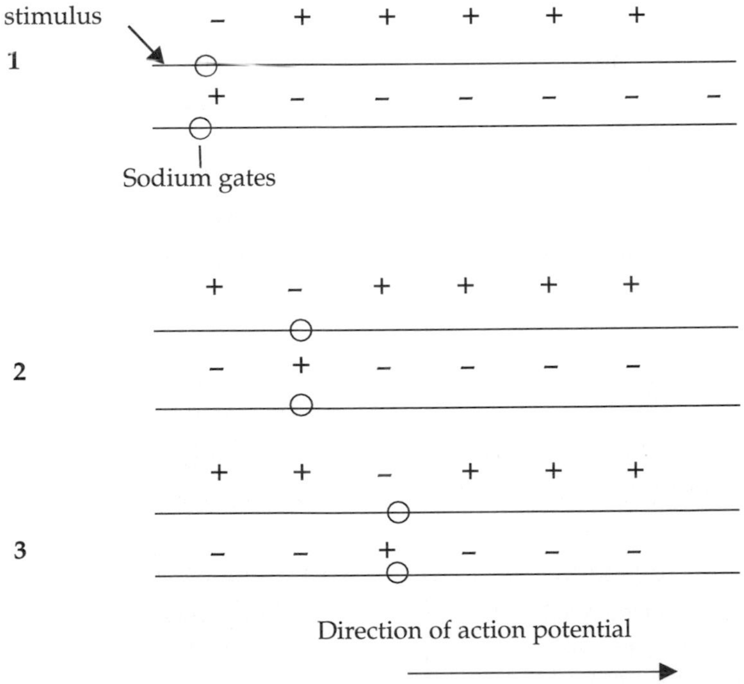

This shows how the action potential travels along the axon of a neurone by changing the polarity as it goes

This change then affects the adjacent portion of the axon, and causes its membrane to depolarise too. This happens again and again, and this process is the nerve impulse or action potential which is shown in the diagram as '+'.

Because '+' is generated anew at each stage along the axon, it does not diminish in strength. A good way to imagine this is to think of a firework fuse. When the fuse is lit, the burning part travels along the whole length of the fuse, but at any one time only one tiny part of the fuse is alight. The speed of travel of '+' can be between two and two hundred miles per hour, depending on the size of the axon and whether or not it is 'myelinated'.

What is myelin you may ask? A myelin sheath is a kind of insulation which is found around most but not all of the axons of neurones. It is not a continuous tube around the axon, but is more like a series of segments with a small area of uncoated axon between each section known as a node of Ranvier.

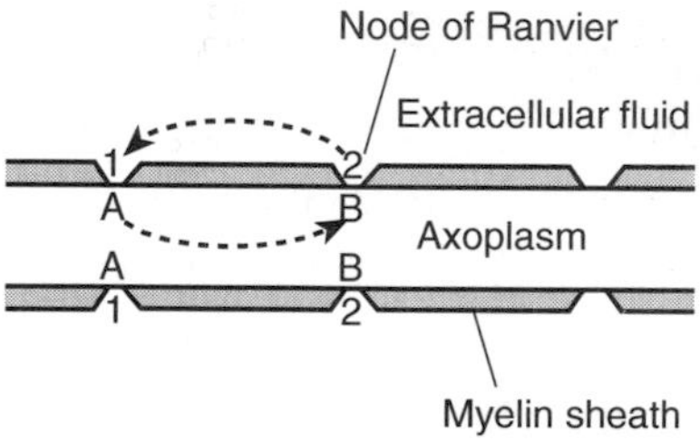

This diagram illustrates how a myelin sheath can speed up neuronal transmission. The sodium gates at position 1 open allowing a change in polarity. The impulse which is generated at A travels down the axoplasm to position B which stimulates the opening of the sodium gates at 2. Meanwhile the sodium gates at 1 have closed. This allows a more speedy transmision of an impulse along the length of the axon.

The purpose of the myelin is to speed up the action potential because each adjacent area of the axon does not need to become depolarised in order for the action potential to travel along. Only the membrane at the node of Ranvier has to change its polarity and this means that the action potential can jump from one area to the next.

It was originally believed that neurones were long fibres which simply merged with each other. It was not until the late 1800s that a method of staining a single nerve cell or neuron, without staining its neighbours, was discovered. This indicated that cells did not actually merge into one another but that each cell was distinct and that a small gap separated one cell from the next. These gaps allowed cells to line up in various different ways which explained why one person's experiences and behaviours were different to the next person.

The next problem was understanding how the electrical impulse got from one neurone to the next across the space between them. This space is known as the synaptic gap and it is here that synaptic junctions are formed between different types of neurones. The process is called synaptic transmission.

When the impulse reaches the end of a neuron where the axon terminates, it stimulates what are called synaptic vesicles which are tiny round packages in the shape of spheres which contain transmitter substances. The term vesicle actually means 'little bladder' and in effect this is what they are. They contain chemicals known as transmitter substances or neurotransmitters which are released from the presynaptic (before the junction) membrane into the synaptic gap.

These neurotransmitter substances are like a number of small keys which fit into keyholes on the membrane of the next neurone which is known as the post-synaptic membrane. Once they are in place, they change the potential of the postsynaptic membrane, allowing the sodium gates to open and the whole process to happen again in the adjacent neurone.

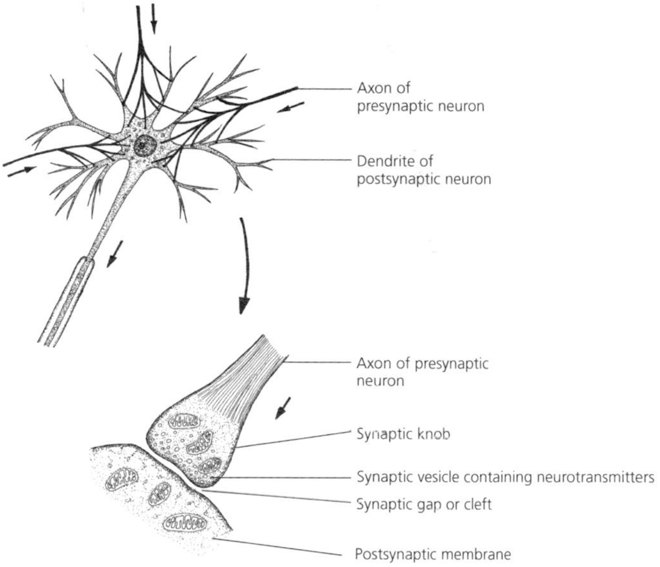

Once this has happened the neurotransmitter is drawn back into the end foot by way of a pump-like mechanism. This means that the postsynaptic receptors only get a very brief exposure to the transmitter substances. This process is known as 'reuptake'.

There are over 40 different types of neurotransmitters found in different areas of the body. Acetylcholine is the most common, being found in many synapses in the brain and spinal cord, especially in an area of the brain called the hippocampus which is relevant in the formation of new memories. Alzheimer's disease involves impairment of memory and other cognitive functioning. It has been found that brain cells producing acetylcholine degenerate in people suffering from Alzheimer's disease and consequently the production of acetylcholine is reduced. This means the transmission of 'messages' are considerably reduced, which explains why Alzheimer patients suffer such problems in their thinking. Also acetylcholine is released at every synapse where a nerve termi-

2 Does what we think about a situation (our cognitions) constitute an emotion, irrespective of our body's physical response?
3 Are emotions actually a mixture of the two?

Just to recap, we know from the section on physiology, that we have a sympathetic division of the autonomic nervous system which is the part which prepares us for emergency action – the fight/flight response. This is the part that increases our heart rate and raises our blood pressure, makes us breathe faster, dilates our pupils and makes us sweat, while things like saliva secretion decrease. All the vital organs necessary for emergency action are supplied with blood and other areas, which are not required in the immediate response, are put on hold.

We also know that when the emergency subsides, the parasympathetic system, the energy conserving system, takes over and returns the organism to its normal state. These activities are triggered by activity in certain critical regions of the brain, including the hypothalamus and parts of the limbic system.

The kind of heightened physiological arousal just described is characteristic of some emotional states such as anger or fear when we must prepare ourselves for some sort of action. The interesting part is that they are also present when we are extremely elated, excited or sexually aroused. It is only when we feel very sad that our bodily processes seem to be depressed or slowed.

So what is the relationship between heightened physiological arousal (the 'physical' bit) and our subjective experiences (the 'felt' bit) of an emotion? If we didn't have the 'physical' bit, would we feel less? What we need to consider is whether or not our perception of our own arousal makes up part of the experience of the emotion?

One way to study this is to look at people who have spinal cord injuries. When the spinal cord is severed or lesioned, the impulses sent by the sensory neurones which enter the spinal cord below the point of injury can't reach the brain because the neurones in the spinal cord have been damaged and so the messages can't get through. Once they are damaged, the neurones in the spinal cord can't repair themselves and so the person suffers permanent lack of sensation. The actor Christopher Reeve suffered just such damage when he fell off a horse and severed his spinal cord at the level of his neck. He has no feeling in any areas of his body below the break, although his body still functions.

Some of the sensations from our body come from the 'somatic system', for example we know if the temperature is hot or cold. Others come from the 'sympathetic nervous system' – we know if our heart is pounding and whether or not we have a dry throat. Therefore if people have suffered a spinal cord lesion they will no longer have an awareness of any bodily response to a situation and will suffer a reduction in any sort of contribution autonomic arousal may make to felt emotion. To put it more simply, if we don't get any sort of feedback from our bodies, and this feedback is essential for the experience of an emotion, then this is why people with spinal cord lesions don't feel any emotion.

Hohmann (1966) studied army veterans who had spinal cord injuries. He divided them into five groups according to where the lesion was on their spine. In one group the lesions were near the neck so there was very little feedback from the sympathetic system. In another group the lesion was near the base of the spine, so that they had far more feedback from the sympathetic nerves. The other three groups fell between these two extremes.

The subjects were interviewed to find out what their feelings were in situations of fear, anger, grief and sexual excitement. They were asked to remember an emotion-arousing event that took place before they were injured. Then to think of a comparable event which occurred after they were damaged, and try to compare their emotional experiences in each case to see if they were greater before the injury was sustained. It seemed that the higher the lesion, (giving less feedback from the autonomic nervous system) the more they reported a decrease in emotionality no matter what the original emotional feeling actually was. This tends to indicate that the less autonomic arousal we have available to us, the less intense the emotions are that we experience.

Patients who had the highest spinal cord lesions suggested that they could react emotionally to arousing situations, but that they did not really *feel* emotional

> 'It's a sort of cold anger. Sometimes I act angry when I see some injustice. I yell and cuss and raise hell, because if you don't do it sometimes, I've learned people will take advantage of you; but it doesn't have the heat to it that it used to. It's a mental kind of anger...'

So we now have a useful but not entirely objective study because the emotional situations would have varied from person to person and subjects rated their own experiences. What may be an intensely emotional experience for you may have been no more than a laugh for me.

Further studies have, however, shown that very similar findings have been made so the conclusions are that the less feedback we get from the autonomic system to the brain, the less intense is the feeling of emotion. So it seems that autonomic arousal *does* contribute to the intensity of emotional experience but does it actually differentiate the emotions? Is it really the case that there is one pattern of physiological activity for joy, another for anger, another for fear?

3 Although you can artificially induce the bodily changes associated with an emotion, for example injecting a drug such as adrenaline (the fight/flight hormone), this still does not produce the experience of a true emotion.

This was demonstrated by a study carried out by Maranon (1924) when he injected his subjects with adrenaline. About 71 per cent of the 210 participants experienced physical symptoms such as a dry mouth or a pounding heart, but none of them felt real emotions. Twenty nine per cent reported that they felt *as if* they were afraid or angry. He did discover that a few of his subjects did actually seem to experience a genuine emotion rather than an 'as if' feeling. When they were asked about what they were feeling, they reported that they were remembering an emotional event from their past or imagining a highly emotional situation. This implies that they were using their cognitions (thoughts) as a way of interpreting the physiological responses they were having and labelling the response with the appropriate emotion for the situation they were in. To put it in easier terms, it seems that the physiological arousal alone is not enough to give the feelings of an emotion unless the person is given (or produces) a suitable cognition such as an upsetting memory.

What we have to remember is that 71 per cent of Maranons's subjects did not report an emotion. However, they knew they were receiving an injection and may well have known what it was and what the effects would be. Consequently they had a completely appropriate explanation as to why they underwent the physiological changes they did. Maybe this was why so few of the subjects reported any emotional experience.

4 Perhaps the physiological changes we associate with various emotions are not even necessary and it is quite possible to feel an emotion without autonomic feedback to the central nervous system.

There is some evidence to support this idea, although the evidence is really quite weak. Cannon (1927) removed the sympathetic nervous system of cats but they still showed a supposedly normal set of emotional responses – the question is, what are the normal emotional responses of a cat?

The Cannon-Bard Theory

As an alternative to the James-Lange theory, Cannon proposed what is known as the Cannon-Bard theory. This suggests that emotions can be felt without any change in the responses of the nervous system.

Cannon pointed out that incoming stimuli are processed through the thalamus in the brain. Messages then pass from the thalamus upwards to the cortex, where conscious emotional experience occurs. At the same time messages are sent downwards to the hypothalamus and then on to the body which would result in physiological arousal and muscle activity. If the spinal cord has been damaged, obviously the messages can't get back down to the body from the brain, so physiological arousal won't occur. However, the messages that are travelling from the thalamus to the cortex won't have been affected and so emotional feelings will still be preserved.

I am sure that you will agree that neither of these theories really explain emotions adequately because, despite what Cannon believed, I don't feel that an emotion could be complete without *both* the thoughts and the physical responses. Can you imagine feeling fear or anger without the stomach going into a knot and the heart pounding? Maybe the James-Lange theory is correct and there are subtly different responses for each emotion, but imagine how fast the interpretation must be of all these physical responses in order for you to work out what you feel almost instantaneously when something happens. Say you see something ambiguous like a light in the sky which may or may not be a flying saucer – you will need to have feedback from every part of your body in order to pick out all the slightly different rates of activity before you can decide if you feel frightened or excited about the object. By this time you may well have been massacred by whatever the object was. I don't think this is really realistic, do you?

Schachter's two factor theory of emotion

Schachter (1964) suggested that there is a relationship between physiological arousal and emotion. He believed that most of the theories about emotions and the role of arousal had ignored the importance of cognition and how we use our cognitions to make sense of the situation. In effect we label the situation according to the cognitions that are available to us. The two factors he referred to were the state of arousal and the cognitions that make sense of the situation.

He argued that when we feel emotions they are *always* about something – either an external stimulus or possibly a memory or thought. How often have you sat alone and thought about things and become very sad, or very happy? You are not feeling these things out of the blue – they are related to past experiences.

When I was at university, I was persuaded to go with a group of mates to hear a band play to a small select invited audience. They had a spare ticket from someone who had dropped out, and rather than waste the space they invited me. The band had originally come from my university, and often returned to the area as a kind of tribute, so instead of having many hundreds of people in the audience there were actually only about one hundred altogether. My friends all raved about them and said how brilliant they were and, although I did not know the band very well, the concert was excellent and I was really aroused in terms of getting into the music and enjoying the atmosphere. Because most of the people there were hardened supporters, I felt a bit awkward because I couldn't instantly recognise the songs from the intros. One particular song went on for ages and I thought it had finished. I started clapping and shouted out something encouraging, when I suddenly realised that no-one else was going for it ... the reason they didn't all clap was because it was simply a pause in that particular song, and they carried on playing. I felt such a complete idiot, I wanted the ground to swallow me up. Everyone in the place turned round and looked at me, and I felt so embarrassed. Even now, all these years later, when I think of this particular experience it makes me wince.

Here the emotion I feel is directly related to a memory. I can feel my heart begin to beat faster and I get this really sick feeling in my stomach, which is so stupid after all this time. Maybe thinking about the event produces the physical response and I then relate that response to the situation and it makes me feel embarrassed again.

If this is the case, Schachter's explanation gives some support to the James-Lange theory that we *do* need to have some kind of physiological response first in order to feel emotions. But Schachter makes the point that it is how we *interpret* the physical response that really makes an emotion, and we do this according to the situation we find ourselves in. What he meant was that when we have a physical response we attribute it to something, and this attribution will suggest whether the emotion is labelled as fear or anger or whatever.

At this point I hope you can accept his theory that an emotion comes from a combination of a state of arousal *and* a cognition that makes best sense of the situation the person is in. Let me give you a couple of examples:

It is a sunny summer afternoon and you have borrowed a car from a friend, with the intention of impressing your girlfriend by taking her out for the day. You decide to drive to a really romantic spot at the top of a steep hill, where there is a wonderful view over the sea. You pull the car up and look out over the landscape, and at your partner, when you begin to feel a very strange sensation. A horrific awareness of what is going on suddenly occurs to you – the car has started to roll down a steep slope and you have no control over it. Not just the handbrake, but all the brakes have failed. You experience the emotion of absolute terror...

Now imagine the situation where the car is part of a roller coaster. The feeling you have will also be one of fear and excitement, but not the blind terror of the first situation. Here, our cognitive appraisal of the situation determines the intensity of the emotional experience.

Schacter developed his two-factor theory (which is also known as 'cognitive labelling theory') in part as a result of past research. Schachter and Singer (1962) had joined forces to conduct some research to look into the notion of cognitive labelling. Their research was intended to test three propositions which would support the idea of the two factor theory of emotion. The study involved manipulating not only the arousal levels of the subjects but also the situations they found themselves in, and the expectations of what the side effects should be. Their explanations of their feelings were the interesting and relevant part for the researchers.

S. Schachter and J.E. Singer (1962) Cognitive, social and physiological determinants of emotional state.

Psychological Review, 69 (5), pp. 379–99

The aim of the study was to investigate the interaction between physiological responses and cognitive factors when experiencing an emotion (the 'two-factor' theory).

In order to do this, three propositions were tested:

1 If a person experiences a state of physiological arousal that they can't explain then they will describe the state in terms of the cognitions available to them at the time. This means that the same state of arousal can be labelled as fear, anger or lust depending on the situation the person is in.
2 If a person experiences a state of physiological arousal that they can explain (a result of an injection), then they are unlikely to try to re-explain the arousal as a result of the situation they are in.
3 If a person is not physiologically aroused they will not experience an emotion even if they are put in a situation which in the past, would have made them feel an emotion. If they are not in a state of arousal they will be more objective about the situation.

Method

Design Laboratory experiment with independent subjects in four groups. Subjects were told by the researchers that the study was to look at the effects on vision of vitamin supplements called 'Suproxin' although it was to investigate the effects of physiological arousal on emotions. The 'Suproxin' which was administered by a doctor, was in fact epinephrine (adrenaline) which produces arousal similar to that when we are in the fight/flight situation – heart beating, increased respirations, pupils dilating etc.

The data was collected by observing the subjects through a one way mirror and by self report measures.

In order to test the hypotheses, the independent variables were manipulated in three ways as follows:

1 Subjects were given either an injection of epinephrine (adrenaline) or saline solution (placebo) in order to manipulate the state of arousal.
2 Subjects were either told of the correct side effects, they were misinformed or they were ignorant in order to manipulate the explanation the individual would give to the state of arousal. In order to operationalise this variable, subjects were divided into four groups:

- **Epinephrine informed**
  Subjects were given an injection that they believed was Suproxin and were told by the doctor of its real side effects which were shaky hands, pounding heart, etc.
- **Epinephrine misinformed**
  Subjects were given an injection that they believed was Suproxin and were told by the experimenter (confirmed by doctor) of possible side effects but these effects were inaccurate (itching, numb feet and headaches).
- **Epinephrine ignorant**
  Subjects were given an injection that they believed was Suproxin and told by the doctor that there would be no side effects.
- **Control group**
  Subjects were given an injection that they believed was Suproxin but was in fact only saline solution and told by the doctor that there would be no side effects.

CONDITIONS	Epinephrine informed	Epinephrine misinformed	Epinephrine Ignorant	Control Group
Euphoric Stooge	Suproxin	Suproxin	Suproxin	Saline
Angry Stooge	Suproxin		Suproxin	Saline

3 In order to manipulate emotional states, subjects were exposed to either a euphoric stooge or an angry stooge (except the epinephrine misinformed group who only saw the euphoric stooge). This was because people evaluate their own feelings by comparing themselves with others around them.

Subjects

184 male college students studying introductory psychology who received extra points towards their exams. Their health records were checked to make sure that the adrenaline would not harm them.

Procedure

Subjects were tested individually. They were told that the aim of the study was to look at the effects of a vitamin injection called Suproxin, on visual skills. They were given an injection of either epinephrine (adrenaline) or a placebo (saline) and tested individually. The effects of epinephrine began after a period of three minutes and lasted up to an hour although the average length of time was 15 to 20 minutes.

The subjects were observed by two experimenters through a one-way mirror during the next stage of the experiment.

Euphoria inducing condition

Subjects in the euphoria condition were put in a room with a stooge for twenty minutes to let the Suproxin be absorbed by the bloodstream before they undertook their vision test. The room was slightly untidy and as soon as the experimenter left, the stooge made a number of friendly comments to the subject and began playing with items left in the room (paper, rubber bands, pencils folders and hula hoops). He encouraged the subject to join in while he played basketball with crumpled paper, made paper airplanes, fired pieces of paper with rubber bands, made a tower of folders and played with one of the hula hoops. The routine was standardised but would be adjusted according to the behaviour of the subject and whether or not he joined in.

Anger inducing condition

Subjects in this condition were put in a room with a stooge and were asked to spend the time waiting for the injection to take effect by filling in a questionnaire. The stooge began trying to wind-up the subject by moaning about having injections. The questionnaire was also intended to annoy the subject by asking increasingly personal questions such as 'Do you bathe and wash regularly,?' 'What is your fathers average annual income?' 'How many times a week do you have sexual intercourse?' and other very personal questions. The stooge then got very angry (again in a standardised routine) ripped up his questionnaire and left. (N.B. In order to prevent any experimenter effects, the stooge had no idea which condition the subject was in.)

For the next stage, the experimenter returned and took the subject's pulse. He told the subject that it was necessary to assess any side effects of 'Suproxin' which may affect their performance on the vision tests and this would involve filling out a questionnaire.

The questionnaire consisted of a number of irrelevant questions about their current mental and physical state. Some required answers on a four point scale, others were open-ended questions. The crucial questions used to measure mood and emotional state were on a five point scale.

How irritated angry or annoyed would you say you feel at present?

I don't feel at all irritated or angry (0)	I feel a little irritated and angry (1)	I feel quite irritated and angry (2)	I feel very irritated and angry (3)	I feel extremely irritated and angry (4)

How good or happy would you say you feel at present?

I don't feel at all irritated or angry (0)	I feel a little irritated and angry (1)	I feel quite irritated and angry (2)	I feel very irritated and angry (3)	I feel extremely irritated and angry (4)

From Schachter and Singer (1962)

Finally the subjects were told about the nature of the experiment and debriefed. Eleven subjects expressed extreme suspicion about a crucial part of the experiment and their data were discarded.

Results

All subjects who had epinephrine showed more signs of sympathetic arousal than controls.

Effects of euphoria condition

The subjects' scores for anger were subtracted from their score of happiness. Therefore if they have a positive value, it means they were feeling more happy than angry.

In the euphoria condition, we can see that the misinformed group were feeling more happy than all the others. The second most happy group was the ignorant group and so on. These results were as predicted because subjects were more

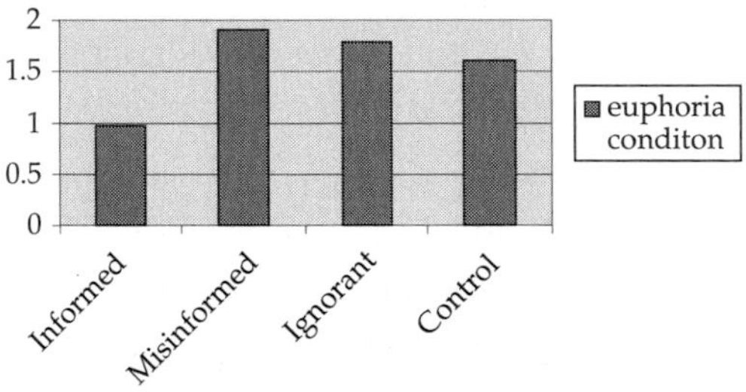

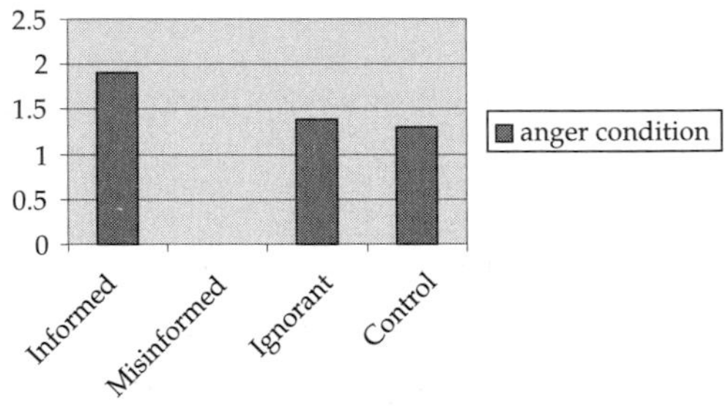

Condition	No of subjects	Self report (happiness – anger)
Informed	25	.98
Misinformed	25	1.90
Ignorant	25	1.78
Control	26	1.61

Condition	No of subjects	Self report (happiness – anger)
Informed	22	1.91
Misinformed	0	
Ignorant	23	1.39
Control	23	1.63

susceptible to the mood of the stooge when they had no explanation of why their body felt as it did. This also indicates that the informed group felt the least happiness because they understood why they felt as they did.

In the anger condition, we can see that the ignorant group were feeling the most angry (or rather the least happy) than all the others. The second most angry group was the placebo group and the group who were informed felt the least upset by the questionnaire, as predicted. Again this was because subjects were more susceptible to the mood of the stooge and the nature of the questionnaire when they had no explanation of why their body felt as it did.

Behaviour

The behaviour of subjects in both conditions matched their self reports. The euphoric condition produced the most manic behaviour from the misinformed group followed by the ignorant group, and in the anger situation the ignorant group produced the most anger. This was probably because there was no misinformed group in the anger condition.

Discussion

The results of the study followed the expectations of the researchers and support Schacter's (1964) idea of cognitive labelling theory which suggests that the physiological arousal in different emotions is the same – we just label it according to our cognitions.
Proposition A it seems that if a person experiences a state of physiological arousal that they can't explain, they do describe this arousal in terms of the situation they are in. They give a 'cognitive' reason for the arousal they were feeling rather than just feeling it and not understanding it.
Proposition B it seems that when a person experiences a state of physiological arousal that they can explain by way of an injection they have received, they are unlikely to try and explain it in any other way.
Proposition C We have a problem because the proposition stated that if a person is not physiologically aroused they will not experience an emotion even if they are put in a situation, which, in the past, would have made them feel an emotion. However, in the ignorant condition, subjects experienced arousal without any obvious reason for it. It may be the case that simply being in an extraordinary situation and having received an injection, they may have become aroused or anxious anyway.

However, the findings were not as impressive as expected. All the subjects in the euphoria and anger conditions were actually not angry (if they were angry, the numbers would have been minus numbers and they were all plus numbers). In fact, the measures were more a measure of levels of happy-neutrality, rather than anger. It seems that the researchers didn't actually manage to make their subjects angry.

Evaluation

Epinephrine does not have the same effect on everyone and five subjects who said they had no physiological symptoms had their data removed from the study. Therefore we can't be sure that they were all experiencing the same level of arousal to start with.

Subjects may have attributed their feelings to the injection despite the fact that they were told in some conditions that it had no side effects. In fact some of the subjects in the ignorant and misinformed conditions reported physical effects which they directly attributed to the injection by stating that it made them feel shivery for example.

It is also likely that subjects who did not have the epinephrine would still have felt aroused, simply because they were taking part in a study. In fact, the subjects mood was not assessed before the study and this might have affected their subsequent behaviour.

One question remains, and that is why were there no subjects in the misinformed/anger condition? Although the results were probably predictable, it would have been far more balanced.

Ethically, the study involved considerable deception although it was necessary in order to produce the conditions.

Key terms

Saline – salt water.

Standardised routine – when the routine or procedure is the same for each condition.

Epinephrine – an alternative name for adrenaline.

Placebo – a harmless or pharmacologically inactive substance used in drug trials or to placate a patient who thinks they should be given some kind of medication. An example would be using a sugar pill as a placebo in a drug trial involving tablet taking.

Key questions

1. Why should the researchers have assessed the mood of the subjects before the start of the study.
2. Is the study ecologically valid?
3. Why do we have no trouble in real life assessing what emotion we feel?
4. Do you think the methods used by Schachter and Singer to measure emotion were valid?
5. What is the main ethical concern in this study?

Circadian rhythms and sleep

Despite what you may think, sleep is actually a behaviour although it is more often defined as a state of consciousness.

> When I was small, I used to think that sleep was the same as being unconscious. This may have had something to do with the fact that it was impossible to wake my parents at 6 o'clock in the morning, even when I poked them and shouted at them to get up and play with me. After jumping around on the bed and trying to pull the covers off, I concluded that they were either dead or unconscious because I couldn't do much more to wake them up. I think the penny dropped when I had children of my own. I remember many mornings when I pretended to be asleep hoping they'd go away and watch the early morning cartoons on the TV and leave me for another half an hour.

Because we all sleep, it is a topic that often crops up in conversation. Here are a list of phrases I am sure you will recognise:

> How are you sleeping?
> I'm so tired.
> I'm NOT tired mum!
> I stayed out till 4 o'clock in the morning and I'm dead today.
> I must get some sleep.
> I can't sleep, I just toss and turn all night.
> I seem to wake up far too early.
> Did the baby sleep all night?
> I wish she'd go to sleep
> If I don't get eight hours sleep I can't function
> I only need four hours sleep a night
> She's overtired, that's why she's in such a bad mood.

and so on…

It's not surprising that sleep is so relevant, after all we spend one third of our lives asleep. We all know that we can't do without it, and yet it seems such a waste of time – I often wish I didn't have to sleep at all. Have you also noticed that during the week when you have to get up, you can't seem to wake up, and at the weekend when you can lie in bed, you wake up really early when you don't have to. That should give you the idea that perhaps our feelings of needing sleep seem also to relate to our state of mind. If we are enjoying ourselves at a party, we find it easy to stay awake, whereas if we are at home, bored, we feel very sleepy. People suffering from depression also feel very tired all the time and sleep more than they would normally.

There are other aspects to sleep – the fact that while we are asleep we have periods of relative quiet and periods when we know we dream. We also vary in the amount of sleep we need throughout the course of our lives. When we are babies, we sleep and wake many times during the course of a day. As we get older, many of us only sleep once at night, although people from very hot countries may well have a siesta during the day when the sun is at its highest in the sky. We also seem to need less sleep when we are in our teens and twenties, and yet with the passing of the years we seem to need more sleep. When we are really antique, our need for sleep often decreases again. The reasons for this are complex and not only to do with our bodily requirements but are related to the stresses and strains of everyday life. In many ways, the most stressful times seem to require the most sleep and yet they seem to be the times when we get the least.

One of the most exciting things about sleep can be the dreams we have. You can be anything in dreams, and yet they are not always about pleasant things. They are sometimes weird, sometimes very enjoyable or erotic, and sometimes they seem to perform the function of giving an insight into the solution of problems. My dreams sometimes seem to go on for hours and I often have such vivid dreams that I wake up believing they were true. I can also remember odd dreams I have had over the years, but whether that was because I told people about them (rehearsal) or simply they were so weird, I'm not sure. The analysis of dreams was one of Freud's interests, and in some of the daily newspapers you will occasionally see articles on how to analyse your dreams. As to whether this dream analysis actually bears any relationship to reality is another matter!

Before we look in any depth at the nature of sleep and its functions (as far as we know), we will look at the rhythms which govern our lives – whether they are twenty four hour rhythms or annual rhythms. The cycles of sleeping and waking and the different levels of sleep seem to form regular patterns which we can identify as part of our lives.

Circadian and circannual rhythms

Rhythms in behaviour and physiological processes are found throughout the plant and animal world. These cycles are generally called circadian rhythms (*Circa* means about and *dies* means day, which explains why circadian rhythms are based on a 24 hour cycle) but they may be circannual (about a year). One of the reasons for these cycles seems to be related to the changing patterns of sunlight and temperature that vary from day to day across the seasons.

Plants and animals respond to these changing patterns by pursuing different behaviours according to the time of year or time of day. Some animals hibernate when the length of day shortens and the temperature falls. Even when the temperature remains mild, they become more sleepy, responding to the change in daylight. Other animals collect stores of food, a process triggered by their internal clocks rather than the conscious decision 'Mmm, the days are getting shorter, I think I'll go and collect acorns for the winter'! Birds migrate south and plants begin to lose their leaves. There are similar positive patterns of behaviour in the spring, when animals, triggered by the increasing length of day and warmer temperature, come out of hibernation and begin to find mates and build nests. Humans, too, follow patterns of behaviour that seem to be stimulated by the length of day and amount of light.

So what happens to make us follow these rhythms – is it just light? The answer to this is no – it's not that simple. Work by Curt Richter (1922) found that rats increase their level of activity every two to four hours, even when the environment is constant. This seems to coincide with stomach contractions. Female rats become even more active every four or five days which is when they become fertile. This was some of the first evidence to suggest that the body can generate rhythms without needing external stimuli. Later work by Gwinner (1986) showed that if birds who would normally migrate were kept in a constant environment with 12 hours of daylight and dark and a constant temperature, then even after a number of years they would become restless every autumn and spring when they should normally be migrating.

This indicates that we must produce endogenous rhythms (rhythms generated from within) which are unrelated to light, although they seem to follow a similar pattern to external cues. What seems to finetune these rhythms are 'zeitgebers' or timegivers, the most powerful being light which can override other environmental cues. The light therefore seems to moderate the rhythms and prevents them from going too fast or too slow. Evidence to show the power of light as a zeitgeber has been collected from animal studies where animals who are kept in constant darkness will reset their internal clock, advancing or retarding it when shown no more than a brief flash of light (Aschoff, 1979). If however, there is no light available, other environmental stimuli such as temperature can serve as a zeitgeber – which is why hibernating animals know when to wake up, even if they are hibernating underground.

It seems that humans have a circadian rhythm which doesn't quite match that of a 24 hour clock. This has been shown by a number of intrepid scientists who have rashly decided to go and live in caves for varying amounts of time.

They obviously had no daylight to keep them on track and simply got up, ate and went to sleep when they felt the urge. The results of these studies have indicated that man has approximately a 25 hour sleep waking cycle. Other studies have tried to retrain the biological clock to days of different lengths, and although some people seem to be able to adapt reasonably well, others had great difficulty in staying awake or sleeping when it would not normally be time to do so. This natural 25 hour clock can explain why, when we are on holiday, we often stay up later than we could do normally, and wake up later too – our biological clock is gaining one hour in 24, so in effect if we had a 24 day holiday and we got up and went to bed when we wanted to, by the end of the holiday we would be back where we started again.

In humans, another cycle which seems to influence our behaviour is our temperature. Under normal circumstances temperature in the body core (not skin temperature) will rise during the middle of the day and dip slightly in mid-afternoon. It will fall again at night, reaching its lowest point in the early hours of the morning whether or not our sleep follows that pattern (this is why we often wake up in the night and feel really cold). You must have heard of morning people and evening people ('larks' and 'owls'). The reason that some people are better in the morning or the evening is connected with their core temperature peaking either earlier or later in the day. We also have other internal cycles of eating, drinking, urinating and secreting hormones, but these are related to when we wake up or sleep and are not governed by any other external cues.

It therefore seems that temperature must have something to do with how well we sleep. Shift workers, for example, have dreadful problems trying to sleep when their body temperature tells them that they should be up and about.

It seems that if we disrupt the circadian rhythms by asking people to do shift work, the extent and timing of disruption affects how serious it is for them. If shift workers go to sleep in the morning or early afternoon after working all night, they won't sleep for very long because their core temperature is rising. They will sleep for longer if they go to sleep in the early or middle part of the night, when their body temperature is still going down. What makes it worse is that the external zeitgebers are consistent so shift workers have to deal with them too.

What about jet lag, that nightmare occurence that can ruin any potential holiday to America! If we are travelling from east to west, we follow the natural course of the sun so although we stay awake later at night and wake later in the morning than we do at home, we will be okay. However, if we travel from west to east, as we would returning home from America, we are actually going back in time and so the effects are greater because we have already done that bit!

'Yeah, but what about this stuff called melatonin. Doesn't that sort out jet lag?' said the fat American Executive as he sat in his Club Class seat on British Airways flight BA 343 from Washington.

The young medical student sitting next to him shook her head in despair. These executives – all they seem to think we need is a pill here and a pill there.

'Melatonin,' she said with an air of superiority, 'is what we make when the natural light goes. It is made by the pineal gland in the brain and it is the stuff that makes us sleepy. It's a hormone that affects brain cells that make serotonin – another substance associated with sleep. In fact melatonin is linked to body temperature and peaks around about 3 or 4 a.m. The minute the sun shines in our eyes this works as a trigger to tell the pineal gland to stop making it which is why we wake up. If you take melatonin it's kind of like taking a sleeping pill. The problem is that lots of the melatonin you can buy isn't very pure and the dose hasn't actually been agreed. Still it's up to you if you want to risk taking drugs that aren't adequately tested.'

'Uh,' said the executive, somewhat gobsmacked (he hadn't anticipated a lecture). He reached to get another sticky doughnut from the plate.

'There you are, you are obviously short in serotonin,' the young woman continued. 'You see, every time you are short of serotonin you tend to crave carbohydrates. Sticky buns, cakes, biscuits, pasta, potatoes, bread: they are all carbohydrates and they are considered to be the food that helps us make serotonin. That's why we eat more stodge in the winter.'

The executive was now totally confused. He wondered why he had bothered to say anything. He just looked at her and made an executive-type decision. He pulled out a pair of ear plugs and a mask to cover his eyes, and settled back to try and sleep for the rest of the journey.

The function of sleep

I have gone on about circadian rhythms and sleep for quite a while but still haven't considered what function sleep serves. I mean we all know we need it, but why? And what happens if we don't sleep?

Horne (1988) has conducted considerable amounts of research into sleep and has reviewed much of the literature on sleep. He points out that everything that is alive has some period of rest during a day – even plants, who seem to go into a period of quiescence or inactivity, at the same time every day. There are really three theories which suggest why we need to sleep: for our bodies, for our minds, or as a result of evolution.

Physiological Restoration – for our bodies

This theory suggests that the main reason we sleep is to allow our bodies to restore themselves after a hard day. Our bodies do seem to undertake certain processes which relate to restoration when we are asleep such as digestion, the removal of waste produces and protein synthesis, but these processes also happen when we are awake so that can't be the only reason. The speed at which cell division takes place is also not affected by sleep – they divide at the normal rate for time of day, irrespective of whether the person is awake or asleep. There does seem to be some effect on the immune system, with a greater likelihood of catching colds or other infections when we are overtired. However, this is probably caused by the stress of knowing that we should be asleep rather than simply the lack of sleep.

Horne and Minard (1985) also point out that if we have had a physically exhausting day, we don't necessarily sleep for longer. Hartmann (1984) noticed that the total amount of sleep may not be longer but during that time a certain type of sleep called non-REM sleep increased over REM sleep. So perhaps non-REM has something of a restorative function (more about these types of sleep later).

Psychological restoration – for our minds

Sleep may not be essential for our bodies but it does seem to be essential for our brains. If we don't sleep we may become dizzy and irritable and find it much harder to concentrate or do complex tasks. Our memories seem less efficient and we may have problems finding the words to explain what we want to say.

'Oh hell, I can't concentrate anymore,' thought Helen turning to the clock. The clock on her bedside table read 4 a.m. She looked at the pile of papers scattered all over the floor and the bed and the few pathetic pages she seemed to have taken hours to write. 'I'm never going to get this essay finished. I can't think of the right words and it's all jumbled up and there's something about some stuff on whether things are real, or whatever that bloke said who did the er, lesson um, when was it, er – if I could just remember, then maybe I could find the notes…' She reached out to get a book from the bookshelf when the pot of pens on the desk tipped over knocking the cup of cold coffee she had forgotten to drink onto the pages she had so laboriously written out.

I will talk in more detail about sleep deprivation studies later in this section. The main finding with all of them is that they illustrate how lack of sleep does causes problems with higher order thinking and this seems directly related to the amount of REM sleep we get. There is evidence that people show higher levels of REM sleep following some kind of stressful life event or trauma. Therefore we can assume that perhaps the restorative function of sleep is not that accurate for the body, but certainly plays a part in restoring our psychological functioning to maximum efficiency.

Evolutionary theory

Because the lengths we sleep don't seem to have any relationship to what we did the day before, it has been suggested that perhaps the function of sleep is similar to hibernation. It is to conserve energy when the environment is hostile, such as having limited food, or when we would be inefficient such as in the dark. It is true that our bodies mimic a kind of mini-hibernation because we have a lower metabolic rate, lower temperature and lower blood pressure when we are asleep.

If we accept this theory, it would make sense in suggesting that animals should vary in how much sleep they need depending on different aspects of their lifestyles. For example, if it takes them long periods of time to search for food, they should sleep less. If their food is low in nutrients, such as cattle and horses, they need to eat a great deal in order to survive so they should sleep less. How safe they are from predators should also enter the equation, with animals such as sheep sleeping less than foxes.

The research evidence supporting this idea comes from the average amount of time various animals spend sleeping. Horses sleep for approximately 2.9 hours per day, while goats and sheep sleep for 3.5 hours per day and cattle for 3.9 hours a day. The reason for this is because none of them are predators; in fact they are prey for other animals and therefore need to keep watch for potential danger in order to survive. In fact, even when they do sleep, they are easily aroused. They are also all herbivores, living on grass and other plant matter which contains little goodness, so they have to consume vast quantities of food throughout the course of the day to fulfil their nutritional requirements.

Humans sleep for an average of 8 hours per day because the food consumed is much higher in nutritional value and can be eaten at more regularly spaced intervals. Most predators, such as foxes and cats, live in relative safety and will only eat one meal a day and that meal will contain all their nutritional requirements. Consequently they can sleep for much longer periods of time in relation to their body size, as foxes sleep for an average of 9.8 hours per day and cats for 14.5 hours per day.

The one problem with this theory according to Hauri (1979) is that sheep and goats are extremely vulnerable to predators, and if sleep was purely an evolutionary activity why would they sleep at all, bearing in mind that the minute they go to sleep they become even more vulnerable than ususal.

How is sleep investigated?

Most of the work undertaken on sleep has been carried out in 'sleep laboratories'. These consist of one or several small bedrooms next to an observation room where the experimenter spends the night and monitors the sleeper's behaviour both by observation and also by wiring the sleeper up to a series of recording instruments. The sleeper may also be videoed to record his behaviour. Can you imagine how difficult it would be not only to sleep in a strange bed but also to know you were being watched. I always imagine some poor soul lying there with his mouth wide open, snoring away and looking really unpleasant! I don't think I would volunteer to take part.

If you remember the first section where I talked about different types of investigations, I briefly mentioned that it is possible to monitor and measure the activity of the nervous system by taking physiological measurements. You can read more about the different types of machines in the next section, but in sleep laboratories subjects would be wired to three types of machines which all work in the same way:

- An EEG measures brain activity (Electroencephalogram) – here the electrodes are placed over the head to record the electrical activity of the underlying neurones.
- An EMG measures muscle activity (Electromyogram) – here the facial and jaw muscle activity is monitored by electrodes being placed on the jaw area.
- An EOG measures eye movements (Electro oculogram) – here the movement of the eyes are recorded by electrodes being placed around the eye socket.

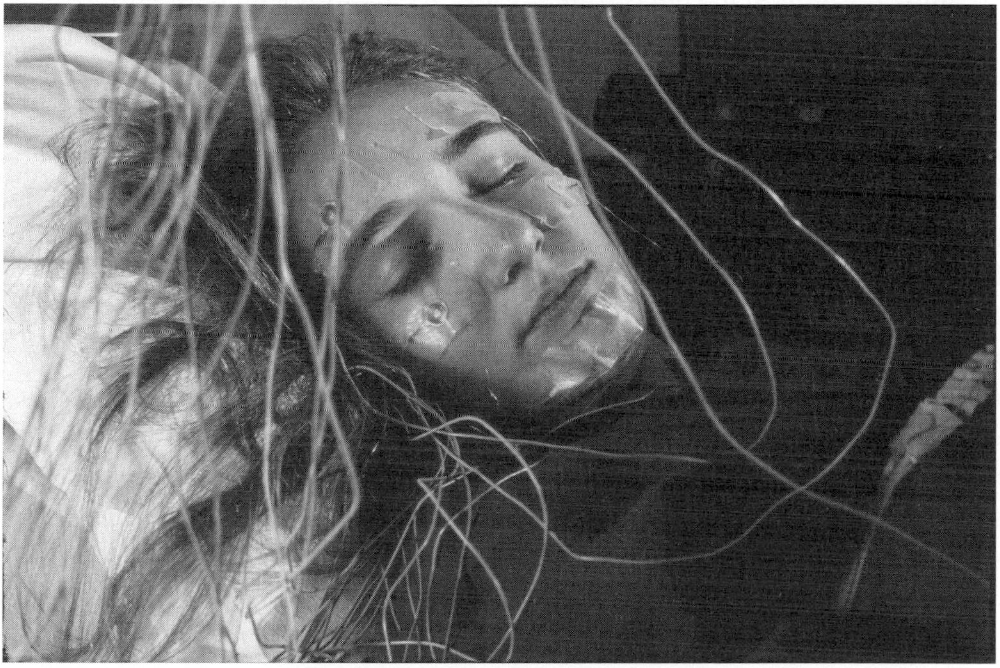

A subject who has been "wired up" before sleeping. Would this affect your quality of sleep?

The subjects who take part in such studies may have been deprived of sleep or allowed to sleep for limited periods. They may even have the type of sleep monitored to see what happens if, for example, they are not allowed to enter REM sleep. The types of measurements taken will give a good indication of what is going on. They may also be woken at regular intervals or specific times and questioned about dreams or feelings they may be having.

It seems that if we are deprived of sleep or sleep is limited for one night it has no serious effects, but what happens is that we will simply fall asleep much more quickly and sleep longer the following night.

> 'What time did you come in last night, Andrew?'
>
> 'Er, um, about three o'clock.'
>
> 'Liar! I know you didn't because I got up at seven this morning and your bed hadn't been slept in. I don't know how you think you are going to manage to concentrate at work today when you have had no sleep.'
>
> 'I'll be fine mum, honest,' said Andrew unconvincingly.

I'm sure you have all been without sleep for one night and managed quite well. It's interesting that whatever you are doing during the night you are up is actually quite relevant. If it's interesting or fun – it's no problem. If you are working it's slightly different. When my children were small, I used to work night shifts in a nursing home and then come home and stay up all the next day with them. I felt absolutely trashed by the following evening, and I'm sure I was probably more scratchy than normal, but I would go to bed at about 9 o'clock and feel fine the next day.

If the amount of time subjects are allowed to sleep is gradually reduced, then they seem to suffer few effects. Webb and Bonnett (1979) (cited in Lahey, 1983) reduced the amount of sleep they allowed a group of volunteers to sleep from eight to four hours a night over a two month period and found they suffered no obvious effects. I actually tried this in my quest to sleep less, but it didn't work for me. However, if sleep is suddenly reduced, say in the case of hospital doctors being on duty, then their ability to perform certain tasks is reduced. If the task is simple, no performance decrement (decrease in performance) is shown, but if it is a complicated task which needs planning and thought, then performance declines. This goes along with the idea that the frontal cortex seems to be the area of the brain that requires sleep as this is the area which is involved in things like higher order thinking, planning and problem solving.

In order to test these effects out, subjects have been given a number of different tasks such as problem-solving tasks, reaction time tasks (to see how quickly they respond to a given stimulus) and also vigilance tasks (where they have to watch screens for example and report a change in the display – a bit like an air traffic controller). Subjects showed a number of symptoms of sleep deprivation such as no originality in their responses, staring into space, memory deficits for recent events or information, a decline in their spatial orientation, word fluency and spelling and finally speaking in a monotone.

If prolonged lack of sleep can be so debilitating, and sleeping in the day is so difficult, it doesn't say much for the people who work at night does it? Think of hospital doctors, nurses, airport staff and so on. Without wishing to unduly concern you, it is interesting to note that two of the most frightening environmental disasters happened in the early hours of the morning.

In March 1979 there was an accident in Unit 2 at the Three Mile Island nuclear power station. As a result of both equipment failure and human error, the core of the reactor was exposed. This generated extremely high temperatures which resulted in damage to the fuel and equipment inside the reactor. It took time to bring it back under control but by then approximately 400,000 gallons of radioactive water had collected on the floor of the reactor building. Radioactive gases had also been released and remained trapped in the concrete container surrounding the reactor.

The incident at Chernobyl in Russia happened in 1986 as result of a well-meaning safety check. It was considered the largest and most hazardous nuclear accident in history and involved an enormous amount of radiation being released into the atmosphere. I remember that there was concern for the contamination of pasture and sheep kept in the Lake District during that time. It involved a huge number of people and the after effects are still being dealt with today.

If these two events were the result of sleep deprivation in key personnel, surely it means that we shouldn't take the effects of sleep deprivation lightly.

There are many studies and reports about the effects of sleep deprivation, and I have only mentioned a few. However, I remember hearing a lecture about sleep some years ago and being told about a 17 year old high school student called Randy Gardner who stayed awake for 264 hours. I am not sure how he did this, but the lecturer claimed that he recovered with 14 hours 40 minutes sleep and could at that point play an arcade game and beat the researcher. Jim Horne of Loughborough University has reported that five to eight days of sleep deprivation has little effect on the body. However, motivation might be impaired and there are sometimes small effects on the immune system but this is caused by the stress of not sleeping rather than the lack of sleep. If, however, we are deprived of sleep, it seems that there is what is called a 'rebound effect'.

Before I can explain about the rebound effect, I need to briefly describe the stages or levels of sleep which can be identified by changes in electrical activity in the brain. When the pineal gland starts to produce melatonin, we start to feel drowsy. If we are in bed, no problem, and so we start to drift off into Stage 1 sleep. Have you ever noticed that just as you are drifting you jerk violently and it sometimes wakes you up. This is where the neurones are randomly discharging before you enter the second stage.

Stage 2 is deeper than level one but we can still be easily woken. The heart rate, breathing and brain activity is slower than stage one.

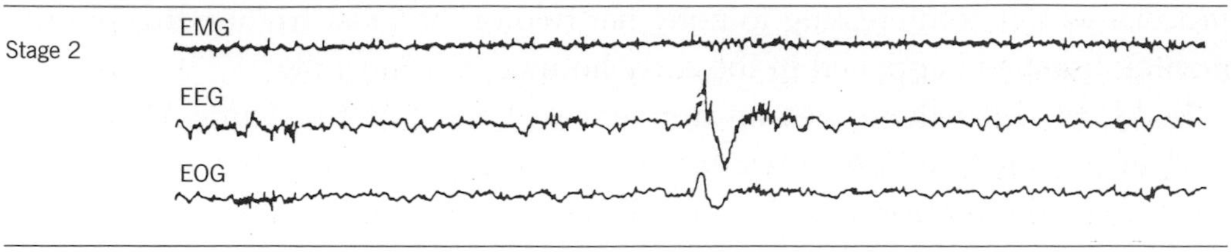

Stage 3 is deeper still with more long, slow delta waves. The person is difficult to wake at this point and their heart rate, blood pressure and temperature are dropping.

Stage 4 is known as delta or quiet sleep. This is the stage where it is hardest to wake the person unless the stimulus is very relevant such as the alarm clock or a baby. This sleep lasts for approximately thirty minute bursts. During this stage we are able to toss and turn or move our limbs as necessary.

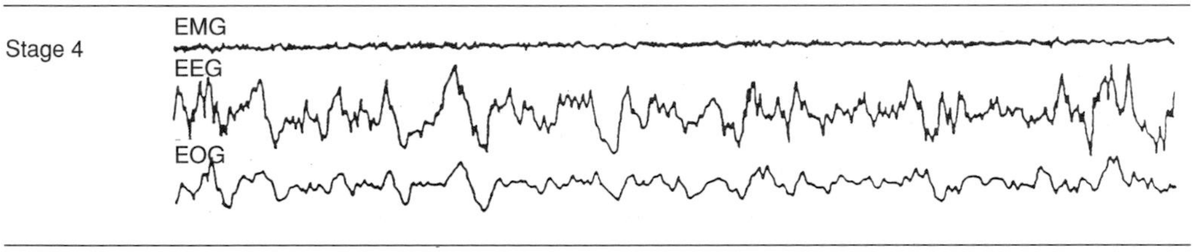

A whole sleep cycle lasts for about 90 minutes and involves us moving 'down' through all the four stages and returning 'up' again during that time.

This 90 minute cycle is present in infants who are fed on demand and has also been noticed in adult activities. We can be engaged in something for about 90 minutes but suddenly have the urge to go and get a cup of coffee or have a break – think of watching television for example.

When we return to where stage 1 would be, we enter a different kind of sleep known as rapid eye movement sleep (REM sleep) where our eyes dart back and forth beneath closed eyelids. It is different because it is an active sleep – active in terms of our brain waves and eye movements, but strangely enough our bodies are actively inhibited from movement. That means that we are paralysed so we don't move during this period of sleep. Because the blood pressure rises, this is the time when men get erections in their sleep although the rest of their bodies are immobile. Our pulse, respiration rates and blood pressure increase and our brain wave patterns look like they would when we are awake. The trouble is, it is even harder to wake someone from this sleep than stage 4. It is sometimes known as 'paradoxical sleep,' a term coined by Michel Jouvet in the late 1950s. Jouvet was carrying out research into insomnia when he noticed how high brain activity occurred that resembled wakefulness but at the same time the body was in extreme relaxation and was very hard to rouse. The term paradoxical literally means 'apparently self-contradictory' as the activity of the brain and body are in total contrast to each other.

It was believed that we only dream during this REM sleep, however it has now been shown that we do dream during stage 4 sleep, though the dreams are not stories like the ones we are used to. If people are awakened from stage 4 sleep they are more likely to report a situation or some kind of feeling or awareness, although some of the most terrifying nightmares occur during stage 4 sleep.

We still don't know the function of dreaming. Some researchers suggest that it is simply a way of putting the events of the day in some kind of order; others like Freud believed that it is our unconscious finally having free rein, and our id running away with itself. Others say it is simply random neuronal firings which trigger some distant memory or thought that we try to make sense of and therefore turn into part of a story. Whatever the reason, it seems that REM sleep is far more important to us than non-REM sleep.

To return to the rebound effect, if we deprive someone of sleep for a night, they will spend more of the next night in REM sleep than normal, but will not necessarily increase the amount of non-REM sleep they have missed. This is called the REM rebound where we seem to compensate for the amount of REM sleep lost. This explains why people aren't too bad at having their sleeping hours slowly reduced. What they do is to pack their REM sleep into a shorter period and reduce the amount of non-REM sleep. There have been a number of reports as to what happens to humans if they are deprived of REM sleep. Although the findings are contradictory, it seems that people may develop a kind of paranoia where they are very suspicious of other people's motives. They may also have what are often called hallucinations but are really visual illusions or distortions – that is they are based on some external stimulus but it is actually interpreted wrongly (Dement 1960).

Most of the research on sleep has either looked at types of sleep, sleep deprivation or dreaming. The key study in this area is one that was undertaken by Dement and Kleitman and looked at the relationship between sleep patterns and dreaming.

W. Dement and N. Kleitman (1957). The relation of eye movements during sleep to dream activity: an objective method for the study of dreaming.

Journal of Experimental Psychology, 53, 339–46.

The aim of the study was to see if the physiological aspects of REM sleep relate to subjects' experience of dreaming.

Design

A laboratory experiment which involved collecting data by observation and questionnaire.

Subjects seven adult males and two adult females, five of whom were studied intensively while the other four were used to confirm the findings.

Materials Sleep laboratory with specialised equipment to objectively measure sleep. Electrodes were attached to subject's eyes to measure eye movement, and to the subject's scalp to measure brain activity. A doorbell was used to wake subjects and a tape recorder was used to record subjects' recollections of what they had been dreaming.

There were 3 hypotheses:

1. There is a significant association between REM and reported dreaming.
2. There is a significant positive correlation between the estimate of time spent dreaming and the measurement of REM sleep.
3. There is a significant association between the pattern of eye movement and reported content of the dream.

Procedure

On the day before testing subjects were told to avoid alcohol and caffeine but to eat normally. They attended the laboratory at their usual sleep time, and had the electrodes applied before sleeping on their own in a quiet dark laboratory. Subjects were woken at various times during the night by a loud doorbell at various times during the night, some of which were during REM or during non–REM. They immediately spoke into a tape recorder to report whether they had been dreaming or not and returned to sleep in less than 5 minutes. There was no contact with the experimenter before dream reports (to avoid any bias) and subjects were not told whether their eyes had been moving.

Testing hypothesis 1

Subjects were woken in one of four ways and asked if they had been dreaming.

Two subjects were woken according to a random numbers table to remove any likely pattern.

One subject was woken at the whim of the experimenter.

One subject was woken during 3 REM periods and 3 non-REM periods.

One subject was woken randomly (having been told he would only be woken during REM sleep).

Testing hypothesis 2

Subjects were woken either 5 or 15 mins after REM sleep began and were asked to estimate the length of their dream by choosing one or other length. They were also asked to relate the content of their dream, and the length of the narrative was correlated with the duration of REM sleep before they were woken.

Testing hypothesis 3

Subjects were woken one minute after one of four patterns of eye movement had occurred. They were asked what they had just dreamed. The patterns were mainly vertical, mainly horizontal, both vertical and horizontal and little/no eye movement.

Results

For all hypotheses, dreaming was accepted if the subject could give a relatively coherent and detailed description of the dream.
All subjects showed periods of REM every night that they slept in the laboratory and this was shown by low voltage fast EEG patterns. The total number of awakenings (for all nine subjects) was 351 times over 61 nights which averaged out at 5.7 awakenings per subject per night.

The average occurrence of REM was one period every 92 minutes for the whole group with variations between 70 and 104 minutes. The length of REM was between 3 minutes and 50 minutes, and they tended to increase in length as the night progressed.

Hypothesis 1

More dreams were reported in REM than non-REM.

When subjects failed to report dreams from non-REM this was earlier in the night. Subjects were woken 132 times when they had ceased REM by more than 8 minutes and, of these, only 6 subjects recalled dreams. However when woken within 8 minutes of ceasing REM, 5 out of 17 reported dreaming. This indicates that the closer subjects were to REM, the more likely they were to be able to recall their dreams.

The table below shows that there were significantly more recollections of dreams from subjects woken in REM sleep than non-REM sleep.

	Rapid Eye Movement		Non-Rapid Eye Movement	
Subject	**Dream Recall**	**No Recall**	**Dream Recall**	**No Recall**
DN	17	9	3	21
IR	26	8	2	29
KC	36	4	3	31
WD	37	5	1	34
PM	24	6	2	23
KK	4	1	0	5
SM	2	2	0	2
DM	2	1	0	1
MG	4	3	0	3
Totals	**152**	**39**	**11**	**149**

	Estimates (in minutes) after 5 minutes REM		Estimates (in minutes) after 15 minutes REM	
Subject	**Right**	**Wrong**	**Right**	**Wrong**
DN	8	2	5	5
IR	11	1	7	3
KC	7	0	12	1
WD	13	1	15	1
PM	6	2	8	3
Total	**45**	**6**	**47**	**13**

Hypothesis 2

There was a significant relationship between subjects' estimate of dream length and amount of time spent in REM for both the 5 and 15 minute period. There was also a significant relationship between length of narrative and REM period. Results of dream-duration estimates after 5 or 15 minutes of rapid eye movements

The table also shows that there were significantly more correct estimates of length of REM than incorrect estimates. It also shows that there were more wrong estimates after 15 minutes REM.

Hypothesis 3

There was a strong association between the pattern of REMs and the content of the dream, with horizontal and vertical movements relating to dream reports of looking up and down or left and right. The kinds of situations reported by subjects were such events as looking up cliff faces, or throwing tomatoes at each other.

Periods where movements were mixed were associated with looking at close objects and the periods where there was little or no movement was associated with dreams of looking at stationary or distant objects.

Discussion

All the subjects showed regular periods of REM whilst they slept. The results obtained by waking subjects strongly support the connection between REM sleep and dreaming. EEG patterns also showed that subjects were at the lightest level of sleep during the REM periods. When subjects were woken during non-REM sleep they occasionally reported feelings of emotional states rather than narrative dreams, such as anxiety or pleasantness. The eye movements of subjects also related to dream content which would indicate that the eyes are moving as if seeing what the subject was dreaming about. However, babies in the womb have periods of REM, and yet they must be unable to recall images of objects and events as they have had no experience of such objects.

Later studies have indicated that not everyone follows this pattern, with some subjects who claim they rarely dream reporting a low level of dreaming during REM sleep. It therefore seems likely that there are individual differences between subjects.

We must remember that this study was looking for a relationship between REM and dreaming. Even though a significant relationship was found, we still cannot confirm whether one causes the other or whether they just happen to coincide by chance.

Evaluation

The situation may have affected the type of sleep shown by subjects; after all sleeping wired up in a laboratory is not conducive to getting an excellent night's sleep. Therefore we could criticise the study for a lack of ecological validity. Also the nature of the method of waking subjects may have affected their ability to recall the dream.

The disproportionate number of males to females may have influenced the study, and the sample size was extremely small. We cannot be sure that the results of this study were not simply biased towards the dream patterns of men rather than women.

Even though there were far more reports of dreaming during REM and no dreaming during non-REM the reason for the lack of reports of dreaming during non-REM may have been something to do with the depth of sleep and the lack of ability of subjects to remember the dream as they awoke from such a deep level of sleep.

The length of dream narrative was influenced by the talkativeness of the subjects with subjects who were naturally more talkative giving a much longer description of their dreams. This in turn might have influenced how quickly they went back to sleep.

Key terms

REM – a period of sleep characterised by rapid eye movements in various directions. During REM people are effectively paralysed.

Non-REM sleep – no eye movements are evident and people can turn over and adjust their position.

Random numbers table – a table of random numbers generated by computer which are often used in experiments to prevent any sort of bias.

Narrative dreams – dreams which involve stories.

Key questions

1. Why were the subjects 'wired up' rather than being observed to look for REM sleep?
2. Why were the subjects woken by bells and asked to report the content of their dreams into tape recorders.
3. Do you think the subject sample was representative?
4. Do you think the individual differences between subjects might influence the way the dreams were reported?
5. Give an explanation as to why people may have problems remembering dreams in non-REM sleep.

Postscript

Much research has shown that the majority of people, when woken from REM sleep, report that they were dreaming. However Dr. Mark Solms of St. Bartholomews and Royal London School of Medicine recently discussed the fact that the relationship my not actually be causal after all. He claimed that the reported relationship has made people accept that REM sleep *is* the physical manifestation of dreaming. The trouble is, we still don't know whether dreaming is simply a by-product of REM sleep or REM sleep is a by-product of dreaming. By this I mean do our eyes move because we are dreaming, or do we start to dream because our eyes are moving? On the other hand, they may not actually have any relationship with each other and just happen to coincide by chance.

Dr. Solms investigated nine patients who had all had their cortical-limbic circuit damaged or destroyed by trauma (stabbing), bacterial infection or pathology (tumors). They all reported that they no longer dreamed, however they still all showed normal REM sleep in terms of eye movements and brain wave patterns.

This intrigued Dr. Solms, and he went on to discover that 70–90 per cent of patients who had undergone lobotomies in the past reported loss of dreams. These were patients who had the same circuit and part of the frontal lobes destroyed in order to control their behaviour. He concluded that as rapid eye movements and their associated brain wave patterns are controlled by a different area of the brain altogether, this would indicate that the relationship between REM and dreams is possibly no more than correlational evidence.

Hemisphere deconnection or (split brains)

As we have already discussed, the brain is divided into two relatively symmetrical halves. We also know that the left hand side of the brain controls the right hand side of the body and vice versa but it is not known why that crossover occurs. The two hemispheres are joined by what are known as commissural fibres and the corpus callosum is by far the largest commissure (cross-hemisphere connection), responsible for carrying the majority of information between the two hemispheres.

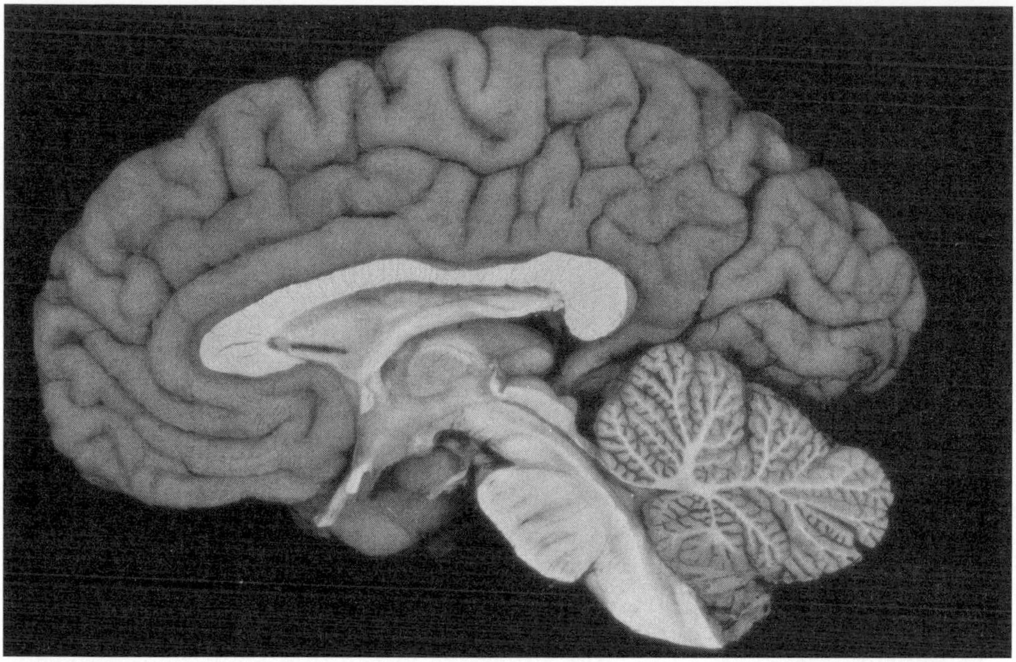

This median section through the centre of a human brain shows the corpus callosum. The large curved central structure if the corpus callosum, connecting the two cerebral hemispheres.

I expect you will have heard that the two hemispheres have different functions. It is true, they do, but nowhere near as different as we are led to believe by the large number of books which seem to suggest that the left hand side of the brain is the clever side, and the right hand side is the spiritual, artistic part!

> When I was younger I remember, finding a book on my mother's bookshelf called 'Drawing with the right side of the brain'. Pulling it down from the bookshelf, I delved into its pages, feeling inspired that perhaps I was too 'left brain dominant' and had lost touch with my creative self. Some time later, after doing many of the exercises it suggested, I decided that either my left brain was so dominant that my right brain had withered up and died a death, or perhaps this idea was just too simplistic. I still couldn't draw...

In most people there is some 'lateralisation of function' which means that one side has a different role to the other. In the majority of people the language centres are on the left hand side – Broca's area is responsible for speech production, and Wernické's area is responsible for speech comprehension. This is so for the majority of right handed people, although people who are left handed may well have their language centres on the right hand side of their brain. However, it is virtually impossible to give exact percentages so it is best to accept the fact that the majority of people, left and right handed, have their speech centres located in the left hemisphere. This would mean that any damage you may get to the left side of your head would probably leave you unable to speak or understand.

Why this is the case is another matter. One suggestion is that having speech centres in both hemispheres is likely to cause stuttering. It would seem quite likely that both centres would be sending impulses to the muscles responsible for speech, and these impulses may well arrive at slightly different times, so that speech will not be synchronized. Jones (1966) performed a number of operations on patients who had blood clots or tumors near their left hemisphere speech centres and who also stuttered. He knew in advance that they were quite unusual because he had discovered, by anaesthetising one hemisphere at a time with sodium amytal, that they could still carry on a conversation. This showed that they had speech centres in both hemispheres. What he discovered after the operations was that their speech was quite normal, and that they had stopped stuttering.

In physiological terms the only difference in the two hemispheres, besides the well known speech centres, is an area of the temporal cortex called the 'planum temporale'. Geschwind and Levitsky (1968) found that it is larger in the left than the right hemisphere for 65 per cent of people, equal for 24 per cent and larger in the right hemisphere for 11 per cent. The differences are apparently visible to the naked eye. This is not as exciting as it sounds because this area is known to be important for language.

Much of the evidence which has been gathered about hemisphere function has come from people who have suffered strokes or 'cerebrovascular accidents', as they are correctly called. This is the most common source of brain damage in old age and is caused by either a blood clot or other obstruction closing off an artery, or an artery rupturing. This will result in the area around the site being deprived of oxygen or nutrients and the relevant neurones dying. Because the left hand side of the brain controls the right hand side of the body, a left sided stroke will result in right sided lack of function. This can be quite mild, for example a non-mobile side of the face, or more severe as with hemiplegia, where the whole of the right side of the body ceases to function. What makes it worse is the fact that the person often loses the ability to either comprehend or produce words, and so not only are they non-mobile but they are also isolated in their own little world.

I once had the privilege to meet a stroke patient who, prior to her accident, was an artist. She had suffered a cerebro-vascular accident in the left hand side of her brain, which left her with hemiplegia and loss of language production, apart from the word "Ascii". She was completely aware of what was going on, understood every word that you said to her, got extremely angry when people treated her as if she was stupid, and was so frustrated with her lack of ability to move that I felt so much for her. When she became frustrated or wanted anything, you would hear 'Assscccciiiiii, Assccii, Ascii,' booming out of her door. Why 'Ascii', I have no idea, but that was the sum total of her linguistic production. I used to think that she must have felt so completely trapped inside her body, unable to communicate in any meaningful way because the words had gone. She could still understand but could no longer turn her thoughts or wants into any sort of linguistic form.

Having made the point that one side of the brain controls the other side of the body, we should note that there are a couple of exceptions to this rule.

Vision

In vision, the input from the left half of each eye goes to the right hemisphere and the input from the right half of each eye goes to the left hemisphere, as seen below.

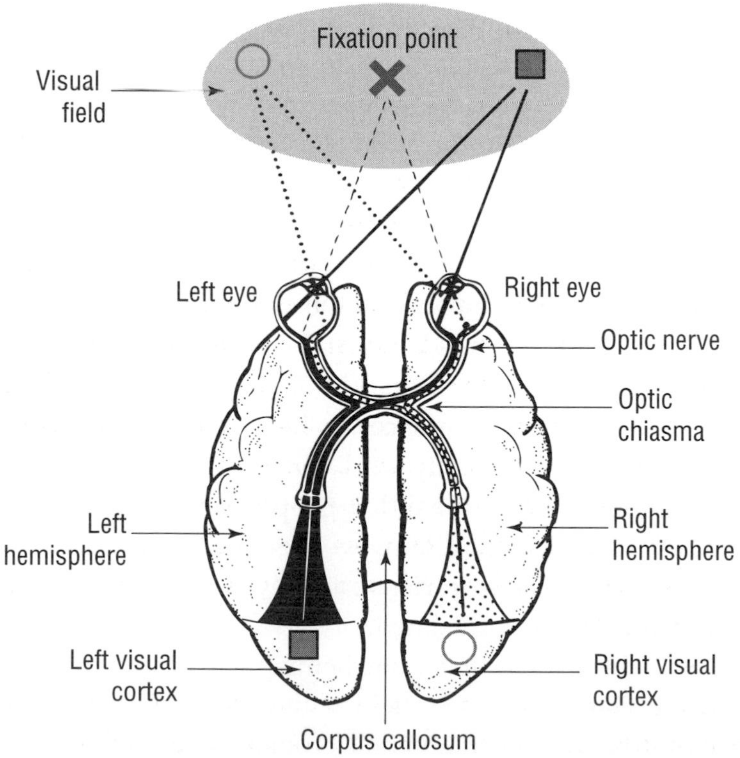

To explain this more simply:

- Light from the world stimulates the receptors at the back of the eye.
- The light from the left half of the world stimulates the receptors on the right half of both eyes (shown by the dotted line), and the light from the right half of the world stimulates the receptors on the left half of both eyes (shown by the black line).
- The right half of each retina connects to the right hemisphere and, thus, the right hemisphere sees the left visual field.

Although this seems complicated, it is actually accurate. But the result is simply that things that appear to the right of your nose are 'seen' by your left hemisphere and things that appear to the left of your nose are 'seen' by your right hemisphere.

Touch

Hands cross over so the information from the right hand goes to the left hemisphere and vice versa.

Hearing

Each ear receives sound from just one side, but sends 90% of its input to the other side of the brain, and retains 10% on the side it entered. The reason for this is so we can pinpoint where a noise is coming from by comparing the input from both ears – we couldn't do this if the information only went to one side.

Smell

Information from each nostril remains on the same side as it enters, so odours that are experienced by the left hand side of the brain are processed on the left.

If you want to look at the differences in hemispheres, there are some fun tasks you can do (although they only work for people with intact brains).

Kimura (1973) found that right handed people move their right hand more often than their left when speaking. However, left handed people show no hand preference. Watch your teachers or friends as they talk and notice whether hand movement and 'handedness' are related.

Kinsborne (1972) discovered that if one hemisphere becomes more active, the eyes tend to turn towards the visual field of that hemisphere. So it someone is trying to work out the answer to a verbal problem, they will gaze to the right significantly more often than they will gaze to the left. Similarly, if someone is trying to work out the answer to a spatial question, such as where something is located on a cognitive map (map inside your head), the eyes will turn significantly more to the left. However, this is only true for right handed people and left handed people are inconsistent in their results. Try this by studying puzzle books or puzzles printed in newspapers.

Hicks (1975) suggested finding a stick that it is quite difficult to balance on your right index finger. Then start talking and see if the task gets harder. In fact you can time how long you can balance it for when you are talking and not talking. However, if you are left handed, again the results may be quite variable.

If we return to the differences in the hemispheres, you will recall that the main differences between the two hemispheres relates to language. Ornstein (1986) suggested that the right hand side of the brain is involved in pulling different things together to form a whole picture or concept whereas the left hand side is better for breaking down information into different units for analysis. This is why the right hand side of the brain is better at spatial tasks and artistic activities and the left hand side is better for analytical thought. There is some evidence to support the idea that the left hand side of the brain is more analytical and logical and the right side is more holistic and sensory (Rasmussen and Milner, 1977). The right brain seems to be related to depression and pessimism. It has also been noted that people who get left brain strokes are often extremely depressed, irrespective of the amount of damage done to the brain, presumably because the right brain is the only normally functioning part now, and its whole outlook on life is more pessimistic than optimistic. On the other hand, right brain damage often leaves the person with an optimistic outlook, even though their prognosis is poor.

Rita Carter (1998) reports the tale of a senior American judge who suffered from a right brain stroke.

> '…he insisted on continuing at the bench despite having lost his ability to weigh evidence in anything like a sensible way. He maintained an exceptionally jolly courtroom, happily allowing serious criminals to go free while occasionally dispatching minor offenders to lifelong prison sentences. He resisted his colleagues' attempts to persuade him to retire and was finally sacked. Thanks to his right brain damage he seemed perfectly content – if puzzled – by this turn of events, and subsequently enjoyed a long and happy retirement.'
>
> *(Carter, 1998, p 36)*

We have now considered that the two symmetrical hemispheres are only slightly different in the tasks they carry out. In order for us to function adequately, these two parts need to communicate with each other and we have mentioned that they do this by means of the corpus callosum. This gives the side of the brain without speech centres access to words and descriptions which it would be without if there was no bridge between the two. It does not take a huge amount of imagination to think what would happen if that bridge was not there. Such a thought gives new meaning to the phrase 'the left hand does not know what the right hand is doing!'

There are rare instances of people having the connections between their two hemispheres severed, either as a result of accidents or more likely as one of the surgical treatments for epilepsy. Epileptic seizures are a result of abnormal electrical discharges of groups of brain neurons, described by Carlson (1986) as the 'wild sustained firing of cerebral neurons'. The source of the hyperactivity is usually in the temporal lobe and results in the person briefly losing contact with reality and even experiencing hallucinations. Sometimes the seizures can be more sustained, and these are known as 'Grand mal' seizures. During one of these, the person becomes unconscious for a few minutes and experiences muscle spasms which may result in them breaking their bones or damaging themselves, and they may also lose bowel and bladder control. When the seizure is over the muscles relax and the person will wake up but often they are extremely disoriented and embarrassed. A seizure like this would obviously be quite debilitating and would put the person in some danger, so any way of trying to reduce the severity or frequency would obviously be of huge benefit.

One way of reducing the problem, developed by the late Wilder Penfield, is to remove the 'focal point' or original source of the seizures from the temporal lobe; operations of this type have been carried out on conscious patients. They need to be conscious in order to make sure that the surgeon doesn't take away too much brain tissue. The patient would be given a local anaesthetic, and the surgeon would remove the skull and layers of dura mata until the brain was exposed. The focus would have been identified by EEG recordings before surgery and checked by more recordings during surgery. The subject would also have areas surrounding the identified focal point stimulated with the tip of a metal electrode in order see what sort of response the patient made. If the area stimulated was part of the speech centre, then obviously that area would be avoided. The benefit of this method is that it prevents excess tissue or essential tissue from being removed. The by-product of these operations was to give us an excellent map of brain function.

An alternative way of preventing the spread of the wildly excited neuronal firings is to sever the corpus callosum, preventing the other side of the brain from becoming involved and thus reducing the severity of the effects. This method was very successful and it was found that it not only stopped the discharges from spreading, it also reduced the epileptic seizures to negligible proportions.

You would think that an operation of this severity would result in lots of side effects, but the extraordinary aspect is that most of the people who underwent surgery actually had very few side effects which were noticeable in their everyday lives. They were in effect living with two brains in a single head, each one functioning adequately and seemingly suffering no real side effects from the surgery. However, there were side effects and it is these effects that form the focus of the key study undertaken by Roger Sperry in 1968.

Before we look at the study itself, I would like to tell you a little about Sperry and his work. It would be useful to explain how the studies were carried out and the expected results. Sperry is a neuropsychologist who has conducted a number of studies on split brain patients whilst working at the California Institute of Technology. In the early 1950's he had undertaken research by 'splitting' the brains of cats and monkeys and discovered, by training the animals, that you could teach one hemisphere a task but the other hemisphere would remain unaware of the information learned. This supported his idea that the brain consisted of two separate modules rather than one unified whole. In fact he shared the Nobel Prize for physiology and medicine with David Hubel and Torsten Wiesel in 1981. (Hubel and Wiesel pioneered a method of studying the physiology of vision by inserting very thin wire electrodes into the columns of neurones in the optic cortex and recording their response to different stimuli. They discovered that the cells of the optic cortex were arranged in columns that seemed to respond to specific stimuli in a particular orientation.)

Many of the effects of splitting brains were investigated in the laboratory with relatively simplistic tasks. These tasks we will look at in greater detail, but they were not the sort of effects that would be noticed in real life situations, so they lacked a degree of ecological validity. They involved presenting information to one or other eye so that the information went to the opposite side of the brain.

If the information was presented to the right eye, it would go to the left hand side of the brain which contain the speech centres. Therefore the person would be able to say what they had just seen. If the information was presented to the left eye, it would go to the right hand side of the brain which has no speech centre. Therefore the person would know what it was, but would not be able to say what they had just seen. However, if this person was then asked to draw the object with their left hand (and their eyes closed), they could draw the object.

From the diagram shown earlier, you may remember that each eye has information that goes to the opposite side of the brain, crossingover at a point called the 'optic chiasma'. (If this crossover point were severed too, this would mean that information from one eye went to one side of the brain only, and in a few cases this has happened.) In order to sort the situation out with the rest of the subjects, they were asked to fixate (fix their eyes) on a spot in the centre of the screen. The image was projected for 1/10th of a second, which was insufficient time for them to move their eyes enough to send information to the opposite side of the brain. Therefore, for any of the split brain studies which involve projecting objects for someone to look at, just accept the fact that the information projected on one side of the fixation point was **only** seen by that eye and **only** went to the opposite side of the brain.

As I said earlier, these studies aren't really ecologically valid because in the real world the situation would not occur, unless they only had one eye. However, a later set of studies on split brain patients was conducted by Gazzaniga et al. (1977) and again, although they lack ecological validity, they also showed how important it is for the two hemispheres to connect.

Gazzaniga et al. developed a contact lens which allowed the presentation of sophisticated images to one side of the retina only and therefore to only one side of the cortex. In one study they presented a female subject, V.P., with a short film showing one person throwing another into a fire. The image was presented to right hemisphere (with no language) and although the woman was fully alert throughout the course of the film she was only aware of having seen some kind of light. She reported that she felt scared and jumpy but was not sure why, and so she explained her feelings by saying that she felt scared of Gazzaniga although she knew she liked him.

It seems she labelled her state of arousal by the situation she was in – namely having contact with her surgeon. She transferred the fear the film had created into a fear of Dr. Gazzaniga. Does this remind you of the study by Schachter and Singer?

Beneath the corpus callosum is another tract of fibres that connect the more primitive part of the brain – the 'limbic system'. If you remember, the limbic system is found under the cortex, and forms the junction between the older, more primitive parts of the brain with their unsophisticated emotional responses, and the more logical, reasoning cortex. Here there is another tract of fibres which connect the two hemispheres – the 'anterior commissure'. Very basic information about emotional responses such as anger or fear are passed from this area to both sides of the cortex, but the more sophisticated responses of the cortex are missing.

R.W. Sperry (1968) Hemisphere deconnection and unity in conscious awareness.

American Psychologist, 23, 723–33

The article by Sperry describes the results of a series of experiments undertaken on people who had already had their corpus callosum severed for epilepsy. The aim was to investigate the effects of this deconnection and to show that each hemisphere has different functions, and that information in one side of the brain is not accessible to the other side.

Method

Design

The design was a quasi experiment which compared 'severed' subjects with 'normals' in both laboratory tests and case studies of all the individual patients.

Subjects

Eleven patients who had already undergone surgery as a result of epilepsy. All subjects had a history of severe epilepsy which had not responded to drug therapy. Two of the patients had been successfully operated on to sever their corpus callosum some time before the experiments. The remaining nine had only recently undergone surgery.

Materials The equipment used allowed for various types of sensory information to be presented to one or other hemisphere, in different combinations. Visual information was presented by projecting images on a screen in front of the subject. Tactile information would be presented to either the left or the right hand without the patients being able to see what the object was. A representation of the apparatus is given below.

Procedure

Subjects had to remain in silence during the studies unless they were asked questions by the experimenter.

Visual investigations

Visual investigations involved showing one stimuli at a time to one visual field or showing two stimuli simultaneously to different visual fields.

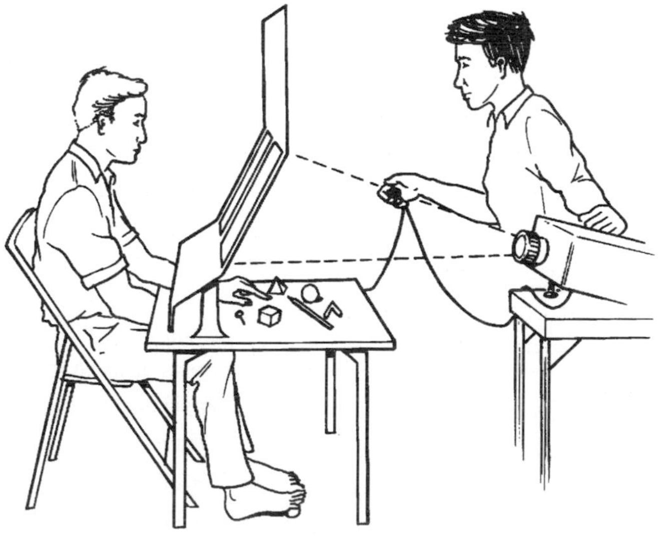

One visual field

These tests require the subject to cover one eye. They are told to look at a fixation point in the centre of the screen. The image would be projected for 1/10th of a second on either the left or the right of the fixation point which would send the image to either the right or left visual field. It was projected for that short space of time to prevent the information going to the wrong half of the visual field if the subject moved their eyes.

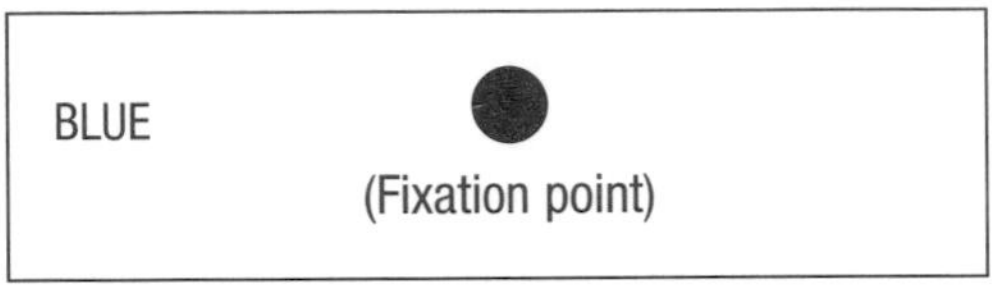

This screen would be sending the image of the word blue to the right side of the brain because it would be seen by the left eye (although in the experiment, pictures of objects were used instead of words).

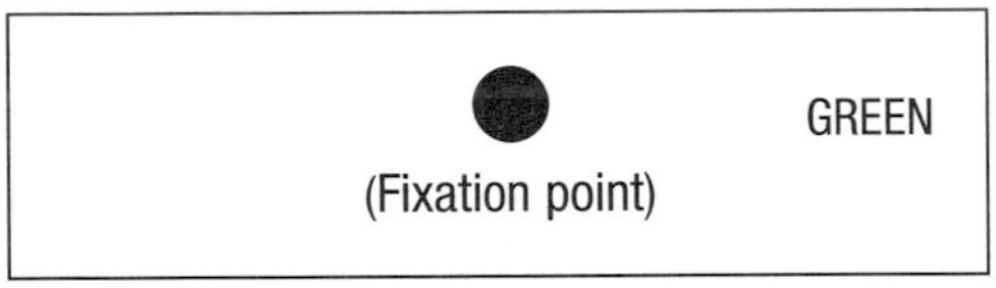

This screen would be sending the image of the word green to the left side of the brain because it would be seen by the right eye.

Both visual fields

The subject would look at the fixation point on the screen while two images are projected simultaneously either side of the fixation point.

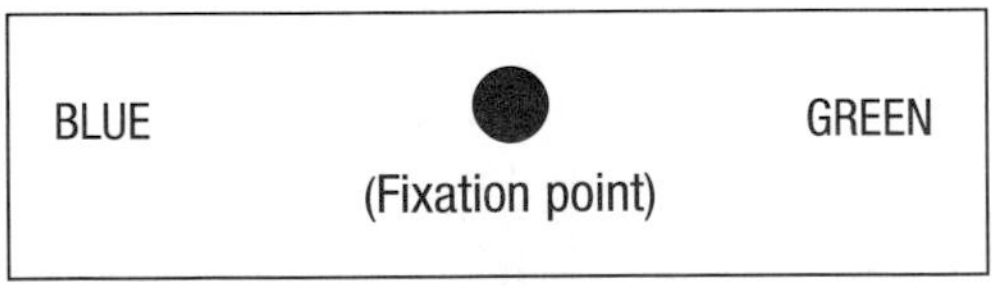

This screen would be sending the image of the word green to the left side of the brain because it would be seen by the right eye and the word blue to the right side of the brain because it would be seen by the left eye.

The subject would then be asked to say what he had seen.

He would then be given a pen with his left hand and be asked to draw what he had just seen.

Tactile Investigations

One hand:

- The object is placed in one hand or other, without the subject being able to see what they are holding and the subject would then be asked to find an object corresponding to what they have seen on the screen.
- The object is placed in one hand or other, without the subject being able to see what they are holding, and then they are asked to say what they have been given.
- The object is placed in one hand or other, without the subject being able to see what they are holding, and then they are asked to point to what they have been given.

Both hands at the same time:

- The subject works with his hands out of sight. He would be given two different objects, one in each hand, and then the objects are taken away.
- The subject is asked to find the objects by touch from a pile of items.
- The subject is asked to say what they have just held.

Tests of the Right hemisphere

Because the right hemisphere does not contain language, in order to test if it has any ability to make mental associations, work logically or experience separate emotions from the left hemisphere, the following tests were undertaken:

- The left eye (therefore right hemisphere) is presented with an object on the screen. The person would then be asked to pick out similar objects by touch from an array of objects.
- Simple mathematical problems were presented to the left eye.
- The left hand is asked to sort objects by touch into shapes or by size or texture.
- An array of geometric shapes are projected to

both visual fields on the screen. In the middle of this array is the picture of a nude which is presented to the left eye only. The subject is later asked if they saw anything other than the geometric shapes.

Results

Visual stimuli presented to one visual field

When subjects were shown an image in one visual field, they would only recognise the image as one they had already seen if it was shown again to the same visual field. The reason for this is because that information would have only gone to one side of the brain and not the other.

- If it was shown to the right eye (left hemisphere) the person was able to say what they had seen, could identify what it was from an array of pictures shown to the right eye by pointing to it, or could find it from an array of objects with their right hand.
- If it was shown to the left eye (right hemisphere) the person was *unable* to name it, but could draw it (with eyes closed) with the left hand, could identify what it was from an array of pictures shown to the left eye by pointing to it, or could find it from an array of objects with their left hand.

Visual stimuli presented to both visual fields

The subject would be able to say what he had seen with his right eye, but would be unaware that he had seen anything else. If he was given a pen with this left hand and asked to draw with his eyes closed, he would again be able to draw what he had seen with his left eye although he would seemingly have no conscious knowledge of having seen anything else and be very surprised when he discovered what he had drawn. He would then be able to name the object, once he had seen his drawing with his right eye.

Tactile investigations

The results of the tactile investigations were the same irrespective of whether one hand held the object at a time or both hands held the objects simultaneously.

- The subject would have no problems identifying an object by name if it was put in the right hand, but if it was put in the left hand they would have no conscious awareness of it. However, they would be able to find it by touch if they put their left hand in a bag full of objects.
- When the objects were placed in one hand or other, subjects could point to what the object was with the same hand that held the object.

Tests of the right hemisphere

- Subjects were able to pick out semantically similar objects, for example if they saw on the screen a picture of wall clock with their left eye (therefore right hemisphere) and the only related item in a tactile array is a toy wrist-watch, this would be the object chosen.
- Right hemispheres can carry out simple mathematical problems.
- Left hands were able to sort objects by shape, size and texture.
- When subjects saw the array of geometric shapes, they would giggle or look embarrassed when the picture of the nude appeared, even though they had no idea what they were responding to. This suggests the right hemisphere has a second conscious entity.

Discussion

The study gave considerable support to the idea that the brain consists of two seemingly independent hemispheres, each with its own consciousness and that there is no transfer of information from one side to the other. For the subjects studied, the dominant hemisphere was the left hand side which contained the speech centres and this explained why, when information was presented to the right hemisphere (via the left eye), they were unable to say what they had experienced. The final tests of the right hemisphere give further support to the idea that the two hemispheres have their own consciousness whereby one responds in a typically human way, by giggling at the nude, while the other one doesn't have a clue what is going on.

Evaluation

The findings of the study would be unlikely to be found in a real life situation because a person with severed corpus callosum who had both eyes would be able to compensate, therefore it lacks ecological validity. The information would be carried to the other hemisphere by speech (but this would indicate that the right hand side of the brain must have some speech abilities, or it would not understand).

The sample was extremely small and this may have influenced the results because there may have been tremendous subject variables. However, as the condition is quite rare, more subjects are difficult to locate.

Key words

Hemisphere – literally means half a sphere divided through the center. It is used to describe half of the cerebral cortex.

Deconnection – two sides of the cerebral cortex when are no longer joined to each other.

Fixation point – the point on the screen on which subjects are asked to fix their eye.

Neuropsychologist – a person who studies the relationship between the brain, the nervous system and behaviour.

Lateralisation of function – different areas of the brain are designated different tasks, such as the left hand side being responsible for speech production and language comprehension.

Key questions

1. What comments can you make about the sample in this study?
2. Why must the researcher make sure that the stimulus is presented for such a short amount of time?
3. Why were the subjects not allowed to see their hands?
4. Do you think the study was ecologically valid?
5. The subjects were all epileptic. Could this have influenced the results?

The Criminal Brain

In the earlier section on learning and aggression, I talked about theories of aggression and how it may be an innate predisposition or was simply learned behaviour. In order to look at the next section, I would very briefly like to clarify what I mean here by aggression because at this point I want to talk about people who are considered criminals. Depending on your concept of aggression, you may feel that crime and aggression are not always one and the same thing.

I recently had a heated debate with one of my lower sixth classes. We were talking about Harold Shipman, the notorious doctor who had killed so many of his patients. I pointed out that we could perhaps try and understand his behaviour by looking at the theories of aggression when one of them said, 'But Harold Shipman wasn't aggressive.'

I have to say that I was horrified! 'How can you say that? Surely murdering all those women in cold blood was the ultimate in aggression?' I shrieked.

'But he didn't hurt them, he was really gentle.'

'But he killed them! Aggression does not have to be overt. We can demonstrate aggression in how we talk to someone or the way we behave, like slamming things around. Think of aggressive career people who don't care who they damage on the way up. None of them are overtly aggressive, but you can't call it anything else.'

'Yes you can, it could be called assertiveness.'

'OK, so imagine a woman who had been brow-beaten by her husband for years, kept short of money and not allowed out unless he was there. For years she did everything for him, looked after the children, always had his dinner on the table, never spoke harshly to him, but was so miserable and unhappy inside. Would you say she was being aggressive if, one night, when he staggered in late from the pub, she decided she couldn't take it any more, and set fire to him as he slept on the sofa?'

'Well, it was an aggressive act.'

'What about if she poisoned him by giving him an overdose of sleeping pills, so he just went to bed and didn't wake up – is that an aggressive act?'

'Um, not really.'

'So would you say she was aggressive?'

'Well… not in this case.'

'But the outcome is the same?'

'Oh hell, I don't know!'

The debate continued for some time and I did understand what that student was saying. Most of us, when we think about aggression, tend to relate it to whacking someone with a large lump of wood or something else quite violent, whereas aggressive acts can be very subtle. Perhaps we need to think of aggression as an act that is intended to harm someone or something but uses a number of different techniques. We can't even say it is anti-social because sometimes aggression may be used as a means of defence. However, what we do need to remember is that criminal behaviour is not always aggressive, but it is always anti-social.

This next section focuses on the ultimate aggressor, one who takes the life of another person. Is their aggression an innate tendency or is it due to the life experiences they have had, and what they have learned?

The innate theories we have looked at so far have simply considered two possible explanations for anti-social behaviour. Lorenz believed that aggression was a biological drive which may be discharged in either anti-social or competitive ways; Dollard said it was only displayed as a result of frustration. Other theories suggest that it is the result of their genetic inheritance: they are born with a predisposition or susceptibility to develop criminal tendencies in later life. It has been suggested that they have a cluster of symptoms which make it impossible to develop the kind of moral control that normal people develop through their childhoods as a direct result of cortical under-arousal. In order to combat this under-arousal, they are hyperactive and inappropriate in their behaviour and are often diagnosed as having 'attention deficit hyperactivity disorder' (ADHD). It has been suggested that this disorder can lead to criminal behaviour where the motive seems irrelevant or nonexistent. However, we should not instantly assume that children diagnosed with ADHD automatically become criminals.

Other theories claim it is due to chromosomal abnormalities. Jacobs et al. (1965) found a higher percentage of people from a prison population in an XYY pattern of chromosomes than a similar sample of the general population. The problem was that even though it was higher than the population as a whole, it was still only 1.5 per cent. This theory has really very little evidence to support it, especially after Witkin et al. (1976) tested over 4500 men and found no evidence that the XYY individuals in the sample were any more aggressive than the rest.

More recent research has suggested that there may be other kinds of biological malfunction, either an excess of hormones or some kind of physiological damage which may have been present at birth or been caused by some kind of accident. It is this aspect of anti-social behaviour we will be looking at in greater detail.

It is not our place here to consider the social explanations of crime, after all we have touched on some of the explanations in earlier parts of this book. Here we are going to consider the idea that perhaps serious criminal actions may be brought about by an abnormality in the functioning of a person's brain. In fact there are a number of studies which have shown that violent offenders have poorer brain functioning than normal controls (Eichelman, 1993, Eysenck and Gudjoinsson, 1989, Elliott, 1987, Lewis et al., 1988, Moffitt, 1988, Raine, 1993). Until recently, however, trying to identify the particular part of the brain that is not functioning properly has been impossible.

Brain imaging techniques

Nowadays, it is possible to use a number of brain imaging techniques in order to assess the functioning of our brains.

EEG machines

I mentioned the EEG machine in the section on sleep, where brain activity is measured by tracing the electrical impulses under the surface of the skull by 'sticking' electrodes to the scalp. The electrical impulses from each of the electrodes are amplified and traced or drawn onto a roll of paper. This is what gives us the information, say, about different types of sleep. They are also used to pick up activity from different areas of the brain, and can be used to detect epilepsy in individuals.

CT scans

CT scans or CAT scans are used for the diagnosis of pathological conditions such as tumors or degenerative diseases. The patient's head is put in a large doughnut shaped ring which contains an x ray tube on one side and opposite an x ray detector. The head is scanned from front to back and then the doughnut is moved around a few degrees and another scan is taken. These images are fed into a computer and this produces a cross-sectional image of the brain. The doughnut can take images of the head from top to bottom so that a whole selection of cross-sectional images can be produced to show the size or site of any abnormalities.

MRI scans

MRI (magnetic resonance imaging) is more precise than the CT scanner as it shows far more detail in soft tissue. It works using strong magnetic field and radio pulses. Patients lie in a round tunnel surrounded by a large magnet which generates a powerful magnetic field. The required part of the anatomy is 'magnetised' and exposed to radio pulses which cause the tissues to give off radio signals that can be measured. Hundred and hundreds of measurements are made which are converted by computer into a two dimensional picture of the area.

PET scans

PET scans (positron emission topography) work in a very different way to the other techniques. PET scans actually look at the different levels of metabolic activity in the brain. Every cell in the body needs energy in the form of glucose, and in the brain neurones use glucose from the bloodstream as their source of energy. Therefore, by injecting a person with glucose which has been mixed with a small amount of a radioactive tracer compound, it is possible to see how much glucose each area of the brain is using. The PET scan measures the amount of radioactivity and sends the information to a computer which will draw cross-sections of the brain, showing the areas using different amounts of glucose as different colours. If an area is really working hard, it is going to require more glucose and this technique makes it easy to see.

By comparing PET scans of normal people with people who have some kind of disorder, it is possible to identify the areas that differ. It is also used to identify which areas work hardest when we are doing specific tasks, such as listening to music or solving mathematical problems.

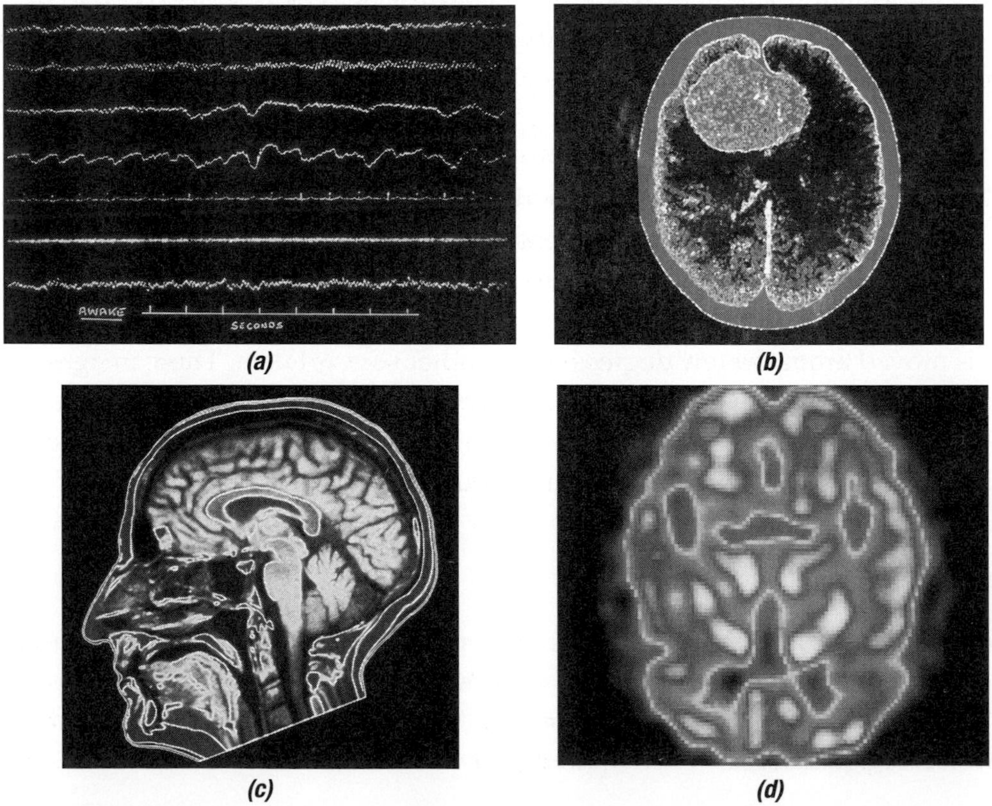

(a) (b) (c) (d)

(a) Traces from EEG, EOG and ECG machines (b) A cross section of the skull from a CT scan (c) An MRI image (d) Activity in the brain from a PET scan which shows areas of differing activity.

Let's return to the people who have committed anti-social acts. I don't know if you remember Peter Sutcliffe, the 'Yorkshire Ripper'. He tried to plead insanity as the reason for his murdering of 13 women – this plea was discounted. One of the biggest problems is that we are really unable to differentiate between the sane and the insane. You will see in the next chapter on abnormality that even people who are totally normal can be judged as insane and admitted to psychiatric hospitals. Wouldn't it be good if we could just stick people in some equipment and scan their brains and then label them accordingly?

'O.K. Mr. Smith, come in. It's time for your annual scan to find out if you are normal or not.'

Mr. Smith edged his way towards the door and kind of hung about, debating whether or not to run. Every year he had to go through this nightmare of being scanned to find out if he could go on living a normal life. His best friend was found abnormal just last month and had been disposed of in the Human Waste Disposal Institute attached to the council offices. He couldn't understand why. His friend wasn't abnormal. The only thing he had ever done wrong was to park on a double yellow line for a few minutes while picking up his daughter but the letter came the next week, saying that his scan was abnormal and he had to attend for termination.

'Come in man, we haven't got all day,' said the official. 'Take off your shirt and lie down on the bed and whatever happens, don't move. You know the procedure, after all it is compulsory for everyone from the age of twelve.'

Mr. Smith didn't run. What was the point? If he got out of the building, he would only be caught and taken back by the authorities, so he might as well do it now.

He lay down on the bed and put his arms down by his sides. The bed slid inside a giant tube and he closed his eyes. As he lay there, he felt the most horrific feeling. He wanted to sneeze. He mustn't move. Whatever happens he must stay still or the reading will show that he's abnormal. He could feel it coming and he tried to swallow and to hold his breath, but suddenly, explosively, he sneezed. The machine whirred.

I probably don't need to go into the ethical implications such a policy might have. I think it's best to leave that idea right now.

We mustn't forget that brain scanning is useful for neurologists and neuropsychologists who look at normal functioning of the structures that make up our brains to understand why people behave as they do and to. You could also conclude that if brain scanning provided positive evidence that people who committed certain crimes (and who later pleaded not guilty because they were insane) really did have some kind of brain abnormality, it would make you much less worried about accepting their plea and treating them accordingly.

In order to look at this topic in an accessible way, I would like to start by introducing the idea of one area of the brain causing problems. If you remember, the hypothalamus helps control our internal environment such as temperature regulation, appetite and thirst. It also influences other motivated behaviours such as sexual behaviour and emotional arousal levels. Therefore if we could find the right part of the hypothalamus and stimulate it, we might be able to produce bizarre aggressive behaviours which are out of character for the situation. This would then indicate that if the hypothalamus was damaged in any way it may influence our behaviour, either making us much more aggressive or very passive.

Animal studies have backed up this idea. It has been shown that by giving certain animals mild electrical stimulation to a region of the hypothalamus aggressive behaviour will result. For example, a cat will hiss, its hair will stand on end and it will attack an object placed in its cage when its hypothalamus is stimulated by electrodes. Another demonstration of the effects of hypothalamic stimulation is when a gentle, non-aggressive rat, who has lived peacefully in the same cage with a mouse, attacks and kills that mouse if its hypothalamus is stimulated. It is believed that the stimulation triggers an innate killing response.

But what has this got to do with humans? Obviously it wouldn't be acceptable to stick electrodes in people's heads and stimulate their hypothalamus in order to get a response; what researchers have done instead is to look at primates. The instinctive patterns of aggression in primates are moderated by the cortex and therefore they are influenced by experience rather than crude arousal. If you have a monkey that is at the top of the dominance hierarchy, he will only attack subordinate males if necessary and will not attack the females. Monkeys at the bottom of the dominance hierarchy are very submissive and won't attack anyone. Research shows that if these two monkeys have their hypothalamus electrically stimulated, the top monkey will attack subordinate males but still not attack females. The bottom monkey will just cower and behave in a more submissive way than normal. This indicates that learned patterns of behaviour and experience have a very strong moderating force on even the electrical stimulation of part of the brain.

The functioning of the tracts of fibres between the two hemispheres, the corpus callosum, could also be assessed. As we looked at in the section on split brains, the patients with split brains couldn't interpret the external environment in the same way as people with intact brains. Some studies have shown that the two hemispheres seem to work at either different speeds or one works harder than the other. The suggestion is that lack of coherence between the two hemispheres may be something to do with the corpus callosum not transferring information between the two hemispheres effectively, although this suggestion hasn't actually been tested.

We could also consider whether another part of the brain which usually moderates the hypothalamic drives is functioning. Supposing you feel really aggressive, under normal circumstances you wouldn't go out and whack someone with a large piece of wood. Something inside should say to you that this behaviour is not really appropriate and therefore you wouldn't do it. The moderator we do have – our cerebral cortex, especially the frontal lobes – seem to act to restrain our behaviours. It is in these frontal lobes that we store all the learned social behaviours and ways of acting which are accepted in our society, and store them as memories to be used when the need arises.

When I was at university I remember, being absolutely transfixed by the story of Phineas Gage, a railway worker who lived in the nineteenth century. He suffered the most horrific injury when a steel rod was blown through his head, entering the socket of his left eye and leaving through the top of his skull. Obviously the damage done to his frontal cortex was immense and yet he survived. As the frontal cortex is the area which is involved in the regulation of behaviour, any damage to that area will result in the person behaving in a less

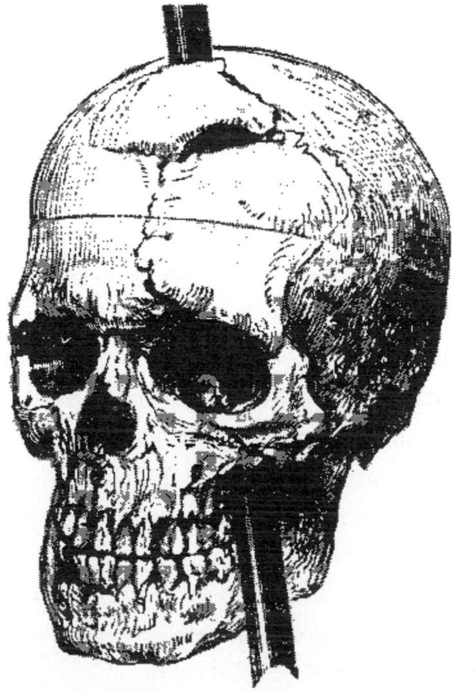

An impression of the skull of Phineas Gage showing the entry and exit points of the steel rod.

acceptable manner. Phineas changed from being a restrained, polite, industrious worker to a drunken waster. He became obstinate and rude, urinated at will and seemed to have no controls on his behaviour. He made plans but never followed them through as he was lacking in any sort of direction. His intellect suffered too, and he became more like a child although he still had the physical strength and drives of a mature man which were no longer modified by acceptable social behaviour.

Damage to our frontal lobes means we can't judge our own performance and compare it to others, and we no longer learn from our mistakes. It can damage our memories and make us absentminded although out long term memory may remain intact. Another problem is that this kind of damage may leave us in a rut in terms of our thought processes – this is known as 'perseveration' and means that problems are always looked at with the same perspective. Perhaps the easiest way to describe this is the Wisconsin Card Sorting Task. Here people are asked to sort playing cards into piles. The cards can be sorted according to shape – the four suits – or into colours – red or black. In fact they are more complex than our usual packs of cards but this is a good analogy. Whichever way subjects choose to sort them, the experimenter will tell them after a while that this is actually wrong. In response most people will try another tack and sort according to a different method, so if they started off with suits they will change to colours and so on. People with frontal lobe injuries will not be able to change their method but will continue sorting according to their original ideas. This kind of perseveration will cause them problems if it is carried into their everyday lives, because they will not be able to adjust their behaviour according to the situation but will continue to operate according to one set of rules.

Mr. Bloome was the nicest sweetest man you could wish to meet. He worked at a very small, all girls school in a quiet village in Suffolk, teaching biology. In fact the school only had four hundred pupils and he knew each of them by name. He was slight of build and had short fair hair which he swept to one side and secretly sprayed with a can of hairspray that he bought one day, claiming it was for his wife. He always wore one of those old tweed jackets with leather patches on the elbows and smelt of peppermint. He had actually never married because he felt he loved his job so much that he would neglect a wife and that would not be fair. All the girls loved him and, although he was quietly spoken, he made his lessons fun by bringing in all sorts of things to demonstrate what he meant. He never raised his voice in the twenty/five years he had worked at the school, but had never had any problems with any of the students, who often stayed behind after lessons asking him about his various hobbies such as butterfly collecting and restoring old radios.

His lessons always started with him wishing the girls good day and then he would follow an age old ritual which took about five minutes. He would slowly put his briefcase on the desk in front of him, and take out a carrier bag which he would place on the floor to the right of his desk. Then he would take out his register placing it squarely on the desk. He would then take out his two pens, one red for marking and one black for the register and place them one inch above the register. He would ensure that the chalk and board rubber were at the top of his desk, and he would look round the room to make sure that at least one window was open. Next, he would do up his case and put it on the floor to the left of his desk, pull out his chair and sit down, pulling his trousers up at the thighs so that his knees did not leave them with stretch marks.

The girls knew this routine and simply waited in anticipation for what sort of goodies he would produce that day from his accompanying carrier bag. He always had something to show them to make the lesson so interesting.

Mr. Bloome was devastated when he heard that the school would have to close. He was promised a job in the local comprehensive school as they were short of a biology teacher, and he was assured that he would teach the same syllabus. The school had 2,500 students and was located in a large housing estate in a nearby town.

The first day of term came and he felt a tear in his eye as he remembered the girls' goodbyes. He clutched his new case, the present from them when they said their final farewells and walked into the main entrance of the school. Bunches of students stood around in huddles, laughing and pointing at him. His first lesson was a year nine, bottom set biology class. He entered the classroom carrying his briefcase containing his carrier bag and pens. He lasted three minutes when...

You can just imagine what happened to him. It makes you realise how important it is to adjust your behaviour to the environment you find yourself in.

As I mentioned in earlier sections, both Piaget and Freud pointed out that young children find it hard to resist their impulses. Piaget said it was because they had not matured sufficiently in their cognitive development, whereas Freud blamed it on the primeval urges of the id, which have not yet been controlled by the ego. Physiologically, this is really because the frontal lobes are slow to mature and are really not fully matured until the person is in their twenties.

There is research evidence to back up what I have suggested so far, that dysfunction of the prefrontal cortex is likely to disrupt the regulation of aggression. Studies by Damasio et al. (1990) have shown this to be the case. Animal studies have indicated that there may be other structures involved in moderating aggression, such as the amygdala and hippocampus, although these are animal studies and are far removed from human beings.

Before we continue, I would like to tell you about a man called Charles Whitman who provided a small amount of evidence that brain malfunction may have something to do with murder.

Charles Whitman seemed quite normal as a small boy, but his behaviour seemed to changed after his mother left home as a result of his father's physical abuse. He often complained of headaches and occasionally fell into a rage for no obvious reason.

When Whitman was 25, he spent much of his time making detailed plans to carry out a massacre at the University of Texas. The date for this massacre, he decided, was to be on 1st August, 1966. He knew his mother would be upset at his plans, so he visited her on 31st July and as she opened the door, he attacked her with a knife, stabbing her and then shooting her in the head. He put the body to bed and tidied up the apartment before returning home to his wife. This gave him time to make his final preparations for the following day before he went upstairs, and using a hunting knife, stabbed her three times in the heart.

The next day he left for the university wearing grey nylon overalls and strolled into the reception area of the observation tower. Here he struck a receptionist over the head with a rifle and ran up the stairs of the tower with an assortment of weapons, before barricading himself in. Two young brothers and their mother and aunt went to go up the stairs, unaware of what was happening, when he shot and killed two of them and seriously injured the other two. He then went back down and shot the receptionist.

Returning to the observation deck where he had an excellent view over the campus, he laid out his weapons. The first person he shot from the tower was a paperboy, cycling across the campus. He then shot and killed another three students before anyone realised what was going on. He then shot a traffic policemen who had come to investigate what was happening.

Over the next 96 minutes the police tried to do everything they could to deal with him including using a low flying aeroplane. When all else failed they charged Whitman's barricade and finally shot and killed him. He had however hit 48 people, many of whom died either instantly or later in hospital.

The curious thing about Whitman was that before he committed these murders he typed out a note saying, 'I am prepared to die. After my death I wish an autopsy on me to be performed to see if there is any mental disorder.' When this was done, he was found to be suffering from a tumor in the region of his hypothalamus. However, no one could ever be sure that this was what actually caused his behaviour.

Although this example is only one instance of possible brain damage leading to anti-social behaviour, this should give you some idea of how important any sort of brain damage or malfunction might be in explaining the behaviour of criminals and why the plea of 'not guilty by reason of insanity' should be considered acceptable. After all, was he responsible for his actions, or was the tumor making it impossible for him to reason about what he actually did? The trouble is we will never know.

Whatever conclusion you may have at the moment, you must always remember that the kind of social environment criminals come from, their early experiences within the family and their experience of the education system can have considerable effects on their later behaviour. It is obvious that this nature-nurture debate is unlikely ever to be completely solved. Perhaps people who have behavioural problems end up in certain social situations, which then make the problems worse. Supposing you have a person with low intelligence who can't get work and ends up eating a poor diet. He may well be married and have children who also have an inadequate diet. This may contribute to their lack of physical development and, at the same time, they will be living in a poor area where perhaps others are engaged in criminal activities as a way of meeting the bills. There may also be an availability of drugs, or drugs and alcohol may be used as a way of making life more tolerable and these may contribute to lack of brain function by destroying neurones. There are so many factors which could result from a deprived childhood that it is impossible to say which came first, the abnormal brain or the abnormal behaviour.

However, each one of these explanations may have a place in our understanding of the causes of anti-social acts, although as yet no one theory has been accepted as the gospel truth. Perhaps that is the way it should be, after all the hardened killer is hardly the same as the single mother who hasn't enough money to survive, and tries to supplement her meagre income with a little bit of petty shoplifting – but they are both considered criminals and they have both carried out anti-social acts.

A. Raine, M. Buchsbaum and L. LaCasse (1997) Brain Abnormalities in Murderers Indicated by Positron Emission Tomography

Biological Psychiatry 1997; 42: 495–508

The aim of the study was to look at direct measures of both cortical and subcortical brain functioning using PET scans in a group of murderers who have pleaded not guilt by reason of insanity (NGRI). The expectation was that the murderers would show evidence of brain dysfunction in their prefrontal cortex as well as in other areas that have been linked to violent behaviour in the past.

Method

Design Laboratory experiment with independent subjects.

Subjects

The experimental group consisted of 41 subjects (39 men and 2 women) with a mean age of 34.3 years. They had been charged with either murder or manslaughter. They had been sent to the University of California imaging centre for one of three reasons:

1. To obtain evidence as to whether they were NGRI.
2. To find out if they were competent to understand the judicial process.
3. To see if there was any evidence of diminished mental capacity which may affect the nature of the sentencing they received.

They were referred for the following reasons:

- 6 had schizophrenia
- 23 had head injuries or organic brain damage
- 3 had a history of psychoactive substance abuse
- 2 had affective disorders
- 2 had epilepsy
- 3 had a history of hyperactivity and learning disability
- 2 had passive-aggressive or paranoid personality disorders

The control group of 41 people were matched by age and sex and had a mean age of 31.7 years which was considered not significantly different to the experimental group. The six schizophrenics in the experimental group were matched with six schizophrenic controls who had not committed murder. The rest of the control group were thoroughly screened and showed no history of psychiatric illness.

Experimental controls All offenders were in custody and were kept medication free for the two weeks before brain scanning. The control group were also medication free. Tests were undertaken to make sure that being left handed or right handed had no effect on behaviour. Fourteen of the murderers were non-white but when they were compared to white murderers on PET measures there was no significant difference between them. Twenty three murderers had a history of head injury, but again they showed no difference between non-head injured murderers except in the functioning of their corpus callosum, and the authors accepted that this may have contributed towards a reduction in the murderers' brain activity.

Materials

- Thermoplastic head holder, individually modelled, to hold the subject's head still while being scanned.
- PET machine to image brain functioning.
- Fluorodeoxyglucose (FDG) tracer injected to trace brain metabolism.
- Continuous performance task (CPT) which was a task which has been shown to make the frontal lobes work especially hard, together with the right temporal and parietal lobes.

Procedure

Ten minutes before the injection they were given practice trials at a CPT so they knew what to expect. Then, thirty seconds before they had their injection, they made a start at the actual task to get over their initial fears. This was to make sure that the feeling of fear did not show up in an increase in the metabolism of glucose and thus confound the results. Once they had been injected they were monitored for 32 minutes and then they were scanned in the PET scanner, having their heads held still in the individually moulded plastic head holders. Their brains were scanned ten times at 10mm intervals to pick up differences in brain metabolism in both the cerebral cortex and the sub-cortical layers.

Results

Although there was no significant difference in the task performance between the two groups, there was evidence of a significant difference in brain metabolism of glucose in a number of areas.

CORTEX

Frontal lobes

The murderers had lower glucose metabolism relative to controls in both the lateral and medial prefrontal cortical areas.

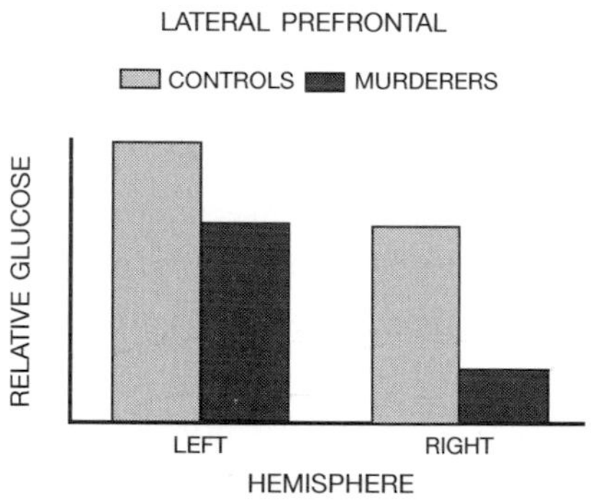

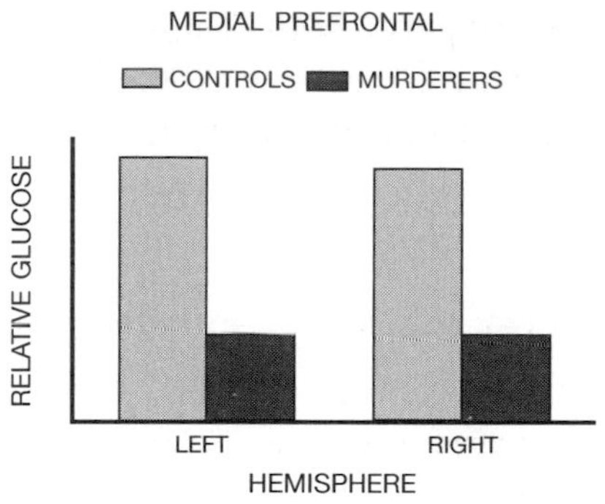

Parietal lobes

Murderers had lower parietal glucose metabolism than controls.

Temporal lobes

Temporal lobe glucose metabolism was identical between the two groups.

Occipital lobes

The murderers had higher occipital lobe glucose metabolism than normals.

SUBCORTICAL REGIONS

Corpus callosum Bilaterally lower glucose metabolism than controls.

Amygdala Reduced left and greater right amygdala activity than controls.

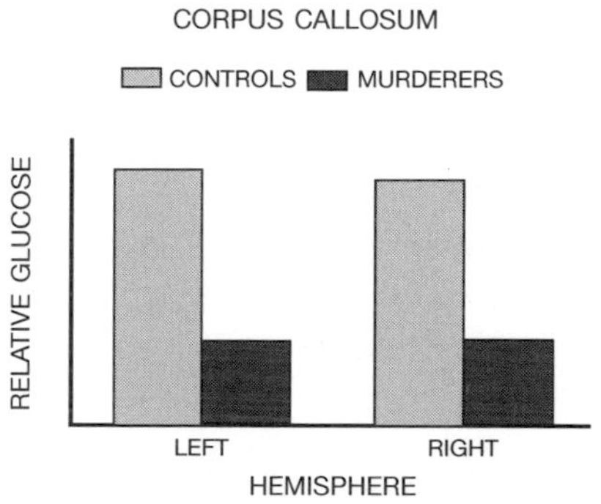

Medial temporal lobe including the hippocampus There was evidence of reduced left and greater right activity in the murderers although the results were not significantly different to controls.

Thalamus Murderers had more right thalamic activity compared to controls.

Group means for murderers and controls for cortical and subcortical glucose metabolism

	Left Hemisphere		Right Hemisphere	
	Control	Murderer	Control	Murderer
Cortical				
Lateral Prefrontal Lobes	1.12	1.09	1.14	1.11
Medial Prefrontal Lobes	1.25	1.20	1.22	1.17
Parietal Lobes:	1.15	1.10	1.17	1.13
Temporal Lobes:	.90	.90	.93	.94
Occipital Lobes:	1.09	1.12	1.11	1.15
Subcortical				
Corpus Callosum	.68	.56	.67	.56
Amygdala:	.97	.94	.83	.88
Medial temporal lobe incl. hippocampus:	.95	.91	.93	.96
Thalamus	1.09	1.09	1.09	1.15

■ Difference (not significant)

■ Difference (significant)

Summary of findings of murderers compared with controls

Lower glucose metabolism
The prefrontal cortex
The parietal lobes
The corpus callosum

Higher glucose metabolism
The occipital lobe

Same glucose metabolism
The temporal lobes

Asymmetries
The amygdala
The medial temporal lobe including the hippocampus
The thalamus

Discussion

The results indicate that murderers pleading NGRI have significant differences in the metabolism of glucose in a number of different areas compared to controls.

Lower glucose metabolism indicates a lack of activity in certain areas, and the findings that there was reduced activity in the prefrontal areas may explain impulsive behaviour, a loss of self control, evidence of immaturity, altered emotionality and the inability to modify behaviour. All of these may make it easier to carry out different kinds of aggressive acts because the normal constraints on behaviour may be reduced (Damasio 1985).

Lee at al. (1988) found that the amygdala plays a role in our ability to recognise socially significant stimuli and the destruction of the amygdala in animals leads to a lack of fear. In man the destruction of the amygdala has been shown to lead to a reduction of autonomic arousal which could be relevant to a 'fearlessness theory' of violence. This means that a situation that most of us would find very frightening would have a minimal effect on violent offenders – this idea has been backed up by findings of reduced autonomic arousal in offenders.

To support this idea still further, Raine (1993) has found that abnormalities in the functioning of the hippocampus, amygdala and thalamus are important to learning; memory and attention. Therefore, any abnormalities may result in problems in learning **relevant** emotional responses as well as the inability to learn from experience, which is often shown by criminal and violent offenders.

Discussion

The study suggests that the neural processes which underlie violent behaviour can't simply be reduced to a single brain mechanism that causes violence. It seems that there are several processes involved and if there are deficits in a number of these processes the likelihood of violent behaviour occurring is much greater.

Murderers show a totally different pattern of brain function to that observed in other mental disorders, for example psychiatric patients show abnormalities in brain structures which are not found in the brains of murderers. The authors even looked at substance abusers and found that none of the brain abnormalities seen in those samples were present in the brains of the murderers. However, the results can't be attributed simply to the fact that the murderers had mental disorders. There are a number of other factors which must be taken into account. Social experiences, situational factors, psychological predispositions and learned responses will all have their part to play and perhaps the physiological elements may only produce predispositions to extreme forms of violent behaviour rather than being a cause in themselves.

Evaluation

The main evaluation of the study is that it shows a correlation and therefore *cannot* be taken as causal. Although all the evidence indicates that brain dysfunction may be responsible for the subjects committing murder, there are too many other factors which have to be taken into account and cannot be measured:

- The authors point out that their findings don't suggest that offenders are not responsible for their actions.
- They point out that PET scans cannot be used to 'diagnose' potential murderers.
- The say that the findings of these abnormalities in brain function cannot be generalised to other types of violent offenders or to non-violent criminals because their study did not contain control groups who matched these criteria.
- Finally they point out that the study gives no indication of the cause of the dysfunction.

Key terms

Hyperactivity – extreme levels of activity.
Tracer – a substance used to be able to trace or track the activity of something.
Cortical areas – the structures comprising the outer layer of the brain.
Subcortical areas – the structures found underneath the cortical areas.
Metabolism – the collective name for chemical reactions which occur in the cells of the body. Metabolism is usually thought of as chemical

reactions which result in the provision of cells with some kind of nutrient or energy form.

Asymmetry – irregularity, not the same in each place or arrangement.

Confound – confuse.

Affective disorders – disorders of mood.

Lateral – on one side.

Bilateral – on both sides.

Medial – the area in the middle.

Key questions

1. Why were the subjects matched so carefully?
2. Why were both groups of subjects kept medication free for two weeks before the study took place?
3. Why was it necessary to have an individually modelled head holder for each of the subjects?
4. Why were the subjects given practice trials on the CPT?
5. Why should the findings of the study be treated carefully?

6 The psychology of individual differences

The last section in this book will look at individual differences, a term often used in psychology. What are individual differences? To put it simply, they are the differences between individuals which make it very difficult to group people together as one bunch or 'type'. Sure, we can find things that people have in common such as their cultural backgrounds or their gender or their ages. We may even be able to identify things about their personality or how clever they are which puts them in a group of others who share similar characteristics. What we must always remember is that every person is unique – and that uniqueness and individuality must be acknowledged, even if we find the way that others behave is not always acceptable.

If we do remember that people are individuals, it makes it easier to understand that if people don't behave in the same way as us, they are not necessarily wrong – they are just different. There are lots of examples of, say, the behaviour of different cultures in terms of family life or group norms which you or I would probably find quite bizarre. Gross (1992) cites a number of studies by people like Margaret Mead and Malinowski who describe patterns of behaviour that are totally different to ours.

Malinowski studied the Trobriand islanders, a South Pacific culture where both male and female had a reputation for being virile. As a way of keeping that reputation intact, groups of women from one tribe would go and seize a man from a different tribe and gang rape him. There was nothing gentle and 'feminine' in the way that this was done, and what made it more extraordinary was that the women would boast of their conquests after the event. I don't suppose the men appreciated the situation but to the women of their own tribe, their behaviour would be quite normal. Can you imagine how a situation like this would be viewed in our society? It would be greeted with shock and horror and we would consider it to be quite abnormal, whereas to the tribe concerned it was perfectly acceptable. However, who is to say that what we believe to be 'femininity' is how women should really be. Perhaps our idea of femininity is purely a social construct rather than what women are really like.

Just to back up this idea that women are not always the sweetness and light that goes with the stereotypical image of femininity, I want you to think of the kind of audience we see portrayed in films like 'The Full Monty'. When groups of women are shown together watching male strippers, they cease to be as quiet and docile as men might imagine them to be. They turn into quite lewd, noisy and raucous groups who are far less reserved than normal, shouting 'Get 'em off' and other unusual phrases! Maybe if western cultural expectations weren't as they are, western women would be a bit more like the Trobriand Islanders. Maybe it's the security of being with a group of women, where there is no threat, that allows them to become completely uninhibited.

Last summer I went on my dream holiday to Thailand. The culture is fascinating, especially the 'ladyboys' or kathoeys who are part of everyday life. These men are known for their cross-dressing and breast development (using female hormones) and often, but not always having their 'bits' surgically removed. Rosalind Morris (1994) suggested that the concept of gender in Thailand is one of three sexes, male, female and hermaphrodite (kathoeys) and that kathoeys are part of the culture. They are generally so beautiful, spending hours pouring over their appearance and many perform in cabarets where they mingle with the audience after the show. The thing was, I found their roles very disconcerting – did they see themselves as women or what?

According to Jackson (1995) they provide the function of providing a safe sexual outlet for unmarried men as Thai women are expected to be virgins when they marry. Firstly, their families would not be as angry as the family of a female who was having a sexual relationship before marriage. Secondly, there is no chance they could get pregnant! The other interesting thing about them is that they do sometimes 'marry' men in the more rural villages with the full acceptance of friends and families.

One of the things I found most unusual was seeing them with their families. One day I was visiting a Buddhist shrine overlooking a bay when I realised that the very tall girl in front of me kept taking out her mirror and checking her appearance. She spoke in a very loud voice and was exaggerated in the way that she walked. Her clothes were immaculate and she was extremely attractive. With her were an older man and woman and a number of slightly younger children who she spoke to and played with as they were walking along. I realised that she was a kathoey and yet it seemed so strange, away from the bright lights and girlie bars, to see one on a family outing – she/he was just one of the family. Later that day I questioned a taxi driver who spoke very good English how the parents felt about their sons becoming kathoey. He said that sometimes they were disappointed but that many of the families were so poor that a child becoming a kathoey was not considered a social stigma because that child would probably do quite well for themselves in terms of income (not always legal) and could help support the family.

Can you imagine how many western parents would react if their sons wanted to become the equivalent of a kathoey? Can you imagine the way kathoeys would be treated by many members of our society? Imagine the reaction of some families when they were informed that their son wanted to marry a transvestite! Hopefully, this gives you an idea of the relevance of taking into account cross-cultural issues when we test and judge other people – because we do ultimately judge people by our own yardstick, as you know, and this is the ultimate, ethnocentrism. Even though I am a psychologist, I found myself doing it too.

This question of individual differences is one of the factors that makes it quite difficult to carry out psychological research. In Chapter One we talked about matching subjects and mentioned the fact that you can only match people on certain things. The problem comes when you try and compare them because perhaps, as you can now appreciate, each one of those subjects will have an individual part of them which is totally unlike anyone else – not just life experiences but also cultural and cross-cultural differences.

The studies in this section will be looking at a number of topics which consider differences between individuals. The first section looks at intelligence and tries to provide some kind of definition as to what intelligence might be. However, if we aren't sure what it is, how can we accurately measure it – man-made tests can only test what man thinks something is, and if he's wrong the test is worthless. The second study looks at the changing pattern of racial identity and preference and how black people have far more pride in their identity nowadays, rather than seeing themselves as being inferior to white people. The third study looks at how we define abnormality – or indeed if we can. The implications here are that if we cannot tell the sane from the insane then does insanity actually exist. The final study looks at multiple personality, one of the most fascinating conditions in the field of psychopathology (the part of psychology that looks at the abnormal workings of the mind).

How clever are you?

Would you like to know what your IQ is? My guess would be that you would love to know, but if it wasn't very high you would probably not want anyone else to know. Have you also thought about what you mean by IQ – do you know what 'an IQ' is?

'So, what is an IQ?' I ask you.

'Everyone knows what an IQ is, it's how intelligent you are,' you answer.

Your clever friend, sitting next to you suddenly adds, 'Actually, it's your Intelligence Quotient.'

'Well excuse me,' you say.

'Yes, but what is an intelligence quotient and how do you measure it?' I ask again.

By this time you would start to look a little perplexed. 'Well, it's kind of how clever you are,' you would answer, 'and you measure it with an IQ test.'

'How clever you are at what?' I would reply.

'Well, er, everything, sums and things like that.'

'What do you mean – academic skills?' I say.

'Yes, that's what I mean'.

'Now think of the amazingly clever, academic professor who can recite theories of quantum physics in his sleep – but put him in a kitchen and ask him to boil an egg or mend a fuse. He may have no idea at all how to do these things, which are really very simple. In fact he may well have no common sense at all. Do you think he has a high IQ?'

'Well, yes of course he has,' you answer.

'But he can't even boil an egg. He wouldn't survive for long if he was dropped in the middle of a jungle, would he? O.K. Now think of the bricklayer who has designed and built an ecologically friendly house with solar heating panels, from recycled building materials. He has no formal training in anything and left school when he was sixteen. He actually can't read very well either. Would you say he was intelligent?'

'Yes.'

'But, he has no academic skills – they are purely practical.'

'No I know, but he knew things from experience.'

'Ah, ha. So does that mean that intelligence comes from experience? What about someone who has done the same job for years and years – they are experienced but are they intelligent?'

And so the conversation would go on. Everything you suggest, I could probably contradict in some way.

I am going to begin by talking about what intelligence is believed to be and how you measure it. When you get to the end of the section and you feel even more confused than ever, don't worry – you can rest assured that you are one of a majority. The other point is that if we, as a profession, find it hard to agree what really is the essence of intelligence, then we must consider whether the techniques used to measure this 'thing' have any validity.

Another thing that is worth taking into consideration is that if we do get it wrong, what are the likely repercussions of labelling someone as either 'intelligent' or, more to the point, 'thick' in terms of self-fulfilling prophecies.

I am your form tutor at school (you are about 14 years old) and I have told you that you are to do a test for me to see how well you are getting on at school. You think you are doing OK. You seem to be at about the same level as your friends and find some subjects hard, but some reasonably easy.

Two weeks later I call you in to my office and tell you that you have an IQ of 150 and that the average IQ is 100. I also tell you that you are in the top 1% of the population in terms of academic ability. How do you think this would make you feel about yourself?

Now imagine the same situation, but instead of telling you you have an IQ of 150, I tell you that you have an IQ of 85. It would probably make you feel that it wasn't worth trying at school any more.

You have probably already realised that defining intelligence is no easy task. It might be worth just jotting down on a piece of paper what you think intelligence is, and then compare this with your thoughts when you finish this section.

Interestingly enough, few concepts in psychology have received more devoted attention and few have proved so difficult to define. Despite many efforts over the years to come up with an adequate definition of the term 'intelligence', all the attempts seem to have remained linked to the techniques developed for its measurement.

Let me explain this further: if you think that intelligence is your ability to use language and do mathematical calculations, the intelligence test you devise will contain these two topics. If you think it is to do with problem solving and spatial awareness, the test will have to cover these topics. It seems to be the case that we can only define intelligence in terms of measurable skills. What is the point of saying that intelligence is something intangible, because if we believe it's intangible it would be impossible to measure – which rather defeats the object.

Intelligence – nature or nurture?

Perhaps it would be useful to look at the arguments about whether intelligence is inherited or whether it is due to our environment. This *may* help us to decide what it actually is and whether it is a single factor or a number of abilities, and then we may be able to determine how we can assess how high or low it is?

Herbert Spencer (1820–1903) and Sir Frances Galton (1822–1911) were the first people to use the term intelligence in the way we use it today. They both believed in the existence of a 'general ability', which affected how well we perform at any sort of intellectual task. This 'general ability' was thought to be distinct from task-specific abilities, for example we might find people who are good at one type of task such as arithmetic calculations or possibly two things, but not very good at all types of tasks. If we found someone good at everything, even if they had never come across the thing before, we could say they have a 'general ability'. Spencer and Galton called this general ability 'intelligence' and believed this ability was inherited.

Galton began the psychological investigation of intelligence in the 1860's. He wrote a paper in which he showed that genius seemed to run in families. He noted that most eminent Victorian gentlemen had eminent fathers, and he concluded that their intelligence must therefore be inherited and this was why they all did so well in society. He seemed to forget that eminent gentlemen had the financial status to educate their children at public schools, and could give them far more opportunity to develop a career than the average person by way of contacts and financial backing. He also thought the rulers of the British Empire must be the most intelligent people in the world (I think we can safely say he was ethnocentric). It was therefore understandable that he should believe that people who held lower positions in society (the working class, women and black people), must be of inferior intelligence.

Galton was actually influenced by Charles Darwin's work on adaptation and survival of the fittest. Darwin believed that intelligence is the factor that adapts humans for survival. If you are intelligent, you are more likely to survive as you have the intellect to work out how to do the best for yourself.

From this Galton formed a movement known as the Eugenics movement. This is the movement that claims that people of inferior abilities should be prevented from having families, because in some way this would result in a feebler society. He claimed that people who lived in poverty or squalor did so because of a 'natural depravity', which was inborn in them. He also suggested that different races who were of inferior origin should not be permitted to interbreed for fear of genetically contaminating the so-called superior races. Jewish people, Gypsies and Poles were some of the races that were considered inferior: this will give you some idea how ridiculous this whole idea actually was. However, this whole idea became very popular earlier in the twentieth century in many countries, especially Nazi Germany and South Africa. In fact it was this ideology that brought about the actions that led to the genocide of the Jews in Germany and the acceptance of apartheid in South Africa, where different races were segregated by law and brought up separately. Despite these beliefs, Galton failed to come up with any successful intelligence tests that could confirm his theories.

One of the people most influenced by Galton was Cyril Burt who I mentioned in Chapter One. If you remember, he was firmly committed to the idea that intelligence was inherited and that it was pointless to educate people beyond the limits of their capacity. Burt, in conjunction with two research assistants, Miss Conway and Miss Howard, produced a large number of research papers which seemed to provide unquestionable proof that intelligence was inherited. This led to the universal testing of children when they reached the age of eleven to see whether they would receive an academic education or more practical training for later life. It was believed that the children who did not pass the eleven plus were less academically able and therefore would not benefit in any way from a more formal, academic education.

In 1974, Kamin questioned Burt's statistical proof. When he analysed the data, he found that much of the evidence was contradictory, and concluded that in terms of a piece of scientific research Burt's findings were not acceptable. Later it emerged that Burt's two research assistants may not have existed (although this is still a matter of controversy) and that he had made up most of his data. It was concluded that because he believed so strongly that intelligence was inherited, he simply adjusted the evidence to support his ideas.

Hans Eysenck, one of the most well known (and controversial) supporters of the nature perspective, believed that intelligence is purely inherited. He was also a firm supporter of Jensen's (1969) idea that there was a difference in the abilities of racial groups. The findings were that, on average, black people's test results were about one standard deviation (15 IQ points) below the average of the white population in IQ. This fact was not disputed but what was disputed was the explanation – that it was due to genetic factors. True, they had achieved a lower average score to the white population, but it was nothing to do with innate ability. The findings were due to the nature of the tests and that they were culturally biased towards the white population (more about this later).

Is IQ Inherited?

There are two ways to investigate whether IQ is inherited or not. One way is to look at identical twins (also known as monozygotic or MZ twins) reared apart in different homes and to see if their IQ's are the same despite their different experiences. Because they are genetically identical, this would test whether their IQ's are caused by genetic factors rather than early experiences. The other way is to look at children who have been adopted and see if their IQ is closer to their adoptive parents or their natural parents.

Before we go on here, you should think about the likelihood of people, even if they do have the same genetic features, achieving exactly the same scores on tests if they have been brought up in different surroundings. Surely their early experiences must count for something?

Daisy and Violet were the twin daughters of Jack and Mary Howard who lived in a tied cottage on a large estate in the West Country where Jack worked as a shepherd and Mary worked in the kitchens. When the twins were born the couple were delighted but in order to keep their house, Mary had to return to work within two weeks of the birth of her daughters. The chief housekeeper had agreed that she could have the babies with her as long as they didn't interfere with her work. This arrangement was fine for the first few weeks, but as the twins grew more and slept less, Mary constantly had to attend to one or other of them until the chief housekeeper said the situation could no longer continue.

Mary was devastated and begged that she be allowed to keep the twins at work, but was told that she could perhaps keep one, but not both of them or she would lose her job. She decided she would have to let one twin go for adoption and as luck would have it a wealthy family had arrived from London and taken over one of the large country houses for a couple of months as a holiday. The wife of the family was unable to have children but desperately wanted a baby and Mary decided to go and visit them and ask if they would be willing to take on one of her twins.

The family agreed to adopt Daisy and raise her as their own. Over the next few years, the child was given everything it could possibly need. She had a personal tutor, numerous books and toys, went to a girl's public school, learned foreign languages, travelled widely and was introduced to the rich and famous.

> Meanwhile Violet stayed with Jack and Mary. She was helping in the kitchen by the age of four, went to the village school and left at the age of twelve to follow in her mother's footsteps. The family remained poor and were unable to provide Mary with many toys. She never left the village she grew up in, and was a shy and nervous young girl.

The difference in the experiences of these two children would be obvious if they were tested for their IQ levels. Even though they shared the same genes, the life led by Daisy would have been far more enriching and stimulating than Violet. Daisy would have had books to read and extra tuition to help her academic development. Violet on the other hand, may never have been able to read, or, if she could, would have been very weak. Imagine if you had experienced an enriched and advantaged life or a poor and impoverished one: what differences would it make to the way that you are? Even something as simple as parental influence will affect a child's development. If parents encourage their children at school and support and help them, they are far more likely to do well than a child whose parents have no interest in education or academic achievement.

This example is one of the ways that psychologists have investigated whether intelligence is innate or learned. They have compared the IQ's of twins reared together with twins who were reared apart and looked at how similar they were. This is done by using a 'correlation coefficient' which is a statistical measure showing a relationship between two sets of data. If there is a relationship, we would expect the scores to go up or down together.

- Twins A have IQ scores of 120 and 118
- Twins B have IQ scores of 102 and 104
- Twins C have IQ scores of 112 and 109
- Twins D have IQ scores of 95 and 96

These scores are very similar and would indicate that there is a relationship between them. This is worked out mathematically to make sure that it is not simply due to chance.

Just to emphasise the point, consider the relationship between these sets of scores.

- Twins A have IQ scores of 120 and 121
- Twins B have IQ scores of 102 and 131
- Twins C have IQ scores of 112 and 111
- Twins D have IQ scores of 95 and 140

Two are very different, and two are similar. This would indicate that there is no relationship between them.

Another study, carried out by Shields (1962), involved looking at 37 pairs of twins who had been reared apart and comparing them with ones who had been brought up together. It was decided that they should have been reared in different homes for at least five years but the study didn't mention how old they should be at the age of separation. In fact some of the separations did not occur until the twins were 7, 8 or even 9 years of age. They would have spent much of their 'formative' years together and this may have affected the results. The other problem was that the 'separated' were often living with other members of the same family, such as one being raised by mother and the other by aunt. Often the twins knew each other and were attending the same school, so in terms of totally different upbringings the findings were really not that valid.

When Shields took these factors into consideration it only left 13 pairs of twins and the correlation in IQ scores between these remaining pairs of twins was quite weak, giving very little support to the idea that IQ was inherited. Further research suffered from similar sampling problems to the Shields study, although Horn (1983) reported on a group of 300 children whose mothers had given them up within a week of birth, thus getting round some of the earlier methodological problems. He found that the MZ twins had very similar IQs whereas the DZ twins had less similar IQs. He concluded that about 80% of the concordance of IQ in twins is due to genetics rather than environmental factors.

Another way of investigating whether IQ is inherited is to look at the relationship in the IQs of fostered or adopted children and comparing them to their natural mothers and adoptive mothers. We would expect, if IQ is inherited, to see a closer relationship between the natural mother than the foster mother.

One quite dated study by Skodak and Skeels (1945) found a closer correlation between adopted children's IQs and those of their biological mothers rather than their adoptive mothers. This seemed to show that there was a stronger genetic influence on intelligence than simply environmental factors. However, this study also had problems. The groups were supposed to be matched for age, sex, parental occupation, educational levels and type of neighbourhood but the adoptive parents were older, more committed and turned out be a more successful group as parents (perhaps because they wanted the children). So overall, the adopted children's IQ's were much higher than their biological mothers, and seemed to be closer to that of their adoptive parents, suggesting that intelligence wasn't inherited.

Let me explain how this happened. The study, which was carried out over 11 years, had a high drop out rate. The children were tested four times over that period and it appears that the majority of adoptive parents who dropped out during the course of the study were not college educated (presumably not seeing the point of the study), leaving a group of similar, college educated, adoptive parents. On the other hand, only eight per cent of the natural parents had attended college. If we look at the mean IQ's of the adopted children (117), it is interesting to note that they were very different to the biological mothers (86). But a correlation does not look at actual scores, simply whether they go up or down together. It may have been the case that the IQ scores followed the same pattern as the biological parents but were in fact closer to the scores of the adoptive parents (unfortunately no one bothered to measure the IQ scores of the adoptive parents).

The following table is an example of how this works.

Child's IQ	Biological Mother's IQ	Adoptive Mother's IQ
117	86	120
120	88	115
110	81	112
114	84	110
125	92	120
122	90	135

The child's IQ and the mother's IQ go up and down together.

The child's IQ and the adoptive mother's IQ are much closer in value but do not go up and down with the same sort of regularity.

Therefore the study indicated that environment probably had more of a part to play in the IQ's of the adopted children than heredity. Further research has shown that environmental experiences have a large effect on the development of IQ. In fact further studies have shown that there is often very little difference between the IQ's of the natural children of adoptive parents and the IQ's of the adopted children.

So what about environment?

Alfred Binet believed that intelligence was not a fixed capacity we are lumbered with at birth. He believed that anyone could learn anything, but that some learned faster than others and therefore the environment in which the child grows up will have a large impact on their achievement. Think back to the example with Daisy and Violet. I'm sure you will all agree that two children with the same genes, brought up either in a stimulating environment or a deprived environment, will score differently on IQ.

- Think of intellectual stimulation (books, conversation, outings), emotional security, rewards for academic success, feedback from parents.
- Also think about nutrition – a study was done looking at the IQ at age 8 of 300 children who were born prematurely. During the initial weeks of life, the

diet of these premature infants was carefully monitored. The type of nutrients consumed had the effect of as much as 10 IQ points difference.

- Another study (Meyer and Harris 1975) showed 20 points difference between severely malnourished and well nourished children.
- Also the more schooling, the higher the IQ – studies suggest that you can lose between .25 and 6 IQ points per year of missed school.
- Toxins in the environment (eg lead in the air from car exhausts) in high doses are certainly toxic and can have severe effects on the central nervous system. Needleman et al. (1990) found that high levels of lead in early childhood are associated in adolescence with low vocabulary and grammatical reasoning scores, slow reaction times, poor hand eye co-ordination and low reading scores.
- Dozens of animal studies have shown that a stimulating environment afffects the structure of the brain. Rats that learn complicated tasks or have lots of toys develop thicker and heavier cortexes and have a richer network of synaptic connections in certain brain areas than do rats in unchallenging environments. (Rosenzweig 1984).
- Family size – the average IQ in a family tends to decline as the number of children rises (perhaps due to less parental time?)
- Individual experiences – why do siblings growing up in the same environment have different IQ's? Dunn and Plomin (1990) have reasoned that it is due to individual experiences like different teachers.
- Parent-child interactions – children who score well on IQ tests have parents who actively encourage their development.

From the evidence so far, it does appear that it is possible to change IQ by varying the environment, which contradicts some of the earlier findings. This idea was the reason for the creation of the Head Start Programmes in the USA, started in 1965 by President Johnson as part of his war on poverty. Congress authorised funds for a number of programs designed to provide learning experiences for 2 to 5 year olds from poor homes. They provided different activities for both parents and children and were seen as a way of giving the children the preschool educational experiences they would have otherwise missed.

Although Head Start did have very positive effects, many of these were not recognised until the children were in their teens. In fact the children who attended Head Start were more likely to complete their schooling and enter higher education than others who didn't go; they also showed a greater likelihood of staying away from delinquency. This experiment and further research have shown that IQ can be increased by early experiences, indicating that it is not such a fixed 'asset' as was originally thought.

But what is intelligence?

I have looked to try to find a really good definition of intelligence in order to be able to find out what intelligence really is. Some psychologists such as Binet view it as 'a general capacity for comprehension and reasoning', while others like Terman (1916) believe it is 'the ability to carry out abstract thinking'.

Wechsler (1958) suggested it is 'the aggregate or global capacity of the individual to act purposefully, to think rationally and to deal effectively with his environment', while Heim (1970) argued that 'intelligent activity consists in grasping the essentials in a situation and responding appropriately to them'.

I interpret these definitions as trying to suggest that intelligence is like some kind of super microchip in our heads that makes us good at thinking things out and responding accordingly. They all imply that intelligence involves thinking and reasoning, but they aren't really that clear, are they? Charles Spearman (1904) questioned whether there is such a thing as 'general intelligence' which is what these other definitions suggest. He said that everyone has 'a general intelligence factor' (which he called 'g') in varying amounts. This 'g' will affect our achievements in various specific areas (which he called 's'). Linguistic skills and numeracy are examples of 's' so if we had a high 'g' we would be good at language and maths. However, if we follow this idea through, it doesn't follow that we have to be good at everything, which would make it easier to accept that the professor who can't boil an egg is intelligent after all!

I could carry on describing different theories of intelligence for pages and pages but, apart from anything else, it all gets very boring. However there is one more theory of intelligence I think it is worth mentioning, and that is Eysenck's theory. I referred to Eysenck earlier and his idea that intelligence is inherited. Eysenck (1986) argued that approaches to intelligence can be categorised into biological approaches, psychometric approaches (which means that they can be measured) and social approaches (which is how we behave in social situations). In short he said that there are actually three meanings of intelligence but he believed that the biological approach was by far the most acceptable and objective.

He suggested that we should try and find out if there were any physical characteristics or mechanisms which were responsible for intelligent behaviour. If we can look at intelligence in terms of biological functioning then it would stand to reason that any measurement would be objective rather than subjective. He said that using physiological measurements such as reaction times and 'evoked potentials' (where you measure the speed of an electrical impulse in the nervous system) and looking to see if these bore any relationship to IQ test scores, it was possible to see that speed of information processing seemed to be a fundamental property of biological intelligence.

There is a little more evidence to back up the fact that there might be a biological component to intelligence. A few years ago, a group of neuroanatomists looked at four tiny pieces of Albert Einstein's brain which had been preserved in case anyone wanted to look at in it detail. In one area, they found more glial cells per neuron than in control brains from 11 non-geniuses (these cells supply nutrients to neurons). But what does this show? Was he clever because had had a lot of glial cells, or did his glial cells multiply because he used his brain more than other people? Most neuropsychologists doubt that the differences in intelligence are due to the anatomy of the brain. It is more likely that the wiring of neural circuits, the amount or efficiency of neurotransmitters, or the metabolic rates of cells are what matter.

To back up the last idea, by using PET scans Parkes et al. (1988) showed that, during certain intellectual tasks, the brains of high performers are less active (use less glucose) than those of low performers. This could be because in high performers fewer neuronal circuits are needed as the ones that are there are more efficient. The problem is that this kind of brain geography could be either the cause of intelligence or the effect of intelligence, but unfortunately there is no way of knowing which is which.

So, we have now gone round in circles. We are no wiser as to what intelligence really is, although I expect you have a better idea of the possibilities. You may well be wondering what was the point of going through all this background as we seem to have achieved very little. Well, the reason is because if we are still not absolutely sure what intelligence is, how on earth can we measure it? This is the area that we are going to focus on next.

Intelligence testing

When we try to test or measure mental characteristics such as this thing called intelligence or even personality, this is known as 'psychometric testing'. It is a way of quantifying what we are, and is believed by many theorists to be possible. These theorists are called 'nomothetic' theorists and they say that we are all made up of the same skills, abilities, characteristics and traits but just have them in lesser or larger amounts, so we should be able to measure them. This also means that we should be able to work out what makes an 'average person', and we can see how far away we are from the average or norm (at this point, I won't even venture into the realms of trying to define personality, because the arguments that hold good for intelligence also seem to exist for personality – that is, what is a 'personality'?). Just to make sure this argument is balanced, it's worth knowing that there are other people who say that it is impossible or pointless to measure and compare people because we are all individuals and, by trying to categorise people, we lose the essence of that individuality. These theorists are called 'ideographic' theorists.

Galton was believed to be the first to try measuring intelligence. He did this by measuring people's sensory sensitivity (ie their ability to distinguish subtly different colours). He believed that these measures would serve as indicators of intelligence because he assumed that more intelligent people would have better discriminating powers when looking at colours or feeling pinpricks. Needless to say, he was not very successful.

He might not have been too good at measuring intelligence, but he wasn't completely unsuccessful. In fact in 1885 Galton was the first person to identify the 'normal distribution curve'. He set up an anthropometric centre as a tourist attraction in London, and people paid to come and have their physical characteristics measured – like height, weight, width of upper arm, lung capacity and strength of grip. He collected reams and reams of data about different physical characteristics from thousands of people. Then he plotted their scores from each characteristic on a graph and found he had a normal distribution curve. He therefore assumed that as mental characteristics were presumably dependent on physical ones, the mental ones would also show a normal distribution curve.

So the normal distribution curve (also known as the 'Gaussian distribution') is a bell shaped curve that has special mathematical properties. The mean or average score falls in the middle because it is the most frequently occurring score – but note this is only the case in a normal distribution. Using another calculation which comes directly from the mean (called the 'standard deviation') allows us to find out the percentage of people who fall either side of the mean. This can be used mathematically to predict how similar or dissimilar someone is to the population as a whole.

If we finally manage to measure IQ and we then look for an average amongst a large number of people in the population, we could then seen how normal or abnormal an individual is, in terms of measured IQ score. However, as we have seen so far, Galton was not the person to achieve this although we do have intelligence tests. We therefore have to go back even further in history to France.

In 1881 the French government passed a law making school attendance compulsory for all children. Then in 1904, the administrators of the Paris school system asked Alfred Binet and Theophile Simon to devise a method of identifying children who found learning in normal classroom settings very difficult. The school system was extremely overcrowded and the idea was that these children should be given the opportunity for special education, which might help them keep up and take some of the pressure off the rest of the classes.

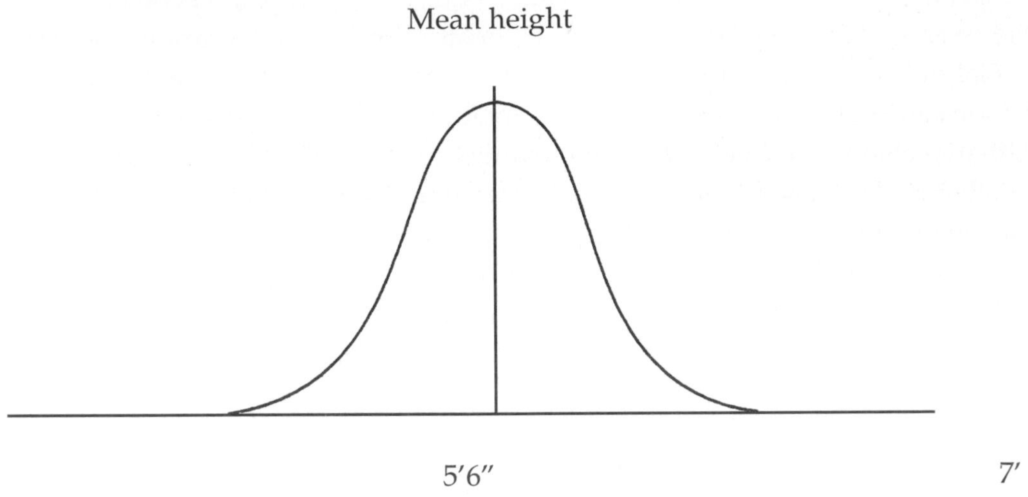

This normal distribution curve illustrates adult height. The curve indicates that most people are 5'6" tall, whereas there are very few who are 4' and very few who are 7'

The few tests that had been given to children in the past had been very simple tests which just looked at things like spelling and adding. Binet decided to put together a new kind of test which involved reasoning and problem solving, areas which are probably more suited to measuring this illusive thing called intelligence. Binet's test was published in 1905 and the format of the test has been the basis for most intelligence tests ever since. Binet believed that a slow or dull child was no different to a normal child but that it took longer for their mental abilities to develop, which meant that they would simply perform like a younger child. Binet was therefore measuring what he called 'mental age', which would then be compared with the child's 'chronological age' (how old they really were).

In 1916, Terman developed a version of Binet's intelligence test which was suitable for North American populations. This became known as the Stanford-Binet test. It's quite interesting to note that Terman held very strong eugenic beliefs and believed that testing people's IQ would result in the identification of those with reduced intellectual skills. He wrote, 'This will ultimately result in curtailing the reproduction of feeble-mindedness and in the elimination of an enormous amount of crime, pauperism and industrial inefficiency' (Terman, 1916). Despite this horrific view, the Stanford-Binet test is still the most well known test for children today. IQ is calculated by comparing a child's mental age, as measured on a test, with their real or chronological age:

The formula used is: $$IQ = \frac{\text{mental age (MA)} \times 100}{\text{chronological age (CA)}}$$

The 100 is used so that the IQ will have a value of 100 when the child's mental age equals their chronological age. If their mental age is lower than their chronological age, their IQ will be less than 100. If it is the other way round the IQ will be more than 100.

The Stanford-Binet test has used a number of different items to test intelligence and until 1986 all the items tested had an equal weighting towards the final IQ score. Since then, verbal reasoning, abstract/visual reasoning, quantitative reasoning and short term memory have become the areas that are used as an acceptable measure of intelligence.

In 1939, Wechsler suggested a way of modifying the formula for calculating IQ to cover adults, because until then it was impossible to measure adult IQ. What is the mental age of a 30 year old adult, or a 40 year old adult or even a 60 year old adult? Are they going to change in their reading and mathematical ability while their chronological age keeps on getting higher: in effect their IQ would decrease the older they get. Weschler suggested measuring a group of people who were similar to the person being tested. This would give an average for that group and give an indication of what you would expect that person's score to be if they were 'normal'. This average score is called a standardised score and is what we use to compare any scores with. Therefore if you have a group of grannies, your standard score would be an average of their scores, compared with a group of business men, or forty year olds, and so on.

Weschler's formula was $$IQ = \frac{\text{actual test score}}{\text{average score for norm group}} \times 100$$

The Wechsler Scales are now probably the most widely used individual intelligence tests of all. They consist of 11 subtests, six of which are designed to measure 'verbal intelligence'. The verbal intelligence subtests are tests of vocabulary, general comprehension, general knowledge, mental arithmetic, identifying similarities between pairs and digit memory span. This is fine for people who are literate and numerate, but what about someone who has problems with language? The remaining tests involve things like spatial relationships and are tested as follows:

- Block design – the person is shown a pattern and asked to recreate it using a set of small red and white blocks.

- Another is picture arrangement, where three or more cards have to be arranged in order that they make a consistent picture completion.
- Picture completion – where a person says what is missing from a picture.
- Object assembly – like a jigsaw.
- Digit symbol – where symbols are used as a kind of code to stand for other digits and the person has to translate as many of these as they can in one and a half minutes.

> At university I remember asking one of the post-grads, who was training to be an occupational psychologist, to test my daughter's IQ. I was interested, having just covered the topic of intelligence, and although she was only seven I thought it might be exciting to find out. I had asked around, automatically assuming that anyone who had a degree could do it and was actually quite shocked to find out that you have to be trained to administer the tests. When I finally sorted it, it took all morning, and I think my daughter Hannah was somewhat bored by the end of it, although they did stop to have a break every so often. I kept thinking, what would happen if you wanted to test large groups of people?

Robert Yerkes (1917) developed a number of what are called 'mass tests' which were developed mainly as screening tests for the US army although they ended up being used as a means of selection for refugees from Europe who wanted to enter the US. The key study looks at the development of these tests and how they were used inappropriately. The first test was called the 'Army Alpha Test', which consisted of a number of different types of questions including questions which asked people to unscramble mixed sentences and say whether they were true or false. They were also asked for the next number in a sequence, to identify words with the same or opposite meanings and so on, all of which were obviously language based questions. Because it was likely that people were not always suitably literate or perhaps didn't speak English, the 'Army Beta Test' was developed which involved tasks like tracing the outcome of a maze, picture completion, counting the number of cubes in a stack and combining several shapes to make others. The tests took about one hour to do, and could be given to lots of people at the same time.

One of the main criticisms of this test was that the pictures which needed completing were extremely culturally biased and consisted of things that were familiar in American culture but certainly not relevant to immigrants. If you look at the pictures above, you will see that so many of them would be alien to people from some other cultures. Supposing you had never used a spoon, or didn't know what one was, then picture four would be impossible to complete.

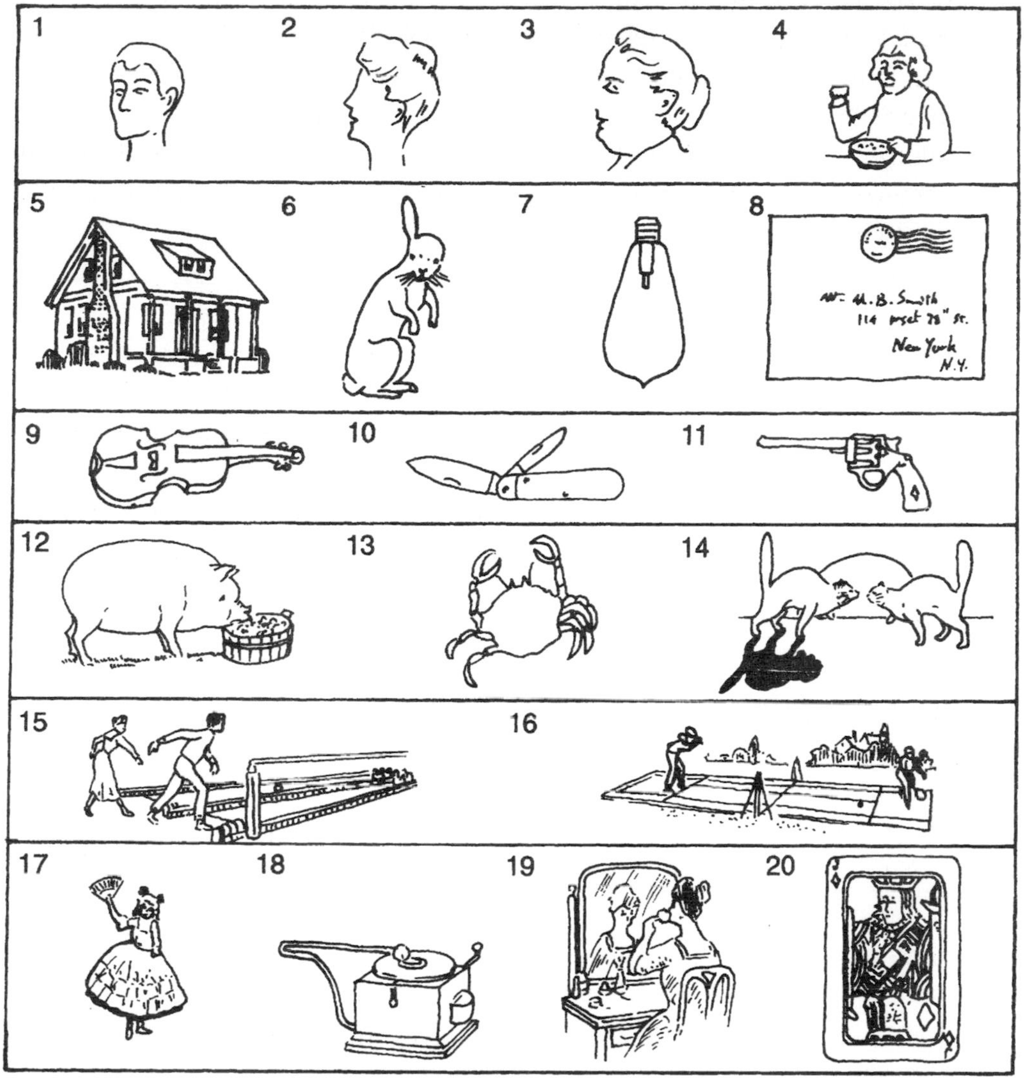

A page of 'picture completion' taken from the Army Beta Test. Note the cultural bias in the pictures.

What about five with its missing chimney pot, or seven without the element from the light bulb, or eight with its stamp missing? What relevance would this have if you had come from an underdeveloped nation? What about the crab – not everyone has seen a crab or a bowling alley or a tennis court or a gramophone.

You would think that having compiled these two mass tests, at least people who had language or literacy problems would be dealt with in a reasonable way, but it is fairly obvious that they weren't as fairly treated as they should have been. Even the people who did have a knowledge of English, and therefore sat the Army Alpha tests, were actually discriminated against because, unless their knowledge of the language was extremely good, they would still have problems with the questions.

Let me give you some examples:

1 Finger is to arm as toe is to...

2 Which is the odd one out: pig/badger/bean/elephant/dolphin

3 Which is the next number in the sequence 2 5 7 12 19 31

4 If the arms of a clock seen in a mirror appear to say 4.30, what is the real time?

5 Which of the following is the opposite of small: lots/large/enormous/big.

6 Does the sentence make sense?
'Mrs. Brown has had no children, and I understand that the same was true of her mother.'

Let's look at the answers:

1 Leg – if you chose foot, and you are a native English speaker, imagine how hard this must be for someone whose native tongue is not English.

2 First of all, we need to understand the meaning of the English words 'odd one out'. The answer could be bean as it's not a mammal but on the other hand it could be dolphin because dolphins live in water. Either way, the person could be forgiven for getting the answer wrong.

3 50 – you simply add the last two numbers together – but what if you don't understand the word sequence?

4 The answer is 7.30. This test of spatial reasoning is not that difficult if you are familiar with the face of a clock.

5 Large would probably be the accepted opposite of small, but enormous and big are not really wrong – again, what if you are not that familiar with the language.

6 The sentence is rubbish – language again.

As you can see, lots of items on intelligence tests assume that you have a good knowledge of cultural objects and a familiarity with the language of the test. Wade and Tavris (1994) point out that cultures differ in the way they teach their children to solve problems. For example, children from white middle class families are typically trained to categorize things – an apple and a peach are similar because they are both fruits. However children from another culture may say they are similar because they taste good; neither are wrong.

Culture bias can be even more subtle – what about class differences and how they can affect people's performance on IQ tests? Perhaps people from what are considered working class backgrounds use less formal language and are more involved in practical problem solving whereas the middle classes use more formal language and abstract problem solving skills. IQ tests use formal English and more abstract problem solving questions which may make them more suitable for people from middle class environments. This could also result in them discriminating against working class candidates.

Do you remember that earlier on in this section I mentioned that it had been found that, on average, black people's test results were about 15 IQ points below the average of the white population. I also mentioned that the findings were not wrong, but the reasons for these findings were the fact that the tests were culturally biased towards the white population. Perhaps you are now getting an idea of how this works. In the early part of this century, American intelligence testers applied tests which had been standardised on white English-speaking Americans to people from other ethnic and cultural groups – especially the Army Alpha Tests. Not surprisingly, they found East European immigrants, Mexicans, American Indians and Blacks to be of much 'lower' intelligence.

These American testers believed that they had shown that white English speaking people were of superior intelligence, but their critics pointed out that they were misusing their tests – tests standardised on one population cannot be used to measure the IQ of people from different populations.

In theory it should be possible to develop tests which look at many different types of skills, and establish norms that are taken from the groups of people likely to be tested. You may therefore have a high standardised score for people who have the same culture as the testers, and a lower score for immigrants from certain countries, but at least the standards would be fair. Then if you get a group of people to complete the test, you could judge them against each other, rather than against the population of the country.

Before we end this section and look at how America was said to be full of morons as a result of misapplied tests, I would like to finish with some ideas that came from Hans Eysenck in 1992. I was driving in my car when I happened to tune into a radio broadcast of an interview with Eysenck. I was transfixed because I had never heard him speak about the issue of intelligence before and had only read reports of his theories. I grabbed a pen and paper and wrote a few notes about what he had to say.

Eysenck claimed that tests do actually serve an important function. They just give the idea that if tests are accurate, they do actually serve an important function.

He reported that IQ tests done on children who lived on the Isle of Wight when they were five years old quite accurately predicted their results in school in later years. He also said that there is a relationship between a newborn infant's brainwave patterns and their IQ, meaning that their brainwave patterns must have a predictive element.

He believed that between 70 and 75 per cent of intelligence is due to heredity and it is both predictive and useful. He maintained that selection is essential for good education – IQ tests are not meant to mark success or failure, but to act as guidance as to what is best for the child. He made the point that IQ tests would show whether the quiet or reserved child had high or low academic ability and this would change teachers' expectations towards that child. I can see his point here, because if a student is very quiet it is often hard to know at first whether they are understanding something or are completely lost. If you had an idea of how intelligent they are, then you are likely to be able to deal with the child who is struggling but is too frightened to say. On the other hand, a good teacher generally knows how well their students are doing anyway but it would help to pick that student up, much earlier.

League tables of school results would be much more relevant if you knew what the IQ levels of the children were, because you have a starting point for progress. Eysenck also said that IQ tests do correlate with academic achievement. Interestingly, in America, IQ has been shown to correlate with parental income with the most wealthy parents having the highest IQ children. Are the parents very wealthy because they are super-intelligent and the children have inherited this, or are the parents just lucky and the children have benefited from lots of extra stimulation and experience?

At the end of the day, can we really measure this elusive ability? What I think we have to accept is that we do all vary and some of us find things easier than others. The concept of intelligence is very useful in life in order to make comparisons and estimations about people but what we must always remember is that it may simply be a concept rather than a reality. So we should never use it as a final judge of a person, but should look at that person as a whole and value them for what they are.

S.J. Gould (1982) A nation of Morons.

New Scientist (6 May 1982), 349–52.

This article is an edited extract from the book 'The Mismeasure of Man'. The book was written by Gould in 1981 and charted the history and problems associated with intelligence testing and documented the efforts by Robert M. Yerkes to establish psychology as a scientific discipline.

The Key Study

Yerkes was a psychologist at Harvard University. Because psychology was perceived as a 'soft' science, he wanted to improve its status and demonstrate that it could be as objective and quantifiable as the other scientific disciplines. Yerkes also believed that intelligence was inherited and therefore could not be changed. He saw an opportunity to give psychology the status it deserved by incorporating his ideas of inherited intelligence and the development of mental testing, which was at the time in its earliest stages. If he could show that intelligence tests were reliable and valid, then surely this quantifiable measure would prove his point.

With the outbreak of the First World War, the now Colonel Yerkes, developed the idea that it might be possible to use American army recruits as a source of sufficient data to show that intelligence testing was scientific. Previous efforts to do this had been insufficiently coordinated or were simply inadequate. He managed to pursuade the government to go along with his idea, and consequently presided over the testing of 1.75 million army recruits.

From May to July 1917, Yerkes, together with a number of colleagues who shared his views on the hereditary nature of intelligence, wrote the army mental tests. Together they developed three types of tests, the first two of which could be given to large groups and took less than an hour.

The Army Alpha Test

Designed for literate recruits, it consisted of eight parts. It included items with which we are totally familiar as part of intelligence testing: analogies and filling in the next number in a sequence. It required a good basic understanding of language skills and a level of literacy (which must come from education). Although the tests were considered to measure 'native intellectual ability' (Gould p. 349), they were in fact extremely culturally biased. After all, how could someone who was unfamiliar with American culture achieve a decent score? The following examples give some idea of the type of questions used in the test:

- Washington is to Adams as first is to…
- Crisco is a: patient medicine, disinfectant, toothpaste, food product?
- The number of Kaffir's legs is 2, 4, 6, 8?
- Christy Matthewson is famous as a: writer, artist, baseball player, comedian?

The Army Beta Test

A pictorial test designed for people who were illiterate or failed the Army Alpha Test consisting of seven parts. It consisted of picture completion tasks, an example of which appears on page 351.

The pictures again were culturally specific and would be extremely difficult to complete if subjects had no knowledge of some of the items. There were also maze tests, counting the number of cubes, finding the next in a series of symbols and translating numerals into symbols if you are given a code to work from. The instructions were written, in three of the seven parts of the Beta Test the answers had to be given in writing and yet this was a test for illiterates who may never have held a pencil.

Individual Spoken Examination

If recruits failed on the other two tests, they were given an individual spoken examination although this rarely happened.

Administration of the tests

Administration of the tests caused numerous problems. Recruits who were illiterate should immediately have been assigned to the Beta Test or given it if they failed the Alpha Test, but this only happened in some camps. Therefore illiterate or immigrant recruits often sat the Alpha Test and came out scoring next to nothing. In fact the levels of literacy amongst Americans, especially black Americans, was much lower than Yerkes anticipated and this confounded the problems further.

Queues for the Beta Test began to build up and this lead to the artificial lowering of standards by the administrators in order to reallocate more men to the Alpha Test. In some camps, the minimum level of schooling was sufficient to warrant sitting the Alpha Test, whereas in others the recruits had to achieve a certain grade. Besides these inconsistencies in administration, further problems arose with men, especially black men, who failed the Alpha Test not being allowed to resit the Beta test and only one fifth of those who failed the Beta Test being allowed to take the individual examinations.

Results

The data was analysed by E.G. Boring, Yerkes's lieutenant, who manipulated the results. Selected data was converted to a common standard to look for racial and national averages. The following 'facts' emerged:

- The average mental age of white American adults stood just above the edge of moronity at a shocking and meagre 13. Terman had previously set the standard at 16' (p.351). This indicated that the country was really 'a nation of morons' and as such was taken by the eugenicists to show that the poor, negroes and the feeble minded had been interbreeding and lowering the overall intelligence of the population.
- The data also showed that European immigrants could be graded by their country of origin with the darker people of Southern Europe and the Slavs of Eastern Europe being less intelligent than the fair people of Western and Northern Europe.
- The black man had an average mental age of 10.41, however the lighter the skin colour the higher the score.

Yerkes had achieved his goal. Data had been collected on 1.75 million men and the first mass produced tests of written intelligence were in use. The tests had a large impact on officer screening. By the end of the war, two thirds of the men who had been promoted were the ones who had taken the tests and achieved good test results. According to Yerkes there was also a 'steady stream of requests from commercial concerns, educational institutions and individuals for the use of army methods of psychological examining or for the adaptation of such methods to special needs.'

The 'fact' that the average mental age of Americans was 13 was concerning but the most important implication these tests had was the differences in racial and national groups. Bearing in mind that these tests were now accepted measures of innate intelligence, here was evidence that there really was a difference between racial and national groups in their levels of intelligence. Interestingly enough, Nordic people from northern Europe had been shown to be the most intelligent. This 'evidence' was used by Carl Brigham, Assistant Professor at Princetown University, in a book which was ideal propaganda for any racists. The book dispelled any possible concerns that might be raised about the accuracy of the findings by some very strange reasoning. Although some Jews were extremely accomplished as scholars, statesmen and performing artists, these were only noticeable because they were unusual exceptions to the rule. The majority had been assessed as having low levels of intelligence.

Although the tests were supposed to be accurate irrespective of country of origin or first language, even Yerkes admitted that the results showed that there was a problem for people who weren't familiar with English. The most recent immigrants were Latins and Slavs who spoke little English, and they had the lowest test scores of all. Also, there was a correlation between the length of time people had been resident in America and their test scores, with people who had been living there the longest having higher scores. This second problem was explained by the fact that the first wave of immigrants had been drawn from the more intelligent, and the latest immigrants had drawn the dregs of Europe in the form of lower-class Latins and Slavs. What an ideal argument to use to restrict immigration!

The Immigration Restriction Act was passed in 1924 by the US Congress and was shaped by Yerkes' findings. People from southern and eastern Europe, and from the Alpine and Mediterranean nations who had low scores on the army tests were not welcome. The way this was controlled was by looking at data from a census of immigrants, which had been conducted in 1890 when immigration from southern and eastern Europe was very low. It was decided that the quota of immigrants allowed into American would be two per cent of each recorded nation taken from the 1890 figures. This would obviously mean that the numbers of 'the unwanted' would be extremely low. Gould makes it clear why the data from another census, conducted in 1920, was not used as the basis – because the proportions of immigrants at that date were very different.

These immigration restrictions were to have horrendous consequences as the immigration from southern and eastern Europe all but ceased. The persecution of the Jews which started before the beginning of the Second World War meant that many Jews tried to escape from their homeland, but there was 'no admittance' to America. Calculations suggest that as many as six million people from southern, central and eastern Europe were denied entry into America between 1924 and 1939, when the war started. We now know the fate of many of them as a result of the Nazi regime.

Discussion

What is intelligence? Surely until we all agree what is meant by this intangible construct, we can't possibly work out how to test it. If we are not sure, even now, what it is, how can a pencil and paper test given to illiterates really determine an accurate measurement? Attempts made to define intelligence rest on the subjective belief of what it constitutes. Until we have a totally accurate and indisputable definition of what intelligence really is, how can we test it?

This argument reinforces Yerkes' point that the testing, which was subjected to huge amounts of experimenter bias, should never have been accepted as a valid test of a supposedly inherited ability. What makes it worse is that Yerkes' evidence supports the idea that IQ test scores can change over time. The immigrants who had been residents of America had higher test scores than the newly arrived immigrants, which does rather support the idea that the tests were culturally biased.

The racial bias of the testing was also astounding, with many of the black recruits being treated differently to their white counterparts. For no other reason, the nature of the testing situation should have been addressed, but racism was far more acceptable in the early years of this century than it is nowadays. In fact Yerkes discovered that the relative levels of education between blacks and whites was significantly different but he explained this by saying that this was because the black people were too stupid to realise how important it was to stay on at school. They couldn't win!

Evaluation

The cultural bias of the tests, the nature of the testing and the situation would have surely filled the recruits with anxiety. Although a degree of arousal is needed for good performance, the more anxious or aroused you are, the worse your performance becomes. The article notes that many of the recruits were terrified, confused and didn't manage to finish the tests in the allocated time, and this would have contributed to their overall level of anxiety. How could such a situation produce a valid measure of intelligence? If we accept that these arguments are fair, surely this points to the injustice of using these tests as a measure of an innate, inherited ability. To make it worse, the results were used as a tool of discrimination which suited the requirements of a political system – a kind of scientific racism.

Any psychometric test is open to abuse and people seem to blindly accept test results without questioning the nature of the test and the theory on which it has been founded. Tests must be administered in a uniform manner with both identical instructions and conditions for each subject. Unless this degree of rigour is achieved, how can the results from one test be compared with another? And yet this was what happened. Even when results are gathered, how those results are interpreted is often very biased. Data that doesn't support the hypothesis can easily be discarded or misinterpreted, yet, who would know?

Key terms

Intelligence – a concept which varies according to the researcher, but seems to focus on using learned information in new situations effectively and rationally and includes abstract thinking and reasoning. However, even this definition is far from adequate.
Literacy – the ability to read and write.
Psychometric tests – tests which are used in the measurement of mental characteristics such as intelligence and personality.
Reliability – consistency.
Validity (in testing) – is something really measuring what it is supposed to be measuring?
Eugenicists – people who believe that some races are inferior to others and therefore should not be allowed to breed. In extreme circumstances, eugenicists would advocate wiping out a particular race.
Scientific racism – the attempt to use the methods of science to justify the racist beliefs of the population.

Key questions

1. Why was it so important for Yerkes to develop intelligence testing?
2. How many reasons can you come up with which might have explained why non-Americans scored so badly on the tests?
3. What are the dangers of being selective with statistics?
4. Can you answer the questions from the Army Alpha test?
5. Look at the pictures on the Army Beta Test and try and identify what is missing?

Stereotyping and discrimination

In the section on ethnocentrism, I started by talking about the perceived differences between men and women drivers. If you remember, Harry was absolutely certain that women drivers were useless. I suggested that if I asked you what your opinions were about women drivers, then you would probably have an opinion and would be able to list a number of characteristics that apply to women drivers. These characteristics may be things like, 'safe', 'reliable', 'aware', 'responsible', 'focused', 'rational' and 'happy to stop and ask the way if they are lost'. On the other hand they may be things like 'dangerous', 'unpredictable', 'slow', 'easily distracted', 'oblivious of other drivers on the road', 'irrational' and 'likely to cause accidents'.

If I asked you about people who drive Volvos, or Americans, or gays, or old people, or vicars, or students, or Japanese, or black people, or scientists, or people who smoke illegal substances, or the Scots, or horseriders, or people called Nigel, or people who play bingo – I am sure that you could come up with some sort of list of characteristics and traits, based on your schema of that group, that would describe a kind of 'prototype'.

Our opinions and ideas about different groups of people are often totally irrational. They are influenced by factors such as our membership of a group (ethnocentrism) and by our experience, no matter how small, of that group. Some of these ideas may be negative and some may be positive but often these opinions or attitudes are based on very little information.

Stereotyping

The process of grouping people together and believing that they are all the same is known as 'stereotyping'. The term stereotype was introduced by Walter Lippman in 1922 and was defined as being an oversimplified view of the world that satisfies our need to see the world as more understandable and manageable than it really is. What he actually meant was that if we can attribute a whole set of characteristics to something, we will not have to analyse the thing each time we meet it in order to know about it.

You are walking down the road in the middle of the night on your own. It is dark and damp and the streets are empty. All the houses are in darkness and everyone is in bed. You turn the corner and coming towards you are a group of eight skinheads with the boots and the turned up jeans and the shaved heads. What is your immediate reaction?

I would imagine it probably isn't to go up and shake their hands and wish them goodnight. It would probably be something along the lines of 'Oh my God! I'd better get out of here.' Why?

The reason would be something to do with your expectations of this particular group's likely behaviour. You may expect them to be somewhat aggressive or provocative and would probably perceive that they were not going to be over-friendly and may even by quite dangerous. However, what you don't know is that they are all really Buddhist monks who have just been to a fancy dress party. Mind you, if you had decided to try to take the time to try to find out, you may well be lying in a large heap by the side of the road before you had the opportunity. What you have done is to use the information that was available to you to help you instantly judge the situation in order to predict what was likely to happen. As I am sure you can see, this process serves to maintain our safety, both physical and also emotional. If we can estimate the basic characteristics of what we are dealing with, we will know how best to behave.

So now we have established that stereotyping involves classifying people according to a set of pre-established criteria such as, if they have shaved heads they may be skinheads; if they walk around in orange robes they are Buddhists; if they are wearing a uniform they are authoritarian. This kind of classification is usually made on the basis of something as superficial as their appearance. What the person is actually like is totally irrelevant because we simply attribute all sorts of characteristics to them on the basis of the group that we have put them with.

An example of how this works is shown in the table below. The table is made up of the results of three different studies that were carried out at Princeton University between 1933 and 1969. The study asked students to ascribe traits to different ethnic and national groups even though many of the students didn't have first hand knowledge of the group in question. The table shows not only the type of traits, but also how often they were used. The ones which were cited most often are shown at the top of each list. It is interesting to notice how stable some of the traits are, even though they have perhaps changed position. It's also interesting to see that some new traits have been included.

Group	1933	1951	1969
Americans	industrious	materialistic	materialistic
	intelligent	intelligent	ambitious
	materialistic	industrious	pleasure-loving
	ambitious	pleasure-loving	industrious
Japanese	intelligent	imitative	industrious
	industrious	sly	ambitious
	progressive	extremely nationalistic	efficient
	shrewd	treacherous	intelligent
	sly		progressive
Jews	shrewd	shrewd	ambitious
	mercenary	intelligent	materialistic
	industrious	industrious	intelligent
	grasping	mercenary	industrious
	intelligent	ambitious	shrewd
Negroes (African Americans)	superstitious	superstitious	musical
	lazy	musical	happy-go-lucky
	happy-go-lucky	lazy	lazy
	ignorant	ignorant	pleasure-loving
	musical	pleasure-loving	ostentatious

Adapted from Katz and Braly, 1933; Gilbert, 1951; and Karlins, Coffman & Walters, 1969.

Prejudice

Sometimes the attitudes we have towards a group of people are extreme, like Harry's attitude towards women drivers, and we call this kind of extreme attitude 'a prejudice'. This prejudice can be either positive or negative depending on the person holding the views – Harry hates women drivers (he is negatively prejudiced) but I think women drivers are the best (I am positively prejudiced). In this example, our opinions are related to whether we are part of the group. Often these extreme attitudes have virtually no foundation in reality and are based simply on some minor attribute like appearance, are influenced by factors such as the media and the way we have been socialised, and tend to ignore characteristics of the individual and the nature of the situation at the time.

Probably the most obvious form of prejudice is racial prejudice. However, it could be gender prejudice known as sexism (Harry and I) ageism, or religious prejudice (sectarianism) such as the situation between the Catholics and Protestants in Northern Ireland. None of these prejudices are rational because there are good and bad people in every category but rationality does not enter the equation here.

I mentioned horseriders in the list of 'types' earlier because something happened to me recently, which made me realise how unfair stereotyping really is. Even when I tried to reason with the person concerned, he was so blinkered and narrow in his opinions that it really upset me and I had a very small insight into how it must feel for people who are stereotyped in every aspect of their lives.

I have two horses who are really family pets and used to be ridden by my children when they were younger. I can't bear to part with them although they aren't ridden as often as they should be. I keep them in a field near where I live, helped by donations from friends who ride from time to time. I wouldn't describe myself as a stereotypical 'horsey' person – I just love animals.

One Sunday morning, I had gone out quite early and was riding with one of my friends. The horse I was riding had 'mud fever' which meant that her poor old legs had become really sore and red from bacteria which are found in mud. I was really worried about getting them muddy and had been so careful for the whole of the ride.

We were just about to go onto a patch of common land and I cut the corner and rode over about 10 feet of grass to avoid a muddy part. Suddenly, this man seemed to leap out of the undergrowth and started having a go at me. 'B***** horse riders. You're all the same. Can't you read? It says bridle path there, not over this grass. I'm sick of you, you're all so arrogant. I drive past and none of you ever say thank you when I slow down. You make me sick.'

I was so flabbergasted at this tirade. I tried to explain that there was a reason, but this just provoked another stack of abuse. The trouble was, in order to protect myself, I started to shout back and had to check myself and just ride on because he was not interested. He had labelled me and that was that. It took me about half an hour to get over it and calm down because it was so unjust. The trouble was, I know many riders are arrogant – but not all. I get cross when I pass horses slowly in my car and the riders don't say thank you, but like all groups of people, there are good and bad in each and you can't judge them all by the experiences you have with a few.

If that situation caused me so much grief, how must it be for people who are stereotyped due to no fault of their own. I have a choice as to whether I ride or not. Supposing someone has something about their appearance that they have no control over – how must they feel? The studies done by Piliavin in the subway showed that people with ugly facial birthmarks were not helped as frequently. Were they being stereotyped on the basis of some external characteristic and consequently suffering from some kind of prejudice to do with the fact that their appearance was not perfect?

One of the most famous studies to have consider the negative aspects of prejudice was a field experiment carried out by a teacher called Jane Elliot which was reported by Aronson and Osherow (1980). The experiment, known as 'The Eye of the Storm' (but is sometimes referred to as the 'blue-eyes brown-eyes' experiment), gives us an insight into how easy it is to create a prejudice.

Jane Elliot was a third grade teacher in Riceville, Iowa, an area where all the families were white. Because of their environment, these nine year olds had no understanding of prejudice and discrimination and the negative effects they can cause, and so she decided to try to teach them what it felt like, as a way of equipping them for later life. She went into the classroom one morning and told the children that she had heard that blue-eyed people had been found to be better than brown-eyed people. They were nicer, more clever and more trustworthy and so the brown eyed children were to wear collars which made it obvious, from a distance, that they were the inferior group. She also told the blue-eyed children that they could have a longer play time, would be allowed second helpings in the dining room and would be given preference over the brown eyed children in any other activity.

It took just half an hour for the situation in that classroom to deteriorate with the blue-eyed children turning into prejudiced little individuals. They refused to play with the brown-eyed children, made fun of them, told tales about them to the teacher and discriminated against them at every opportunity. The brown-eyed children responded by becoming depressed and unmotivated. The work they produced was of a poorer standard than normal and they went home tearful and unhappy. The situation had not only caused the blue-eyed children to become prejudiced towards the brown-eyed children, but had also resulted in a kind of self-fulfilling prophecy, whereby the brown-eyed children believed they were useless and responded accordingly.

The following morning, Jane Elliot came into the classroom and confessed to having made a serious mistake. She had got it the wrong way round and it was really the brown-eyed children who were superior and the blue-eyed children would have to wear the collars. The brown-eyed children were elated and responded by being even more unpleasant to the blue-eyed children.

On the third day, she explained that really none of them were superior, and this was simply an exercise to teach them about prejudice and how it feels to be the subject of discrimination as a result of something beyond your control. She likened the situation to skin colour and explained that how they felt was how people who had black skins felt if they were treated as inferior. The children discussed what they had done to each other and how miserable each group had felt. Jane Elliot arranged for the students to attend a reunion when they were in their twenties with children of their own, and even then they remembered the experience and claimed that it had helped them to understand the negative consequences of holding irrational prejudices.

Even when prejudices are irrational, if they are maintained or perpetuated by society they can have very dangerous consequences for the person concerned. The person who is on the receiving end of the prejudice is likely to develop very low self-esteem, seeing themselves as less worthy than the people holding their prejudiced views. They will probably feel unhappy and have very low expectations which will lead to depression. I am sure you will have experience of someone who is depressed. It doesn't matter what you suggest, they won't go for it because they think they won't be any good.

If someone is really demoralised and their self-esteem has been lowered for a prolonged period of time, you can imagine the long term consequences on their behaviour. Perhaps because the effects are more subtle they may actually become even more severe as there is nothing obvious to rebel against. It's a bit like a dripping tap that keeps on dripping and eroding the self confidence until it's all washed away and the person has no energy left to fight.

Now imagine the same situation in terms of group morale. If you think back to the section on ethnocentrism where I mentioned how belonging to a group gives a kind of self-identity: if that group's morale and self-esteem is low, it will make the people who belong to the group feel worthless too.

In the 1930's, America was still extremely prejudiced against black people and areas were legally designated as either black or white areas. The opportunities for betterment for black people were few and far between and they had little access to education, jobs and state welfare. A study carried out in 1947 by Clark and Clark showed that African American children who were as young as three were already demoralised about their skin colour and felt that to be white was preferable over being black. They were offered the choice of playing with a black or a white doll and most of them chose the white doll because they thought it was better than the black doll. This study was cited by Thurgood Marshall, Chief Counsel for the National Association for the Advancement of Coloured people, when he argued in the Supreme Court that there should be an end to the legalised racial segregation that went on in schools. Clark stated that 'Human beings .... whose daily experience tells them that almost nowhere in society are they respected and granted the ordinary dignity and courtesy accorded to others, will, as a matter of course, begin to doubt their self worth' (K.B. Clark, 1965, p.64). The result of this case was that the Court ruled that schools should no longer be segregated.

There is evidence to show that if you have an expectation that people will be prejudiced towards you, this may in fact lead you to perceive a situation in a different way to people who have no expectation of prejudice. This was demonstrated by a study done by Kleck and Strenta (1980) who applied make-up to their participants to make them look as if they had an extremely large, ugly facial scar. After checking their appearance in a mirror, the researchers applied some cream to 'set' the make up but what it actually did was to remove the scar. The participants then spent some time interacting with another person and reported back on whether the scar affected their interactions. Even though there was no disfigurement, the participants reported that their appearance had influenced the way the other person behaved towards them. This suggests that people may well explain the way people behave towards them as being due to their membership of a particular group. This helps us understand the perceptions of minority racial groups who *believe* they are being persecuted, even when this is not the case.

Despite what we know about prejudices, they still seem to exist. Aronson et al. (1997) reported how the trial in the same year of O.J. Simpson, the American sportsman-cum-actor, seemed to have two different meanings depending on whether the observers were black or white. O.J. had been charged with murdering his wife Nicole Brown Simpson and her friend Ron Goldman in 1994, although he was found not guilty. Aronson reported that the majority of black people believed that the evidence against him was unconvincing, whereas the majority of white people believed he was guilty. He suggests that this prejudice towards one racial group or the other may in fact be due to the different experiences of various racial groups in America with the criminal justice system.

The problem is that attitudes are often developed over a number of years and are very resistant to change. There is a whole body of psychological research that considers how attitudes develop and the methods we can use to change them, but the bottom line is that most people have an attitude, and they can't really be bothered to find out enough about the situation to work out if they

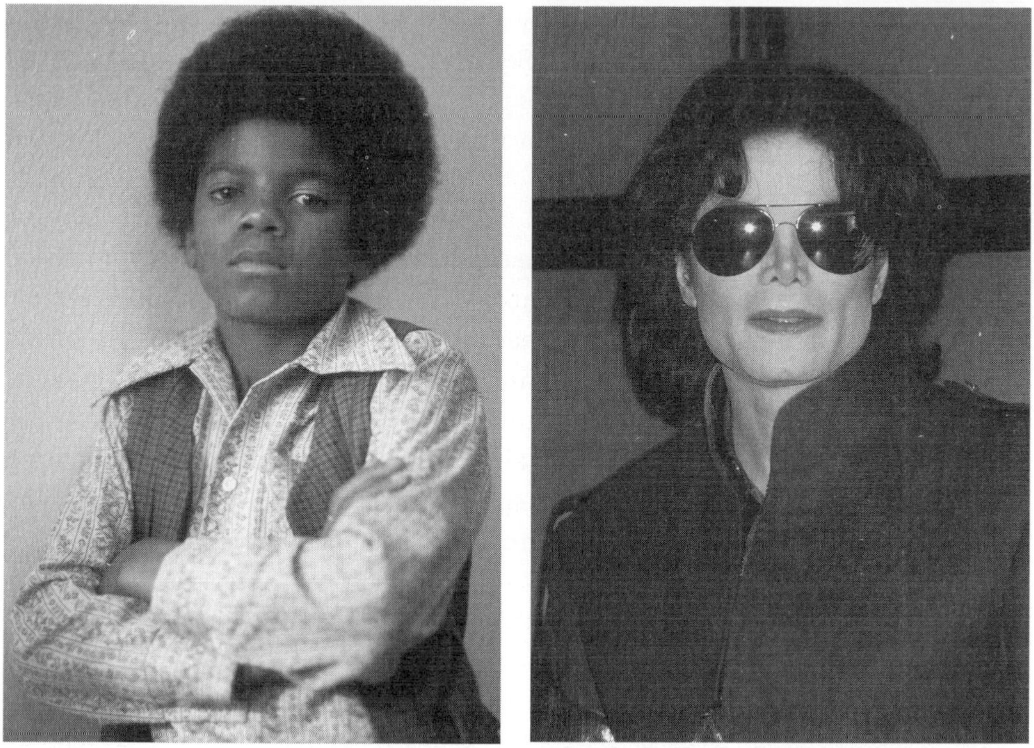

Michael Jackson as a young boy and how he appears today. He went to extreme lengths, helped by extensive plastic surgery, to change his external appearance.

want to change their minds or not. There is also the idea that if it is that easy to convince us that some of our attitudes are wrong, we might have to question all our beliefs and ideas about the world and this makes us feel quite insecure as to who we really are.

Discrimination

It should be evident now that if we hold a prejudiced belief, it is likely to lead to some kind of discriminatory behaviour. Discrimination can therefore be described as the way we act towards a group of people as a result of our prejudices. The group in question will either be given an advantage or a disadvantage, depending on whether our prejudice is positive or negative.

Allport (1954) looked into racial or ethnic prejudice and found that there seems to be five possible stages to the development of the ultimate form of discrimination – that is extermination. However, they can only develop to the extreme if they are found in a society that tolerates or encourages racism.

- **Anti-locution** – verbal abuse and racist propaganda
- **Avoidance** – keeping the ethnic group separate from the dominant group in society (eg ghettos).

- **Discrimination** – when the minority group is excluded from civil rights, employment, housing etc. (think of South Africa).
- **Physical attack** – against the group.
- **Extermination** – indiscriminate violence against an entire group of people (eg the Jews).

An example of how symbolic prejudice can lead to the ultimate discrimination – extermination – has been shown relatively recently in what was Yugoslavia. Sears (1988) describes the type of prejudice that developed there as 'symbolic prejudice'. This is where the in-group are seen as being all but perfect, while at the same time the feelings of hatred towards the out-group increase because they are seen as being a threat. This situation seems to be self-perpetuating because the more the out-group are feared, the more they are hated; and the more they are hated, the more the in-group are seen as wonderful.

After the end of the First World War, four multi-ethnic empires collapsed (the Russian, German, Austro-Hungarian and Ottoman Empires). This resulted in the creation of new countries with new boundaries. Yugoslavia was one of the last to be 'put together' and because it was done in a hurry, it was not very well thought out. It was decided that this new country would take in territory from the Austro-Hungarian Empire (Slovenia, Croatia and Bosnia-Herzegovina) and Montenegro and Serbia. This new grouping was to form 'the Kingdom of Slovenes, Croats and Serbs', which was too much of a mouthful, so its name was changed to Yugoslavia. Although the population was mixed, the majority of people were Serbian and it was ruled as a monarchy with a Serb King.

The people who were now living in this new country, the Serbs, Croatians and Moslems, originally all came from the same racial stock. Because of this they all speak virtually identical languages, so in theory they should get on well. However, the main differences between them were religious and we all know from Ireland that religious differences can account for a great deal of hatred and bloodshed.

Economically, Yugoslavia became a successful example of a cooperative type of Communism during the 50s and 60s, unlike some of the other communist countries that relied heavily on Russia. As a result of the oil crisis in the early 70s, Yugoslavia got herself into debt and this was made worse when interest rates on the loans she had taken out increased. This caused the economy to take a downturn and many people lost their jobs, although the levels of unemployment stayed more or less the same after the initial falls. The problem was that the unemployment level was much higher in the less economically developed southern republics of Yugoslavia. It was below 10% in Croatia in 1990, but roughly 20% in Serbia proper, and almost 40% in Kosovo – increasing the perceived differences in the people.

By 1988, Yugoslavia was in a serious economic crisis as inflation rocketed to 1,200% per year, and the annual growth rate declined into negative numbers. Can you imagine how horrific this must have been with prices rising and rising? The people felt a sense of hopelessness about their situation – an ideal breeding ground for prejudice and discrimination to develop. Although the groups had been living peacefully side-by-side up to this point, in order to support their own needs they turned against each other as a way of surviving the now lower standard of living they had to deal with.

Extreme nationalist leaders in both Serbia and Croatia argued for the interest of their own nation at the expense of others. This made the people of Serbian descent began to feel threatened by Croatians and Moslems. Slobodan Milosevic, the head of the Serbian Communist Party, was extremely nationalistic and in response to the situation began proclaiming the historic rights of his people and produced an upsurge of nationalistic feeling. The result – military campaigns which were intended to increase the Serbian territories either by 'ethnic cleansing' or by driving members of other groups from their homelands.

We have all heard about the kind of extreme behaviours that come from this example of symbolic prejudice. The television has been filled with images of people, not dissimilar to us, being driven from their homes, clutching their few remaining possessions and being forced to live in mass camps miles from where they had lived. We collected clothes and bedding for them, dispatched lorries full of material support for the people of Kosovo, but what we need to consider is whether anything can make up for the kind of extreme prejudice that many millions of innocent people had to suffer as a result of seemingly irrational fears. The in-group unity and out-group fear and hatred resulted in the killing of hundreds of thousands of people and millions more becoming homeless refugees – the ultimate discrimination.

Do prejudices have any sort of function?

We mentioned earlier about how stereotyping can be seen as having an important function, in that we do not have to go through the process of analysing everyone individually but can make broad generalisations in order to assess the situation quickly (remember the skinheads?). This means that stereotyping and prejudice can be seen as having a survival function. In fact Ardrey (1966) suggested that people have a basic instinct to defend their territory against all possible invaders and in order to do that we need to identify who is one-of-us and who is one-of-them. He said that here people are acting according to what he called a territorial imperative. The problem is that we may not necessarily be defending a territory in terms of a plot of land – back to the skinheads again – but if we consider that our bodies are a kind of territory, then this makes sense.

Richard Dawkins (1976), who wrote the book 'The Selfish Gene', suggests that prejudice is to do with protecting our genes. This xenophobia (which is a fear of strangers and therefore hostility towards them) stems from our desire to protect the purity of our genes, both in ourselves and in those directly related to us.

Other theories are based on the idea that prejudice is really no more than an outlet for our innate aggressions. If you remember, Freud claims that we have innate aggressive tendencies and Lorenz suggests that aggression is a 'dripping tap' which needs channelling from time to time. Therefore we vent our aggressions towards people who we believe are responsible for depriving or disadvantaging us. This idea is known as 'scapegoating' and has some evidence to back it up. Hovland and Sears (1940) analysed the number of lynchings that took place in the southern states of the U.S.A. and found that they correlated with the price of cotton. What was happening was that the number of lynchings increased whenever the price of cotton went down. The farmers were blaming the black people for the poor cotton prices – using them as scapegoats and directing their aggression towards them.

Scapegoating also happened in the U.K. The economic recession and high levels of unemployment in the 1960's resulted in very high anti-immigrant feelings. Enoch Powell delivered his anti-immigration speeches and emotions ran

Since the fall of communism in eastern Europe, bringing with it new market conditions and unemployment, minorities like these gypsies in Hungary have been experiencing increased persecution and deprivation.

high. People from extremist groups suggested that the black and Asian immigrants were taking all the available jobs and consequently there was a high number of racial incidents. In order to see how ridiculous it was to use the immigrants as scapegoats, you only had to look at the types of jobs they were doing. The jobs were more often than not the ones that the white unemployed refused to do!

Although we have talked about discrimination being an action or set of actions we take as a result of our prejudice, this is not always the case. La Piere (1934) discovered that holding a prejudiced attitude towards a racial group does not automatically result in discrimination. In the 1930s in America, there was quite a lot of prejudice towards Asian people. La Piere had arranged to travel across America with a young Chinese couple but he was concerned how they would be received in hotels and restaurants on the way. They visited a total of 251 places but only one of those actually refused to serve them. He found this quite an interesting situation and decided that perhaps how they felt, and how they behaved may not necessarily be the same. In order to check this out, he wrote to all the places they had visited and 90 per cent of them reported that they would not serve Chinese visitors, should they arrive. As La Piere himself agreed, there were a number of reasons why the results may have been so different, not least because it was not a controlled study. He was not even sure that the people who answered the letters were the same ones that actually served him. However, later research studies that were much more closely controlled drew the same conclusions (Wicker, 1969).

We know the way to reduce prejudice and discrimination which was discussed in the section on ethnocentrism. Equal status contact and the pursuit of common goals are believed to be the two main methods and, although these are put to effect in many areas of life, what we need to ask ourselves is, despite all this knowledge, are things any different today? The key study in this area, which was a study replicating the Clark and Clark (1947) study, suggests that things are different and that black people at least, no longer suffer from such low self-esteem. Martin Luther King, the black American Baptist minister, was partly responsible for this change in attitude towards black people and by black people in America when he helped found the non-violent civil rights movement against racism and discrimination. This resulted in increased opportunities for black people and consequently raised their expectations of achievement. Today black people hold positions of importance in America but the majority of black people are still likely to be found in the poorest sections of American society.

Authors such as Aronson, (1997) point out that racism does still exist in America, although it takes on a different form. He calls it modern racism and claims that '... it has become more subtle' (Aronson, 1997 p. 511). What he means is that we are now no longer blatantly prejudiced because we are all concerned with and aware of 'political correctness'. We aren't prepared to express our prejudiced views any more for fear of appearing 'racist'. What we do instead is to simply act them out in a very subtle way by offering less help or charging more to members of different racial groups for the same services or goods. Jones and Sigall (1971) demonstrated this with something they called the 'bogus pipeline'. This was a machine covered in dials, which participants believed was a kind of lie detector machine. Jones and Sigall compared the responses of their participants on either a pencil and paper questionnaire of prejudice (where they could easily lie) and their responses on the 'bogus pipeline'. They found that participants showed far more racial prejudice and gender prejudice when they were questioned using the 'bogus pipeline' than when they had to fill in the questionnaires.

One real life demonstration of modern racism comes from a study of car sales in America. Ayers et al. (1991) visited 90 garages selling cars in the Chicago area. The researchers all used the same technique to negotiate the minimum price the salesmen would take for their cars, and found that there was a substantial difference in the lowest price according to who was buying. This study confirms my belief that garages see women coming a mile off! They found that a new car, which cost the dealer about $11,000 would be sold to white males for an average price of $11,362, to white females for $$11,504, to black males for $11,783 and to black females for $12,237. Isn't this appalling?

Perhaps it is fitting that I should end this section on prejudice with an excerpt from the famous speech given by Martin Luther King on August 28th 1963 at the Lincoln Memorial in Washington D.C.

> 'I have a dream that one day this nation will rise up and live out the true meaning of its creed: "We hold these truths to be self-evident; that all men are created equal."
>
> I have a dream that one day on the red hills of Georgia the sons of former slaves and the sons of former slaveowners will be able to sit down together at the table of brotherhood.
>
> I have a dream that my four little children will one day live in a nation where they will not be judged by the colour of their skin but by the content of their character.'

J. Hraba and G. Grant (1970) Black is beautiful: A re-examination of racial preference and identification.

Journal of Personality and Social Psychology, 16, 398–402.

This study was a replication of a study by Clark and Clark (1939) which was designed to investigate children's racial preference, racial awareness and racial self-identification by using a set of black and white dolls.

Design

This study was a quasi-experiment where the independent variable was the child's race (white or black) and the dependent variable was the child's racial preference, racial awareness and racial self-identification.

Subjects

160 children between the ages of four and eight years of age who were at five primary schools in Lincoln, Nebraska took part in the study. 89 children were black *(Note: this was 60 per cent of all the black children attending the five schools, the total number of black children being about 150. Lincoln's black population was 1.4 per cent of the total and the proportion of black children in each school averaged just under 7 per cent. 70 per cent of the black children reported that they had white friends.)* 71 white children were white and came from mixed race classes.

The black children were also classified according to skin tone: 'light' (practically white), 'medium' (light brown to dark brown) and 'dark' (dark brown to black).

Materials

A set of four dolls, two black and two white which were identical apart from skin colour.

Procedure

The children were on their own when they were asked the following questions:

1 Give me the doll that you want to play with
2 Give me the doll that is a nice doll
3 Give me the doll that looks bad
4 Give me the doll that is a nice colour

These four items measure ***racial preference***

5 Give me the doll that looks like a white child
6 Give me the doll that looks like a coloured child
7 Give me the doll that looks like a Negro child

*These three items measure '****racial awareness or knowledge****'*

8 Give me the doll that looks like you.

This last item measures ***racial self-awareness***

The children were then asked to name the race of their best friend and the children's teachers were asked for the same information. This was to find out if their racial preferences and awareness actually had any behavioural consequences.

Results

The results show a comparison between the findings of Clark and Clark (1939) and Hraba and Grant (1970).

Question 1

Give me the doll that you want to play with.

	Clark and Clark (1939): Blacks	Lincoln (1969): Blacks	Lincoln (1969): Whites
White Doll	67	30	83
Black Doll	32	70	16
Don't know (no response)			1

In the Lincoln study, black and white children preferred the doll of their own race.

Question 2
Give me the doll that is a nice doll.

	Clark and Clark (1939): Blacks	Lincoln (1969): Blacks	Lincoln (1969): Whites
White Doll	59	46	70
Black Doll	38	54	30

Here the position has changed and the black children see the black doll as being nicer, although if you look the numbers aren't that different: 46 to 54, only slightly more than half.

The white children were significantly more ethnocentric than the black children on this question and question 1.

Question 3
Give me the doll that looks bad.

	Clark and Clark (1939): Blacks	Lincoln (1969): Blacks	Lincoln (1969): Whites
White Doll	17	61	34
Black Doll	59	36	63
Don't know (no response)		3	3

Again a change in the black response to colour. No difference in ethnocentrism on this question between whites and blacks.

Question 4
Give me the doll that is a nice colour.

	Clark and Clark (1939): Blacks	Lincoln (1969): Blacks	Lincoln (1969): Whites
White Doll	60	31	48
Black Doll	38	69	49
Don't know (no response)			3

Black children are much more ethnocentric on this question whereas the white children are more or less evenly divided.

Questions 5 to 8 obtained answers similar to Clark and Clark. The children made few errors of racial identification or personal identification and any errors that did occur disappeared with the older children.

The effect of skin tone
In the Clark and Clark study, the children of light skin colour had a greater preference for the white doll and the dark children the least. This was not found in this study.

Age
The Clarks found that black children of all ages preferred white dolls in this study black children of all ages preferred the black dolls.

Race of friends
There was also no apparent relationship between doll preference and the race of friends from either black or white children.

Discussion

The results can be interpreted or explained in a number of different ways, but on face value they indicate that children have little problem with racial identification and are not necessarily oriented to favour whites, unlike the findings of 1939.

The findings indicate that black people are now much more proud of their race than they were in 1939 and therefore are more willing to choose dolls that have their own skin colour than white dolls. However, we are simply looking at doll preference and we need to question whether choosing a doll is really that valid as a measure of attitudes towards other human beings. If this was the case, all the black children should just have had black friends but this was not the case. This may have been due in part to the fact that there were far more white children anyway, and although we can suggest that children's choice of friends may be to do with race, it may also be to do with the nature of the other child. We like some people and not others because of the type of person they are, irrespective of their appearance.

The reason for the findings may be to do with a greater sense of black pride. Hraba and Grant point out that over the two years before the study, a black pride campaign was directed towards the adolescents and young adults in Lincoln, and this may have influenced the feelings of the children who took part in their research.

Another explanation may be that children in Lincoln in 1939 may also have chosen black dolls if the original Clark and Clark study had been carried out in the same area, but as it was carried out elsewhere, we will never know.

Evaluation

There are a number of evaluative issues which ought to be considered. We have already mentioned whether doll choice is really a valid measure of racial preference. Secondly, children in Lincoln might not have been representative of the population as a whole. The black community in Lincoln was only 1.4 per cent of the whole and the chances are that they would have integrated far more with the white community than if they had been a much larger group. Their cultural differences would therefore also have been small, whereas if there is a large group of people of a certain ethnicity then they are more likely to stay together and retain their cultural norms.
It was suggested that the race of the interviewers might have influenced the answers given by the children, although Hraba and Grant maintain that this problem was controlled for and had no significant effect on the results.

The technique used was called a 'forced choice technique'. This means that there are no half measures and so the attitude that is expressed may appear to be much more strongly held than it really is. After all, it doesn't give subjects the chance to say 'I'll choose this one, but I really like that one too and tomorrow I might change my mind'. This method therefore doesn't give any indication of the strength of attitude.

One of the questions is really rather dubious. The question which states, 'Give me the doll that looks bad,' could be interpreted in a number of ways. Does the question mean does it look horrible, or does it look naughty? If we have a problem working out what was meant by the question, what do you think the children thought? This raises the question that perhaps some of the results may have been due to the children responding to demand characteristics and trying to work out what the experimenters wanted them to say. This may have been more evident in the 1939 study, when racial discrimination was far more in evidence universally than it is nowadays.

Key terms

Stereotyping – to categorize people as being all the same according to one (usually physical) characteristic.
Racism – a feeling of either rivalry or hatred between races, which comes from a belief in the fact that some races are inherently superior compared with others and therefore have the right to be dominant. These feelings or attitudes often lead to discrimination.
Xenophobia – a fear of strangers and therefore a hostility towards them.
Scapegoating – using a group of people
Racial preference – preferring your own race over and above other races.
Racial awareness – being aware that there is actually a difference between races.
Racial self-identification – being able to say which race you belong to.

Key questions

1 Why might the race of the interviewer have had an effect on the choices made by the black or white children?
2 What would have been an alternative to the 'forced choice technique'?
3 Why did the researchers ask the children about the colour of their best friends?
4 Why were the teachers asked about the children's choice of best friends?
5 Can you think of any other way of measuring racial or cultural identity?

What is abnormality?

Has it ever worried you how psychiatrists and psychologists determine whether someone is abnormal? I mean we all go through stages of being a bit weird don't we but where do we draw the line between weird and actually 'abnormal'? And if we are abnormal, does that mean we are mentally ill?

One thing that can change our behaviour quite dramatically is the run up to impending exams. Have you suddenly discovered how housework takes on new meaning? Bedrooms suddenly get tidied and even the washing up seems a better prospect than going and getting your head down to some really serious work. Isn't this sudden fascination with housework some kind of weird, abnormal behaviour? Then as the exam gets closer, you feel more and more stressed and unhappy, and instead of being your normal, happy-go-lucky self, you become totally anti-social and very quiet. We could say that your behaviour has showed 'substantial change' but does that mean you have actually become 'abnormal'? Well maybe it is abnormal for you – but there is a reason for it, and surely that makes a difference. It is no more than a kind of temporary abnormality, because as soon as the exams are over, you will revert back to your normal self.

Also our behaviour in one situation may be very different from our behaviour in another situation and so we ought to take that into consideration when looking at abnormality.

'Simon's gone loopy. Look at him. What on earth is he doing running and up and down the high street at ten o'clock on a Saturday night with only a pair of boxers on?'
'It's the beer, mate!'

Is Simon abnormal? No, he's just probably quite happy and that, plus the alcohol which will have removed some of his inhibitions, has resulted in his decision to run around in his underpants! I hope that you are beginning to see how the label abnormal is not quite as clear cut as it seemed earlier.

In order to look at this whole situation, we need to try and work out what we really mean by 'abnormal' and how we can tell it from normality. It isn't as simple as just judging someone's behaviour. Already you will have realised that we have to take into account how the person has been over a period of time. We need to consider the situation they are in and whether there was a reason for the way they were behaving. Finally we ought to take into account whether there was any kind of drug involved which may have been a cause of their behaviour.

Defining abnormality

There have been a number of attempts to try to find out a way of differentiating the normal from the abnormal. The problem is that, as you will see, none of them are really satisfactory.

Statistics

We could begin to look at abnormality by considering some kind of statistical formula which would help us define who is and who isn't abnormal. If you remember, Galton showed that when we measure large numbers of people the data will fall into a normal distribution curve. Perhaps we could consider the people who, when measured, are statistically rare and fall at either end of the distribution curve as the ones who are abnormal. There can't be very many adults over the height of 7 feet or under 4 feet, so maybe they're abnormal.

However, physical appearance doesn't tell us much about behaviour (although it might have some effect) so what about IQ as a measure. People who have very low IQ's or very high IQ's could certainly be considered abnormal. People with very low IQ's may actually need some support to help them deal with life and look after themselves but what about the ones with very high IQ's? We are far more likely to see them as lucky rather than abnormal in any way. Other people who score low or high on any sort of psychometric test may still be living their lives quite contentedly. I am sure you will have heard of the term 'extrovert' (and its opposite, 'introvert') and have some idea what they mean. Extroversion is a personality trait or characteristic that has been identified by Eysenck (1947), who describes an extrovert as very outgoing, liking lots of company, someone who seeks excitement and doesn't mind taking chances. On the other hand, the introvert is quiet and reserved, tends to keep his feelings to himself, prefers his own company or the company of small groups of other people and is often believed to be shy. If we were measured, most of us would fall somewhere between the two extremes.

Extroversion — Introversion

However, if we had an exceptionally high extroversion score, we would be statistically rare but probably considered the life and soul of the party. If we had an exceptionally high introversion score, we would again be statistically rare and would probably spend lots of time on our own, but we would be quite happy with that. So being statistically rare, doesn't actually help when we are trying to work out what we mean by abnormal (in terms of mental illness).

Non-conformity

An alternative way to consider how we define abnormality is to look at whether people's behaviour conforms to what society expects. Have you ever been in the company of someone who has started behaving in a really weird way, and you just get dreadfully embarrassed and want to remove yourself from the situation. I used to know someone who did just that whenever he was out with his friends. He would pretend to be seriously 'intellectually challenged' and he would go up to people and say really personal things about how they looked. He would stroke their jackets or hair and say how nice their clothes were and then ask how much they cost. He sometimes asked whether their hair colour came out of a bottle! I hated it. It made me feel really uncomfortable and I either ran away or felt I had to try to explain his behaviour. You could see that the people he targeted also felt really uncomfortable and just wanted to escape.

If someone's behaviour makes another person uncomfortable, then perhaps they are abnormal, but it must depend on the audience. After all, not everyone feels uncomfortable about the same things, so it seems the definition here is very much to do with the people watching rather that the person doing the actions.

Social control

Perhaps abnormality doesn't actually exist, so the concept is no more than a means of social control. When we mentioned Simon's bizarre behaviour on a Saturday night, we realised that he was behaving in only a *slightly* abnormal way because it was Saturday and he had been on the beer. What would happen if unusual behaviour wasn't seen in context? Supposing someone behaved in a way that was seen as a weird or unacceptable and this was enough to have him caught and confined and labelled as being mentally ill? How would he convince people that he wasn't actually mad? I remember being quite moved by a cartoon I saw sometime ago that was written by a patient at a psychiatric hospital. If you read it, it will make you realise that by labelling someone as abnormal, just because they don't behave the same way as everyone else, has enormous ethical implications.

Once upon a time, there was a happy man called Joe Odd. He lived in a little hut on the side of a hill with his dog and from his window he could see right in to the distance. Around the hut was a beautiful garden where he grew flowers and vegetables and lots of lupins because lupins were his favourite flowers.

On weekdays he went to work in the valley where all the people lived in little boxes all looking just the same, but afterwards he could go home to his little hut and watch the sunset. The people who lived in the boxes thought Joe was very strange because they all watched television. At first they said, 'Why don't you live in a box like us?' So they broke his windows and made up bad stories about him and the police said he was causing a breach of the peace…'Ain't Joe weird - I bet he's queer…or maybe into little boys…yeh, a child molester.' 'And he hates everyone…he's dangerous…let's get him.'

So Joe locked his door and barred his windows and was afraid to go out. The garden became overgrown with weeds and died. Only his dog stayed by his side. One day a man came to the hut and said, 'Mr Odd, this hut is unhealthy because there is no bathroom, so we are going to pull it down, but we cannot rehouse you because you do not meet the requirements.'

Joe wandered from place to place and stole bottles of milk from doorsteps. One day the police caught him and a social worker came to take his dog to the R.S.P.C.A. Joe was so upset that he hit the social worker…so she said he could not be in his right mind and would have to be assessed. They sent Joe to mental hospital where the doctor examined him and asked him lots of questions about his childhood and his bowel movements…then wrote on some labels and hung them round his neck. Then another social worker wrote a report about how Joe had lived in a hut with the doors and windows barred. So the doctor hung another label round his neck saying 'PERSECUTION COMPLEX'…and gave him some pills to make him feel better. Joe didn't like the pills because they made him feel strange and he wouldn't take them, so the doctor hung an 'UNCOOPERATIVE' label round his neck and gave him an injection instead.

Every week the doctor asked him lots of questions to find out what was wrong with him, but Joe didn't answer anymore, so he hung an 'UNCOMMUNICATIVE' label round his neck as well. After a long time they told Joe he was better and they found him a regulation box to live in under the rehabilitation scheme. Joe lived in his little box and from his window he could see lots of other boxes, all looking just the same.

The welfare workers told him he was coping very well, but sometimes Joe still had a feeling he wanted to hit people, only he couldn't remember why he felt like that, because the pills made his head feel sleepy. The social worker looked at Joe's labels and told him that this was all part of his illness and that it might take a long time before he felt really better. One night he thought he heard a voice in his head saying, 'Come with me…I know a beautiful place…come with me.' 'I can't. I am very ill. Can't you see all those labels round my neck?' 'Take them off, Joe,' said the voice again and again and again.

At last Joe lifted the labels from around his neck and threw them away. He was surprised how easy it was, and his head felt so much lighter. He opened the door and followed the voice. He walked for miles and miles and came to a beautiful place with lots of other odd people. He grew some more lupins and played music and painted pictures and flew in balloons, and he brought a cat who followed him everywhere, and everybody there loved Joe. Then one day the people in the boxes found out where he was and said he would have to come back because he was very ill.

A fleet of police cars and ambulances came after him with sirens screaming and Joe ran along the beach into the waves to escape the noise for ever and ever, and ever….

Can you see how abnormality is actually quite a frightening concept because it implies that there is some kind of 'normal' way of behaving and if we don't fit into that, we can be removed rather than cause our society any sort of discomfort. Although this is a cartoon, the situation can actually become more serious when people who aren't willing to conform to the behaviour that society expects, like political objectors, are made to conform by being removed and locked up under the pretext that they are abnormal and therefore mentally ill.

This 'social control hypothesis' idea, has been used to help to explain some of the worst cases of psychiatric abuse. In his book 'The Gulag Archipelago', Alexander Solzhenitsyn wrote about the chain of prison camps stretching across the Soviet Union which were full of people who wouldn't conform to rules and regulations they believed were wrong. The frightening thing is that these situations continue today, for example in areas where non-democratic governments are trying to maintain control. Another example comes with Japan's drive for industrial success. 'Bins' (as in loony-bins) are used to 'dump' those who are unwilling to conform to the demands of industry. Therefore, in order to instil the appropriate terror, the 'bins' must be sufficiently unattractive. In fact conditions in Japanese mental hospitals are similar to the old Victorian asylums in the UK, being overcrowded, dirty and often brutal in their discipline. Between 1955 and 1990, the number of inpatients in Japanese mental hospitals increased from 100,000 to around 400,000.

What better answer than to label someone who disagrees with policy, or refuses to conform, as a looney? In fact Amnesty International is an organisation dedicated to the maintenance of human rights and actually spends most of its time trying to pressurise governments for the release of political objectors who have been locked up on the pretext that they are mentally ill.

Abnormality as coping

Abnormal behaviour could be seen as no more than a way of coping with life. I went to a lecture in London given by Gary Craven where he talked about forming relationships. He related the story of a man who found a very bizarre way of coping with a problem he had. Below is a version of the story he told.

> There was an advertisement in the local paper for an adult education class, the purpose of which was to help people who were having problems forming relationships with members of the opposite sex. At the first class, the students sat in a circle sharing their experiences with each other. It was Edward's turn and he was very nervous. He pulled anxiously at his Ben Sherman shirt collar and wiped a bead of sweat from his forehead. Edward wasn't unattractive. In fact he was quite a good looking man, but there was something rather strange about him.
>
> At first, the students shared their interests with each other as a kind of ice-breaker. Edward explained that his great interest was lifts and he proceeded to fascinate everyone with tales of the lifts he had visited all over the world. He thrilled them with stories of the speed of lifts in New York which rose 60 storeys in a matter of seconds. He filled them with terror when he related stories of the older lifts in Russia, which creaked and groaned and stopped and started as they slowly slid up the shafts. However, half an hour later they were all semi-comatose.
>
> Then came the time to talk about his experiences with women. When he began to explain that he had never had much luck with members of the opposite sex, suddenly the people became more interested again. He told them how, every time he started talking to a woman, she seemed to move away from him. Suddenly his eyes lit up. 'But I have noticed that when I am in a lift, it is much better. They seem to talk to me there and I get on so well with them, but then the minute the lift doors open, they disappear.'
>
> The instructors were puzzled. However, by the end of the evening, the explanation for this little situation was clear to them. Edward had no concept of personal distance, and just stood too close to whoever he was talking to. Most

of the time, people made their excuses and left, but in a lift – he had a captive audience – there was nowhere to go!

Edward's real problem was that he had never learned the concept of personal space due to having been brought up within another culture where people's need for personal space is very different to that of our culture. The people there were quite happy to stand almost nose-to-nose while having conversations. He therefore had no idea that there was anything unusual about his behaviour, but he was aware that people didn't seem to like him very much. As a way of coping with this situation, he simply adjusted his behaviour until he found a way to make people talk to him. Not understanding the underlying reasons, but having found himself a reasonable solution, his behaviour had become quite abnormal.

A much more simple example of how abnormal behaviour is simply a coping strategy can be seen in people who are fanatical about tidiness, to the extent that every little thing has to be in its place. This fanaticism can become obsessive and can take over their lives. In order to understand the reasons for this we need to look at the rest of the person's life. It may be that they have no confidence in themselves and feel inadequate, so they can only just cope with work and their other responsibilities. Extra problems or burdens would just become too much for them, so in order not to make things more stressful they need to be sure that their home life or office is totally ordered and organised.

Remember the idea I suggested at the beginning of this chapter: when exams are imminent, it isn't uncommon to kind of socially withdraw and this is yet another way of using 'abnormal' behaviour as a coping strategy. The reason for this is because quite often things like exams cause us to become very aroused, in fact far more than normal. High levels of arousal are fine in the short term and can often mean that we will actually work better, but if they last for a prolonged period, as in the time when we approach exams, we start to find ourselves becoming what we call 'stressed'. The body doesn't function too well when it is stressed and so we unconsciously seek ways of reducing that level of arousal. One way of coping with this over-arousal is to actively remove ourselves from situations which would seek to increase the arousal, hectic parties and social events. I know when I get stressed like I just want to go and hide and be away from everyone until I get back to normal again.

The final kind of abnormality I want to mention here is multiple personality disorder. This mechanism of splitting the personality into a number of sub-personalities is really the ultimate form of coping. Here, part of the personality may then deal with specific situations, thereby protecting other parts from harmful situations such as abuse. You will read about it in the next section which focuses on multiple personality.

Cultural relativity

I am sure by now you have begun to realise that defining abnormality is going to be extremely difficult, if not impossible. It seems that there is no one thing that allows us to say, without hesitation, this is what we mean by abnormality. If we try and take abnormality as a theoretical concept first and foremost, we should perhaps see if the people who are considered abnormal all share the same features. However, even this doesn't seem to work because what is considered abnormal in one culture is seen as perfectly normal in another.

I mentioned a number of cultural differences in behaviour at the beginning of this chapter when I talked about the work of Malinowski and Mead, and talked about the kathoeys in Thailand. We see these behaviours as very strange and somewhat abnormal but within their cultures they are accepted as part of life. Another example comes from the film called 'Little Big Man' starring Dustin Hoffman where one of the Indians in the tribe that adopted him when he was a small boy said and did everything the opposite way to the way it should be. I remember the screen image of him washing in mud rather than water and walking backwards and yet he was accepted and considered an important member of the tribe. Perhaps levels of tolerance also have an influence on the definition of abnormality.

Cultural differences can be either between cultures or within cultures. Between cultures means between different cultures such as western and eastern peoples; within means either in terms of areas such as north and south, or over time, say comparing medieval England with the present day. In England, men would be considered somewhat abnormal if they wore skirts with no underpants, and yet in Scotland, no one thinks twice about doing it (though usually only for a special occasion). In fact if you look back at our early history, the village 'idiot' was lovingly tolerated rather than locked away although in later years he was seen as a threat and removed from the village. Despite the fact that most people on the surface understand that cultural differences do exist, they seem to be somehow forgotten by the people who are responsible for diagnosing abnormality.

Many practitioners in the western world assume that the behaviours of the white population are normal and therefore any deviation from this normality by another ethnic group shows some racial or cultural pathology. It should be obvious that what is normal behaviour for that person can only really be judged in relation to the patient's background and culture. The trouble is that because this is not always understood in Britian, West Indian men are more likely to be admitted to psychiatric hospitals, and psychotic black patients are twice as likely as whites or white immigrants to be in hospital involuntarily. Black patients are more often seen by a junior rather than a senior doctor and, even when they are diagnosed with the same disorder as a white person, are more likely to be given more radical treatments (Littlewood and Lipsedge, 1989). These treatments may be major tranquillizers or Electro Convulsive Therapy (ECT) whereby people have electrodes placed over part of their brain and are given an electric shock which induces a convulsion. ECT has been shown to be effective against depression, but there is no real understanding of how it works, and therefore it is considered an ethically dubious form of treatment. It is also well known that in America, more black people than white are diagnosed as being Schizophrenic every year.

Other research has shown that the compulsory detailing of patients in secure hospitals is higher for Afro-Caribbeans than any other groups. Ineichen et al. (1984) looked at hospital admissions in Bristol. They found that non-white groups (West Indian plus other non-whites) accounted for 32 out of 89 compulsory admissions, but only 30 out of 175 voluntary admissions – notice the difference in the proportions here. McGovern and Cope (1989) found that two thirds of hospital detained psychotic patients in Birmingham were Afro-Caribbean (both migrants and British born), with the remaining one-third white and Asian. They also found that up to 16 per cent of Afro-Caribbeans were diagnosed with cannabis induced psychosis, whereas none of the white or Asian patients were given this diagnosis. Cochrane (1981) found the diagnosis of alcohol related admissions in Indian born men was more than twice that of white native born men.

The features of abnormality

Rosenhan and Seligman (1989) tried to get round the problems of identifying what is meant by abnormality. They suggested that if we identify the major features that are more likely to be found in abnormal individuals, we could do a kind of tally – the more you have, the more abnormal you are – and the more abnormal you are, the more likely it is to do with mental illness! They came up with seven features that are based on statistical rarity and social deviance.

1 Suffering

Suffering is often seen amongst people who are mentally ill. The problem here is that some people have no concept of suffering, say people with psychopathic personality disorders, and many normal people suffer, say when they lose someone they love.

The pearly kings and queens from the East End of London are vivid and unconventional. Would you consider them abnormal?

2 Maladaptiveness

If someone suffers from maladaptive behaviour, it means that their behaviours are not the sort of behaviours which will allow them to have a fulfilling life because they will probably prevent them from achieving success or happiness. An example of a maladaptive behaviour is when someone has an irrational fear or phobia about something, for example flying, and can't go anywhere or do anything where that behaviour may be necessary.

3 Vividness and unconventionality

This refers to behaviour that is very obviously unusual or unconventional. I often see an old lady who lives in a village near me on my way home from college. She always wears long flowing black or purple clothes and big floppy hats, and she looks like she is conducting the London Philharmonic Orchestra as she dances up the street. Her behaviour is substantially different from the way we would expect most people to behave. The trouble is there are always unconventional people who are just eccentric rather than mentally ill.

4 Unpredictability and loss of control

Think back to Simon and his escapade in his boxer shorts. His behaviour was certainly unpredictable, and we aren't sure how much beer he actually consumed, because he may well have lost it later on and removed them too! However, most of us are relatively predictable and our behaviour is reasonably well controlled most of the time. Therefore, is this a good measure of abnormality and mental illness?

5 Irrationality and Incomprehensibility

Pre-menstrual tension sometimes causes women to behave in an abnormal and incomprehensible way – at least it probably seems like that to the male members of society. Once the reason for the behaviour is explained, however, it no longer seems quite so irrational and incomprehensible. We therefore have to be careful when judging someone's behaviour as being irrational because we can never be sure that the reason for their behaviour doesn't have a good cause.

6 Observer discomfort

I mentioned the behaviour of the man who thought it was amusing to go up to people and pretend that he was 'intellectually challenged' and how he made me feel really uncomfortable. I also remember a colleague who never actually looked at me when she was talking to me. She used instead to gaze at my shoulder and I always had this urge to crouch down so she had to look into my eyes because I found it really difficult to have a conversation with her when she wouldn't look at me. How about someone who stands just a little too close – this also makes us feel really uncomfortable. This is because our social behaviour is governed by a set of rules that we seem to learn but are never actually taught. We learn them as we grow up by monitoring other people's responses to our behaviours. When the rules are broken by another person, we generally become very uncomfortable. This will affect how we feel about that person and whether or not we want to go on associating with them – we find it hard to deal with someone whose behaviour is abnormal compared with the normal rules of our society.

7 Violation of moral and ideal standards

If a man rapes a woman, we would consider that to be a transgression of the accepted moral standards of our society. Although this is a very extreme example, it gives you an idea that we would find the perpetrator of this kind of behaviour abnormal because he is not following the unwritten moral code.

These seven features do not actually help us a great deal because most of them can be explained in a number of different ways. Although they could be adapted to fit into different cultures, they also involve an element of subjectivity because it would depend very much on the perception of the person doing the judging. What I may see as vivid and unconventional, you may see as perfectly normal! However, if you add them together, you can begin to get a picture of someone who falls beyond what most of us would accept as normal. So where do we go from here?

> During my time as a nurse, I spent some time in a psychiatric unit in London. I remember being very frightened when I first started because the patients seemed very uncontrolled and strange in many of their behaviours. However, as time went by, I became less and less concerned about the things they did and more and more fond of many of them. I remember one woman who had what was called 'manic depressive psychosis'. It was the middle of the night and for some reason or the other she suddenly decided that everything on the ward had to be washed. She started to gather all the clothes she could find and take them to the laundry room, followed by the sheets and blankets. Not satisfied with that, she started to pull the bedcovers and sheets of the beds of the sleeping patients. At this point, the staff on the ward realised what was going on. She became very angry and violent because she was so convinced that this washing had to be done and she got really upset when we tried to stop her, and punched out at the charge nurse. She ran down to the other end of the ward and started to pull down the curtains around the beds, causing the remaining patients who were still asleep to panic and get up. Soon there was pandemonium on the ward as some of the patients who were depressed started to cry, and others started rocking back and forwards while others washed their hands or ran up and down the corridor to try and find somewhere to hide.

I think it was at this point that I decided that perhaps abnormality was a useful concept because if we can decide that someone 's behaviour is 'seriously abnormal' and we have an idea what form that abnormality takes, then we should have some idea how to make the situation more tolerable for them. The washing woman was convinced that the laundry needed doing and had no grasp of the fact that it was 2 o'clock in the morning. Surely being able to alleviate her distress, and the distress caused to the people around her, can't be all bad? It has been recognised that there are lots of different types of abnormality, and each one of these types seem to have a number of common features. Although there is danger in trying to put people into categories and label them accordingly, if they are categorised as carefully and accurately as possible it means that medical professionals don't have to spend ages trying to work out what is going on for each individual person and can perhaps help them that much more quickly. After all, we know that someone with 'say' depression will have a whole list of symptoms which are likely to follow on, such as problems with sleeping. These problems could be addressed without having to wait to see how the course of the disorder progresses.

There are a number of critics of this labelling process' such as Szasz (1962). He says that the basic assumption that psychiatrists make when categorising mental illness is that it is caused by physiological factors – disorders of the functioning of the nervous system. This results in the treatment of these disorders by the use of drugs, which will deal with the abnormal behaviours by reducing them to a manageable level. However, many abnormal behaviours are actually caused by problems in coming to terms with life, mislearning or early experiences which may have left that person psychologically damaged in some way. We have actually looked at how early experiences can affect behaviour in later life. Szasz suggests that what we should do is to try to differentiate between the two causes and perhaps separate the two rather than lump them together.

The other problem that arises is when the categorisation is wrong. The person may well have been labelled and treated accordingly by medical professionals. Unfortunately, many of the labels of mental disorders automatically suggest to the layperson a set of ideas about what the person is like and how they should be treated. I'll give you a really common example. Take the case of schizophrenia. I would imagine a vast number of people would describe a schizophrenic as someone who has a split personality and they would come up with all sorts of behaviours that they might expect to be associated with that categorisation. Well they would be wrong, because first of all schizophrenia is a kind of *disorganised* personality not a split personality. Split personality is known as 'multiple personality disorder' (MPD) or 'dissociative identity disorder' (DID). Secondly, many diagnosed schizophrenics who are receiving treatment have no symptoms at all.

So what is the answer?

Classificatory systems

There are two classificatory systems which are used to identify mental disorders but they both owe much to the work of Emil Kraepelin (1856–1926). He suggested that groups of symptoms seemed to occur together on a regular basis. This meant that these groups of symptoms (syndromes) could perhaps be classed as diseases. He also believed that they had a biological basis and should be treated in the same way as any other illness. He suggested (1896) that there were two groups of serious mental illness: 'dementia praecox' (later called schizophrenia) and 'manic-depressive psychosis'. If nothing else, he must be acknowledged for recognising that many mental disorders had a biological basis rather than caused by external factors such as evil spirits or possession by demons.

The International List of Causes of Death was originally compiled by the World Health Organisation as a way of monitoring causes of death throughout the world. In 1939 they added mental disorders to the list and in 1948 the list expanded further and became known as the International Classification of Diseases (ICD). However, the mental disorders section was not widely accepted and was superceded by the DSM (see below). The current version is the ICD-10 which focuses on descriptions which are grouped according to similarities and differences in signs and symptoms rather than looking at the other aspects of people's functioning in their everyday lives. As some of the signs and symptoms appear in a number of disorders, this makes its use inadequate for psychiatrists. The lack of categories also makes it difficult to make specific diagnoses. One example is the category entitled 'Neurotic, stress related and somatoform disorders' which appears as one category on the ICD-10 but actually appears as four separate categories on the DSM (anxiety disorders, somatoform disorders, dissociative disorders and adjustment disorders).

The Diagnostic and Statistical Manual of Mental Disorders (DSM) was first published in 1952 by the American Psychiatric Association in response to the ICD. The current version is the DSM IV (1994) and it differs from the ICD because it has a greater number of discrete categories. It also looks at the influence of outside factors on a person as part of the diagnosis. This is obviously much more valid because the life experiences of a person are very likely to contribute to any kind of disorder.

The DSM consists of 5 axes or dimensions that are not only used as a diagnostic tool but also help with the planning of treatment and prediction of outcomes. Each person is assessed on every axis to give a much broader picture of what is going on in their lives, which as we have seen is extremely important if we are to give a fair diagnosis.

The Five DSM Axes

Axis 1: *Clinical syndromes* – contains lots of clinical syndromes such as mood disorders, anxiety disorders, sexual disorders etc. It also includes various conditions that cannot be put down to a mental disorder but which may require attention or treatment, such as marital problems.

Axis 2: *Developmental disorders and personality disorders* – contains disorders not listed on Axis 1 but which are often found in patients who are suffering from one of the Axis 1 disorders. This axis covers disorders that typically start in childhood or adolescence, such as mental retardation and learning disorders.

Axis 3: *Physical disorders and conditions* – any medical problems which may appear to be of relevance to the psychological ones such as cancer or heart disease.

Axis 4: *Psychosocial stressors* – this refers to the situations that the patient has been subjected to, for example whether they have lost their parent or husband/wife or whether their partner has committed suicide. These factors would probably have an influence on the course of treatment as well as how the patient feels at the time.

Axis 5: *Global assessment of functioning at the present time and during the past year.* – questions that would be asked are whether or not the person has been working, whether they have been suicidal, violent and so on.

It should be obvious that the whole topic of abnormality is one fraught with problems. There are so many issues that need to be considered before we risk planting some kind of label on a person which may well be with them for the rest of their lives. Schizophrenia, for example, is an incurable illness. If someone is diagnosed, they will only ever become a schizophrenic in remission. Therefore we can't risk making a mistake.

The key study in this area emphasises just how easy it is to make mistakes when diagnosing mental illness and how, once someone has been labelled, all their behaviours are seen in a different perspective. If we can't tell the sane from the insane then it doesn't leave us with much hope. At least the diagnostic criteria are far more sophisticated than they were at the time of the key study which was carried out in 1973. The DSM II was in use at the time and this second version didn't have the five axes but just had much more simplistic diagnostic labels. Therefore the system we now use for categorisation, we hope, is much less likely to be abused than it was in the past.

D.L. Rosenhan (1973) On being sane in insane places.

Science, 179, 250–58.

The purpose of this two part study was to see if psychiatrists really were able to differentiate the sane from the insane.

STUDY ONE: The purpose of this study was to see if sane people could get themselves admitted to psychiatric hospitals.

Design

Field study which took place in a number of psychiatric hospitals. One subject was the author of the study and was therefore a participant observer.

Subjects The pseudopatients consisted of 8 sane people (5 men and 3 women) who were a psychology graduate in his 20s, three psychologists, a paediatrician, a psychiatrist, a painter and a housewife. All used fake names to protect their health records in the future, and the subjects who were working in the health service pretended they were in other occupations.

Procedure Twelve hospitals, old and new, were selected in different states in the USA. The pseudopatients phoned the hospitals for an appointment and on arrival complained that they had been hearing voices which were unfamiliar, of the same sex and said 'empty', 'hollow', and 'thud'. Any other information given by the subjects was completely honest including details of their family and personal background and recent life experiences.

These symptoms were chosen because they simulated existential symptoms which come from the realisation that life is really meaningless and so, as moral free agents, we have to create our own values through our actions and accept the responsibility for those actions – we can't blame our lives on anyone else. Also, there are no reports of existential psychosis in any literature on mental illness and therefore it was thought that this would make the diagnosis harder to recognise.

One part of the study involved patients approaching staff members with friendly conversation or simple polite requests about their condition or date of discharge to see how many times their questions were answered. In order to have a comparison group, Rosenhan carried out a similar study in a university faculty with a female student asking similar questions of tutors and in the university medical centre where she asked where she could find a doctor or a psychiatrist.

Results

All the pseudopatients were admitted to the hospitals where they remained for between seven and 52 days (mean length of stay 19 days), and seven out of eight were diagnosed as schizophrenic. When they were finally discharged, it was with the diagnosis of 'schizophrenia in remission'.

Once the pseudopatients were admitted, they stopped showing any signs of abnormality. They were all extremely concerned that they would be discovered, shocked by how easy it was to be admitted and some were nervous as they had never been into a psychiatric hospital before. On admission, they had nothing to do and so they kept notes of their experiences and mealtimes became one of the few events in their daily schedule. Their behaviour was observed by the members of staff, and although they were totally normal, their behaviour was either overlooked or misinterpreted because they had been 'labelled' as mentally ill.

Patient experiences

The pseudopatients made notes about their experiences, quite openly in front of staff and other patients. None of the staff asked them what the notes were but simply assumed the behaviour was part of their illness making comments in the records such as 'Patient engages in writing behaviour'. If anything went wrong and a patient became upset or distressed by the behaviour of the staff, the response was seen to be because of their illness not due to the situation (and extreme case of making dispositional not situational attributions). On one occasion, patients waiting outside the cafeteria for lunch were described as displaying the oral-acquisitive syndrome, rather than simply being hungry.

Rosenhan also mentions the fact that there is a tremendous overlap between normal and abnormal behaviours. We all get angry or upset and sometimes there is no obvious reason but when looked at as a proportion of the whole, these episodes have really very little relevance. However, if someone has been labelled as insane, those behaviours will be perceived in a totally different way because this label will distort the interpretation of even the most normal activity or event. This is what happened when medical practitioners made notes about the subjects. One pseudopatient talked about his upbringing and family which seemed a typical example of how we experience changes in relationships with our parents as we get older. Sometimes we are closer to one parent at a young age, but when we reach adolescence, we find that we have become closer to the other. This may be due to one of our parents finding it harder to relate to small children, but enjoying a new found closeness as the child matures. Similarly with marital relationships, they do not always run smoothly and occasionally minor rows can develop which are relatively meaningless. However, the case notes of this particular pseudopatient talked about him having 'a long history of considerable ambivalence in close relationships, which begins in early childhood'. The notes continue by saying that his relationship with his father changes from being distant to 'becoming very intense. Affective stability is absent.' This last sentence means that his feelings have no stability – implying he has emotional swings. The report goes on to describe the fact that his efforts to 'control emotionality with his wife and children are punctuated by angry outbursts and, in the case of the children, spankings'.

Pseudopatients' visitors said that they saw no changes in their behaviour as a result of being hospitalised but a number of real patients recognised they were fakes and made comments like 'You're not crazy, you're a journalist or a professor. You're checking up on the hospital,' probably as a result of the fact that they were making notes.

Rosenhan reports that 2100 pills were handed out to the pseudopatients during their stays in the hospitals although all but two were flushed down the toilet. As long as the behaviour of the patients was acceptable whilst on the wards, such actions were not noticed.

The staff tended to keep themselves away from the patients except for administrative or practical duties. The doctors were even more remote than the nurses and seemed to maintain the greatest distance except on admission and discharge. Patients spent on average, under seven minutes a day with senior members of staff over the course of their stay. Surely it should have been the other way around with these senior members of staff who wield the most power being the most familiar with the patients case histories, and yet the doctors tended to see patients on arrival and departure only.

The following table shows the responses received by the pseudopatients versus a female student asking simple questions.

	Psychiatric hospital	Psychiatric hospital	University campus	University medical centre	University medical centre
Responses (%)	**Psychiatrists**	**Nurses**	**Faculty**	**'Looking for a psychiatrist'**	**'Looking for a doctor'**
Moves on, head averted	71	88	0	0	0
Makes eye contact	23	10	0	11	0
Pauses and chats	2	2	0	11	0
Stops and talks	4	0.5	100	78	100
No. of respondents	13	47	14	18	15
No. of attempts	185	1283	14	18	15

Note the lack of response towards the pseudopatients compared with controls in both eye contact and conversation. Students were talked to 100 per cent of the time whereas the pseudopatients were only talked to 4 per cent of the time by psychiatrists and 0.5 per cent by nurses. The other really interesting thing about this table is that even when the student asked where they could find a psychiatrist, the per cent response they got decreased to 78 per cent which indicates that people find mental illness quite hard to deal with.

The other major impact on the pseudopatients was their complete lack of power in the psychiatric wards. Their movements were watched and restricted, they had virtually no contact with staff and their notes were available to all members of staff. They also suffered from a minimum of personal privacy for example some hospitals had no toilet doors and examinations were conducted in semi-public rooms. It was also found that there were instances of serious physical abuse to patients. Sometimes these were observed by other patients who were presumably seen as being irrelevant, but such abuses of power were immediately stopped when another member of staff appeared – yet another example of how irrelevant the patients were considered in terms of witnessing such acts.

STUDY TWO:

The purpose of the second part was to see if hospitals who had been told that they were going to be approached by pseudopatients, would be able to tell the insane from the sane.

Rosenhan told the staff at a large hospital, who had heard about the first part of the study, that some time during the next three months, one or more pseudopatients would attempt to gain admittance to the hospital. Each member of staff was asked to rate on a ten point scale the likelihood of the patients who appeared as being pseudopatients. The fact was that no pseudopatients actually presented themselves, and out of 193 genuine patients who attended for psychiatric treatment, 41 were judged to be pseudo patients by at least one member of staff and 19 of these were thought to be acting by two members of staff, one of which was a psychiatrist. The conclusion by Rosenhan was that psychiatric hospitals were unable to distinguish the sane from the insane.

Discussion

The results indicate that psychiatric diagnosis is extremely inaccurate and that Rosenhan's claim that 'we cannot distinguish the sane from the insane in psychiatric hospitals' is actually given considerable support. However, he also acknowledges that hospitals seem to be special environments where behaviour gets easily distorted and patients are treated in such a way as to perpetuate any problems they may have rather than providing the kind of environment which would help and support them.

The study also showed how significant labelling can be in producing expectations and influencing behaviour which was demonstrated by the actions of the staff towards the patients. If nothing else, this study highlights how careful the health profession should be when diagnosing any kind of psychiatric disorder. The pseudopatients found the whole experience extremely unpleasant, not from associating with the patients but because of their experiences with staff. At least they had the advantage of knowing that they were sane; the real patients don't have that luxury and therefore must find the sense of powerlessness and depersonalisation even worse.

Evaluation

Although the study highlights the ease with which the pseudopatients were misdiagnosed, we must remember that psychiatrists would not expect normal people to want to gain admittance to a psychiatric hospital. The same situation applies for the second part of the study.

Although the patients, once they had been admitted, believed they had stopped showing any signs of abnormality, we cannot be sure that this was the case. If they were anxious and nervous, this might well have influenced their behaviour, both prior to diagnosis and after they had been admitted to the wards.

The doctors were not completely wrong in their diagnoses, because after a period of observation they did diagnose the pseudopatients as having schizophrenia in remission. This, of course, presumed that the original diagnosis was correct, because schizophrenia rarely, if ever, disappears completely.

The ethical considerations of the study involve deception in the first study, whereby the medical practitioners were deceived by the pseudopatients in the symptoms they claimed to be experiencing. The second study on the other hand has far more important ethical implications, because it involved 19 supposedly real patients being turned away. However, we are not to know if they really were genuinely ill, but the chances are that people, in general, would not choose to go into a psychiatric hospital except in the course of scientific research!

Key words

Schizophrenia – a psychiatric disorder which results in the patient suffering from a disorganised personality. They are likely to experience hallucinations, usually auditory, and delusions of grandeur or delusions of persecution.
Pseudopatients – normal people pretending to have schizophrenic symptoms.
Affective stability – stability of emotions.
Existential symptoms – symptoms which come from the realisation that life is really meaningless and therefore the only meaning it will have is the meaning that we give it.
Labelling – giving someone a label which is really like putting them into a category and this label will be used to explain their behaviour and to define how they are treated.

Key questions

1. How did the pseudopatients feel once they had been admitted to the psychiatric hospitals?
2. Why did the patients suffer the effects of deindividuation?
3. Why were patients considered irrelevant when it came to witnessing the mistreatment of other patients?
4. Do you think this type of misdiagnosis could happen today?
5. What ethical issues does this study raise?

Multiple personality

I have touched on the topic of personality twice so far, the first when looking at psychometric testing and the second time in the section on defining abnormality when we mentioned extroversion and introversion. Like intelligence, personality is a concept which varies according to the theorist although we all have a pretty good idea what the concept means to us. Therefore, it is virtually impossible to give the ultimate definition of personality – suffice to say, we know that each one of us has something unique about us which separates us from others, and we tend to refer to that as our personality.

The Far Side © Farworks, Inc. Reprinted with permission of Creators Syndicate International. All rights reserved.

Although we are unique, we do have things about us that are similar. When I discussed psychometric testing, I mentioned that we all have a measure of extroversion/introversion that we can use as a means to compare ourselves with others. Even if we found someone with very similar measures on a number of different traits, it does not mean that they will be like the next person. Some of us achieve great things, while others achieve a very modest amount in their lives and these differences seem to be as much to do with our genetic inheritance, our socio-economic class, our family experiences, and our culture as much as the type of person we seem to be. The whole package is too closely linked to be able to extract one aspect and leave all the others behind.

It has been suggested that we do inherit certain predispositions such as high or low arousal levels and these will influence our experiences of the environment we grow up in. If we have low levels of arousal, we will seek out more arousing and exciting experiences. If we come from a lower socio-economic class, our experiences may be limited compared to others, due to lack of funds. If we have grown up in an institution, we may have had little experience of close personal relationships. This may then influence whether we form successful long-term relationships, and even whether we become good parents. If we live in certain cultures, our expectations will be different and this in turn may influence our experiences and subsequently affect our personalities.

If we accept that all these things are going to influence our personality, we have to accept that *all* these factors are also going to influence the way that we perceive and interpret the same event. Therefore the way that we perceive situations will be very different to each other. What we mustn't do is to fall into the trap of thinking that the study or understanding of personality is no more than an extension of our efforts to try and understand perception.

Lawrence Pervin (1984) made the point that

> 'Personality research is not the study of perception but rather of how individuals differ in their perceptions and how these differences relate to their total functioning. The study of personality focuses not only on a particular psychological process but also on the relationships of different processes. Understanding how these processes act together to form an integrated whole often involves more than understanding each of them separately. People function as organised wholes, and it is in the light of such organisation that we must understand them.'
>
> *(Pervin, 1984, p. 3)*

The point that Pervin is making is that we really need to look at all the processes that make up personality and *how* these processes fit together to make an individual. Each one of us has a childlike part of us that makes us react in an egocentric or irrational way. We all have a logical and analytical part which allows us to assess situations and make decisions. We have parts which make us sociable or insular, parts which make us jealous, parts which make us frightened, parts which make us resentful, inquisitive, compassionate and so on. Many of these parts fit in with Freud's theory of personality whereby the id, the ego and the super-ego all have a role to play. Other parts don't fit so well with his theory but, nevertheless, still exist. Each one of us, therefore, is made up of lots of different characteristics in lesser or larger amounts which, put together, make us the individuals we are. But what happens when these parts don't fit together to make a unified whole?

One of the most fascinating mental disorders is multiple personality disorder or dissociative identity disorder, (DID) as it is now known. It is fascinating partly because it is so rare and causes such bizarre behaviour, and secondly because it is a disorder which has a purely psychological basis. As I have already mentioned it is not the same as schizophrenia, although the terms tend to be used interchangeably by people who don't know the difference. People who suffer from DID seem to have all the different aspects of their personality, but each part is contained in a separate unit. Pervin suggested that all these processes act together to form an integrated whole which is what our personalities are, but it seems that in DID they don't form an integrated whole. Instead they stay as individual units, each one taking on the aspects of an individual personality so it is as if one body contains lots and lots of different people.

Someone who suffers from DID can therefore have any number of different personalities and each split is locked into its own personal role. Each personality has its own characteristics and likes and dislikes. Each may even live its own life alongside the others, while being contained within one body. Therefore we will have the childlike part, the sensible part, the jealous part, the fun loving part and so on, all as individual units which are often given different names.

In order to be diagnosed as having dissociative identity disorder, the DSM IV says the person must have at least two separate 'personalities' which they call ego states or 'alters', and each one must have its own way of feeling and acting that is totally independent from any of the other 'alters'. Each one of these alters has to come forward and take control at different times. Their existence can't be temporary either – they must exist for some time and should cause the person quite a lot of disruption rather than simply being, say, the result of taking drugs or drinking too much.

People who suffer with DID are extremely likely to have gaps in their memories. If they are aware of one alter but there are, say, three, they will not know what is going on when the other two take turns of being in control. It will be as if they keep having blackouts or lapses in memory, which must be really frightening. What must be even worse is if one unrecognised alter does something and the person is unaware of it, when the second alter arrives, it will have to deal with the consequences. In fact, it could be quite embarrassing.

'Hi Jude. How do you feel after your exploits last night?'

'My exploits – what do you mean?' said Jude looking puzzled.

'You know – after we left the pub last night.' Kathy chuckled.

'I don't know what you are talking about,' said Jude feeling angry.

'Yeah, right. So how do you explain the garden gnomes that are sitting in your front garden?'

Jude felt a sort of icy shiver. When she went out to get in her car this morning, she wondered why there were literally hundreds of garden gnomes sitting on her lawn. Her mum was out, and she didn't remember seeing them the night before.

'And what about Kevin?'

'Who's Kevin?' asked Jude, still trying to work out where the gnomes had come from.

'Who's Kevin – you're joking. He's the one that ran off with your bra and put it on the statue in the High Street – you must have been well gone.'

'I er, I um, I don't know what you mean – No, I mean I REALLY don't know what you are talking about.'

'So I suppose you don't remember moving that bench from outside Boots, into the middle of the High Street and dancing on it with three balloons and not a lot else to cover your modesty! We were thinking of putting out a hat and collecting money from passers by.'

Jude at this point, removed herself from the conversation.

If each alter has its own memories and patterns of behaviour and relationships, then each one will act in the way it feels is appropriate. Some alters may know about others but not all of them, and some may be unaware of the existence of *any* other personality. There are often primary alters and subordinate alters. The primary alters are the main personalities which manifest most often. The subordinate alters have lesser relevance and are rarely present, or may even be undetected for some time after the disorder is recognised. Often the subordinate alters may hear the voices of the others but not be aware of who they belong, in other instances some of the alters may even talk to each other. Each alter will usually be very different, possibly even of the opposite sex. Some may be older than others, some may be extrovert and some introvert. Each one will have its own patterns of behaviour, its own experiences, its own memories and its own relationships with other people. It is literally like having a number of different people living in the same body, each one making their own decisions and acting out their own roles. They may even have different physical characteristics for example one may be left handed, another right handed. One may even like one type of food whilst the next may find it disgusting.

Symptoms and causes of DID

In order to understand what the disorder actually is and how it develops, we have to return to Zimbardo's study of prisoners and guards. The most influential factor on their behaviour was the role they believed they were playing. If we consider ourselves, we know our lives are made up of a number of roles and each one is played out according to the situation we find ourselves in. Supposing one of those situations is really horrific, then if we can keep that role separated from the rest of our lives, it is a way of protecting us from damage. In effect, it's an abnormality which has been 'produced' as a coping mechanism.

There are in fact four kinds of dissociative disorders which affect the person's sense of identity and each one may well have a very similar cause. They all result in the person becoming dissociated (or disconnected) from who they were before they developed the condition. This may be caused by 'simple amnesia' ('dissociative amnesia') or the amnesia may be so dense that the person takes on a new life without realising they can't remember the past ('dissociative fugue'). It may be that they lose their sense of self and take on an almost robotic role ('depersonalisation disorder') or it may be due to the fragmenting of the personality ('dissociative identity disorder'). However, DID is considered more chronic and serious than other dissociative disorders and the chances of a full recovery are less.

The condition usually starts in early childhood but may well be unrecognised as it is quite rare and is less likely to be the first diagnosis the practitioner arrives at. Ross (1991) undertook a study on 454 adults in Winnipeg, Canada. He found that 1.3 per cent developed DID which is an amazingly high number but the sample was not representative of the population as a whole and there were no independent interviewers to confirm the diagnosis, so perhaps the estimate is too high.

Although DID was recognised in the nineteenth century, it seems that there was a fall in reported cases between 1920 and 1970, but then it increased again. This may well have been due to the popularity of schizophrenia as a diagnosis in the intervening years. One thing that was quite interesting was that there was a rise in the number of alters of diagnosed patients that seemed to coincide with the publication of a book called 'Sybil' (Schreiber, 1973) which told the story of a woman with sixteen personalities. Before Sybil, the number of alters was two or three but after the book the average rose to ten.

There are a number of theories to explain the cause of DID, but it is recognised today that it is often associated with some kind of traumatic childhood event such as sexual abuse, although the event is not always sexual in nature. Putnam et al. (1983) surveyed therapists who work with DID clients and found that 80 per cent of them had suffered physical abuse in their childhood and 70 per cent had been incest victims. Other research has indicated an even higher incidence.

According to Freud, DID develops as a result of repression of wishes or desires. If you remember, Freud claims that children have sensual desires which focus on their opposite sex parent when they pass through the Oedipal stage. They manage to curb the desires but if they re-emerge in adulthood, the person may do something rash and impulsive of a sexual nature. If this happens, a way of dealing with it would be to repress the memory into the unconscious (motivated forgetting). If this does not work, another way of dealing with the problem would be to actually split that part of the personality from conscious awareness (Buss, 1966) or, alternatively, cope with the memory by giving the 'part of them' that carried out the act a new independent identity.

Probably the most accepted theory is that DID occurs in early childhood as a way of coping with traumatic or disturbing events. Learning theorists suggest that the child learns how to deal with the stressful memories by adopting an avoidance technique. The child 'hypnotises' or fools itself into believing that the events haven't happened to them but to someone else, and this someone else becomes another alter. Bliss (1983) discovered that people suffering from DID are easier to hypnotise than controls and suggested that this might support the idea.

Not surprisingly, women are more likely to develop DID than men. This may well be affected by the fact that the instances of girls experiencing sexual abuse are higher than boys. A study of 796 college students found that 19 per cent of the women and 8.6 per cent of the men had been sexually abused as children (Finkelhor 1979). The women often present with other symptoms such as depression or headaches before the DID is acknowledged. It seems that DID is frequently accompanied by substance abuse, self-abuse or suicide attempts – all of which go along with low self-esteem or guilt. It isn't surprising that some poor little scrap, who experienced such damaging events, may end up feeling so bad about themselves. They would be dealing with an extreme form of anxiety caused by the fact that adults are always right, but what this adult is doing is wrong. The dissonance caused would have to be dealt with and the way the child might make sense of the situation is to change their conscious belief that maybe it isn't wrong – and simply repress the fact that they know it is. This would leave the child unable to trust their own judgement and to feel that they were inadequate and useless – hence the low self-esteem.

Jackson et al. (1990) found that children who had been victims of abuse had more severe problems than controls in later relationships and also suffered from low self-esteem and depression. It also seems that one of the long term effects of child sexual abuse is an increase in the persons vulnerability to further sexual assault (Alexander and Lupfer, 1987) probably because the person would have an expectation that that sort of behaviour was all they deserved.

It's not surprising then, that children who have been through such traumatic relationships feel find it hard to deal with what happened. Of course they would need to protect themselves from any further hurt and perhaps this fragmentation would be a way of doing it. If this is the case, the treatment must involve trying to convince the person that it is not necessary to split their personality in order to deal with their earlier traumas and to help them to reintegrate – but first of all, they have to acknowledge their split of other parts. It seems that hypnosis is a good technique to use as it gives the person access to hidden portions of the personality. But as you will see, it may actually result in the belief that there are other alters – even when there aren't!

Diagnosis of DID

It's essential that there are very stringent criteria for the diagnosis of DID because it has been used as a legal defence in a number of court cases. An example is the case of the serial killer known as the 'Hillside Strangler' who was brought to trial in California in the 1980's. Ken Bianchi pleaded not guilty by reason of insanity, because he claimed he was suffering from DID. A number of researchers were very sceptical about his defence and, as a result of this, decided to conduct some research to find out if it was possible to fake the disorder by using the same method as Bianchi's interviewer had done.

Spanos, Weekes and Bertrand (1985) told a group of undergraduate subjects that they would, for the purposes of the study, take the role of an accused murderer who had pleaded not guilty even though there was lots of evidence that they had in fact committed the murder. The researchers also told the subjects that they would be interviewed as if they had done the crime and may be hypnotised as part of the role play. They then met the 'psychiatrist' who was in fact a confederate of the researcher.

The independent variable was the nature of the interview.

- In the first condition using the same technique as Bianchi's interviewer, subjects were given a very basic hypnotic session and asked to let a second personality come forward.
- In the second condition, subjects were also hypnotised and told that they may have blocked off parts of themselves, but were given no other information.
- In the final condition which was really the control, they weren't hypnotised and were given virtually no information about the fact that they may have a hidden part of their personality.

At this point in all three conditions, the 'psychiatrist' asked questions about the murder. He also asked questions to try and get at the possible existence of a second personality and amazingly enough many of the subjects agreed that there was another personality within them.

In a later session it was found that the first condition brought forth more 'second personalities'. In fact 81 per cent of them gave their second personality a name and many of these 'new' personalities admitted the murder! They were then asked to take two personality tests. They had to do both tests twice so that each personality within them could do both and even these showed a considerable difference between the two.

This evidence casts quite a lot of doubt on the existence of DID but nevertheless there are still a large number of professionals who accept DID as a real disorder, even if it is extremely rare. The final criteria which is used as a kind of make-or-break test is the amount of difference between the alters. Sometimes physiological measures such as EEGs are used because of their lack of subjectivity and these have been found to produce significant differences between the personalities in DID sufferers compared with controls.

Unfortunately, at the end of the day, we still can't be 100 percent sure that DID exists. If you believe something for long enough, you can almost make it happen – a kind of self-fulfilling prophecy. Supposing you have been convicted of a murder, and you really don't feel that you were acting rationally when you committed that murder, then it might be possible to convince yourself that it was really another part of you that did it, not your normal self. If you believe this for long enough, you will have had lots of practice imagining yourself as another person, and this in itself may be enough to make the measures significantly different.

One of the implications of DID is to do with the status of different alters and the law. Elyn Saks (1992), from the University of Southern California Law Centre, argued that the body should only be considered a container for the

Joanne Woodward played the part of Eve in a film called 'The three faces of Eve'. The photographs show how she portrayed Eve Black and Eve White.

person. It is therefore the person who should be to blame and not the body. Obviously in a 'normal' person, they are the same thing but not in a situation where the body contains a number of different 'people'. The problem comes when one 'alter' knows what the other one is doing – does that make them both to blame? An alternative to this is if one alter knows what the other one has done but can't actually stop it – by law the alter who hasn't actually committed the act isn't guilty. Surely the one who didn't commit the act is guilty because it should have reported the act of the other.

Confusing isn't it?

One case where DID was accepted was the case of Eve White. This was the most carefully documented report of dissociative identity disorder at the time and as such deserves a place with the key studies. It is interesting to note that the whole idea behind the therapy was to try and reintegrate the alters into a whole person. This method of treatment recognises the significance of each part of our personality as components of a whole and acknowledges that we really are complex beings with many different sides – a little like a Rubik's cube.

C.H. Thigpen and H. Cleckley (1954). A case of multiple personality.

Journal of Abnormal and Social Psychology, 49, 135–51.

The aim of this case study was to document the psychotherapeutic treatment of a 25 year old woman who was presented with a history of severe headaches and blackouts (periods where she had no recollection of what was going on) but was later discovered to have multiple personality disorder (now known as DID). This study gives fairly strong support for the existence of the condition.

The alters

Eve White

At the time of the first consultation, the patient, Eve White, was aged 25. She had been married for six years with one daughter Bonnie, aged four. She had twin sisters who were younger than her and she had left school early, getting a job as a telephone operator to help support the family. Her marriage was in trouble and during the course of the treatment she temporarily moved away from her husband to live in a city about 100 miles away, leaving her daughter with grandparents.

Eve White was neat, colourless, demure, very conservative and totally honest. Her discussions were always serious and she was conscientious about details. She was also very anxious about all sorts of things, especially the difficulties in her relationship with her mother and her husband and showed great concern for the welfare of her daughter. She was a serious Baptist, as were her parents, but her husband Ralph White was a strict Catholic. She had recently suffered a miscarriage which had precipitated the onset of serious headaches. Eve had no awareness of the other alters.

Eve Black

Eve Black was almost the complete opposite of Eve White. She was mischevious and childish with little concern for either the husband or the child (they weren't her husband or child!).

She had no desire to help Eve White with her problems and pretended she was co-operating when she wasn't.

Jane

Mature, sincere, capable and interesting. She was aware of the other two personalities but had no access to their memories before she emerged. She could only emerge through Eve White but felt free from Eve White's responsibilities and attachments although that didn't mean she couldn't feel genuine devotion and love.

She took over from Eve White and stayed 'out' more and more but couldn't displace Eve Black or communicate through her. It was believed that if they could all be integrated through her, the patient would regain full health.

The researchers

At the time of the case study, Dr Thigpen was the Associate Clinical Professor and Dr. Cleckley was Professor of Psychiatry and Neurology at the Medical College of Georgia. They both became involved when it was evident that the case being investigated was more complex than usual.

The study

Eve White had been irregularly attending for interview over several months due to her headaches and the blackouts which followed on after the headaches. During that time it became obvious that she had a number of emotional difficulties originating from disagreements with her husband about the fact that he wanted Bonnie to be raised as a Catholic. She also claimed she had no memory of a recent trip to her cousin and an argument that had occurred with Ralph, but this was dealt with by hypnosis to replace the missing memories. Ralph also claimed that from time to time the woman he was with seemed very different from his wife and was loud and boisterous, but the next minute she would be her normal self.

After her visits and reassurance from her therapist, her symptoms improved. A number of days after one of her visits, a letter arrived which caused confusion. The letter was written by Eve White but was unfinished. At the bottom of the letter was a final paragraph which looked as if it had been written by a child and had nothing to do with the rest of the letter. The final paragraph stated 'baby please be quite dear lord don't let me lose patience with her she's too sweet and innocent and my self-control….'

The therapist wondered whether Eve White could 'as a puerile prank, have decided to disguise her characteristic handwriting and add this inconsequential note?' although he found this possibility extremely unlikely.

Within a week Ralph called the therapist explaining that Eve had gone into town and had bought an array of expensive clothes – he asked if she could attend the next day. When she arrived, she denied sending the letter although she remembered writing it, saying it was unfinished. She also explained that she had no awareness of the clothes that hung in the wardrobe which were extremely expensive and totally out of character. Then she explained for the first time that she heard voices which were becoming more and more frequent and expressed a fear that she was going mad. Then she was silent for a moment, looked dazed and then changed her posture.

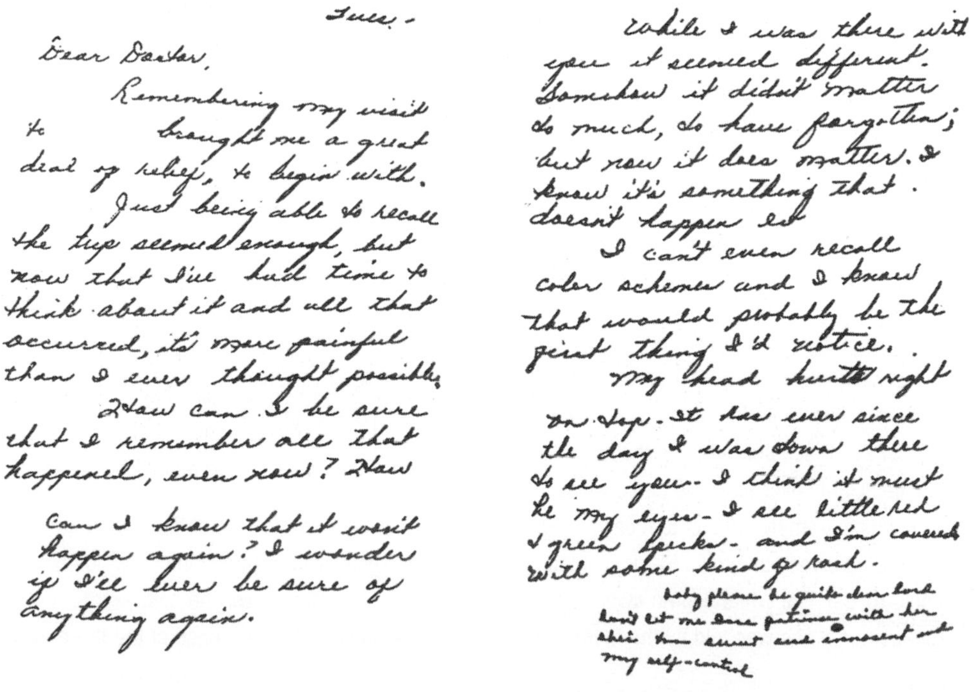
Tues. -

Dear Doctor,

Remembering my visit to brought me a great deal of relief, to begin with. Just being able to recall the trip seemed enough, but now that I've had time to think about it and all that occurred, it's more painful than I ever thought possible. How can I be sure that I remember all that happened, even now? How can I know that it won't happen again? I wonder if I'll ever be sure of anything again.

While I was there with you it seemed different. Somehow it didn't matter so much, so have forgotten; but now it does matter. I know it's something that doesn't happen ...

I can't even recall color schemes and I know that would probably be the first thing I'd notice.

My head hurts right on top. It has ever since the day I was down there to see you. I think it must be my eyes. I see little red & green specks – and I'm covered with some kind of rash.

baby please be quite dear lord don't let me lose patience with her she's too sweet and innocent and my self-control

> 'An alien, inexplicable expression then came over her face… Closing her eyes, she winced as she put her hands to her temples, pressed hard, and twisted them as if to combat sudden pain. A slight shudder passed over her entire body.
>
> Then the hands dropped. She relaxed easily into an attitude of comfort the physician had never before seen in this patient. A pair of blue eyes popped open. There was a quick reckless smile. In a bright unfamiliar voice that sparkled, the women said, 'Hi, there, Doc!'
>
> *Thigpen and Cleckley, 1954, p.26*

The physician was impressed with Eve Black: 'Perhaps because of the easy laxness of this girl's posture and her more vigorous movements, the lines of her body seemed somehow a little more voluptuously rounded.' The new Eve talked about Eve White using the words that she was 'always respecting the strict bounds of a separate identity'. The physician had little doubt that this was another person: 'It was immediately apparent that this new voice was different, that the basic idiom of her language was plainly not that of Eve White.'

The new Eve explained the blackouts that Eve White suffered from were when she was 'out' but that Eve White had no awareness of her. This explained the strange bouts of behaviour that Ralph talked about, and the incident when Eve Black bought the wardrobe full of clothes. In fact Eve Black's behaviour involved all the things that Eve White hated: drinking in bars, flirting with numerous men, dancing, wearing slinky clothes and so on. Over the next 14 months, Eve White and Eve Black were interviewed for a total of 100 hours. At first, Eve White had to be hypnotised in order to let Eve Black out but later she appeared unexpectedly, until over time she came when called. It was extremely difficult to recall Eve White when Eve Black was out as Eve Black seemed to become stronger. Eve White had no awareness of the situation until she was told by the therapists and although Eve Black knew of Eve White's actions this was not the case in reverse.

Throughout this therapy, Eve Black talked of events that had occurred in their childhood where Eve White had been in trouble for things Eve Black had done. Because Eve Black was considered to be an unreliable liar, these episodes were confirmed by Ralph and her parents. Eve Black showed very little concern for her 'twin' although she wasn't cruel on purpose. She simply wanted to enjoy her life and sought excitement where ever she could find it. She kept away from people who might recognise her but was able to master the art of acting to hide her identity if she was 'out' and found herself in the company of acquaintances.

Eve White was taken into hospital and while she was there the therapist told her about the other Eve. Although she found it hard to accept, it explained many of the situations she had experienced. She also found she had an element of control over when Eve Black appeared and Eve Black's behaviour become less extreme. After eight months, Eve White seemed to have made progress and had far fewer headaches and blackouts than before. Then the headaches returned, followed by blackouts which could not be explained even by Eve Black.

At one of the therapy sessions, Eve White became very sleepy whilst talking about childhood memories. She opened her eyes and asked in a totally unfamiliar voice 'Who are you?' This was the emergence of a third alter, Jane, who was aware of the other two alters but was distinctly different. From the time she emerged, Jane seemed to be the most balanced of the three. She could only get out through Eve White but knew of both Eves. She also showed compassion towards Bonnie and was able to take over Eve White's tasks at her job and fill in for her at home. It was suggested that if Jane could stay in charge, the patient would probably finally recover from the condition which had caused her such problems over the past years.

Evidence of the existence of the three alters:

Psychological tests	Eve White	Eve Black	Jane
Wechsler Intelligence tests:*	110	104	tests not done
Wechsler memory tests:*	Superior	Inferior	tests not done
Drawings of human figures*	Healthier than Black. Some anxiety, obsessive compulsive traits, rigid and hostile.	Less healthy than White. Hysterical tendencies.	tests not done
Electro-encephalogram (EEG)	11 cycles per second (normal)	12.5 cycles per second (slightly fast – sometimes associated with psychopathic personality)	11 cycles per second (normal)
Personality dynamics	Repressive of her feelings	Regressive	tests not done
Hypnosis	Easily hypnotised	Not hypnotisable	tests not done

The tests show a distinct difference between Eve White and Eve Black indicating that they are two distinct alters. The EEG recording for all three alters indicates a close link between Eve White and Jane, but a faster recording for Eve Black which has sometimes been linked to psychopathic personality disorder.

Discussion

Although the study was undertaken over quite some time, the therapists, by their own admission, questioned the possibility that they had been deceived. They seemed to be convinced that the study demonstrated a clear case of multiple personality disorder rather than any other hysterical conversion or dissociation. Certainly the external data from family and husband supported the idea that there were two distinct personalities. The lack of awareness by Eve White of Eve Black's existence and the totally different behaviours between the two alters does indicate that something strange was going on. Perhaps Eve was simply dealing with the cognitive dissonance created by her two lifestyles by introducing another person, rather than another belief.

Evaluation

The major concern with this case study is the subjectivity that occurred between the authors and the Eves. However, most of the objective measures held up to scrutiny. Correlations of each personality with itself was higher than correlations between personalities. A film was taken and analysed frame by frame of all three persons and minute measurements of the eyes indicated that there was a different pattern of measures for each person.

Key words

Psychopathic personality disorder – a personality disorder based on Bowlby's affectionless psychopath, where the person feels no real empathy for other people and is totally egocentric and amoral (without morals).
Rorschach ink blot test – a projective test which requires people to look at ink blots that have been squashed between folded paper and look like butterflies. Patients are required to say what they look like. The test has been shown to have little reliability or validity.
Repressive – contained, suppressing feelings and emotions.
Regressive – reverting backward towards a childlike stage.
Hypnosis – a state of deep relaxation where patients feel less inhibited and can, according to Freud, gain access to their unconscious mind.
Electroencephalogram – electrodes placed on the head measure brain wave patterns from the different lobes of the brain.

Key questions

1. Multiple personality disorder and schizophrenia are different disorders. What is the difference between the two?
2. What is the most accepted cause for multiple personality disorder?
3. What evidence does the key study give for the existence of multiple personality disorder?
4. What is the weakness of the methodology used in this key study?
5. Why legally, is it so important to make sure of a diagnosis of DID?

Postscript

The real name of the subject for this key study was Chris Sizemore. She wrote a book called 'I'm Eve' (Sizemore and Pittillo, 1977) where she maintained that Thigpen and Cleckley's case study was really the tip of the iceberg. She reported that her personality continued to fragment after the end of the therapy until 21 separate alters inhabited her body. She stated that there were nine before the time of her therapy and that Thigpen and Cleckley never managed to make contact with them. There were a number of traumatic events in her childhood which may have caused this fragmentation, although none of them were sexual in nature. She had seen a man drown when she was about two years of age and had witnessed another cut into pieces by the saw at a timberyard. One event which left her traumatised, and may well have been the core of the fragmentation, was when she was held high off the floor by her mother and made to touch the face of her dead grandmother. She was five years old at the time, but even as an adult could remember the clammy cold cheek. Sizemore believes that the reason she developed these separate personalities was as a way of coping with the harshness of life.

NOTE: Some of the quotations for this study come from the book, The Three Faces of Eve, by Thigpen and Cleckley.

Perhaps this is a fitting study to end with because I am sure you will agree, despite what we know about people, they still continue to confuse us. I do hope that this book, however, has given you some insight into human behaviour and thought. Don't you think we are amazing? I still find after all this time that the complexities and intricacies of humans present us with a continuous puzzle to try to work out why we behave the way that we do – but all the puzzling in the world, at the end of the day, only leaves us with ideas which may not necessarily be facts!

I expect you have also found that when you tell people that you are studying psychology, they will instantaneously assume that you are psychoanalysing them, and you are now in a position to put them straight. Doesn't it make you want to shout at them that it is not that easy! Even when you know as much as you do now, all you can do is to pick up patterns and trends in behaviour when you first meet someone. It takes a long time to really get to know people and to fully understand what makes them tick because we are all individuals and what motivates one person may have no influence on the next. But part of the fun is getting to know them, and the other part of the fun is trying to work it all out. Even then, you may well get some of it wrong but if it makes you more tolerant of human weaknesses, then I have done my job.

We are all different and yet we all have so much in common. At least the majority of us have only got ourselves to deal with. Imagine having numerous versions of yourself inside your body and having to cope with all of them … the mind boggles!

Answers to key questions

Chapter 2 – Cognitive psychology

E.F. Loftus and J.J. Palmer (1974) Reconstruction of automobile destruction: An example of the interaction between language and memory.

See pages 40–43

1 *To look at the effects of leading questions on memory.*
2 *Ecological validity – it was not the same as a real life event where the person might be upset or the subjects may not have been honest in their answers or not taken the study seriously. Subjects would also have known that they were going to answer questions so may have taken more notice than in real life when you would not have the expectation that you would have to answer questions about what you see.*
Subjects – the subjects were all students.
3 *To ensure that the results were due to the manipulation of the verb and not due to chance.*
4 *The state you are in at the time, eg drunk, tired, aroused. Also whether you are actually interested in the event or not.*
5 *Try and set up a real life study where people are asked what they actually saw about a staged event.*

Jan B. Deregowski (1972). Pictorial perception and culture. Scientific American, 227, 82–88.

See pages 64–67

1 *Whether drawings are a universal means of communication amongst all cultures and whether all cultures perceive pictures in the same way.*
2 *The evidence they presented was anecdotal and therefore likely to be inaccurate.*
3 *Because he gave them more than one test and they performed similarly on each test.*
4 *You can see all aspects of the object on a split style drawing.*
5 *Because the natives' drawing abilities were being judged by western standards.*

Simon Baron-Cohen, Alan M. Leslie and Uta Frith (1985) Does the autistic child have a 'theory of mind'?

See pages 81–83

1 *Because if a lack of theory of mind was a core deficit in autism alone, then other two groups would have had a theory of mind. If they too lacked a theory of mind it would therefore have meant that it could not have been the core deficit for autism alone. We have to remember that whatever group had been chosen, it is virtually impossible to find an ideal control group with whom to compare the autistic children.*

2 *The autistic children actually had an estimated mental age higher than the other two groups. This gave them an advantage rather than a disadvantage. Therefore if they still failed the theory of mind test it would have made the results more valid because they were almost advantaged to succeed over the other groups.*
3 *The Verbal age of the Down's syndrome children was much lower than that of the other two groups. This may have disadvantaged them in terms of linguistic skills but they still managed to achieve almost the same scores as the normal children, so the answer would have to be 'no'.*
4 *The memory question was intended to make sure that the child's answer on the belief question was not simply due to a memory failure, but was actually due to their lacking the ability to see a situation from someone else's point of view.*
5 *We could answer that the study was not ecologically valid because it took place in a laboratory and was therefore unlike a normal daily situation and may therefore have frightened the subjects. More important was the fact that the children were being asked to attribute beliefs to dolls and not to real people.*

R. Allan Gardner and Beatrice T. Gardner (1969). Teaching Sign Language to a Chimpanzee

See pages 98–100

1 *Because if the chimp had learned language with the ease of a child, it would have meant that language was not unique to humans.*
2 *The study gave lots of rich data about how chimps learn language and help to highlight how it differs from human language.*
3 *They tend to be very subjective.*
4 *It would be very difficult as chimps gesticulate anyway and so it may be hard to interpret which is a sign and which is an arm wave.*
5 *Probably not!*

Chapter 3 – Social psychology

S. Milgram (1963). Behavioural Study of Obedience

See pages 115–118

1 *To look at obedience levels amongst members of the public to a perceived legitimate authority figure.*
2 *Because subjects were deceived as to the purpose of the study. They were not given the right to withdraw and they may have suffered long terms psychological effects.*
3 *By newspaper advertisement and mail shots.*
4 *The subjects are a self selecting group and are therefore not representative of the population as a whole.*
5 *At home and at school.*

I.M. Piliavin, J.A. Rodin and J. Piliavin (1969) Good samaritanism: An underground phenomenon?

See pages 139–142

1 *To look at bystander intervention and to see if the nature of the victim affected helping behaviour.*
2 *If the victim was not helped spontaneously, the model would come to their aid to prevent them from having to lie on the ground with no-one helping them.*
3 *So they did not have to take part in too many trials as the trails were embarrassing, especially in the drunk condition. They may also have been effective if the situation had been seen before but not the new set of students and therefore people may have believed that this was another genuine incident.*
4 *No because subjects weren't asked for their informed consent, weren't given the opportunity to refuse to take part and weren't debriefed afterwards.*
5 *Previous studies had only had one potential helper and were based in laboratories which were not ecologically valid. This study had a large number of potential helpers and was far more ecologically valid.*

Haney, Banks and Zimbardo (1973), A study of prisoners and guards in a simulated prison

See pages 151–153

1 *To look at how far our behaviour is influenced by the social roles we play rather than our own personalities.*

2 *Ecological validity – it was not really a prison and the subjects were not really prisoners or guards. Ethical considerations – the subjects suffered physical and psychological traumas as a result of the research.*

3 *The findings were valid because the subjects were so affected by the roles that they were playing.*

4 *People lose their individuality when they are wearing uniforms.*

5 *By setting up another situation such as a hospital. However the same questions about the ecological validity would apply as the people undertaking those roles would still not be 'real', nurses for example.*

H. Tajfel. (1970) Experiments in intergroup discrimination.

See pages 165–168

1 *To investigate how simply putting people in categories would demonstrate discrimination.*

2 *Ecological validity – it lacked ecological validity because the study was carried out in a laboratory and the groups weren't like groups that occur in real life because they were meaningless and artificial. Also the boys weren't really giving each other money – it was purely a pencil and paper test.*
Demand characteristics – because the matrices were obvious, subjects may have given the responses they thought were expected of them.
Subjects – the subjects were all boys aged between 14 and 15.

3 *Because they were young boys, they may have been more competitive than girls.*

4 *No because the boys were deceived as to the nature of the investigation.*

5 *This is quite tough because you are no longer a naïve subject. As we have seen, your gender and age may also make a difference but in many instances people do tend to favour their in-group, even though they know they shouldn't.*

Chapter 4 – Children's development

J. Samuel and P. Bryant (1984). Asking only one question in the conservation experiment.

See pages 190–192

1 *To find out if the ages that children could conserve as suggested by Piaget were correct or were simply due to the nature of the methodology.*

2 *To make sure that the children who saw the transformation and then answered the post-transformation question correctly were using information they had gained by watching the transformation from one state to another rather than simply guessing.*

3 *To ensure that order effects did not occur and that some children came to each one of the three tasks with enthusiasm. Otherwise, if all the children had done the same test last, they may have been so bored that they did not do it properly which would have influenced the results.*

4 *Ecological validity – the study was carried out in a laboratory setting which was not true to life.*
The subjects may have been responding to demand characteristics.

5 *To use sweets and drinks for example, where the child would be far more motivated to pay attention.*

A. Bandura, D, Ross and S.A. Ross (1961) Transmission of aggression through imitation of aggressive models.

See pages 205–210

1 *Because the raters knew the children before the start of the study and may have had prior expectations of what they were like.*
2 *By showing that the ratings from the two researchers significantly correlated with each other.*
3 *To make sure that they were aroused and therefore more likely to be aggressive than if they had not been aroused in this way. It was also thought that the subjects who saw the aggressive behaviour may have been less likely to be aggressive themselves, because they would have had their aggressive feelings 'released' by watching the aggressive role model. Finally, if the subjects in the non-aggressive condition were subsequently made angry but then didn't demonstrate their anger, it would suggest that watching a non-aggressive role model might have had an inhibitory effect on their behaviour.*
4 *Because the children were very small and a five foot high doll may have been intimidating*
5 *You may be teaching children to be aggressive when they would not normally have experienced such a situation.*

J. Hodges and B. Tizard (1989) Social and family relationships of ex-institutional adolescents.

See pages 229–231

1 *To see if the results were due to the early experiences. If all subjects experienced the same problems, it would indicate that early experiences were perhaps of little relevance and that something else was causing them.*
2 *Subject attrition is a problem in longitudinal studies because the subjects who are no longer available may have completely changed the results. They may all have been quite happy and settled with no further problems, or they may have been all experiencing tremendous difficulties, both of which could influence the findings and make them seem either better or worse than the study indicated.*
3 *The restored group may have had the most problems getting on with family members because they probably felt let down or resentful about the reasons for their being taken into care in the first place and lacked trust in their parents.*
4 *Perhaps because they still felt insecure and wanted to gain attention and affection from adults. They may also have weaknesses in their understanding of acceptable social behaviours due to their early experiences.*
5 *Many of the ex-institutionalised adolescents were reasonably well adjusted, especially the adopted group who knew they were wanted. Their adoptive parents were willing to spend more time with them than other groups and were more accepting of their behaviours. This would indicate that later experiences can overcome the problems which may be encountered at an earlier age because the adolescents would have developed a sense of security and a greater sense of self-worth.*

S. Freud (1909) Analysis of a phobia in a five-year-old boy.

See pages 248–252

1 *Case studies give much more data than snapshot studies and can show how a situation may actually change or develop over time, whereas a snapshot study looks at behaviour for that one specific moment and gives no insight into how it might change in the future.*
2 *Because most of it came second hand from Hans' father (who was biased) by letter to Freud.*
3 *The study was made to support the Oedipus complex, because if the study was interpreted in another way, say using the theories of John Bowlby, it would not have given any support to the idea of the Oedipus complex.*

4 *Most children get upset or at least slightly insecure with the birth of a sibling but this usually goes very quickly if the parents make sure that the older child is not ignored or 'demoted'. However, if Hans felt insecure about his mother's love, the birth of Hanna and the fact that he was separated from mother may have made the situation worse.*
5 *It is extremely likely that we are not always aware of what makes us react to certain situations or behave in certain ways. However, according to Freud, we occasionally get insights into our unconscious when we make errors in our speech – Freudian slips as they are known. These are when you say things like 'Mum' to your teacher. It may be because you were thinking about your mother, your teacher reminds you of your mother or that you wish your teacher was your mother!*

Chapter 5 – Physiology

S. Schachter and J.E. Singer (1962) Cognitive, social and physiological determinants of emotional state.

See pages 278–282

1 *Because the mood before the study may well have influenced the way they responded in the laboratory.*
2 *No because real life experiences of emotion are very different to the drug-induced manipulations in a laboratory. We would have a number of different cues around us as to the situation and we would be aware of events before the onset of the arousal levels.*
3 *Because we know the situation we are in and this gives us information which we use to interpret our physical responses.*
4 *Observations were probably more valid than the questionnaire because people are not always honest in questionnaires or do not take them seriously. Whatever method you use, at the end of the day you cannot really get at how someone feels.*
5 *Deception. The health of the subjects was checked before the study so it was extremely unlikely they would have suffered any side-effects from the injections.*

W. Dement and N. Kleitman (1957). The relation of eye movements during sleep to dream activity: an objective method for the study of dreaming.

See pages 297–300

1 *If they had been observed this may have prevented them from going to sleep.*
2 *To prevent experimenter bias.*
3 *The sample was very small from one country and consisted of more men than women which may have influenced the results. It is much better to have an equal number of subjects of opposite sexes, especially in such a small sample, or gender variables may influence the results.*
4 *The length of dream narrative was influenced by the talkativeness of the subjects.*
5 *They are in the deepest stage of sleep and may therefore forget the dream as they come out of that stage.*

R.W. Sperry (1968) Hemisphere deconnection and unity in conscious awareness.

See pages 310–313

1 *Sample size was very small and not representative, but there are not many people to choose from who have a severed corpus callosum.*
2 *Otherwise the subject would have been able to move their eyes and see the object with their other eye.*
3 *For the same reason and they may have then said what they saw and informed the other hemisphere.*

4 *Probably not, because the nature of the tasks were not true to life.*
5 *It may have done, but we will never know because they were not tested before their operations.*

A. Raine, M. Buchsbaum and L. LaCasse (1997) Brain Abnormalities in Murderers Indicated by Positron Emission Tomography

See pages 325–329

1 *In order to see if any differences were due to the nature of the murderers brains and not due to chance.*
2 *Drugs may have influenced the functioning of their brains.*
3 *To ensure that the readings were accurate and not affected by subjects moving their heads.*
4 *So that task novelty would not be labelled by the tracer.*
5 *They are correlational and not causal.*

Chapter 6 – The psychology of individual differences

S.J. Gould (1982) A nation of Morons.

See pages 354–357

1 *Because he wanted to find a way of making psychology an indisputable scientific discipline which involved quantifying and calculating.*
2 *They were unfamiliar with the culture and so could not answer the questions. They may have had problems with the language. They may never have held a pencil before and were very nervous. They may have been put into the wrong tests.*
3 *You may be able to manipulate them to show what you want to show and therefore invalidate the results.*
4 *Washington is to Adams as first is to second (Washington was the first president of the United Sates and Adams was the second).*
Crisco is a food product.
The number of Kaffir's legs is 2. (A Kaffir is a black African).
Christy Matthewson is famous as a baseball player
5 *Mouth, eye, nose, spoon, chimneypot, ear, filament, stamp, strings, rivet, trigger, tail, leg, shadow, ball, net, arm, horn from the gramophone, reflection of arm, diamond.*

J. Hraba and G. Grant (1970) Black is beautiful: A re-examination of racial preference and identification.

See pages 371–374

1 *They may have felt intimidated by the colour of the interviewer and answered responding to the interviewer's colour.*
2 *To allow the children to rate the dolls on a likert scale but the disadvantage of that may be that the young children would not understand the methodology.*
3 *The children would have perceived their friends as being nice, and this may have affected their doll choice if the friend's colour was not the same as their own.*
4 *In order to make sure the information the children gave was accurate.*
5 *One way might be to show photographs of groups of people rather than using dolls. This would at least look at their responses to people rather than objects. Recent research by Barrett et al. (in print) has indicated that many children have an idea of their cultural identity by the age of six using a complex and involved system of interviews and questionnaires. When these measures are cross-checked against each other, the reliability and validity of the results should be high.*

D.L. Rosenhan (1973) On being sane in insane places.

See pages 389–393

1 *Frightened and concerned about being discovered and concerned that they would have problems convincing the staff that they were not insane.*

2 *They were all seen as one group of people who were abnormal and therefore any individual elements of their personalities or their lives were no longer valid.*

3 *They were seen as a group with no power or status and therefore not credible witnesses.*

4 *Unlikely as the criteria for psychiatric diagnosis has been tightened up with the DSMIV, although Davison & Neale (1994) claim that some problems still exist.*

5 *One could argue that the first study was unethical in so far as the pseudopatients deceived the practitioners but the study would not have been possible without this deception. The second study was unethical in so far as it may have prevented genuine patients from getting treatment.*

C.H. Thigpen and H. Cleckley (1954). A case of multiple personality.

See pages 403–407

1 *MPD is a fragmented personality or split personality – Schizophrenia is a disorganised personality.*

2 *Sexual abuse in childhood.*

3 *The different result of independent tests.*

4 *Subjectivity – the researchers knew Eve well, and would have perhaps been biased in their interpretation of events.*

5 *Should it be is used as a defence in a court of law, people could be found not guilty when in fact they are.*

Bibliography

Ahrens, S.R. (1954) Beiträge zur Entwicklung des Physiolgnoimie und Mimikerkenntnisse (Contributions on the development of physiognomy and mimicry recognition). *Seitschrift für Experimentelle und Angewandte Psychologie 2:* 412–454.

Aitchison, J. (1983) *The articulate mammal* (2nd edition) London: Hutchinson.

Alexander, P.C. & Lupfer, S.L. (1987) Family characteristics and long-term consequences associated with sexual abuse. *Archives of Sexual Behaviour*, 16, 235–245.

Allen, V.L. & Levine, J.M. (1971) Social pressures and personal influence. *Journal of Experimental Social Psychology* 7: 122–124.

Allport G.W. (1954) *The Nature of Prejudice*. Wokingham: Addison-Wesley.

Allport, F.H. (1955) *Theories of Perception and the Concept of Structure*. Wiley.

Ardrey, R. (1966) *The Territorial Imperative*. New York: Dell.

Arendt, H. (1965) *Eichmann in Jerusalem: A report on the banality of evil*. New York: Viking.

Aronson, E. (1976) *The social animal*. San Francisco: W.H. Freeman & Co.

Aronson, E. (1994) *The social animal* (7th edition) New York: W.H. Freeman & Co.

Aronson, E., & Osherow, N. (1980) Co-operation, prosocial behaviour and academic performance: Experiments in the desegregated classroom. In L. Bickman (Ed.), *Applied social psychology annual, Vol. 1*. Beverley Hills, California: Sage Publications.

Aronson, E., Wilson, T.D. & Akert, R.M. (1997) *Social Psychology* (3rd edition). New York: Longman.

Asch, S.E. (1951) Effect of group pressure upon the modification and distortion of judgements. In H. Guetzkow (Ed) *Groups, leadership and men*. Pittsburg, Pennsylvania: Carnegie Press.

Aschoff, J. (1979) Circadian rhythms: General features and endocrinological aspects. In *Endocrine Rhythms*, edited by D.T. Krieger. New York: Raven Press.

Atkinson, R.C., & Shiffrin, R.M. (1968) Human memory: a proposed system and its control processes In K.W. Spence and J.T. Spence (Eds) *The Psychology of Learning and Motivation 2*. London: Academic Press.

Atkinson, R.L., Atkinson, R.C., Smith, E.E. & Bem, D.J. (1993) *Introduction to Psychology* (11th edition). New York: Harcourt Brace Jovanovich.

Ax, A.F. (1953) The physiological differentiation between fear and anger in humans. *Psychosomatic Medicine*, 15: 433–442.

Ayers, I. (1991) Rair driving: Gender and race discrimination in retail car negotiations. *Harvard Law Review*, 104.

Bandura, A. (1977) Self-efficacy: toward a unifying theory of behavioural change. *Psychological Review 84*: 191–215.

Bandura, A. (1977) *Social Learning Theory*. Englewood Cliffs, New Jersey: Prentice Hall.

Banyard, P. & Grayson, A. (1996) *Introducing Psychological Research*. Basingstoke: Macmillan Press.

Bard, B. & Sachs, J. (1977) *Language Acquisition Patterns in Two Normal Children of Deaf Parents*. Paper presented to the 2nd Annual Boston University Conference on Language Acquistion October 977, cited in J.G. de Villiers & P.A. de Villiers (1978) *Early Language*. London: Fontana.

Barrett, M.D. (1986) Early semantic representations and early word usage. In S.A. Kuczaj & M.D. Barrett (Eds) *The development of word meaning*. New York: Springer Verlag.

Bates, E., Bretherton, I., & Snyder, L. (1988). *From first words to grammar: Individual differences and dissociable mechanisms*. Cambridge: CUP.

Bee, H. (1939) *The Growing Child*. New York: Harper Collins.

Berne, E. (1964), *Games People Play*. London: Penguin.

Blakemore, C. (1988) *The Mind Machine*. London: BBC Books.

Bliss, E.L. (1983) Multiple personalities, related disorders, and hypnosis. *American Journal of Clinical Hypnosis*, 26, 114–123.

Bowlby, J. 1951. *Maternal Care and mental health*. Geneva: World Health Organisation.

Bowlby, J. 1953 *Childcare and the Growth of Love*. London: Penguin.

Brown, G. L., Goodwin, F.K., Ballenger, J.C., Goyer, P.F. & Major, L.F. (1979). Aggression in human correlates with cerebrospinal fluid amine metabolites. *Psychiatry Research*, 1, 131–139.

Brown, R., (1973) *A First language*. Cambridge, MA: Harvard University Press.

Brown, R. (1986) *Social Psychology* (2nd edition). New York: The Free Press.

Bruner, J.S., & Goodman, C.C. (1947) Value and need as organising factors in perception. *Journal of Abnormal and Social Psychology*, 42, 33–44.

Burnstein, E., Crandall, C., & Kitayama, S. (1994) Some neoDarwinian decision rules for altruism: Weighing cues for inclusive fitness as a function of the biological importance of the decision. *Journal of Personality and Social Psychology*, 67, 773–789.

Burt, C. (1912) The evidence for the concept of intelligence. *British Journal of Educational Psychology*, 25 158–77.

Burt, C. (1966) The examination at eleven plus. *British Journal of Educational Studies*, 7 99–117.

Buss, A.H. (1966). *Psychopathology*. New York: Wiley.

Buss, A.R. (1966) Instrumentality of aggression, feedback and frustration as determinants of physical aggression. *Journal of Personality and Social Psychology* 3

Cannon, W.B. (1927) The James-Lange theory of emotions: A critical examination and an alternative. *American Journal of Psychology*, 39, 106–124.

Cannon, W.B. (1929) *Bodily changes in pain, hunger, fear and rage*. New York: Appleton-Century-Crofts.

Carey, S. (1978). The child as word learner. In M. Halle, J. Bresnan & G. Miller (Eds), *Linguistic Theory and Psychological Reality*. Cambridge, Mass.: MIT Press.

Carlson, N.R. (1986) *Physiology of Behaviour* (3rd edition). London: Allyn and Bacon.

Carter, R. (1998) *Mapping the Mind*. London: Weidenfeld & Nicolson.

Chomsky, N. (1965) *Aspects of the theory of syntax*. Cambridge, Massachusetts: MIT Press.

Chomsky, N. (1968) *Language and mind*. New York: Harcourt Brace Jovanovich.

Clark, K. & Clark, M. (1947) Racial identification and preference in Negro children. In T.M. Newcombe & E.L. Hartley (Eds), *Readings in social psychology* (pp.169–178). New York: Holt.

Clarke, A.M., and Clarke, A.D.B. (1976) *Early experience: Myth and evidence*. London: Open Books.

Craik, F., & Lockhart, R. (1972) Levels of processing. *Journal of Verbal Learning and Verbal Behaviour*, 11, 671–684.

Crutchfield, R.S. (1962) cited in R. Gross (1992) *Psychology: The Science of Mind and Behaviour* (2nd edition). London: Hodder and Stoughton.

Curtiss, S. (1977) *Genie: A psycholinguistic study of a modern-day 'wild child'*. London: Academic Press.

Dabbs, J. M, Carr, T.S. Frady, R.L., & Riad, J.K. (1995) Testosterone, crime and misbehaviour among 692 male prison inmates. *Personality and Individual Differences*, 18., 627–633.

Damasio, A.R., Tranel, D. & Damasio, H. (1990) *Individuals with sociopathic behaviour caused by frontal damage fail to respond autonomically to social stimuli. Behavioural Brain Research* 41: 81–94.

Darley, J.M. & Batson, C.D. (1973) From Jerusalem to Jericho: A study of situational and dispositional variables in helping behaviour. *Journal of Personality and Social Psychology*, 27, 100–108.

Darley, J.M. and Latané, B. (1968) Bystander intervention in emergencies: Diffusion of responsibility. *Journal of Personality and Social Psychology*, 8, 377–383.

Darley, J.M. & Latané, B. (1970) Norms and normative behaviour: field studies of social interdependence. In J. Macauley and L. Berkowitz (Eds) *Altruism and Helping Behaviour*. New York: Academic Press.

Davidson, G. & Neal, J. (1996) *Abnormal Psychology* (6th edition). New York: Wiley.

Dawkins, R. (1976) *The Selfish Gene*. Oxford: Oxford University Press.

Dement, W. (1960) The effect of dream deprivation. *Science*, 131: 1705–1707.

Diamond, S., Baldwin, R., & Diamond, R. (1963) *Inhibition and choice*. New York: Harper & Row.

Diener, E. (1979) Deindividuation, self-awareness and disinhibition. *Journal of Personality and Social Psychology*, 37 1160–1171.

Diener, E. (1980) Deindividuation: The absence of self-awareness and self-regulation in group members. In P.B. Paulus (Ed) *Psychology of group influence*. Hillsdale, N.J.: Lawrence Erlbaum.

Diener, E., Fraser, S.C., Beaman, A.L. & Kelem, R.T. (1976) Effects of deindividuation variables on stealing among Halloween trick-or-treaters. *Journal of Personality and Social Psychology*, 33: 178–183.

Dobson, C.B., Hardy, M., Heyes, S., Humphreys, A. & Humphreys, P. (1993) *Understanding Psychology*. London: Weidenfeld and Nicolson.

Dollard J., Doob, L., Miller, N., Mowrer, O.H. & Sears, R.R. (1939) *Frustration and aggression*. New Haven, CT: Yale University Press.

Donaldson, M. (1978) *Children's Minds*. London: Fontana.

Dunn, J & Kendrick, C. (1979) Interaction between young siblings in the context of family relationships. In M. Lewis & L.A. Rosenblum (Eds) *The Child and its Family*. New York: Plenum Press.

Dunn, J. (1988) *The Beginnings of Social Understanding*. Oxford: Blackwell.

Dunn, J. & Munn, P. (1985) Becoming a family member: family conflict and the development of social understanding in the first year. *Child Development*, 50: 306–318.

Dunn, J. & Plomin, R. (1990) *Separate lives: Why siblings are so different*. New York: Basic Books.

Dunn, J., Kendrick, C. & MacNamee, R. (1981) The reaction of first-born children to the birth of a sibling: mother's reports. *Journal of Child Psychology and Psychiatry*, 22: 1–18.

Eagley, A.H. (1987) *Sex differences in social behaviour: A social-role interpretation*. Hillsdale, NJ: Erlbaum.

Eagly, A.H. & Crowley, M. (1986) Gender and helping behaviour: A meta-analytic review of the social psychological literature. *Psychological Bulletin*, 100, 283–308.

Eichelman, B. (1993) Bridges from the animal laboratory to the study of violent or criminal individuals. In S. Hodgins (Ed), *Mental Disorder and Crime*. Newbury Park, CA: Sage, pp 194–207.

Eysenck, H.J. (1947) *Dimensions of personality*. London: Routledge and Kegan Paul.

Eysenck, H.J. (1952) The effects of psychotherapy: An evaluation. *Journal of Consulting Psychology*, 16: 319–324.

Eysenck, H.J. (1970) *Crime and personality*. London: Paladin.

Eysenck, H.J. (1973) *The Inequality of Man*. London: Temple Smith.

Eysenck, H.J. & Gudjoinsson, G.H. (1989) *The Causes and Cures of Criminality*. New York: Plenum.

Fantz, R.L. (1961) The origin of form perception. *Scientific American*, 204, 66–72.

Finkelhor, D. (1979). *Sexually victimised children*. New York: Free Press.

Fiske, S.T. & Taylor, S.E. (1991) *Social cognition* (2nd edition). New York: McGraw-Hill.

Flavell, J.H. (1985) *Cognitive Development*. London: Prentice Hall.

Freud A. & Dann, S. (1951) An experiment in group upbringing. *Psychoanalytic study of the child*, 6, 127–68.

Freud, S. (1930) *Civilisation and its discontents*. London: Hogarth Press.

Frith, U. (1990) *Autism*. Oxford: Blackwell.

Gazzaniga, M.S., LeDoux, J.E. & Wilson, D.H. (1977) Language, praxis and the right hemisphere: Clues to some mechanisms of consciousness. *Neurology*, 27: 1144–1147.

George Butterworth & Margaret Harris (1994) *Principles of Developmental Psychology*. Lawrence Erlbaum Associates Ltd.

Gerard, H. & Miller, N. (1975) *School Desegregation*. Cited in: R. Brown. (1986) *Social Psychology* (2nd edition) New York: The Free Press.

Gergen, K.J., Gergen, M.M. & Barton, W. (1973) Deviance in the dark. *Psychology Today* 7: 129–130.

Geschwind, N. & Levitsky, W. (1968) Human brain: left-right asymmetries in temporal speech region. *Science*, 161: 186–187.

Gilbert, G.M. (1951). Stereotype persisitence and change among college students. *Journal of Abnormal and Social Psychology*, 46, 245–254.

Gluhbegovic, N., & Williams, T.H. (1980) *The Human Brain: A Photographic Atlas*. Hagerstown, Md.: Harper & Row.

Goldfarb, W. (1943) The effects of early institutional care on adolescent personality. *Journal of Experimental Education*, 12, 106–129.

Gregory, R. (1977) *Eye and Brain*. Weidenfeld and Nicolson.

Gross, R. (1992) *Psychology: Science of Mind and Behaviour*. (2nd edition). London: Hodder & Stoughton.

Gross, R. (1999). *Key Studies in Psychology* (3rd edition). London: Hodder and Stoughton.

Gwinner, E. (1986) Circannual rhythms in the control of avian rhythms. *Advances in the Study of Behaviour*, 16: 191–228.

Harris, P.L. & Muncer, A. (1988) Autistic Children's Understanding of Beliefs and Desires. Paper Presented at the British Psychological Society Developmental Section Conference, Coleg Harlech, Wales.

Harris, M., Jones, D., Brookes, S., & Grant, J. (1986) Relations between the non-verbal context of maternal speech and rate of language development. *British Journal of Developmental Psychology*, 4, 261–268.

Harris, P.L. (1988). *Children and Emotion: the Development of Psychological Understanding*. Oxford: Blackwell.

Hartmann, E. (1973) *The functions of sleep*. New Haven: Yale University.

Hartmann, E. (1984) *The Nightmare*. New York: Basic Books.

Hauri, P. (1979) What can insomniacs teach us about the functions of sleep? In R. Drucker-Colin, M. Shkurovich and M.B. Sterman (Eds) *The functions of sleep* (pp.251–271). New York: Academic.

Hayes, K.H. & Hayes, C. (1951) Intellectual development of a house-raised chimpanzee. *Proceedings of the American philosophical Society*, 95: 105–109.

Hayes, N. (1993) *Principles of social psychology*. Hove, UK: Psychology Press.

Heim, A. (1970) *Intelligence and Personality*. Harmondsworth: Penguin

Hetherington, E.M. & Parke, R.D. (1987) *Child Psychology: A Contemporary Viewpoint*. New York: McGraw-Hill.

Hicks, R.E. (1975) Intrahemispheric response competition between vocal and unimanual performance in normal adult human males. *Journal of Comparative and Physiological Psychology*, 89: 50–60.

Hinde, R.A. (1987) *Individuals, Relationships and Culture: Links between Ethology and the Social Sciences*. Cambridge: Cambridge University Press.

Hobbes, T. (1986). *Leviathan*. Harmondsworth, England: Penguin Press. (Original work published 1651).

Hockett, C.F. (1959) Animal 'languages' and human language. *Human Biology*, 31:32–39.

Hofling, K.C., Brotzman, E., Dalrymple, S., Graves, N. & Pieces, C.M. (1966) An experimental study in the nurse-physician relationshp. *Journal of Nervous and Mental Disorders*, 143: 171–180.

Hohmann, G.W. (1966) Some effects of spinal cord lesions on experienced emotional feelings. *Psychophysiology*, 3, 143–156.

Horn, J.M. (1983) The Texas adoption project: Adopted children and their intellectual resemblance to biological and adoptive parents. *Child Development*, 54, 268–275.

Horne, J. (1988) *Why we sleep? The functions of sleep in humans and other mammals*. Oxford: Oxford University Press.

Horne, J.A. & Minard, A. (1985) Sleep and sleepiness following a behaviourally 'active' day. *Ergonomics,* 28: 567–575.

Hovland, C.I. & Sears, R.R. (1940) Minor studies in aggression: 6. Correlation of lynchings with economic indices. *Journal of Psychology*, 9, 301–310.

Hubel, D.H. & Wiesel, T.N. (1979) Brain mechanisms of vision. *Scientific American* 241(3) 150–162.

Huesmann, L.R., & Eron, L.D. (1984) Cognitive processes and the persistence of aggressive behaviour. *Aggressive Behaviour* 10, 243–251.

Huesmann, L.R., & Eron, L.D. (1986) *Television and the aggressive child: A cross national comparison*. Hillsdale, NJ: Erlbaum.

Hughes, M. (1975) *Egocentrism in preschool children*. Unpublished PhD thesis, University of Edinburgh.

Huston, T.L., Ruggiero, M., Conner, R., & Geis, G. (1981) Bystander intervention into crime: A study based on naturally-occurring episodes. *Social Psychology Quarterly*, 44, 14–23.

Ineichen, B., Harrison, G. & Morgan, H.G. (1984) Psychiatric hospital admissions in Brison: 1. Geographical and ethnic factors. *British Journal of Psychiatry*, 145: 600–604.

Jackson, J.L., Calhoun, K.S., Amick, A.E., Maddever, H.M. & Habif, V.L. (1990). Young adult women who report childhood intrafamilial sexual abuse: Subsequent adjustment. *Archives of Sexual Behaviour*, 19, 211–221.

Jackson, P. (1995) *Dear Uncle Go: Male Homosexuality in Thailand*. Bangkok: Bua Luang Books.

Jacobs, P.A., Brunton, M. & Melville, M.M. (1965) Aggressive behaviour, mental abnormality and the XXY male. *Nature* 208: 1351–1352.

James, W. (1884) What is an emotion? *Mind* 19: 188–205.

Janet Wilde Astington, (1994). *The Child's discovery of the Mind*. Fontana Press.

Jensen, A.R. (1969) How much can we boost IQ and scholastic achievement? *Harvard Educational Review* 39: 1–123.

Jones, E. (1953-1957) *Sigmund Freud: Life and Work*. 3 Vols. London.

Jones, E.E., & Sigall, H. (1971) The bogus pipeline: A new paradigm for measuring affect and attitude. *Psychological Bulletin*, 76, 349–364.

Jones, R. K. (1966) Observations on stammering after localized cerebral injury. *Journal of Neurology, Neurosurgery and Psychiatry*, 29: 192–195.

Kalat, J.W. (1988) *Biological Psychology*. Belmont: Wadsworth.

Kamin, L. (1974) *The Science and Politics of IQ*. Harmondsworth: Penguin.

Kanner, L. Autistic Disturbances of Affective Contact, *Nervous Child*, 2, (1943): 217–150.

Kanner, L. & Eisenberg, L. (1955). Notes of the follow-up studies of autistic children. In P. Hoch and J. Zubin (Eds) *Psychopathology of Childhood*. New York: Grune and Stratton.

Karau, S.J. & Williams, K.D. (1993) Social loafing: A meta-analytic review and theoretical integration. *Journal of Personality and Social Psychology*, 65, 681–706.

Karlins, M., Coffman, T.L. & Walters, G. (1969). On the fading of social stereotypes: Studies in three generations of college students. *Journal of Personality and Social Psychology*, 13, 1–16.

Katz, D., & Braly, K.W. (1933). Racial stereotypes of 100 college students. *Journal of Abnormal and Social Psychology*, 28, 280–290.

Kaufman, L & Rock, I. (1962) The moon Illusion. *Science*, 136, 1023–1031.

Kelley, H.H. (1973) The process of causal attribution. *American Psychologist*, 28: 107–128.

Kellogg, W.N. & Kellogg, L.A. (1933) *The ape and the child*. New York: McGraw Hill.

Kelman, H.C. (1958) Compliance, identification and internalisation: Three processes of attitude change. *Journal of Conflict Resolution*, 2: 51–60.

Kelman, H.C. & Hovland, C.I. (1953) Reinstatement of the communication in delayed measurement of opinion change. *Journal of Abnormal and Social Psychology*, 48: 327–335.

Kilham, W. & Mann, L. (1974) Levels of destructive obedience as a function of transmitter and executant roles in the Milgram obedience paradigm. *Journal of Personality and Social Psychology* 29: 696–702.

Kimura, D. (1973a) Manual activity during speaking – I. Right handers. *Neuropsychologia*, 11: 45–50.

Kimura, D. (1973b) Manual activity during speaking – II. Left handers. *Neuropsychologia*, 11: 51–55.

Kinsborne, M. (1972) Eye and head turning indicates cerebral lateralisation. Science, 176: 539–541.

Kolb, B. & Wishaw, I.Q. (1990) *Fundamentals of Neuropsychology* (3rd edition). New York: W.H. Freeman.

La Piere, R.T. (1934) Attitudes vs Actions. *Social Forces*, 13, 230–237.

Lahey, B.B. (1983). *Psychology: An introduction*. Dubuque, Iowa: William C. Brown Co.

Latané, B. & Darley, J.M. (1968), Group inhibition of bystander intervention. *Journal of Personality and Social Psychology*, 10, 215–221.

Latané, B. & Rodin, J. (1969) A lady in distress: Inhibiting effects of friends and strangers on bystander intervention. *Journal of Experimental Social Psychology*, 5, 189–202.

Latané, B. & Darley, J.M. (1970) *The unresponsive bystander: Why doesn't he help*. Englewood Cliffs, NJ: Prentice Hall.

Le Bon, G. (1895) *The crowd: a study of the popular mind*. London: T. Fisher Unwin.

LeDoux, J., Wilson, D.H., & Gazzaniga, M. (1977). A divided mind. *Annals of Neurology*, 2, 417–21.

Lenneberg, E. (1967) *Biological foundations of language*. New York: Wiley.

Lewis, D.O. Pincus, J.H., Bard, B. et al (1988) Neuropsychiatric, psychoeducational, and family characteristics of 14 juveniles condemned to death in the United States. *American Journal of Psychiatry* 154: 584–589.

Liebert, R.M & Baron, R.A. (1972) Some immediate effects of televised violence on children's behaviour. *Developmental Psychology*, 6, 469–475.

Littlewood, R. & Lipsedge, M. (1989) *Aliens and Alienists: Ethnic Minorities and Psychiatry*. London: Unwin Hyman

Loew, C.A. (1967) Acquisition of a hostile attitude and its relationship to aggressive behaviour. *Journal of Personality and Social Psychology* 5: 335–341.

Loftus, E.F. & Burns, H.J. (1982) Mental shock can produce retrograde amnesia. *Memory and Cognition* 10: 318–323.

Lorenz, K. (1950) The comparative method in studying innate behaviour patterns. *Symposium of the Society of Experimental Biology* 4: 221–268.

Lucas, A., Morley, R., Cole, T.J., Lister, G. & Leeson-Payne, C. (1992) Breast milk and subsequent intelligence quotient in children born pre-term. *The Lancet*, 399: 261–264.

Maccoby, E.E. & Jacklin, C.N. (1974) *The Psychology of sex differences*. Stanford, CA: Standford University Press.

Malinowski, B. (1927) *Sex and Repression in Savage Society*. New York: Harcourt Brace Jovanovitch.

Mantell (1971) Cited in R. Gross, (1992) *Psychology: Science of Mind and Behaviour* (2nd edition). London: Hodder & Stoughton.

Maranon, G. (1924) Contribution à l'étude de l'action emotive de l'adrénaline. *Revue Francaise d'Endocrinologie* 2:301–325.

McGarrigle, J. & Donaldson, M. (1974) Conservation accidents. *Cognition* 3: 341–350.

McGovern, D. & Cope, R. (1987) The compulsory detention of males of different ethnic groups, with special reference to offender patients. *British Journal of Psychiatry*, 150: 505–512.

Mead, M. (1928) *Coming of Age in Samoa*. Harmondsworth: Penguin.

Meadows, S. (1993) *The Child as a Thinker*. London: Routledge.

Meeus, W.H.J. & Raaijmakers, Q.A.W. (1986) Administrative obedience; Carrying out orders to use psychological-administrative violence. *European Journal of Social Psychology*, 16: 311–324.

Milgram, S. (1974) *Obedience to Authority*. New York: Harper Torchbooks.

Miller, G. (1956) The magical number seven, plus or minus two: some limits on our capacity for processing information. *Psychological Review* 63: 81–97.

Moffitt, T.E. (1988) Neuropsychology and self-reported early delinquency in an unselected birth cohort. In Moffitt, T.E., Mednick, S.A. (Eds) *Biological Contributions to Crime Causation*. New York: Martinus Nijhoff, pp 93–120.

Mullen, B. (1986) Atrocity as a function of lynch mob composition: A self-attention perspective. *Personality and Social Psychology Bulletin* 12: 187–197.

Murdock, B.B. (1962) The serial position effect of free recall. *Journal of Experimental Psychology* 64: 482–488.

Needleman, H.L., Schell, A., Bellinger, D., Leviton, A. & Allred, E. (1990) Lead-associated intellectual deficit. *New England Journal of Medicine*, 322: 83–88.

Nelson, K. (1973). Structure and strategy in learning to talk. *Monographs of the Society for Research in Child Development* 38. (1 & 2).

Nigel Hawkes. *The Times*, London 27th January 1999 reported in *Psychology Review* Vol 6 no. 3 Feb 2000.

Olweus, D., (1980) Familial and temperamental determinants of aggressive behaviour in adolescent boys. A causal analysis. *Developmental Psychology*, 16, 644–666.

Orne, M.T. (1962) On the social psychology of the psychological experiment; With particular reference to demand characteristics and their implications. *American Psychologist*, 17, 776–783.

Ornstein, R. (1986) *The physiology of consciousness* (2nd edition). Harmondsworth, Middlesex: Penguin.

Pavlov, I.P., (1927) *Conditioned reflexes*. London: Oxford University Press.

Perner, J. (1991) *Understanding the Representational Mind*. Cambridge, Mass.: Bradford Books/MIT Press.

Perner, J., Leekam, S. & Wimmer, H. (1987) Three year olds' difficulty in understanding fasle belief: cognitive limitation, lack of knowledge or pragmatic misunderstanding? *British Journal of Developmental Psychology* 5: 125–137.

Pervin, L.A. (1984) *Personality* (4th edition). New York: John Wiley.

Piaget, J. & Inhelder, B. (1956) *The child's conception of space*. London: RKP.

Piliavin, I.M. Piliavin, J.A. & Rodin, J. (1975) Costs, diffusion and the stigmatised victim. *Journal of Personality and Social Psychology*, 32, 429–438.

Piliavin, J.A. Dovidio, J.F., Gaertner, S., & Clark, R.D. III. (1981) *Emergency Intervention*. New York: Academic Press.

Putnam, F.W., Post, R.M. & Guroff, J.J. (1983) 100 cases of multiple personality disorder. *Paper presented at the annual meeting of the American Psychiatric Association. New York.*

Rasmussen, T. & Milner, B. (1977) The role of early left-brain injury in determining lateralisation of cerebral speech functions. *Annals of the New York Academy of Sciences* 299: 355–369.

Rehm, J., Steinleitner, M. & Lilli, W. (1987) Wearing uniforms and aggression. A field experiment. *European Journal of Social Psychology*, 17:357–360.

Richter, C.P. (1922). A behaviouristic study of the activity of the rat. *Comparative Psychology Monographs*, 1: 1–55.

Ringelmann, M. (1913). Recherches sur les moteurs animés: Travail de l'homme. *Annales de l'Institut National Argonomique*, 2e série, tom 12, 1–40.

Rivers, W.H.R. (1901) Vision. In A.C. Haddon (Ed) *Reports of the Cambridge Anthropological Expedition to the Torres Strait*s, Vol. 2, part 1. Cambridge: Cambridge University Press.

Rosalind Morris (1994) Three sexes and Four Sexualities: Redressing the Discourses on Gender and Sexuality in Contemporary Thailand'. *Positions* 2(1): 15–43.

Rose, S.A. & Blank, M. (1974) The potency of context in children's cognition: an illustration through conservation. *Child Development* 45: 499–502.

Rosenhan, D.L, & Seligman, M.E.P. (1989) *Abnormal Psychology* (2nd Ed). New York: Norton.

Rosenzweig, M.R. (1984) Experience, memory and the brain. *American Psychologist*, 39: 365–376.

Ross, L. & Nisbett, R.E. (1991) *The person and the situation*. New York: McGraw Hill.

Rutter, M. (1981) *Maternal Deprivation Reassessed* (2nd edition). Harmonsworth: Penguin.

Sacks, O. (1985). The twins. In *The man who mistook his wife for a hat and other clinical tales*. New York: Harper & Row.

Sapir, E. (1929) The status of linguistics as a science. *Language* 5: 207–214.

Savage-Rumbaugh, S. (1988) A new look at ape language: comprehension of vocal speech and syntax. *Nebraska Symposium on Motivation* 35: 201–255.

Schachter, S. (1964) The interaction of cognitive and physiological determinants of emotional state. In L. Berkowitz (Ed) *Advances in experimental social psychology*. Vol. 1 New York: Academic press.

Schaffer, H.R. (1971) *The growth of sociability*. Harmondsworth: Penguin.

Schaffer, H.R. & Emmerson, P.E. (1964) The development of social attachments in infancy. *Monographs of Social Research in Child Development* 29. no. 94.

Schreiber, F.R. (1973) *Sybil*. Harmondsworth: Penguin.

Sears, D.O., (1988). Symbolic racism. In P. Katz and D. Taylor (Eds), *Eliminating racism. Profiles in controversy* (pp. 53–84). New York: Plenum.

Seashore, R.H. & Eckerson, L.D. (1940). The measurement of individual differences in general English vocabularies. *Journal of Educational Psychology*, 31, 14–38.

Segall, M.H., Campbell, D.T. & Herskovits, M.J. (1963) Cultural differences in the perception of geometric illusions. *Science*, 139: 769–771.

Seligman, M.E.P. (1975) *Helplessness: on Depression, Development and Death*. San Francisco: Freeman.

Shallice, T. & Warrington, E.K. (1970) Independent functioning of verbal memory stores: a neuropsychological study. *Quarterly Journal of Experimental Psychology*, 22:261–273.

Sheridan, C.L. & King, K.G. (1972) Obedience to authority with an authentic victim. *Proceedings of the 80th Annual Convention of the American Psychological Association*, 7:165–166.

Sherif, M. (1966) *Group conflict and co-operation: Their social psychology*. London: RKP.

Shields, J. (1962) *Monozygotic Twins Brought Up Apart and Brought Together*. London: Oxford University Press.

Shotland, R.L. & Straw, M.K. (1976) Bystander response to an assault: When a man attacks a woman. *Journal of Personality and Social Psychology*, 34, 990–999.

Sigman, M., Mundy, P., Sherman, T. & Ungerer, J.A. (1986) Social interaction of autistic, mentally retarded and normal children and their caregivers. *Journal of Child Psychology and Psychiatry* 27: 647–55.

Sime, J.D. (1983). Affiliative behaviour during escape to building exits. *Journal of Environmental Psychology*, 3, 21–41.

Skinner, B.F. (1938) *The behaviour of organisms*. New York: Appleton-Century-Crofts.

Skinner, B.F. (1957). *Verbal behaviour*. New York: Appleton-Century-Crofts.

Slobin, D.I., 1975. On the nature of talk to children. In E.H. Lenneberg & E. Lennenerg (Eds.) *Infant development*. Hove, East Sussex: Lawrence Erlbaum Associates Ltd.

Spanos, N.P., Weekes, J.R. & Bertrand, L.D. (1985) Multiple personality: A social psychological persepctive. *Journal of Abnormal Psychology*, 94, 362–376.

Spearman, C. (1904) General intelligence, objectively determined and measured. *American Journal of Psychology*, 15, 201–293.

Springer S.P., & Deutsch, G. (eds) 1993. *Left brain/Right brain* (4th edition). New York: W.H. Freeman.

Stang, D.J. (1973) Conformity, ability and self-esteem. *Representative Research in Social Psychology*, 3:97–103.

Stern, D. (1977) *The First Relationship: Infant and Mother*. London: Fontana.

Storr, A. (1989) *Freud*. Oxford: Oxford University Press.

Szasz, T.S. (1960) The myth of mental illness. *American Psychologist*, 15, 113–118.

Tajfel, H. (1970) Experiments in intergroup discrimination. *Scientific American*. 223. 96–102.

Tajfel, H. (1982) *Social identity and intergroup relations*. Cambridge, England: Cambridge University Press.

Terman, L.M. (1916) *The Measurement of Intelligence*. Boston: Houghton Mifflin.

Thibaut, J.W. & Kelley, H.H. (1959). *The social psychology of groups*, New York: Wiley.

Tizard, B. & Hodges, J. (1978) The effects of early institutional rearing on the development of eight-year-old children. *Journal of Child Psychology and Psychiatry*. 19: 99–118.

Tizard, B. & Rees, J. (1974) A comparison of the effects of adoption, restoration to the natural mother and continued institutionalisation on the cognitive development of four-year-old children. *Child Development* 45: 92–99.

Tulving E. (1972) Episodic and semantic memory. In E. Tulving and W. Donaldson (Eds) *Organisation of Memory*. London: Academic Press.

Turnbull, C.M. (1961) *The Forest People*. New York: Simon and Schuster.

Valins, S. (1966) Cognitive effects of false heart-rate feedback. *Journal of personality and Social Psychology*, 4:400–408.

Watson, J.B., & Rayner, R. (1920). Conditioned emotional reactions. *Journal of Experimental Psychology*, 3, 1–14.

Watson, R.I. (1973) Investigation into deindividuation using a cross-cultural survey technique. *Journal of Personality and Social Psychology* 25: 342–345.

Wechsler, D. (1958) *The measurement and appraisal of adult intelligence* (4th edition). Baltimore: Williams and Wilkins.

Weiner, B. (1992). *Human motivation: Metaphors, theories and research.* Newbury Park, *CA.*: Sage.

Whyte, W.F. (1943) *Street Corner Society*. Chicago: University of Chicago Press.

Wicker, A.W. (1969). Attitudes versus actions: The relationship between verbal and overt behavioural responses to attitude objects. *Journal of Social Issues*, 25, 41–78.

Williams, K., Harkins, S. & Latané, B. (1981). Identifiability as a deterrent to social loafing: Two cheering experiments. *Journal of Personality and Social Psychology*, 40, 303–311.

Williams, T.M. (Ed) (1986) *The impact of television: A national experiment in three communities*. New York: Academic Press.

Wimmer, H. & Perner, J. (1983) Beliefs about beliefs: representation and constraining function of wrong beliefs in young children's understanding of deception. *Cognition* 13: 103–128.

Witkin, H.A., Mednick, S.A., Schulsinger, F., Bakkestrom, E. Christansen, K.O., Goodenough, D.R., Hirschhorn, K., Lundsteen, C., Owen, D.R., Philips, J., Rubin, D.B. & Stocking, M. (1976) Criminality in XYY and XXY men: the elevated crime rate of XYY males is not related to aggression. *Science* 193: 547–555.

Zimbardo, P.G. (1969/1970) The human choice: Individuation, reason and order versus deindividuation, impulse & chaos. In W.J. Arnold and D. Levine (Eds) *Nebraska Symposium on Motivation*. Lincoln: University of Nebraska Press.

Index

Note: the names of people who are cited appear with their initials only. Those who are the subjects of case studies have their given names spelled out in full.

abnormality 336, 377–378, 390
  as coping 382–383, 400
  defining 378–383
  features of 385–388
accommodation 178
  of the eyes 52
acetylcholine 267
acoustic (phonetic) encoding 24
adaptation 175
adopting, cost of 125
adrenaline (epinephrine) 278, 282, 286
affectionless psychopathy 218, 222
affective
  disorders 332
  stability 394
agentic state 119
aggression 171, 196, 199, 242, 317–318
  in animals 325
  innate or learned 195–202
  sex differences in 199
  and television violence 213–214
  through imitation 207–211
  and uniforms 150
Allport, G.W. 367
alters (ego states) 391–401, 402, 404–405
altruism 124–134, 140, 206
  and selfishness 125
Alzheimer's disease 267
ambiguous
  figures 68, 69
  situations 144
American Psychological Association 119
American Sign Language (ASL) 100
amnesia 23, 31
  infantile 248
Amnesty International 381
amygdala 270, 271
analysis of a phobia 252–256
anarchy 113
anger 283, 284, 285
animal
  communication 95, 97
  studies 61
animism 184
Anna O (Freudian case study) 237
answers to key questions 412–418
anthropometric centre 347
anti-social behaviour 318, 327
anxiety 104–5, 107, 108, 118, 246, 402
Ardrey, R. 369
Army Alpha and Beta tests 351, 354, 356
arousal 151, 312, 383–384, 398
  autonomic 214
  and emotion 276, 279, 281
Asch, S.E. 108, 109, 110
asking one question only 192–194
Asperger's syndrome 77
assimilation 178
Atkinson, R.C. 27–28, 29, 33
attachment 229, 230
  and autism 78–79

attention deficit hyperactivity disorder (ADHD) 318
attribution theory 129
attributions 138, 142, 280, 361
attrition 230, 234
authority
  figures 111, 113, 114
  forms of 112
  questioning of 123
autism 76–83
  and attachment 78–79
  causes of 81–82
  and language 79–80
  and spontaneous play 79
  symptoms of 78–80
autokinetic effect 107
autonomic nervous system (ANS) 259, 260, 275
axons 262–263

babbling 88–89
Bandura, A. 201, 206–207
Bartlett, F.C. 38
basal ganglia 270
behaviour
  and arousal 151
  anti-social 318, 327
  norms of 146
  in presence of others 131
  and roles 154
  shaping 205
Berne, E. 241–242
bias 1–2, 45, 58, 101
  cultural 340, 353, 354, 358–359
see also ethnocentricity
  in-group 157, 161
Binet, A. 174, 343, 345, 348, 349
binocular cues to vision 52–53
black people and prejudice 353, 384
Black Room Experiment 157
Blank, M. 191
blue eyes brown eyes experiment (Elliot) 364–365
bonobo chimpanzees 98–99
Bowlby, J. 215, 216–218, 221–223
brain 258
  abnormalities in murderers 328–332
  composition of 268–272
  criminal 317
  electrical stimulation of 322
  and hearing 308
  lateralisation of function 305
  localisation of function in 272
  parasympathetic system of 259, 260, 274
  scanning 15, 319–320, 328–332, 345
  and the senses 307–30
  sympathetic system of 259, 260, 274
  and vision 307–308
brainstem 269, 270
Breuer, J. (associate of Freud) 237
British Psychological Society (BPS) 18
Broca's area 272, 305
Brown, R. 90
Bryant, P. 192
Bulger, Jamie (abduction of) 128
Burt, Sir Cyril 4, 339
bystander
  behaviour 130, 136, 145
  effect 133

Calley, William (American soldier) 115
cannabis 268
Cannon, W. 277–279
Cannon-Bard theory of emotion 278–279
carer deprivation 228
carers 135, 226, 233
carpentered world hypothesis 64
case studies 5, 14, 256
castration fear 247, 254, 255
CAT (CT) computerised axial tomography scans 15, 319–320
cathartic method 237
Causal Schemata Model 138
central nervous system (CNS) 259
central sulcus 272
centration 183–184, 189
cerebral cortex 270
Charcot, J. 236–237
Chernobyl incident 297

Child Care and the Growth of Love (Bowlby) 215
Children's Minds (Donaldson) 187
Chomsky, N. 94, 95
chromosomal abnormalities 318
chronological age 85
chunking 27–28
circadian rhythms 287–290, 292
circannual rhythms 288
Clark, K.B. 366, 373
Clark, M. 366, 373
classificatory systems 389–390
Cleckley, H. 406
clinical interviews 71
closed questions 14–15
cognition 21, 104–105, 171, 279
cognitive
  development 173–174
    concrete operational stage 185
    formal operational stage 186, 189
    pre-operational stage 180–185, 189, 194
    sensorimotor stage 179–180
    stages in 177
  dissonance 119, 120, 403
labelling theory of emotion (Schachter) 281
  operations 185
  psychology 21, 171
  maps 308–309
competence 135
compliance 110, 120
computerised axial tomography (CAT) scans 15, 319–320
concordance rates 81, 342
concrete operational stage of cognitive development 185
conditioning 112, 202–212
  operant 93–94, 100, 205–206
conflict reduction 165
conformity 105–110, 111, 115, 145
  experiments 108–110, 117–119
  and obedience 115
confounding variables 19
conscious mind 237
consciousness 257
conservation 182–183, 192–193, 194
  of liquid 176
  of number 190
content validity 17
convergence 52
conversion 120
corpus callosum 271, 304–305, 307, 309–310, 322
correlation 5, 15–17, 331, 358
  coefficient 341
cost/benefit analysis 136, 140
covert observation 13
creativity 102
criterion validity 17
critical periods 92, 217–218, 220
cross-cultural
  issues 335
  studies 63–69, 122–123, 248–249
CT (CAT) scans 15, 319
cultural
  bias 340, 353, 354, 358–359
  differences in perception 64
relativity 384–385
cupboard love theory 224

Dann, S. 228
Darley, J.M. 131, 132, 138–139
Darwin, C. 338
Dawkins, R. 370
debriefing 19, 119
deindividuation 146–149, 151–152, 154–155, 156
  and identification 148
delayed imitation 101
demand characteristics 7, 170, 211
Dement, W. 299, 300
dementia praecox (schizophrenia) 389
dendrites 261
dependent variables 6, 167
depersonalisation 394, 400
depolarisation 265
depression 154, 201, 288, 384, 388

deprivation
maternal 214–218, 221–222, 224, 229, 234
of sleep 296, 297
social 225
depth perception 49, 51, 65, 69
designs, experimental 9–10
determinants of emotional states 282–286
development
cognitive 173–174
emotional 224–225
of language 86–93
psycho-sexual (Freud) 173
Diagnostic and Statistical Manual of Mental Disorders, The (DSM) 390, 398
five axes of 390–391
diffusion of responsibility 115, 132, 133, 142–143, 144
discrimination 169, 347
in babies 59–60
and ethnocentrism 157, 162, 360, 365
and prejudice 367–369, 371
disembedded thinking 189
displacement 102
dissociative identity disorder (DID) 389, 399, 401–405
dissolution of responsibility 133, 144
distance judgement 54–55
Donaldson, M. 187
Down's syndrome 82, 83, 85
dreams 258, 288, 303
analysis of 238, 250, 288
and eye movements 300–303
drugs 268, 378, 389

echoic memory 27
echolalia 79
ecological validity 44, 45, 84, 119, 144
lack of 123, 154, 211, 302, 311–312
ego 240, 241, 242
states (alters) 399–401, 402, 404–405
egocentrism 70–71, 181–182, 187, 240
Eichmann, Adolf (SS Officer) 114, 116
Einstein, A. 346
Electra complex 247
electric shocks used in experiments 117–119, 123
electrical stimulation of the brain 322
Electro Convulsive Therapy (ECT) 385
electro oculogram (EOG) 295, 298
electroencephalogram (EEG) 15, 295, 298, 310, 319, 404, 410
electromyogram (EMG) 295, 298
Elliot, Jane 364
emasculation 154, 155
emotion
Cannon-Bard theory of 278–279
cognitive labelling theory of (Schachter) 281
James-Lange theory of 276–278, 279, 280
Schachter's two factor theory of 279–281
emotional
development 224–225, 229–230
states 282–286
emotions 258, 273
and cognition 274
physical response in 273
empathy 126, 144
encoding
acoustic (phonetic) 24, 34
semantic 24–25, 34
visual 24
endogenous rhythms 289
environment and IQ 343–344
epilepsy 258, 310, 313
episodic memory 37
Eros (Freud) 197, 242
ethical considerations 18–19, 144, 154, 321
ethnic groups 166
ethnocentrism 63, 69, 101, 157–160, 162, 360
and conflict 166
removing 166, 371
in Robbers Cave experiment 164, 165

eugenics 339, 359
euphoria 283, 284, 285
evoked potentials 345
ex-institutional adolescents 232–234
existential symptoms 394
expectancy bias 7, 58
expectations 3, 366
experimental, designs 9–10
  mortality (drop out rate) 342
experimenter
  bias 101
  effect 8
experiments 5–12
  in intergroup discrimination 167–170
extraneous variables 19
extrinsic rewards 126, 144
extroversion 269, 378–379, 397
eye movements and dreams 300–303
eyewitness testimony 40–41
Eysenck, H.J. 251, 269, 339, 345, 354, 355, 378

face validity 17
false beliefs 75
fatigue effects 10
fear
  irrational 253
  of castration 247, 254, 255
field experiments 12
fight/flight mechanism 260, 274
firing of neurones 263
fixation 243, 245, 249
fixed action patterns 199
forebrain 268, 270–272
forgetting 28
formal operational stage of cognitive development 186, 189
fraternal, (dyzygotic, DZ), twins 81
free association 238
Freud, A. 228, 237
Freud, S. 14, 172, 197, 217, 235–236
  historical background of 236–242
Freudian
  developmental theory 242, 397
    anal stage 243–245
    genital stage 248–251
    latency stage 248
    oral stage 243
    phallic stage 245–248
    as untestable 248–249, 255
  slips 238
frontal lobes 272, 323, 324
frustration-aggression hypothesis (Dollard) 200]

Gage, Phineas (case study) 323–324
Galton, Sir Francis 338–339, 347, 378
Games People Play (Berne) 241
general ability 'g' 338, 345
generalisation 101, 102
genes 125
Genie (case study) 92–93
Genovese, Kitty (murder of) 127–128, 130, 145
Gibson, J. 48
Good Samaritan behaviour 137, 141–144
Gould, S.G. 356
grammar 86–87, 90, 97
grand mal seizures (epilepsy) 310
Grant, G. 373
Gregory, R. 55, 62
group
  behaviour 150
  harmony 108
  norms 107, 115, 119
Gulag Archipelago, The (Solzhenitsyn) 381

habituation 13
Head Start programmes 344
Harlow, H. 224–225
Heim, A. 345
helping behaviour 132
  cost of 130, 136–137, 143
  and the nature of the helper 130, 135–136
  and nature of the situation 130–135
  and nature of the victim 130, 137
  and racial differences 140
  sex differences in 137
hemisphere deconnection 304
  and awareness 313–317

hierarchical, society 119
hindbrain 268–269
hippocampus 267, 270, 271
Hodges, J. 230, 232
Holocaust 114, 116
holophrases 89
Hraba, J. 373
Hughes, M. 187–188
human behaviour, understanding of 1
hyperactivity 331
hypnosis 237, 250, 403, 409
hypothalamus 270, 274, 322, 326
hypotheses 4, 6
hysteria 238

iconic
  memory 27
  processing 33–34
id 240, 241, 242
identification 110
  and deindividuation 148
imbalance of power 124
imitation of aggression 207–211
Immigration Restriction Act (USA) 358
imprinting 219
in-groups 157, 161, 162, 170, 369
  preferences of 164
independent
  subjects design 10, 43
  variables 6, 167, 282
individual differences 333–336
infantile amnesia 248
inferences 37
information
  encoding 24–25
  processing 33, 35, 259, 345
  retrieval 25–26
  storage 25
Inhelder, B. 181
inheritance and IQ 340–343
institutional care 216, 230–231, 232–234
intelligence 336, 359
  of adults 349
  definition of 335, 337–338, 345–346, 346
  measurement of 337, 347
  and nature/nurture debate 338–344
  quotient (IQ) *see* IQ
  tests 174, 346–355
inter-rater reliability 14, 212
interaction
  with environment 175, 178, 225
  and language 91–92
intergroup discrimination, experiments in 167–170
International Classification of Diseases (ICD) 390
Interpretations in psychoanalysis 256
interviews 5, 14–15
intrinsic rewards 144, 206
introspection 1
introversion 269, 378–379, 397
intuition 180, 183
IQ 4, 336, 349, 378
  and environment 343–344
  as inherited 340–343
  tests 80, 353
  and toxins 344
irrational fear 253

James, W. 276
James-Lange theory of emotion 276–278, 279, 280
Jensen, A.R. 339
jet lag 290
Jones, E. 239
judgement of distance 54–55

Kamin, L. 339
kathoeys 334–335, 384
Kelley, H.H. 136, 138
kin selection 126
King, M.L. 371, 372
Kleitman, N. 299, 300
Kraepelin, E. 389

La Piere, R.T. 371
labelling 388, 390, 395
Lange, C. 276
language 180, 272, 309
  acquisition 93–95, 220
    device (LAD) (Chomsky) 94

and autism 79–80
definition of 96, 97
development 86–93
and interaction 91–92
and memory 42–44
sign 89, 96
studies with primates 98–99, 100–102
and thought 96
Latané, B. 131, 132, 138–139
lateralisation of function in the brain 305, 316
Le Bon, G. 147, 148
leading questions 42
learned helplessness (Seligman) 80, 201, 222
learning
of object names 89
sets 56
Lenneberg, E. 92
levels of processing model of memory 35–36
libido 242
limbic system 270, 312
Linguistic Relativity Hypothesis 96
Lippman, W. 360
Little Hans (case study) 14, 173, 252–256
localisation of function in the brain 272
location and obedience 121
long term memory 24, 26, 28–29
longitudinal studies 72, 230, 232, 234
Lorenz, K. 197–198, 218–221, 318
lynching 370

McGarrigle, J. 189
magnetic resonance imaging (MRI) scans 15, 319–320
Malinowski, B. 333, 383
manic depressive psychosis 389
mass (group) tests 350–355
matched pairs design 9
maternal deprivation 214–218, 221–222, 224, 229, 234
maturation 21, 86, 179
Mead, M. 333, 384
melatonin 291, 297
membrane potential 264
memory 22–24
echoic 27
episodic 37
iconic 27
and language 42–44
levels of processing model 35–36
long term 24, 26, 28–29
multi-store model of 29–33
primacy effect in 30
recency effect in 30
repression of 173
and schema theory 39–41
semantic 37
sensory 26–27
short term 24, 26, 27–28, 29, 32
mental age 85, 349
metabolism 268, 293, 329, 330, 331
midbrain 268, 269–270
Milgram, S. 11, 104, 116, 117–119
Miller, G. 27
mind 237
mind-body problem 257–258
Mismeasure of Man, The (Gould) 356
mnemonics 25
mob psychology 147, *see also* deindividuation
modelling 207–211
monocular cues to vision 49–52
moral standards 387–388
morons, a nation of 356–359
motherese 91–92
motion
parallax 51
perception of 56–57
Müller-Lyer illusion 55, 56, 64
multi-store model of memory 29–33
multiple personality 336, 397–401
case study of 406–410
disorder (MPD) 383, 389
murder of Kitty Genovese 127–128, 130, 145
murderers, brain abnormalities in 328–332
My Lai massacre 115
myelination 266

nature/nurture debate 21, 59–62, 86, 98, 327
and intelligence 338–344
naughty teddy experiments 189
nervous system 258
neurones 261, 262, 297
firing of 263
neurophysiological measurements 5, 15
neurosis 249, 256
neurotransmitters 267, 268
nightmares 299
nodes of Ranvier 266
non rapid eye movement (non-REM) sleep 292, 299, 303
non-conformity 379 *see also* conformity
normal distribution (Gaussian) curve 347, 348, 378
norms of behaviour 146

obedience 7–8, 111–116, 122–123 behavioural study of (Milgram) 117–119
blind 114, 115
and conformity 115, 119
and location 121
and socialisation 119
and uniforms 121–122
in the workplace 123
Obedience to Authority (Milgram) 121
object permanence 180, 187
objectivity 2, 3, 13–14
observation 5, 12–14
observational studies 2, 12–14
obsessive-compulsive behaviour 249–250
occipital lobe 271
Oedipus complex 239, 246, 256, 401
and Little Hans 254, 255
open questions 14–15
operant conditioning 93–94, 100, 205–206
operations in Piaget's theory 181
opportunity samples 11
Orne, M.T. 7
out-groups 170, 369
overgeneralisation 90, 91
overt observation 12–13
paradoxical sleep 299
parasympathetic division of the brain 259, 260, 274
parents, influence of 341, 344
parietal lobe 271
participant observation 13
participants 6
pathology of power 154
Pavlov, I. 202
Penfield, W. 310
perceived competence 135
perception 46–47
cultural differences in 64, 66–69
of depth 49, 51, 65, 69
of motion 56–57
and sensations 47
visual 47–53
perceptual sets 57–59
peripheral nervous system (PNS) 259
perseveration 324
personal
responsibility 111
space 382
personality, multiple 336, 396–400 *see also* multiple personality
perspective 49, 66
Pervin, L. 398, 399
PET (positron emission tomography) scans 15, 320, 328–332
phobias 204, 252–256
physiological measurements 295, 345
Piaget, J. 70, 74, 174–177
Piaget's theory of cognitive development 177–186
criticisms of 186–191
Piliavin, I.M. 141–144
Piliavin, J.A. 104, 139, 140–144, 364
pineal gland 291, 297
pituitary gland 270
pivot words 90
placebo 283, 286
planum temporale 306
play, symbolism in 180
pleasure principle 240
pluralistic ignorance 131, 143, 144

political correctness 372
Ponzo illusion 55
populations 11
positron emission tomography (PET) scans 15, 320, 328–332, 346
Powell, E. 370
power 124, 154
practice effects 10
pre-concepts 184
pre-menstrual tension 386
pre-operational stage of cognitive development 180–185, 189, 194
preconscious mind 237
predictive validity 17
prejudice 2, 158, 362–367, 369–372
  and black people 384
  and discrimination 367–369, 371
primacy effect in memory 30
primates, language studies in 98–99, 100–102
prison simulation experiment (Zimbardo) 152–155, 400
privation 228 *see also* deprivation
processing
  iconic 33–34
  of information 33
projection 249
pseudopatients 392–395
psychiatric hospitals and sane people 392–395
psycho-sexual development (Freud) 173
psychoanalysis 250–251, 256
psychodynamic theory 242
psychometric testing 346, 359
psychopathic personality disorder 409

quasi-experiments 85, 232
questioning of authority 123
questionnaires 5, 14–15
questions 14–15
quota samples 11

racial
  differences, and helping 140
  identity 335, 373–375
  preference 373–375
  segregation 366, 367, 371
racism 372, 375
  scientific 359
random samples 11
rapid eye movement (REM) sleep 292–293, 295, 298, 299, 303, 304
rationalisation 128
Rayner, R. 204
reality principle 241
rebound effect in sleep 297
recall 25, 26
recency effect in memory 30
recognition 25
recovery of sight 62
reducing
  conflict 165
  ethnocentrism 166, 371
reflexes 177, 179, 202, 204, 240
rehearsal 29
reinforcement 93, 94, 201, 206
rejection 226
relationships 103, 104, 171–172, 228, 229
  social 232–234
reliability 3, 16, 17, 359
  inter-rater 14
repeated measures design 9–10
replication 4, 186
repression 249, 256, 401
research
  designs 2
  methods 5
responses 202–204
responsibility
  diffusion of 115, 132, 133, 142–143, 144
  dissolution of 133, 144
  personal 111
  sharing of 109
  shifting of 122
Reticular Activating System (RAS) 269
retrieval 25–26
reuptake 267
reversibility 183
rewards 126, 144, 206
Robbers Cave Study 163–167
roles 145–147, 151

Roschach ink blot test 410
Rose, S.A. 191
Rosenhan, D.L. 391
Rousseau, J.J. 197
Rutter, M. 227–228

sampling 10–12, 20
Samuel, J. 192
sane people in psychiatric hospitals 391–394
Sapir, E. 96
scapegoating 370–371, 375
scattergrams 16–17
Schachter, S. 279
Schachter's two factor theory of emotion 279–281
schema theory 36–39
  and memory 39–41
schemata 178, 185
schizophrenia 77–78, 385, 389, 395
scientific
  method 3–4
  racism 359
self-esteem 110, 159, 161, 365, 401–402
self-fulfilling prophecy 159, 160, 172, 364
self-satisfaction 126
self-selecting samples 11
Selfish Gene, The (Dawkins) 370
semantic
  encoding 24–25
  memory 37
semanticity 102
sensations and perception 47
sensitive periods 220
sensorimotor stage of cognitive development 179–180
sensory
  deprivation 103
  memory 26–27, 29
  receptors 260–261
separation anxiety 255
seriation 184–185
serotonin 268, 291
sex role identification 247
sexual abuse 238, 401
shaping of behaviour 205
Sherif, M. 110, 163
Shields, J. 342
Shiffrin, R.M. 27–28, 29, 32
short term memory 24, 26, 27–28, 29, 32
siblings 234
sign language 89, 96, 100
significance 19
Simpson, O.J. 366
Skinner, B.F. 93, 95, 205
sleep 287–288
  cycles 298
  deprivation 296, 297
  and dreaming 258
  evolutionary theory of 293–294
  laboratories 294–297
  need for 292, 294, 296
  non rapid eye movement (non REM) 292, 299, 303
  paradoxical 299
  as physiological restoration 292
  as psychological restoration 292–293
  rapid eye movement (REM) 292–293, 295, 298, 299, 303, 304
  rebound effect in 297
  temperature changes in 290
slips of the tongue (Freudian slips) 238
social
  cognition 104–105
  contagion 155
  control 379–381
  deprivation 225
  harmony 113
  influence 116, 145
  interaction 103–104
  loafing 133–135, 144
  relationships 232–234
Social Exchange Theory 136, 137
socialisation 92, 171
  and obedience 119
society, hierarchical 119
sodium gate in neurones 265
Solzhenitsyn, A. 381
somatic nervous system 259, 260
Spearman, C. 345
special education 348

Spencer, H. 338
Sperry, R.W. 311, 313
spinal cord lesions 274–275
spirit as an entity 257–258
split
  brains 304, 311–312, 322
  drawings 68, 69
standard deviation 348
standardised scores 350
Stanford-Binet test 349
statistical tests 2, 19
stereopsis 53
stereotypes 2, 157
stereotyping 360–362, 369, 375
stimuli 202–204
stratified samples 11
stress 383
strokes 306, 309
stuttering 306
subject attrition 230, 234
subjectivity 1, 255, 387
subjects 6
sulci 271
superego 240, 241, 242
surveys 5, 14–15
symbolism in play 180
sympathetic division of the brain 259, 260, 274
synapses 266, 268
syndromes 389
syntax 96, 97
Szasz, T.S. 389

Tajfel, H. 104, 167
telegraphic speech 90
television violence and aggression 213–214
temperature changes in sleep 290
temporal lobes 272, 310
Terman, L.M. 345, 349, 357
territorial imperative 369
testosterone 199
texture gradient and vision 50
Thailand 334
thalamus 270
Thanatos (Freud) 197, 242
theory of mind 75–76, 83
Thibault, J.W. 136
Thigpen, C.H. 406
thinking, disembedded 189
thought and language 96
Three Faces of Eve, The (Thigpen and Cleckley) 411
Three Mile Island incident 297
three mountains task 181, 187–188
time sampling 14
Tizard, B. 230, 231, 232
toxins and IQ 344
traits 361–362
transactional analysis 241
transparent matrices 170
Trobriand Islanders 333–334
twins
  fraternal, (dyzygotic, DZ) 81
  identical (monozygotic, MZ) 81, 340
two word utterances 90

ulterior motives 125
unconscious mind 237, 255
uniforms, and aggression 150
  and anonymity 146–147, 152
  and obedience 121–122, 149, 151
unconscious mind 237

validity 17, 359
  ecological *see* ecological validity
  criterion *see* criterion validity
  face *see* face validity

variables 6, 19, 167
verbal age 85
vision and the brain 307–308
visual
  cliff apparatus 60–61
  constancies 53–56, 65
  encoding 24
  perception 47–53
    binocular cues to 52–53
    monocular cues 49–52
    and motion parallax 51

and overlap 50
perspective in 49
and texture gradient 50
vocabulary growth 87–88

Washoe (chimpanzee) 100–102
Watson, J.B. 204
Wearing, Clive (case study) 31
Wechsler, D. 345, 349
Wechsler scales 350
Wernické's area 272, 305
White, Eve (case study) 406–411
Whitman, Charles (case study) 326
Whorf, B.L. 96
Whyte, W.F. 13
Wisconsin Card Sorting Task 324
words and meaning 97
World Health Organisation (WHO) 389

xenophobia 370, 375

Yerkes, R. 350, 356
Yorkshire Ripper 321
Yugoslavia 368–369

zeitgebers (timegivers) 289, 290
Zimbardo, P.G. 104, 148, 152–155